中国政府白皮书汇编
（2020 年）

人民出版社　外文出版社 FOREIGN LANGUAGES PRESS

目　录

中国军队参加联合国维和行动 30 年

（2020 年 9 月）

新时代的中国能源发展

（2020 年 12 月）

中国交通的可持续发展

（2020 年 12 月）

第二部分　英文版

Fighting Covid-19 China in Action

（June 2020）

Employment and Labor Rights
in Xinjiang

（September 2020）

China's Armed Forces:
30 Years of UN Peacekeeping Operations
(September 2020)

Energy in China's New Era
(December 2020)

Sustainable Development of
Transport in China

(December 2020)

第一部分　中文版

抗击新冠肺炎疫情的中国行动

（2020 年 6 月）

中华人民共和国
国务院新闻办公室

前　言

　　新型冠状病毒肺炎是近百年来人类遭遇的影响范围最广的全球性大流行病,对全世界是一次严重危机和严峻考验。人类生命安全和健康面临重大威胁。

　　这是一场全人类与病毒的战争。面对前所未知、突如其来、来势汹汹的疫情天灾,中国果断打响疫情防控阻击战。中国把人民生命安全和身体健康放在第一位,以坚定果敢的勇气和决心,采取最全面最严格最彻底的防控措施,有效阻断病毒传播链条。14亿中国人民坚韧奉献、团结协作,构筑起同心战疫的坚固防线,彰显了人民的伟大力量。

　　中国始终秉持人类命运共同体理念,肩负大国担当,同其他国家并肩作战、共克时艰。中国本着依法、公开、透明、负责任态度,第一时间向国际社会通报疫情信息,毫无保留同各方分享防控和救治经验。中国对疫情给各国人民带来的苦难感同身受,尽己所能向国际社会提供人道主义援助,支持全球抗击疫情。

　　当前,疫情在全球持续蔓延。中国为被病毒夺去生命和在抗击疫情中牺牲的人们深感痛惜,向争分夺秒抢救生命、遏制疫情的人们深表敬意,向不幸感染病毒、正在进行治疗的人们表达祝愿。中国坚信,国际社会同舟共济、守望相助,就一定能够战胜疫情,走出人类历史上这段艰难时刻,迎来人类发展更加美好的明天。

为记录中国人民抗击疫情的伟大历程,与国际社会分享中国抗疫的经验做法,阐明全球抗疫的中国理念、中国主张,中国政府特发布此白皮书。

一、中国抗击疫情的艰辛历程

新冠肺炎疫情是新中国成立以来发生的传播速度最快、感染范围最广、防控难度最大的一次重大突发公共卫生事件,对中国是一次危机,也是一次大考。中国共产党和中国政府高度重视、迅速行动,习近平总书记亲自指挥、亲自部署,统揽全局、果断决策,为中国人民抗击疫情坚定了信心、凝聚了力量、指明了方向。在中国共产党领导下,全国上下贯彻"坚定信心、同舟共济、科学防治、精准施策"总要求,打响抗击疫情的人民战争、总体战、阻击战。经过艰苦卓绝的努力,中国付出巨大代价和牺牲,有力扭转了疫情局势,用一个多月的时间初步遏制了疫情蔓延势头,用两个月左右的时间将本土每日新增病例控制在个位数以内,用 3 个月左右的时间取得了武汉保卫战、湖北保卫战的决定性成果,疫情防控阻击战取得重大战略成果,维护了人民生命安全和身体健康,为维护地区和世界公共卫生安全作出了重要贡献。

截至 2020 年 5 月 31 日 24 时,31 个省、自治区、直辖市和新疆生产建设兵团累计报告确诊病例 83017 例,累计治愈出院病例 78307 例,累计死亡病例 4634 例,治愈率 94.3%,病亡率 5.6%(见图 1、2、3、4)。回顾前一阶段中国抗疫历程,大体分为五个阶段。

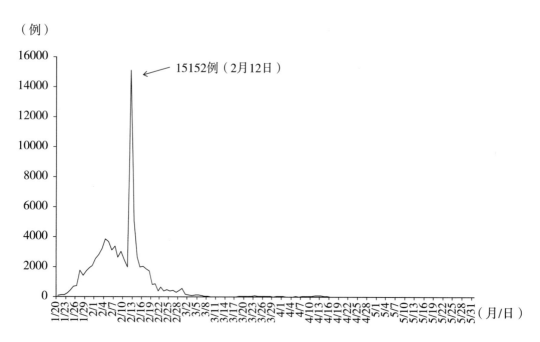

图 1　中国境内新冠肺炎新增确诊病例情况

注:2 月 12 日报告新增确诊病例 15152 例(湖北省累计 13332 例临床诊断病例一次性计入当日新增确诊病例)

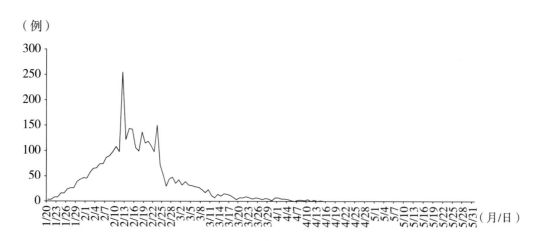

图 2　中国境内新冠肺炎新增死亡病例情况

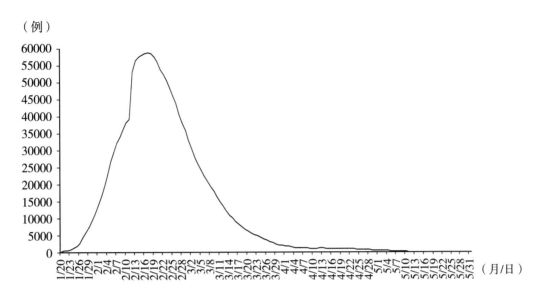

图 3　中国境内新冠肺炎现有确诊病例情况

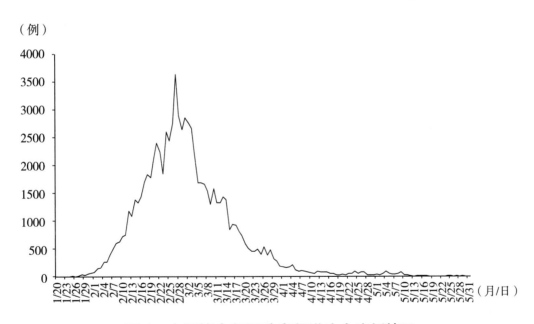

图 4　中国境内新冠肺炎新增治愈病例情况

（一）第一阶段:迅即应对突发疫情

（2019 年 12 月 27 日至 2020 年 1 月 19 日）

湖北省武汉市监测发现不明原因肺炎病例,中国第一时间报告疫情,迅速采取行动,开展病因学和流行病学调查,阻断疫情蔓延。及时主动向世界卫生组织以及美国等国家通报疫情信息,向世界公布新型冠状病毒基因组序列。武汉地区出现局部社区传播和聚集性病例,其他地区开始出现武汉关联确诊病例,中国全面展开疫情防控。

（1）2019 年 12 月 27 日,湖北省中西医结合医院向武汉市江汉区疾控中心报告不明原因肺炎病例。武汉市组织专家从病情、治疗转归、流行病学调查、实验室初步检测等方面情况分析,认为上述病例系病毒性肺炎。

（2）12 月 30 日,武汉市卫生健康委向辖区医疗机构发布《关于做好不明原因肺炎救治工作的紧急通知》。国家卫生健康委获悉有关信息后立即组织研究,迅速开展行动。

（3）12 月 31 日凌晨,国家卫生健康委作出安排部署,派出工作组、专家组赶赴武汉市,指导做好疫情处置工作,开展现场调查。武汉市卫生健康委在官方网站发布《关于当前我市肺炎疫情的情况通报》,发现 27 例病例,提示公众尽量避免到封闭、空气不流通的公众场合和人多集中地方,外出可佩戴口罩。当日起,武汉市卫生健康委依法发布疫情信息。

（4）2020 年 1 月 1 日,国家卫生健康委成立疫情应对处置领导小组。1 月 2 日,国家卫生健康委制定《不明原因的病毒性肺炎防控"三早"方案》;中国疾控中心、中国医学科学院收到湖北省送检的第一批 4 例病例标本,即开展病原鉴定。

（5）1 月 3 日,武汉市卫生健康委在官方网站发布《关于不明原因的病毒性肺炎情况通报》,共发现 44 例不明原因的病毒性肺炎病例。国家卫生健康委组织中国疾控中心等 4 家科研单位对病例样本进行实验室平行检测,进一步开展病原鉴定。国家卫生健康委会同湖北省卫生健康委制定《不明原因的病毒性肺炎诊疗方案（试行）》等 9 个文件。当日起,中国有关方面定期向世界卫生组织、有关国家和地区组织以及中国港澳台地区及时主动通报疫情信息。

（6）1 月 4 日,中国疾控中心负责人与美国疾控中心负责人通电话,介绍疫情有关情况,双方同意就信息沟通和技术协作保持密切联系。国家卫生健康委会同湖北省卫生健康部门制定《不明原因的病毒性肺炎医疗救治工作手册》。

（7）1 月 5 日,武汉市卫生健康委在官方网站发布《关于不明原因的病毒性肺炎情况通报》,共发现 59 例不明原因的病毒性肺炎病例,根据实验室检测结果,排除流感、禽流感、腺病毒、传染性非典型性肺炎和中东呼吸综合征等呼吸道病原。中国向世界卫生组织通报疫情信息。世界卫生组织首次就中国武汉出现的不明原因肺炎病例进行通报。

（8）1月6日，国家卫生健康委在全国卫生健康工作会议上通报武汉市不明原因肺炎有关情况，要求加强监测、分析和研判，及时做好疫情处置。

（9）1月7日，中共中央总书记习近平在主持召开中共中央政治局常务委员会会议时，对做好不明原因肺炎疫情防控工作提出要求。

（10）1月7日，中国疾控中心成功分离新型冠状病毒毒株。

（11）1月8日，国家卫生健康委专家评估组初步确认新冠病毒为疫情病原。中美两国疾控中心负责人通电话，讨论双方技术交流合作事宜。

（12）1月9日，国家卫生健康委专家评估组对外发布武汉市不明原因的病毒性肺炎病原信息，病原体初步判断为新型冠状病毒。中国向世界卫生组织通报疫情信息，将病原学鉴定取得的初步进展分享给世界卫生组织。世界卫生组织网站发布关于中国武汉聚集性肺炎病例的声明，表示在短时间内初步鉴定出新型冠状病毒是一项显著成就。

（13）1月10日，中国疾控中心、中国科学院武汉病毒研究所等专业机构初步研发出检测试剂盒，武汉市立即组织对在院收治的所有相关病例进行排查。国家卫生健康委、中国疾控中心负责人分别与世界卫生组织负责人就疫情应对处置工作通话，交流有关信息。

（14）1月11日起，中国每日向世界卫生组织等通报疫情信息。

（15）1月12日，武汉市卫生健康委在情况通报中首次将“不明原因的病毒性肺炎”更名为“新型冠状病毒感染的肺炎”。中国疾控中心、中国医学科学院、中国科学院武汉病毒研究所作为国家卫生健康委指定机构,向世界卫生组织提交新型冠状病毒基因组序列信息,在全球流感共享数据库(GISAID)发布,全球共享。国家卫生健康委与世界卫生组织分享新冠病毒基因组序列信息。

(16)1月13日,国务院总理李克强在主持召开国务院全体会议时,对做好疫情防控提出要求。

(17)1月13日,国家卫生健康委召开会议,部署指导湖北省、武汉市进一步强化管控措施,加强口岸、车站等人员体温监测,减少人群聚集。世界卫生组织官方网站发表关于在泰国发现新冠病毒病例的声明指出,中国共享了基因组测序结果,使更多国家能够快速诊断患者。香港、澳门、台湾考察团赴武汉市考察疫情防控工作。

(18)1月14日,国家卫生健康委召开全国电视电话会议,部署加强湖北省、武汉市疫情防控工作,做好全国疫情防范应对准备工作。会议指出,新冠病毒导致的新发传染病存在很大不确定性,人与人之间的传播能力和传播方式仍需要深入研究,不排除疫情进一步扩散蔓延的可能性。

(19)1月15日,国家卫生健康委发布新型冠状病毒感染的肺炎第一版诊疗方案、防控方案。

(20)1月16日,聚合酶链式反应(PCR)诊断试剂优化完成,武汉市对全部69所二级以上医院发热门诊就医和留观治疗的患者进行主动筛查。

(21)1月17日,国家卫生健康委派出7个督导组赴地方指导疫情防控工作。

（22）1月18日,国家卫生健康委发布新型冠状病毒感染的肺炎第二版诊疗方案。

（23）1月18日至19日,国家卫生健康委组织国家医疗与防控高级别专家组赶赴武汉市实地考察疫情防控工作。19日深夜,高级别专家组经认真研判,明确新冠病毒出现人传人现象。

（二）第二阶段:初步遏制疫情蔓延势头

(1月20日至2月20日)

全国新增确诊病例快速增加,防控形势异常严峻。中国采取阻断病毒传播的关键一招,坚决果断关闭离汉离鄂通道,武汉保卫战、湖北保卫战全面打响。中共中央成立应对疫情工作领导小组,并向湖北等疫情严重地区派出中央指导组。国务院先后建立联防联控机制、复工复产推进工作机制。全国集中资源和力量驰援湖北省和武汉市。各地启动重大突发公共卫生事件应急响应。最全面最严格最彻底的全国疫情防控正式展开,疫情蔓延势头初步遏制。(图5)

（1）1月20日,中共中央总书记、国家主席、中央军委主席习近平对新型冠状病毒感染的肺炎疫情作出重要指示,指出要把人民生命安全和身体健康放在第一位,坚决遏制疫情蔓延势头;强调要及时发布疫情信息,深化国际合作。

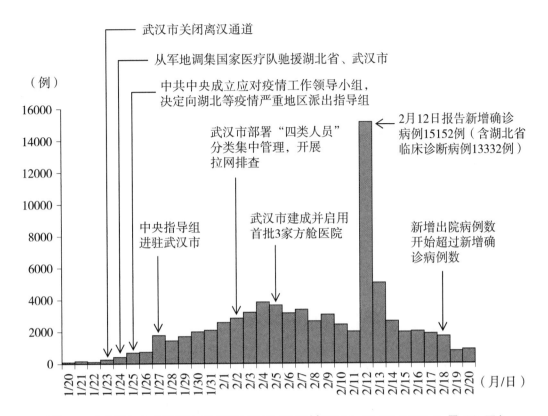

图5 中国境内新冠肺炎新增确诊病例情况（1月20日至2月20日）

（2）1月20日，国务院总理李克强主持召开国务院常务会议，进一步部署疫情防控工作，并根据《中华人民共和国传染病防治法》将新冠肺炎纳入乙类传染病，采取甲类传染病管理措施。

（3）1月20日，国务院联防联控机制召开电视电话会议，部署全国疫情防控工作。

（4）1月20日，国家卫生健康委组织召开记者会，高级别专家组通报新冠病毒已出现人传人现象。

（5）1月20日，国家卫生健康委发布公告，将新冠肺炎纳入传染病防治法规定的乙类传染病并采取甲类传染病的防控措施；将新冠肺炎纳入《中华人民共和国国境卫生检疫法》规定的检疫传染病管理。国家卫生健康委发布《新型冠状病毒感染的肺炎防控方案（第二版）》。

（6）1月22日，中共中央总书记、国家主席、中央军委主席习近平作出重要指示，要求立即对湖北省、武汉市人员流动和对外通道实行严格封闭的交通管控。

（7）1月22日，国家卫生健康委发布《新型冠状病毒感染的肺炎诊疗方案（试行第三版）》。国务院新闻办公室就疫情举行第一场新闻发布会，介绍疫情有关情况。国家卫生健康委收到美方通报，美国国内发现首例确诊病例。国家生物信息中心开发的2019新型冠状病毒信息库正式上线，发布全球新冠病毒基因组和变异分析信息。

（8）1月23日凌晨2时许，武汉市疫情防控指挥部发布1号通告，23日10时起机场、火车站离汉通道暂时关闭。交通运输部发出紧急通知，全国暂停进入武汉市道路水路客运班线发班。国家卫生健康委等6部门发布《关于严格预防通过交通工具传播新型冠状病毒感染的肺炎的通知》。1月23日至29日，全国各省份陆续启动重大突发公共卫生事件省级一级应急响应。

（9）1月23日，中国科学院武汉病毒研究所、武汉市金银潭医院、湖北省疾病预防控制中心研究团队发现新冠病毒的全基因组序列与SARS—CoV的序列一致性有79.5%。国家微生物科学数据中心和国家病原微生物资源库共同建成"新型冠状病毒国家科技资源服务系统"，发布新冠病毒第一张电子显微镜照片和毒株信息。

（10）1月24日开始，从各地和军队调集346支国家医疗队、4.26

万名医务人员和 965 名公共卫生人员驰援湖北省和武汉市。

（11）1 月 25 日，中共中央总书记习近平主持召开中共中央政治局常务委员会会议，明确提出"坚定信心、同舟共济、科学防治、精准施策"总要求，强调坚决打赢疫情防控阻击战；指出湖北省要把疫情防控工作作为当前头等大事，采取更严格的措施，内防扩散、外防输出；强调要按照集中患者、集中专家、集中资源、集中救治"四集中"原则，将重症病例集中到综合力量强的定点医疗机构进行救治，及时收治所有确诊病人。会议决定，中共中央成立应对疫情工作领导小组，在中央政治局常务委员会领导下开展工作；中共中央向湖北等疫情严重地区派出指导组，推动有关地方全面加强防控一线工作。

（12）1 月 25 日，国家卫生健康委发布通用、旅游、家庭、公共场所、公共交通工具、居家观察等 6 个公众预防指南。

（13）1 月 26 日，中共中央政治局常委、国务院总理、中央应对疫情工作领导小组组长李克强主持召开领导小组第一次全体会议。国务院办公厅印发通知，决定延长 2020 年春节假期，各地大专院校、中小学、幼儿园推迟开学。国家药监局应急审批通过 4 家企业 4 个新型冠状病毒检测产品，进一步扩大新型冠状病毒核酸检测试剂供给能力。

（14）1 月 27 日，中共中央总书记习近平作出指示，要求中国共产党各级组织和广大党员、干部，牢记人民利益高于一切，不忘初心、牢记使命，团结带领广大人民群众坚决贯彻落实党中央决策部署，全面贯彻"坚定信心、同舟共济、科学防治、精准施策"的要求，让党旗在防控疫情斗争第一线高高飘扬。

（15）1月27日，受中共中央总书记习近平委托，中共中央政治局常委、国务院总理、中央应对疫情工作领导小组组长李克强赴武汉市考察指导疫情防控工作，代表中共中央、国务院慰问疫情防控一线的医护人员。同日，中央指导组进驻武汉市，全面加强对一线疫情防控的指导督导。

（16）1月27日，国家卫生健康委发布《新型冠状病毒感染的肺炎诊疗方案（试行第四版）》。国家卫生健康委负责人应约与美国卫生与公众服务部负责人通话，就当前新型冠状病毒感染的肺炎疫情防控工作进行交流。

（17）1月28日，国家主席习近平在北京会见世界卫生组织总干事谭德塞时指出，疫情是魔鬼，我们不能让魔鬼藏匿；指出中国政府始终本着公开、透明、负责任的态度及时向国内外发布疫情信息，积极回应各方关切，加强与国际社会合作；强调中方愿同世界卫生组织和国际社会一道，共同维护好地区和全球的公共卫生安全。

（18）1月28日，国家卫生健康委发布《新型冠状病毒感染的肺炎防控方案（第三版）》。

（19）1月30日，国家卫生健康委通过官方渠道告知美方，欢迎美国加入世界卫生组织联合专家组。美方当天即回复表示感谢。

（20）1月31日，世界卫生组织宣布新冠肺炎疫情构成"国际关注的突发公共卫生事件"。国家卫生健康委发布《新型冠状病毒感染的肺炎重症患者集中救治方案》。

（21）2月2日开始，在中央指导组指导下，武汉市部署实施确诊患者、疑似患者、发热患者、确诊患者的密切接触者"四类人员"分类集中管理，按照应收尽收、应治尽治、应检尽检、应隔尽隔"四应"要求，持续开展拉网排查、集中收治、清底排查三场攻坚战。

（22）2月2日，国家卫生健康委负责人致函美国卫生与公众服务部负责人，就双方卫生和疫情防控合作再次交换意见。

（23）2月3日，中共中央总书记习近平主持召开中共中央政治局常务委员会会议，指出要进一步完善和加强防控，严格落实早发现、早报告、早隔离、早治疗"四早"措施；强调要全力以赴救治患者，努力"提高收治率和治愈率""降低感染率和病亡率"。

（24）2月3日，中央指导组从全国调集22支国家紧急医学救援队，在武汉市建设方舱医院。

（25）2月4日，中国疾控中心负责人应约与美国国家过敏症和传染病研究所负责人通电话，交流疫情信息。

（26）2月5日，中共中央总书记、国家主席、中央军委主席、中央全面依法治国委员会主任习近平主持召开中央全面依法治国委员会第三次会议，强调要始终把人民生命安全和身体健康放在第一位，从立法、执法、司法、守法各环节发力，全面提高依法防控、依法治理能力，为疫情防控工作提供有力法治保障。

（27）2月5日，国务院联防联控机制加强协调调度，供应湖北省医用N95口罩首次实现供大于需。

（28）2月5日，国家卫生健康委发布《新型冠状病毒感染肺炎诊疗方案(试行第五版)》。

(29)2月7日,国务院联防联控机制印发《关于进一步强化责任落实做好防治工作的通知》,国家卫生健康委发布《新型冠状病毒感染肺炎防控方案(第四版)》。

(30)2月8日,国家卫生健康委在亚太经合组织卫生工作组会议上介绍中国防疫努力和措施。国家卫生健康委向中国驻外使领馆通报新型冠状病毒防控、诊疗、监测、流行病学调查、实验室检测等方案。中美两国卫生部门负责人再次就美方专家参加中国—世界卫生组织联合专家考察组的安排进行沟通。

(31)2月10日,中共中央总书记、国家主席、中央军委主席习近平在北京调研指导新冠肺炎疫情防控工作,并通过视频连线武汉市收治新冠肺炎患者的金银潭医院、协和医院、火神山医院,强调要以更坚定的信心、更顽强的意志、更果断的措施,紧紧依靠人民群众,坚决打赢疫情防控的人民战争、总体战、阻击战;指出湖北和武汉是疫情防控的重中之重,是打赢疫情防控阻击战的决胜之地,武汉胜则湖北胜,湖北胜则全国胜,要打好武汉保卫战、湖北保卫战;强调要按照集中患者、集中专家、集中资源、集中救治"四集中"原则,全力做好救治工作;强调要坚决抓好"外防输入、内防扩散"两大环节,尽最大可能切断传染源,尽最大可能控制疫情波及范围。

(32)2月10日,建立省际对口支援湖北省除武汉市以外地市新冠肺炎医疗救治工作机制,统筹安排19个省份对口支援湖北省武汉市以外16个市州及县级市。

（33）2月11日，国务院联防联控机制加强协调调度，供应湖北省医用防护服首次实现供大于求。

（34）2月11日，中国疾控中心专家应约与美国疾控中心流感部门专家召开电话会议，沟通和分享疫情防控信息。

（35）2月12日，中共中央总书记习近平主持召开中共中央政治局常务委员会会议，指出疫情防控工作到了最吃劲的关键阶段，要毫不放松做好疫情防控重点工作，加强疫情特别严重或风险较大的地区防控；强调要围绕"提高收治率和治愈率""降低感染率和病亡率"，抓好疫情防控重点环节；强调要全面增强收治能力，坚决做到"应收尽收、应治尽治"，提高收治率；强调要提高患者特别是重症患者救治水平，集中优势医疗资源和技术力量救治患者；强调人口流入大省大市要按照"联防联控、群防群控"要求，切实做好防控工作。

（36）2月13日，美国卫生与公众服务部相关负责人致函中国国家卫生健康委负责人，沟通双方卫生和疫情防控合作等有关安排。

（37）2月14日，中共中央总书记、国家主席、中央军委主席、中央全面深化改革委员会主任习近平主持召开中央全面深化改革委员会第十二次会议，指出确保人民生命安全和身体健康，是中国共产党治国理政的一项重大任务；强调既要立足当前，科学精准打赢疫情防控阻击战，更要放眼长远，总结经验、吸取教训，针对这次疫情暴露出来的短板和不足，抓紧补短板、堵漏洞、强弱项，完善重大疫情防控体制机制，健全国家公共卫生应急管理体系。

（38）2月14日，全国除湖北省以外其他省份新增确诊病例数实现"十连降"。

（39）2月15日，国务院新闻办公室首次在湖北省武汉市举行疫情防控新闻发布会。至2月15日，已有7个诊断检测试剂获批上市，部分药物筛选与治疗方案、疫苗研发、动物模型构建等取得阶段性进展。

（40）2月16日开始，由中国、德国、日本、韩国、尼日利亚、俄罗斯、新加坡、美国和世界卫生组织25名专家组成的中国—世界卫生组织联合专家考察组，利用9天时间，对北京、成都、广州、深圳和武汉等地进行实地考察调研。

（41）2月17日，国务院联防联控机制印发《关于科学防治精准施策分区分级做好新冠肺炎疫情防控工作的指导意见》，部署各地区各部门做好分区分级精准防控，有序恢复生产生活秩序。

（42）2月18日，全国新增治愈出院病例数超过新增确诊病例数，确诊病例数开始下降。中国国家卫生健康委复函美国卫生与公众服务部，就双方卫生与疫情合作有关安排进一步沟通。

（43）2月19日，中共中央总书记习近平主持召开中共中央政治局常务委员会会议，听取疫情防控工作汇报，研究统筹做好疫情防控和经济社会发展工作。

（44）2月19日，国家卫生健康委发布《新型冠状病毒肺炎诊疗方案（试行第六版）》。

（45）2月19日，武汉市新增治愈出院病例数首次大于新增确诊病例数。

（三）第三阶段：本土新增病例数
逐步下降至个位数

（2月21日至3月17日）

　　湖北省和武汉市疫情快速上升势头均得到遏制，全国除湖北省以外疫情形势总体平稳，3月中旬每日新增病例控制在个位数以内，疫情防控取得阶段性重要成效。根据疫情防控形势发展，中共中央作出统筹疫情防控和经济社会发展、有序复工复产重大决策。（图6）

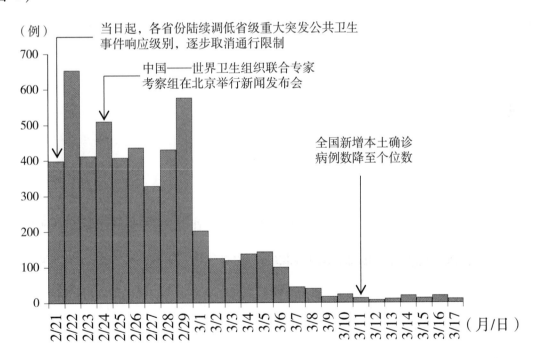

图6　中国境内新冠肺炎新增确诊病例情况（2月21日至3月17日）

　　（1）2月21日，中共中央总书记习近平主持召开中共中央政治局会议，指出疫情防控工作取得阶段性成效，同时，全国疫情发展拐点尚未到来,湖北省和武汉市防控形势依然严峻复杂;强调要针对不同区域情况,完善差异化防控策略,坚决打好湖北保卫战、武汉保卫战,加强力量薄弱地区防控,全力做好北京疫情防控工作;强调要建立与疫情防控相适应的经济社会运行秩序,有序推动复工复产。

(2)2月21日,国务院联防联控机制印发《企事业单位复工复产疫情防控措施指南》,国家卫生健康委发布《新型冠状病毒肺炎防控方案(第五版)》。

(3)2月21日起,各地因地制宜,陆续调低省级重大突发公共卫生事件响应级别,逐步取消通行限制。至2月24日,除湖北省、北京市外,其他省份主干公路卡点全部打通,运输秩序逐步恢复。

(4)2月23日,中共中央总书记、国家主席、中央军委主席习近平出席统筹推进新冠肺炎疫情防控和经济社会发展工作部署会议,通过视频直接面向全国17万名干部进行动员部署,指出新冠肺炎疫情是新中国成立以来在我国发生的传播速度最快、感染范围最广、防控难度最大的一次重大突发公共卫生事件,这是一次危机,也是一次大考,经过艰苦努力,疫情防控形势积极向好的态势正在拓展;强调疫情形势依然严峻复杂,防控正处在最吃劲的关键阶段,要坚定必胜信念,咬紧牙关,继续毫不放松抓紧抓实抓细各项防控工作;强调要变压力为动力、善于化危为机,有序恢复生产生活秩序,强化"六稳"举措,加大政策调节力度,把发展巨大潜力和强大动能充分释放出来,努力实现今年经济社会发展目标任务。

(5)2月24日,中国—世界卫生组织联合专家考察组在北京举行新闻发布会,认为中国在减缓疫情扩散蔓延、阻断病毒人际传播方面取得明显效果,已经避免或至少推迟了数十万人感染新冠肺炎。至2月24日,全国新增确诊病例数已连续5天在1000例以下,现有确诊病例数近一周以来呈现下降趋势,所有省份新增出院病例数均大于或等于新增确诊病例数。

(6)2月25日起,全面加强出入境卫生检疫工作,对出入境人员严格健康核验、体温监测、医学巡查、流行病学调查、医学排查、采样监测,防止疫情跨境传播。

(7)2月26日,中共中央总书记习近平主持召开中共中央政治局常务委员会会议,指出全国疫情防控形势积极向好的态势正在拓展,经济社会发展加快恢复,同时湖北省和武汉市疫情形势依然复杂严峻,其他有关地区疫情反弹风险不可忽视;强调要继续集中力量和资源,全面加强湖北省和武汉市疫情防控;强调要准确分析把握疫情和经济社会发展形势,紧紧抓住主要矛盾和矛盾的主要方面,确保打赢疫情防控的人民战争、总体战、阻击战,努力实现决胜全面建成小康社会、决战脱贫攻坚目标任务。

(8)2月27日,全国除湖北省以外其他省份,湖北省除武汉市以外其他地市,新增确诊病例数首次双双降至个位数。

(9)2月28日,国务院联防联控机制印发《关于进一步落实分区分级差异化防控策略的通知》。

(10)2月29日,中国—世界卫生组织新型冠状病毒肺炎联合考察报告发布。报告认为,面对前所未知的病毒,中国采取了历史上最勇敢、最灵活、最积极的防控措施,尽可能迅速地遏制病毒传播;令人瞩目的是,在所考察的每一个机构都能够强有力地落实防控措施;面对共同威胁时,中国人民凝聚共识、团结行动,才使防控措施得以全面有效的实施;每个省、每个城市在社区层面都团结一致,帮助和支持脆弱人群及社区。

(11)3月2日,中共中央总书记、国家主席、中央军委主席习近平在北京考察新冠肺炎防控科研攻关工作,强调要把新冠肺炎防控科研攻关作为一项重大而紧迫任务,在坚持科学性、确保安全性的基础上加快研发进度,为打赢疫情防控的人民战争、总体战、阻击战提供强大科技支撑;指出尽最大努力挽救更多患者生命是当务之急、重中之重,要加强药物、医疗装备研发和临床救治相结合,切实提高治愈率、降低病亡率;强调要加快推进已有的多种技术路线疫苗研发,争取早日推动疫苗的临床试验和上市使用;指出要把生物安全作为国家总体安全的重要组成部分,加强疫病防控和公共卫生科研攻关体系和能力建设。

(12)3月3日,国家卫生健康委发布《新型冠状病毒肺炎诊疗方案(试行第七版)》,在传播途径、临床表现、诊断标准等多个方面作出修改和完善,强调加强中西医结合。

(13)3月4日,中共中央总书记习近平主持召开中共中央政治局常务委员会会议,指出要加快建立同疫情防控相适应的经济社会运行秩序,完善相关举措,巩固和拓展来之不易的良好势头;强调要持续用力加强湖北省和武汉市疫情防控工作,继续保持"内防扩散、外防输出"的防控策略。

（14）3月6日，中共中央总书记、国家主席、中央军委主席习近平出席决战决胜脱贫攻坚座谈会，指出到2020年现行标准下的农村贫困人口全部脱贫，是中共中央向全国人民作出的郑重承诺，必须如期实现；强调要以更大决心、更强力度推进脱贫攻坚，坚决克服新冠肺炎疫情影响，坚决夺取脱贫攻坚战全面胜利，坚决完成这项对中华民族、对人类都具有重大意义的伟业。

（15）3月6日，全国新增本土确诊病例数降至100例以下，11日降至个位数。

（16）3月7日，国家卫生健康委发布《新型冠状病毒肺炎防控方案（第六版）》。

（17）3月10日，中共中央总书记、国家主席、中央军委主席习近平赴湖北省武汉市考察疫情防控工作，指出经过艰苦努力，湖北和武汉疫情防控形势发生积极向好变化，取得阶段性重要成果，但疫情防控任务依然艰巨繁重，要慎终如始、再接再厉、善作善成，坚决打赢湖北保卫战、武汉保卫战；指出武汉人民识大体、顾大局，不畏艰险、顽强不屈，自觉服从疫情防控大局需要，主动投身疫情防控斗争，作出了重大贡献；指出抗击疫情有两个阵地，一个是医院救死扶伤阵地，一个是社区防控阵地，要充分发挥社区在疫情防控中的重要作用，使所有社区成为疫情防控的坚强堡垒；强调打赢疫情防控人民战争要紧紧依靠人民，把群众发动起来，构筑起群防群控的人民防线。

（18）3月11日，世界卫生组织总干事谭德塞表示，新冠肺炎疫情已具有大流行特征。

（19）3 月 11 日至 17 日,全国每日新增本土确诊病例数维持在个位数。总体上,中国本轮疫情流行高峰已经过去,新增发病数持续下降,疫情总体保持在较低水平。

（20）3 月 17 日,首批 42 支国家援鄂医疗队撤离武汉。

（四）第四阶段:取得武汉保卫战、湖北保卫战决定性成果

（3 月 18 日至 4 月 28 日）

以武汉市为主战场的全国本土疫情传播基本阻断,离汉离鄂通道管控措施解除,武汉市在院新冠肺炎患者清零,武汉保卫战、湖北保卫战取得决定性成果,全国疫情防控阻击战取得重大战略成果。境内疫情零星散发,境外疫情快速扩散蔓延,境外输入病例造成关联病例传播。中共中央把握疫情形势发展变化,确定了“外防输入、内防反弹”的防控策略,巩固深化国内疫情防控成效,及时处置聚集性疫情,分类推动复工复产,关心关爱境外中国公民。（图 7）

（1）3 月 18 日,中共中央总书记习近平主持召开中共中央政治局常务委员会会议,强调要落实外防输入重点任务,完善应对输入性风险的防控策略和政策举措,决不能让来之不易的疫情防控持续向好形势发生逆转;指出要加强对境外中国公民疫情防控的指导和支持,保护他们的生命安全和身体健康。

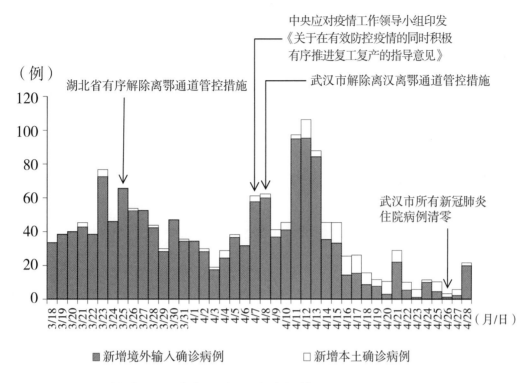

图7 中国境内新冠肺炎新增确诊病例情况（3月18日至4月28日）

（2）3月18日，国务院办公厅印发《关于应对新冠肺炎疫情影响强化稳就业举措的实施意见》。

（3）3月18日，全国新增本土确诊病例首次实现零报告。至19日，湖北省以外省份连续7日无新增本土确诊病例。

（4）3月25日，中共中央总书记习近平主持召开中共中央政治局常务委员会会议，听取疫情防控工作和当前经济形势的汇报，研究当前疫情防控和经济工作。

（5）3月25日起，湖北省有序解除离鄂通道管控措施，撤除除武汉市以外地区所有通道（市际、省界通道）检疫站点。湖北省除武汉市以外地区逐步恢复正常生产生活秩序，离鄂人员凭湖北健康码"绿码"安全有序流动。

(6)3月25日,23个省份报告了境外输入确诊病例,防止疫情扩散压力依然很大。

(7)3月26日,国家主席习近平出席二十国集团领导人特别峰会,发表题为《携手抗疫 共克时艰》的讲话。

(8)3月27日,中共中央总书记习近平主持召开中共中央政治局会议,指出要因应国内外疫情防控新形势,及时完善疫情防控策略和应对举措,把重点放在"外防输入、内防反弹"上来,保持疫情防控形势持续向好态势;强调要在疫情防控常态化条件下加快恢复生产生活秩序,力争把疫情造成的损失降到最低限度,努力完成全年经济社会发展目标任务;强调要在做好疫情防控的前提下,支持湖北有序复工复产,做好援企、稳岗、促就业、保民生等工作。

(9)3月29日至4月1日,中共中央总书记、国家主席、中央军委主席习近平前往浙江,就统筹推进新冠肺炎疫情防控和经济社会发展工作进行调研,指出要把严防境外疫情输入作为当前乃至较长一段时间疫情防控的重中之重,增强防控措施的针对性和实效性,筑起应对境外疫情输入风险的坚固防线;强调要准确识变、科学应变、主动求变,善于从眼前的危机、眼前的困难中捕捉和创造机遇;强调要在严格做好疫情防控工作的前提下,有力有序推动复工复产提速扩面,积极破解复工复产中的难点、堵点,推动全产业链联动复工。

(10)4月1日,中国海关在所有航空、水运、陆路口岸对全部入境人员实施核酸检测。

(11)4月4日清明节,举行全国性哀悼活动,全国各地各族人民深切悼念抗击新冠肺炎疫情斗争牺牲烈士和逝世同胞。

（12）4月6日，国务院联防联控机制印发《关于进一步做好重点场所重点单位重点人群新冠肺炎疫情防控相关工作的通知》和《新冠病毒无症状感染者管理规范》。

（13）4月7日，中央应对疫情工作领导小组印发《关于在有效防控疫情的同时积极有序推进复工复产的指导意见》，国务院联防联控机制印发《全国不同风险地区企事业单位复工复产疫情防控措施指南》。各地做好复工复产相关疫情防控，分区分级恢复生产秩序。

（14）4月8日，中共中央总书记习近平主持召开中共中央政治局常务委员会会议，指出要坚持底线思维，做好较长时间应对外部环境变化的思想准备和工作准备；强调"外防输入、内防反弹"防控工作决不能放松；强调要抓好无症状感染者精准防控，把疫情防控网扎得更密更牢，堵住所有可能导致疫情反弹的漏洞；强调要加强陆海口岸疫情防控，最大限度减少境外输入关联本地病例。

（15）4月8日起，武汉市解除持续76天的离汉离鄂通道管控措施，有序恢复对外交通，逐步恢复正常生产生活秩序。

（16）4月10日，湖北省在院治疗的重症、危重症患者首次降至两位数。

（17）4月14日，国务院总理李克强在北京出席东盟与中日韩（10+3）抗击新冠肺炎疫情领导人特别会议并发表讲话，介绍中国统筹推进疫情防控和经济社会发展的经验，提出全力加强防控合作、努力恢复经济发展、着力密切政策协调等合作倡议。

（18）4月15日，中共中央总书记习近平主持召开中共中央政治局常务委员会会议，听取疫情防控工作和当前经济形势汇报，研究疫情防控和经济工作。

（19）4月17日，中共中央总书记习近平主持召开中共中央政治局会议，强调要抓紧抓实抓细常态化疫情防控，因时因势完善"外防输入、内防反弹"各项措施并切实抓好落实，不断巩固疫情持续向好形势；强调要坚持稳中求进工作总基调，在稳的基础上积极进取，在常态化疫情防控中全面推进复工复产达产，恢复正常经济社会秩序，培育壮大新的增长点增长极，牢牢把握发展主动权。

（20）4月17日，武汉市新冠肺炎疫情防控指挥部发布《关于武汉市新冠肺炎确诊病例数确诊病例死亡数订正情况的通报》，对确诊和死亡病例数进行订正。截至4月16日24时，确诊病例核增325例，累计确诊病例数订正为50333例；确诊病例的死亡病例核增1290例，累计确诊病例的死亡数订正为3869例。

（21）4月20日至23日，中共中央总书记、国家主席、中央军委主席习近平在陕西考察，指出要坚持稳中求进工作总基调，坚持新发展理念，扎实做好稳就业、稳金融、稳外贸、稳外资、稳投资、稳预期工作，全面落实保居民就业、保基本民生、保市场主体、保粮食能源安全、保产业链供应链稳定、保基层运转任务，努力克服新冠肺炎疫情带来的不利影响，确保完成决战决胜脱贫攻坚目标任务，全面建成小康社会。

（22）4月23日，国务院总理李克强主持召开部分省市经济形势视频座谈会,推动做好当前经济社会发展工作。

(23)4月26日,武汉市所有新冠肺炎住院病例清零。

(24)4月27日,中共中央总书记、国家主席、中央军委主席、中央全面深化改革委员会主任习近平主持召开中央全面深化改革委员会第十三次会议,强调中国疫情防控和复工复产之所以能够有力推进,根本原因是中国共产党的领导和中国社会主义制度的优势发挥了无可比拟的重要作用;强调发展环境越是严峻复杂,越要坚定不移深化改革,健全各方面制度,完善治理体系,促进制度建设和治理效能更好转化融合,善于运用制度优势应对风险挑战冲击。

(25)4月27日,经中共中央总书记习近平和中共中央批准,中央指导组离鄂返京。

(五) 第五阶段:全国疫情防控进入常态化

(4月29日以来)

境内疫情总体呈零星散发状态,局部地区出现散发病例引起的聚集性疫情,境外输入病例基本得到控制,疫情积极向好态势持续巩固,全国疫情防控进入常态化。加大力度推进复工复产复学,常态化防控措施经受"五一"假期考验。经中共中央批准,国务院联防联控机制派出联络组,继续加强湖北省疫情防控。(图8)

(1)4月29日,中共中央总书记习近平主持召开中共中央政治局常务委员会会议,指出经过艰苦卓绝的努力,湖北保卫战、武汉保

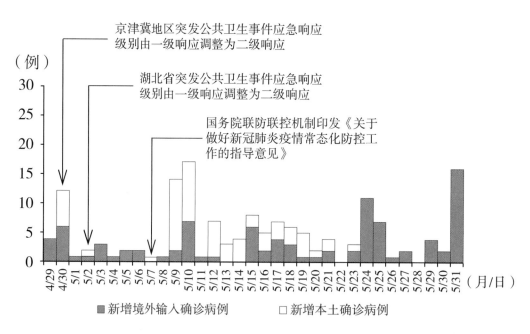

图 8　中国境内新冠肺炎新增确诊病例情况（4 月 29 日至 5 月 31 日）

卫战取得决定性成果,全国疫情防控阻击战取得重大战略成果;强调要抓好重点地区、重点群体疫情防控工作,有针对性加强输入性风险防控工作。

（2）4 月 30 日,京津冀地区突发公共卫生事件应急响应级别由一级响应调整为二级响应。

（3）5 月 1 日,世界卫生组织宣布,鉴于当前国际疫情形势,新冠肺炎疫情仍然构成"国际关注的突发公共卫生事件"。

（4）5 月 2 日,湖北省突发公共卫生事件应急响应级别由一级响应调整为二级响应。

（5）5 月 4 日,经中共中央批准,国务院联防联控机制设立联络组,赴湖北省武汉市开展工作。

（6）5 月 6 日,中共中央总书记习近平主持召开中共中央政治局常务委员会会议,指出在党中央坚强领导和全国各族人民大力支持下,中央指导组同湖北人民和武汉人民并肩作战,下最大气力控制疫情流行,努力守住全国疫情防控第一道防线,为打赢疫情防控的人民战争、总体战、阻击战作出了重要贡献;指出中共中央决定继续派出联络组,加强对湖北省和武汉市疫情防控后续工作指导支持,继续指导做好治愈患者康复和心理疏导工作,巩固疫情防控成果,决不能前功尽弃。

(7)5月7日,国务院联防联控机制印发《关于做好新冠肺炎疫情常态化防控工作的指导意见》。

(8)5月8日,中共中央召开党外人士座谈会,就新冠肺炎疫情防控工作听取各民主党派中央、全国工商联和无党派人士代表的意见和建议,中共中央总书记习近平主持座谈会并发表重要讲话,强调面对突如其来的疫情,中共中央高度重视,坚持把人民生命安全和身体健康放在第一位,果断采取一系列防控和救治举措,用一个多月的时间初步遏制了疫情蔓延势头,用两个月左右的时间将本土每日新增病例控制在个位数以内,用3个月左右的时间取得了武汉保卫战、湖北保卫战的决定性成果;指出对一个拥有14亿人口的大国来说,这样的成绩来之不易。

(9)5月11日至12日,中共中央总书记、国家主席、中央军委主席习近平赴山西,就统筹推进常态化疫情防控和经济社会发展工作、巩固脱贫攻坚成果进行调研,强调要坚持稳中求进工作总基调,坚持新发展理念,坚持以供给侧结构性改革为主线,扎实做好"六稳"工作，全面落实"六保"任务，努力克服新冠肺炎疫情带来的不利影响，在高质量转型发展上迈出更大步伐，确保完成决战决胜脱贫攻坚目标任务，全面建成小康社会。

（10）5月14日，中共中央总书记习近平主持召开中共中央政治局常务委员会会议，指出要加强重点地区、重点场所内防反弹工作，近期发生聚集性疫情的地区要有针对性加强防控措施；强调要针对境外疫情的新情况新趋势，采取更加灵活管用的措施，强化外防输入重点领域和薄弱环节。

（11）5月15日，中共中央总书记习近平主持召开中共中央政治局会议，讨论国务院拟提请第十三届全国人民代表大会第三次会议审议的《政府工作报告》稿，指出做好今年工作，要紧扣全面建成小康社会目标任务，统筹推进疫情防控和经济社会发展工作，在常态化疫情防控前提下，坚持稳中求进工作总基调，坚持新发展理念，坚持以供给侧结构性改革为主线，坚持以改革开放为动力推动高质量发展，坚决打好三大攻坚战，扎实做好"六稳"工作，全面落实"六保"任务，坚定实施扩大内需战略，维护经济发展和社会稳定大局，确保完成决战决胜脱贫攻坚目标任务，全面建成小康社会。

（12）5月18日，国家主席习近平在第73届世界卫生大会视频会议开幕式上发表题为《团结合作战胜疫情 共同构建人类卫生健康共同体》的致辞。

（13）5月21日至27日，全国政协十三届三次会议在北京举行。5月22日至28日，十三届全国人大三次会议在北京举行。

二、防控和救治两个战场协同作战

面对突发疫情侵袭,中国把人民生命安全和身体健康放在第一位,统筹疫情防控和医疗救治,采取最全面最严格最彻底的防控措施,前所未有地采取大规模隔离措施,前所未有地调集全国资源开展大规模医疗救治,不遗漏一个感染者,不放弃每一位病患,实现"应收尽收、应治尽治、应检尽检、应隔尽隔",遏制了疫情大面积蔓延,改变了病毒传播的危险进程。"通过全面执行(中国)这些措施可以争取到一些时间,即使只有几天或数周,但这对最终减少新冠肺炎感染人数和死亡人数的价值不可估量。"①

(一) 建立统一高效的指挥体系

在以习近平同志为核心的中共中央坚强领导下,建立中央统一指挥、统一协调、统一调度,各地方各方面各负其责、协调配合,集中统一、上下协同、运行高效的指挥体系,为打赢疫情防控的人民战争、总体战、阻击战提供了有力保证。

习近平总书记亲自指挥、亲自部署。习近平总书记高度重视疫

---

① 世界卫生组织网站:《中国—世界卫生组织新型冠状病毒肺炎(COVID-19)联合考察报告》(Report of the WHO-China Joint Mission on Coronavirus Disease 2019 (COVID-19))。https://www.who.int/publications-detail/report-of-the-who-china-joint-mission-on-coronavirus-disease-2019-(covid-19),2020年2月28日。

情防控工作,全面加强集中统一领导,强调把人民生命安全和身体健康放在第一位,提出"坚定信心、同舟共济、科学防治、精准施策"的总要求,明确坚决打赢疫情防控的人民战争、总体战、阻击战。习近平总书记主持召开14次中央政治局常委会会议、4次中央政治局会议以及中央全面依法治国委员会会议、中央网络安全和信息化委员会会议、中央全面深化改革委员会会议、中央外事工作委员会会议、党外人士座谈会等会议,听取中央应对疫情工作领导小组和中央指导组汇报,因时因势调整防控策略,对加强疫情防控、开展国际合作等进行全面部署;在北京就社区防控、防疫科研攻关等进行考察,亲临武汉一线视察指导,赴浙江、陕西、山西就统筹推进常态化疫情防控和经济社会发展工作、巩固脱贫攻坚成果进行考察调研;时刻关注疫情动态和防控进展,及时作出决策部署。

加强统筹协调、协同联动。中共中央政治局常委、国务院总理、中央应对疫情工作领导小组组长李克强主持召开30余次领导小组会议,研究部署疫情防控和统筹推进经济社会发展的重大问题和重要工作,赴北京、武汉等地和中国疾控中心、中国医学科学院病原生物学研究所、北京西站、首都机场及疫情防控国家重点医疗物资保障调度等平台考察调研。中央指导组指导湖北省、武汉市加强防控工作,以争分夺秒的战时状态开展工作,有力控制了疫情流行,守住了第一道防线。国务院联防联控机制发挥协调作用,持续召开例会跟踪分析研判疫情形势,加强医务人员和医疗物资调度,根据疫情发展变化相应调整防控策略和重点工作。国务院复工复产推进工作机制,加强复工复产统筹指导和协调服务,打通产业链、供应链堵点,增强协同复工复产动能。

各地方各方面守土有责、守土尽责。全国各省、市、县成立由党政主要负责人挂帅的应急指挥机制,自上而下构建统一指挥、一线指导、统筹协调的应急决策指挥体系。在中共中央统一领导下,各地方各方面坚决贯彻中央决策部署,有令必行、有禁必止,严格高效落实各项防控措施,全国形成了全面动员、全面部署、全面加强,横向到边、纵向到底的疫情防控局面。

(二) 构建全民参与严密防控体系

针对春节期间人员密集、流动性大的特点,中国迅速开展社会动员、发动全民参与,坚持依法、科学、精准防控,在全国范围内实施史无前例的大规模公共卫生应对举措,通过超常规的社会隔离和灵活、人性化的社会管控措施,构建联防联控、群防群控防控体系,打响抗击疫情人民战争,通过非药物手段有效阻断了病毒传播链条。

采取有力措施坚决控制传染源。以确诊患者、疑似患者、发热患者、确诊患者的密切接触者等"四类人员"为重点,实行"早发现、早报告、早隔离、早治疗"和"应收尽收、应治尽治、应检尽检、应隔尽隔"的防治方针,最大限度降低传染率。关闭离汉通道期间,武汉对全市421万户居民集中开展两轮拉网式排查,以"不落一户、不漏一人"标准实现"存量清零",确保没有新的潜在感染源发生。持续提升核酸检测能力,增强试剂盒供应能力,扩充检测机构,缩短检测周期,确保检测质量,实现"应检尽检""即收即检"。湖北省检测周期从2天缩短到4—6小时,日检测量由疫情初期的300人份提升到4月中旬的5万人份以上,缩短了患者确诊时间,降低了传播风险。在全国范围内排查"四类人员",以社区网格为基础单元,采取上门排查与自查自报相结合的方式展开地毯式排查。全面实行各类场所体温筛查,强化医疗机构发热门诊病例监测和传染病网络直报,实行2小时网络直报、12小时反馈检测结果、24小时内完成现场流行病学调查,及时发现和报告确诊病例和无症状感染者。加强流行病学追踪调查,精准追踪和切断病毒传播途径,截至5月31日,全国累计追踪管理密切接触者74万余人。

第一时间切断病毒传播链。对湖北省、武汉市对外通道实施最严格的封闭和交通管控,暂停武汉及湖北国际客运航班、多地轮渡、长途客运、机场、火车站运营,全国暂停入汉道路水路客运班线发班,武汉市及湖北省多地暂停市内公共交通,阻断疫情向全国以及湖北省内卫生基础设施薄弱的农村地区扩散。对湖北以外地区实施差异化交通管控,湖北省周边省份筑牢环鄂交通管控"隔离带",防止湖北省疫情外溢蔓延。全国其他地区实行分区分级精准防控,对城乡道路运输服务进行动态管控,加强国内交通卫生检疫。采取有效措施避免人员聚集和交叉感染,延长春节假期,取消或延缓各种人员聚集性活动,各类学校有序推迟开学;关闭影院、剧院、网吧以及健身房等场所;对车站、机场、码头、农贸市场、商场、超市、餐馆、酒店、宾馆等需要开放的公共服务类场所,以及汽车、火车、飞机等密闭交通工具,落实环境卫生整治、消毒、通风、"进出检"、限流等措施,进入人员必须测量体温、佩戴口罩;推行政务服务网上办、预约办,推广无接触快递等"不见面"服务,鼓励民众居家和企业远程办公,有效减少人员流动和聚集;在公共场所设置"一米线"并配以明显标识,避免近距离接触。全国口岸实施严格的出入境卫生检疫,防范疫情通过口岸扩散蔓延。实施最严边境管控,取消非紧急非必要出国出境活动。

牢牢守住社区基础防线。城乡社区是疫情联防联控的第一线,是外防输入、内防扩散的关键防线。充分发挥基层主体作用,加强群众自治,实施社区封闭式、网格化管理,把防控力量、资源、措施向社区下沉,组建专兼结合工作队伍,充分发挥街道(乡镇)和社区(村)干部、基层医疗卫生机构医务人员、家庭医生团队作用,将一个个社区、村庄打造成为严密安全的"抗疫堡垒",把防控有效落实到终端和末梢。按照"追踪到人、登记在册、社区管理、上门观察、规范运转、异常就医"的原则,依法对重点人群进行有效管理,开展主动追踪、人员管理、环境整治和健康教育。武汉市全面实施社区24小时封闭管理,除就医和防疫相关活动外一律禁止出入,由社区承担居民生活保障。其他地方对城市社区、农村村落普遍实施封闭式管理,人员出入检查登记、测量体温。加强居民个人防护,广泛开展社会宣传,强化个体责任意识,自觉落实居家隔离以及跨地区旅行后隔离14天等防控要求,严格执行外出佩戴口罩、保持社交距离、减少聚集等防护措施,养成勤洗手、常通风等良好生活习惯。大力开展爱国卫生运动,提倡文明健康、绿色环保的生活方式。

实施分级、分类、动态精准防控。全国推行分区分级精准施策防控策略,以县域为单位,依据人口、发病情况综合研判,划分低、中、高疫情风险等级,分区分级实施差异化防控,并根据疫情形势及时动态调整名单,采取对应防控措施。低风险区严防输入,全面恢复生产生活秩序;中风险区外防输入、内防扩散,尽快全面恢复生产生活秩序;高风险区内防扩散、外防输出、严格管控,集中精力抓疫情防控。本土疫情形势稳定后,以省域为单元在疫情防控常态化条件下加快恢复生产生活秩序,健全及时发现、快速处置、精准管控、有效救治的常态化防控机制。全力做好北京市疫情防控,确保首都安全。做好重点场所、重点单位、重点人群聚集性疫情防控和处置,加强老年人、儿童、孕产妇、学生、医务人员等重点人群健康管理,加强医疗机构、社区、办公场所、商场超市、客运场站、交通运输工具,托幼机构、中小学校、大专院校以及养老机构、福利院、精神卫生医疗机构、救助站等特殊场所的管控,覆盖全人群、全场所、全社区,不留死角、不留空白、不留隐患。针对输入性疫情,严格落实国境卫生检疫措施,强化从"国门"到"家门"的全链条、闭环式管理,持续抓紧抓实抓细外防输入、内防反弹工作。

为疫情防控提供有力法治保障。依法将新冠肺炎纳入《中华人民共和国传染病防治法》规定的乙类传染病并采取甲类传染病的预防、控制措施,纳入《中华人民共和国国境卫生检疫法》规定的检疫传染病管理,同时做好国际国内法律衔接。一些地方人大常委会紧急立法,在国家法律和法规框架下授权地方政府在医疗卫生、防疫管理等方面,规定临时性应急行政管理措施。严格执行传染病防治法及其实施办法等法律法规,出台依法防控疫情、依法惩治违法犯罪、保障人民生命健康安全的意见,加强治安管理、市场监管,依法惩处哄抬物价、囤积居奇、制假售假等破坏疫情防控的违法犯罪行为,强化防疫物资质量和价格监管,加大打击虚假违法广告力度,保障社会稳定有序。加强疫情防控期间行政执法监督,严格规范执法,公正文明执法,依法化解与疫情相关的法律纠纷,为疫情防控和企业复工复产提供法律保障和服务。加强普法宣传,引导公众依法行事。

遵循科学规律开展防控。新冠病毒是新病毒,对其认识需要有个过程。积极借鉴以往经验,紧密结合中国国情,遵循流行病学规律,探索行之有效的方法手段,用中国办法破解疫情防控难题。注重发挥病毒学、流行病学、临床医学等领域专家作用,及时开展疫情形势分析研判,提出防控策略建议,充分尊重专家意见,增强疫情防控的科学性专业性。秉持科学态度,加强病毒感染、致病机理、传播途径、传播能力等研究,与世界卫生组织及其他国家和地区保持沟通交流。随着对病毒认识的不断深化,及时调整和优化工作措施,不断提升防控水平。根据疫情形势变化和评估结果,先后制修订6版新冠肺炎防控方案,科学规范开展病例监测、流行病学调查、可疑暴露者和密切接触者管理以及实验室检测等工作。针对重点人群、重点场所、重点单位发布15项防控技术方案、6项心理疏导工作方案,并细化形成 50 项防控技术指南,进一步提高疫情防控的科学性精准性。

(三) 全力救治患者、拯救生命

医疗救治始终以提高收治率和治愈率、降低感染率和病亡率的"两提高""两降低"为目标,坚持集中患者、集中专家、集中资源、集中救治"四集中"原则,坚持中西医结合,实施分类救治、分级管理。对重症患者,调集最优秀的医生、最先进的设备、最急需的资源,不惜一切代价进行救治,大幅度降低病亡率;对轻症患者及早干预,尽可能在初期得以治愈,大幅度降低转重率。

集中优势资源加强重症救治。疫情突发导致武汉市医疗资源挤兑。针对疫情初期患者数量激增与床位资源不足的突出矛盾,集中资源和力量在武汉市建设扩充重症定点医院和救治床位,将全部重症危重症患者集中到综合实力最强且具备呼吸道传染性疾病收治条件的综合医院集中开展救治。建成火神山、雷神山两座各可容纳1000 多张床位的传染病专科医院,改扩建一批定点医院,改造一批综合医院,使重症床位从 1000 张左右迅速增加至 9100 多张,解决了重症患者大规模收治难题。优化重症救治策略,制定个体化医疗救治方案。建立专家巡查制度,定期组织专家团队对武汉市定点医院重症患者救治进行巡诊,评估患者病情和治疗方案。针对超过 80%的重症患者合并严重基础性疾病情况,实行"一人一策",建立感染、呼吸、重症、心脏、肾脏等多学科会诊制度,并制定重症、危重症护理规范,推出高流量吸氧、无创和有创机械通气、俯卧位通气等措施。严格落实疑难危重症患者会诊制度、死亡病例讨论制度等医疗质量安全核心制度,强化对治愈出院患者健康监测,确保重症患者救治质量。开展康复者恢复期血浆采集和临床治疗工作,建立应急储备库,截至5月31日,全国共采集恢复期血浆2765人次,1689人次患者接受恢复期血浆治疗,取得较好治疗效果。

对轻症患者及早干预治疗。及时收治轻症患者,及早实施医疗干预,尽量减少轻症转为重症。完善临床救治体系,全国共指定1万余家定点医院,对新冠肺炎患者实行定点集中治疗。建立全国医疗救治协作网络,通过远程会诊方式提供技术支持。武汉市针对患者数量急剧增长、80%左右是轻症的情况,集中力量将一批体育场馆、会展中心等改造成16家方舱医院,床位达到1.4万余张,使轻症患者应收尽收、应治尽治,减少了社区感染传播,减少了轻症向重症转化。16家方舱医院累计收治患者1.2万余人,累计治愈出院8000余人、转院3500余人,实现"零感染、零死亡、零回头"。方舱医院是阻击重大传染病的重大创新,使"应收尽收""床位等人"成为现实,有力扭转了防控形势。英国《柳叶刀》社论认为,"中国建造的方舱庇护医院对于缓解医疗卫生系统所承受的巨大压力有着至关重要的作用"。[1]

---

[1] 《柳叶刀》:《中国持续遏制新冠肺炎疫情》(Sustaining containment of COVID-19 in China) https://www.thelancet.com/journals/lancet/article/PIIS0140-6736(20)30864-3/fulltext,2020年4月18日。

及时总结推广行之有效的诊疗方案。坚持边实践、边研究、边探索、边总结、边完善,在基于科学认知和证据积累的基础上,将行之有效的诊疗技术和科技研究成果纳入诊疗方案。先后制修订7版新冠肺炎诊疗方案,3版重型、危重型病例诊疗方案,2版轻型、普通型管理规范,2版康复者恢复期血浆治疗方案,1版新冠肺炎出院患者主要功能障碍康复治疗方案,提高了医疗救治工作的科学性和规范性。最新的第7版新冠肺炎诊疗方案增加病理改变内容,增补和调整临床表现、诊断标准、治疗方法和出院标准等,并纳入无症状感染者可能具有感染性、康复者恢复期血浆治疗等新发现。目前,第7版诊疗方案已被多个国家借鉴和采用。强化治愈出院患者隔离管理和健康监测,加强复诊复检和康复,实现治疗、康复和健康监测一体化全方位医疗服务。注重孕产妇、儿童等患者差异性诊疗策略,实现不同人群诊疗方案的全覆盖。

充分发挥中医药特色优势。坚持中西医结合、中西药并用,发挥中医药治未病、辨证施治、多靶点干预的独特优势,全程参与深度介入疫情防控,从中医角度研究确定病因病机、治则治法,形成了覆盖医学观察期、轻型、普通型、重型、危重型、恢复期发病全过程的中医诊疗规范和技术方案,在全国范围内全面推广使用。中医医院、中医团队参与救治,中医医疗队整建制接管定点医院若干重症病区和方舱医院,其他方舱医院派驻中医专家。中医药早期介入、全程参与、分类救治,对轻症患者实施中医药早介入早使用;对重症和危重症患者实行中西医结合;对医学观察发热病人和密切接触者服用中药提高免疫力；对出院患者实施中医康复方案，建立全国新冠肺炎康复协作网络，提供康复指导。中医药参与救治确诊病例的占比达到92%。湖北省确诊病例中医药使用率和总有效率超过90%。筛选金花清感颗粒、连花清瘟胶囊/颗粒、血必净注射液和清肺排毒汤、化湿败毒方、宣肺败毒方等"三药三方"为代表的针对不同类型新冠肺炎的治疗中成药和方药，临床疗效确切，有效降低了发病率、转重率、病亡率，促进了核酸转阴，提高了治愈率，加快了恢复期康复。

实施患者免费救治。 及时预拨疫情防控资金，确保患者不因费用问题影响就医，确保各地不因资金问题影响医疗救治和疫情防控。截至5月31日，全国各级财政共安排疫情防控资金1624亿元。及时调整医保政策，明确确诊和疑似患者医疗保障政策，对确诊和疑似患者实行"先救治，后结算"。对新冠肺炎患者（包括确诊和疑似患者）发生的医疗费用，在基本医保、大病保险、医疗救助等按规定支付后，个人负担部分由财政给予补助。异地就医医保支付的费用由就医地医保部门先行垫付。截至5月31日，全国确诊住院患者结算人数5.8万人次，总医疗费用13.5亿元，确诊患者人均医疗费用约2.3万元。其中，重症患者人均治疗费用超过15万元，一些危重症患者治疗费用几十万元甚至上百万元，全部由国家承担。

加强医疗机构感染控制和医务人员防护。 制定感染控制技术指南和制度文件，明确医疗机构重点区域、就诊流程"三区两通道"建筑布局要求。加强对医务人员的感染控制培训，开展全国督导，确保感染控制措施落实。对疫情严重、院内感染风险高、医疗救治压力大的重点地区重点医院,有针对性地开展指导。加强医疗废物分类收集、运送贮存,做好病亡者遗体处置。在援鄂援汉医疗队中配置感染控制专家,全国支援湖北省和武汉市的医务人员没有感染病例。2月份以后,全国医务人员感染病例报告数明显减少。关心关爱医务人员,制定一系列保障政策,开展心理疏导,妥善安排轮换休整,缓解身体和心理压力,保持一线医务人员战斗力。

（四）依法及时公开透明发布疫情信息

在全力做好疫情防控的同时,中国以对生命负责、对人民负责、对历史负责、对国际社会负责的态度,建立最严格且专业高效的信息发布制度,第一时间发布权威信息,速度、密度、力度前所未有。持续、权威、清晰的疫情信息,有效回应了公众关切、凝聚了社会共识,为其他国家提供了参考和借鉴。

建立严格的疫情发布机制。依法、及时、公开、透明发布疫情信息,制定严格规定,坚决防止瞒报、迟报、漏报。武汉市从 2019 年 12 月 31 日起依法发布疫情信息,并逐步增加信息发布频次。2020 年 1 月 21 日起,国家卫生健康委每日在官方网站、政务新媒体平台发布前一天全国疫情信息,各省级卫生健康部门每日统一发布前一天本省份疫情信息。2 月 3 日起,国家卫生健康委英文网站同步发布相关数据。

建立分级分层新闻发布制度。坚持国家和地方相结合、现场发布与网上发布相结合,建立多层次多渠道多平台信息发布机制,持续发布权威信息,及时回应国内外关注的疫情形势、疫情防控、医疗救治、科研攻关等热点问题。截至 5 月 31 日,国务院联防联控机制、国务院新闻办公室共举行新闻发布会 161 场,邀请 50 多个部门 490 余人次出席发布会,回答中外媒体 1400 多个提问;湖北省举行 103 场新闻发布会,其他省份共举行 1050 场新闻发布会。

依法适时订正病例数据。本土疫情得到控制后,为确保公开透明、数据准确,武汉市针对疫情早期因收治能力不足导致患者在家中病亡、医院超负荷运转、死亡病例信息登记不全等原因,客观上存在迟报、漏报、误报现象,根据相关法律规定,在深入开展涉疫大数据与流行病学调查的基础上,对确诊和死亡病例数进行了订正,并向社会公开发布。

多渠道多平台传播信息。国家卫生健康委中、英文官方网站和政务新媒体平台设置疫情防控专题页面,发布每日疫情信息,解读政策措施,介绍中国抗疫进展,普及科学防控知识,澄清谣言传言。各省(自治区、直辖市)政府网站及政务新媒体平台及时发布本地疫情信息和防控举措。大力开展应急科普,通过科普专业平台、媒体和互联网面向公众普及科学认知、科学防治知识,组织权威专家介绍日常防控常识,引导公众理性认识新冠肺炎疫情,做好个人防护,消除恐慌恐惧。加强社会舆论引导,各类媒体充分传递抗击疫情正能量,同时发挥舆论监督作用,推动解决疫情防控中出现的问题。

（五）充分发挥科技支撑作用

科学技术是人类同疾病较量的锐利武器，人类战胜大灾大疫离不开科学发展和技术创新。面对人类未知的新冠病毒，中国坚持以科学为先导，充分运用近年来科技创新成果，组织协调全国优势科研力量，以武汉市为主战场，统筹全国和疫情重灾区，根据疫情发展不同阶段确定科研攻关重点，坚持科研、临床、防控一线相互协同和产学研各方紧密配合，为疫情防控提供了有力科技支撑。

实施科研应急攻关。遵循安全、有效、可供的原则，加快推进药物、疫苗、新型检测试剂等研发和应用。适应疫情防控一线的紧迫需求，围绕"可溯、可诊、可治、可防、可控"，坚持产学研用相结合，聚焦临床救治和药物、疫苗研发、检测技术和产品、病毒病原学和流行病学、动物模型构建5大主攻方向，组织全国优势力量开展疫情防控科技攻关，加速推进科技研发和应用，部署启动83个应急攻关项目。按照灭活疫苗、重组蛋白疫苗、减毒流感病毒载体疫苗、腺病毒载体疫苗、核酸疫苗等5条技术路线开展疫苗研发。目前，已有4种灭活疫苗和1种腺病毒载体疫苗获批开展临床试验，总体研发进度与国外持平，部分技术路线进展处于国际领先。组织科研团队开展科学溯源研究。

坚持科研攻关和临床救治、防控实践相结合。第一时间研发出核酸检测试剂盒，推出一批灵敏度高、操作便捷的检测设备和试剂，检测试剂研发布局涵盖核酸检测、基因测序、免疫法检测等多个技术路径。坚持"老药新用"基本思路,积极筛选有效治疗药物,探索新的治疗手段,在严谨的体外研究和机制研究基础上,不断总结救治经验,推动磷酸氯喹、恢复期血浆、托珠单抗和中医药方剂、中成药等10种药物或治疗手段进入诊疗方案,获得4项临床批件,形成5项指导意见或专家共识。开展试验性临床治疗,加快推广应用临床验证有效的诊疗方法和药物。强化实验室生物安全监管,加强新冠病毒临床检测血液样本和实验室检测生物样本管理。

运用大数据、人工智能等新技术开展防控。充分利用大数据、人工智能等新技术,进行疫情趋势研判,开展流行病学调查,努力找到每一个感染者、穷尽式地追踪密切接触者并进行隔离。建立数据库,依法开展疫情防控风险数据服务,对不同风险人群进行精准识别,预判不同地区疫情风险,为促进人员有序流动和复工复产提供服务。通过5G视频实时对话平台,偏远山区的流行病学调查团队可以与几千公里之外的高级别专家实时互动交流。经公民个人授权,推广个人"健康码""通信大数据行程卡"作为出行、复工复产复学、日常生活及出入公共场所的凭证,根据查询结果进行管控通行和分类处置,实现分区分级的精准识别、精准施策和精准防控。利用大数据技术绘制"疫情地图",通过社区名称、地址和位置,标明疫情传播具体地点、距离、人数等,为公众防范传染提供方便。

此次新冠肺炎疫情防控,为应对重大突发公共卫生事件积累了宝贵经验，同时也暴露出国家公共卫生应急管理体系存在的不足。中国将认真总结疫情防控和医疗救治经验教训，研究采取一系列重要举措，补短板、强弱项。改革完善疾病预防控制体系，建设平战结合的重大疫情防控救治体系，健全应急物资保障体系，加强构建关键核心技术攻关新型举国体制，深入开展爱国卫生运动，不断完善公共卫生体系，切实提高应对突发重大公共卫生事件的能力和水平，更好维护人民生命安全和身体健康。

三、凝聚抗击疫情的强大力量

面对未知病毒突然袭击,中国坚持人民至上、生命至上,举全国之力,快速有效调动全国资源和力量,不惜一切代价维护人民生命安全和身体健康。中国共产党以人民为中心的执政理念,中国集中力量办大事的制度特点,改革开放40多年来特别是中共十八大以来积累的雄厚综合国力和国家治理现代化建设的显著成效,中华民族同舟共济、守望相助的文化底色,中国人民深厚的家国情怀、天下情怀,汇聚成抗击疫情的强大合力。

(一) 人的生命高于一切

在新冠肺炎疫情突袭,人民生命安全和身体健康受到严重威胁的重大时刻,中国共产党和中国政府始终以对人民负责、对生命负责的鲜明态度,准确分析和把握形势,既多方考量、慎之又慎,又及时出手、坚决果敢,以非常之举应对非常之事,全力保障人民生命权、健康权。

在人民生命和经济利益之间果断抉择生命至上。疫情暴发后,以宁可一段时间内经济下滑甚至短期"停摆",也要对人民生命安全和身体健康负责的巨大勇气,对湖北省和武汉市果断采取史无前例的全面严格管控措施。同时,在全国范围内严控人员流动,延长春节假期,停止人员聚集性活动,决定全国企业和学校延期开工开学,迅速遏制疫情的传播蔓延,避免更多人受到感染。英国《柳叶刀》社论认为,"中国的成功也伴随着巨大的社会和经济代价,中国必须做出艰难的决定,从而在国民健康与经济保护之间获得最佳平衡"。[①] 在疫情防控的关键阶段,准确把握疫情形势变化,作出统筹推进疫情防控和经济社会发展的重大决策,有序恢复生产生活秩序,推动落实分区分级精准复工复产,最大限度保障民生和人民正常生产生活。随着本土疫情防控取得重大战略成果,及时采取"外防输入、内防反弹"的防控策略,坚决防止来之不易的持续向好形势发生逆转,坚决防止人民生命安全再次面临病毒威胁。

不惜一切代价抢救生命。疫情初期,病毒感染者急剧增多,中国把提高治愈率、降低病亡率作为首要任务,快速充实医疗救治力量,把优质资源集中到救治一线。采取积极、科学、灵活的救治策略,慎终如始、全力以赴救治每一位患者,从出生仅30个小时的婴儿至100多岁的老人,不计代价抢救每一位患者的生命。为了抢救病患,医务人员冒着被感染的风险采集病毒样本,没有人畏难退缩。为满足重症患者救治需要,想尽一切办法筹措人工膜肺(ECMO)设备,能买尽买,能调尽调。武汉市重症定点医院累计收治重症病例9600多例,

---

① 《柳叶刀》:《中国持续遏制新冠肺炎疫情》(Sustaining containment of COVID-19 in China) https://www.thelancet.com/journals/lancet/article/PIIS0140-6736(20)30864-3/fulltext,2020年4月18日。

转归为治愈的占比从 14% 提高到 89%,超过一般病毒性肺炎救治平均水平。对伴有基础性疾病的老年患者,一人一案、精准施策,只要有一丝希望绝不轻易放弃,只要有抢救需要,人员、药品、设备、经费全力保障。疫情发生以来,湖北省成功治愈 3000 余位 80 岁以上、7 位百岁以上新冠肺炎患者,多位重症老年患者是从死亡线上抢救回来的。一位 70 岁老人身患新冠肺炎,10 多名医护人员精心救护几十天,终于挽回了老人生命,治疗费用近 150 万元全部由国家承担。

关心关爱海外中国公民。国家时刻挂念海外中国公民的安危,敦促、支持有关国家政府采取有效措施保障当地华侨、留学生、中资机构人员等安全。派出医疗专家组、工作组,开设远程医疗服务平台,为海外中国公民提供科学专业的疫情防控指导。协调外方全力救治在国外确诊感染的中国公民,充分调动国内专家、援外医疗队等资源,积极支持配合外方开展救治。驻外使领馆尽力履行领事保护职能,通过各种渠道宣介疫情防护知识,向留学生发放 100 多万份"健康包"。协助在海外确有困难的中国公民有序回国。

以国之名悼念逝者。4 月 4 日清明节,中国举行全国性哀悼活动,深切悼念抗击疫情斗争牺牲烈士和逝世同胞,为没有等来春天的生命默哀,向所有用生命守护生命的英雄致敬。从最高领导人到普通民众,14 亿中国人民以最深的怀念为牺牲烈士和逝世同胞送行。中国以国家之名和最高仪式祭奠逝者,是国家对人民个体尊严与生命的尊重与敬畏,是 14 亿中国人民集体情感背后的团结和力量。

（二）举全国之力抗击疫情

一方有难，八方支援。疫情发生后，全国上下紧急行动，依托强大综合国力，开展全方位的人力组织战、物资保障战、科技突击战、资源运动战，全力支援湖北省和武汉市抗击疫情，在最短时间集中最大力量阻断疫情传播。"中方行动速度之快、规模之大，世所罕见，展现出中国速度、中国规模、中国效率"。①

开展新中国成立以来规模最大的医疗支援行动。调动全国医疗资源和力量，全力支持湖北省和武汉市医疗救治。自 1 月 24 日除夕至 3 月 8 日，全国共调集 346 支国家医疗队、4.26 万名医务人员、900多名公共卫生人员驰援湖北。19 个省份以对口支援、以省包市的方式支援湖北省除武汉市以外 16 个地市，各省在发生疫情、防控救治任务十分繁重的情况下，集中优质医疗资源支援湖北省和武汉市。人民解放军派出 4000 多名医务人员支援湖北，承担火神山医院等 3家医疗机构的医疗救治任务，空军出动运输机紧急运送医疗物资。各医疗队从接受指令到组建 2 小时内完成，24 小时内抵达，并自带 7天防护物资，抵达后迅速开展救治。在全国紧急调配全自动测温仪、负压救护车、呼吸机、心电监护仪等重点医疗物资支援湖北省和武汉市（表 1）。从全国调集 4 万名建设者和几千台机械设备，仅用 10 天

---

① 谭德塞：《习近平会见世界卫生组织总干事谭德塞》，新华网，http://www.xinhuanet.com/politics/leaders/2020-01/28/c_1125508831.htm，2020 年 1 月 28 日。

建成有 1000 张病床的火神山医院,仅用 12 天建成有 1600 张病床的雷神山医院。短短 10 多天建成 16 座方舱医院,共有 1.4 万余张床位。加强临床血液供应,10 个省份无偿支援湖北省红细胞 4.5 万单位,血小板 1762 个治疗量,新鲜冰冻血浆 137 万毫升(不含恢复期血浆)。大规模、强有力的医疗支援行动,有力保障了湖北省和武汉市救治,极大缓解了重灾区医疗资源严重不足的压力。

表1:疫情发生以来调往湖北省医疗物资情况(截至 4 月 30 日)

序号	类别	品种	单位	数量
1	医疗设备	全自动测温仪	台	20033
2		负压救护车	辆	1065
3		呼吸机	台	17655
4		心电监护仪	台	15746
5	消杀用品	84 消毒液	吨	1874
6		免洗洗手液	万瓶	71.4
7	防护用品	医用手套	万副	198.7
8		防护服	万套	773
9		医用 N95 口罩	万只	498
10		医用非 N95 口罩	万只	2720
11	防控药品	磷酸氯喹	万片/粒	40
12		阿比多尔	万片/粒	360

大力加强医疗物资生产供应和医疗支持服务。疫情防控阻击战,也是后勤保障战。疫情初期,武汉市医疗防护物资极度短缺,为了节省防护用品、争分夺秒抢救病患,一线医护人员克服困难,最大限度地延长防护用品使用时间。为尽快解决医疗资源短缺和病患急剧增多的突出矛盾,中国充分发挥制造业门类全、韧性强和产业链完

整配套的优势,克服春节假期停工减产等不利因素,开足马力,深挖潜力,全力保障上下游原料供应和物流运输,保证疫情防控物资的大规模生产与配送。医疗企业克服工人返岗不足等困难,以最快速度恢复医疗用品生产,最大限度扩大产能。其他行业企业迅速调整转产,生产口罩、防护服、消毒液、测温仪等防疫物资,有效扩大了疫情防控物资的生产供应。快速启动防控医疗物资应急审批程序,全面加强质量安全监管,确保以最快的速度批准上市、促产保供,截至5月31日,共应急批准17个药物和疫苗的19件临床试验申请,附条件批准2个疫情防控用药上市。在各方共同努力下,医用物资产能不断提升,医用物资保供实现从"紧缺"到"紧平衡""动态平衡""动态足额供应"的跨越式提升(表2)。2月初,医用非N95口罩、医用N95口罩日产量分别为586万只、13万只,到4月底分别超过2亿只、500万只。畅通供应链条和物流渠道,建立联保联供协作机制,源源不断地把全国支援物资运送到疫情防控重点地区。

表2:重点医疗物资生产情况(截至4月30日)

	类别	指标产品	日产能	日产量	日产量较疫情初期(1月底)增长倍数
1	防护用品	医用防护服(万套)	189	80	90.6倍
2	消杀用品	免洗手消毒液(吨)	409	308	2.6倍
		84消毒液(万箱)	36.6	11.7	1.6倍
3	医疗设备	全自动红外测温仪(万台)	1.07	0.34	23.3倍
4	检测用品	病毒检测试剂(万人份)	1020	760	58倍

统筹协调生活物资保障。离汉通道关闭后,武汉市近千万人居家隔离,每天需要消耗大量的粮食、蔬菜、肉蛋奶。加强联动协调,建立央地协同、政企联动的 9 省联保联供协作和 500 家应急保供企业调运机制,加大粮油供应力度,投放中央冻猪肉储备,提升蔬菜大省产品供应能力,组织紧急物资运输队伍,全力保障湖北省特别是武汉市居民生活必需品的生产、库存、供应和价格稳定。1 月 27 日至 3 月 19 日,全国通过铁路、公路、水运、民航、邮政快递等运输方式向湖北地区运送防疫物资和生活物资 92.88 万吨,运送电煤、燃油等生产物资 148.7 万吨,煤、电、油、气、热等能源供应充足,保障了湖北省、武汉市社会正常运转和隔离措施顺利实施。武汉市将生活物资配送纳入社区服务,打通生活物资配送从商场、超市到小区的最后环节,通过无接触配送方式将经过检疫、符合防疫标准的蔬菜直送社区,保障了隔离期间居民生活需要和防疫安全。

社会力量广泛参与。工会、共青团、妇联等人民团体和群众组织,组织动员所联系群众积极投身疫情防控。城乡居民、企业、社会组织等纷纷捐款捐物、献出爱心。各级慈善组织、红十字会加强捐赠资金和物资的调配和拨付,将捐赠款物重点投向湖北省和武汉市等疫情严重地区。截至 5 月 31 日,累计接受社会捐赠资金约 389.3 亿元、物资约 9.9 亿件,累计拨付捐款资金约 328.3 亿元、物资约 9.4 亿件。

疫情发生后,港澳台同胞和海外侨胞通过各种方式和渠道伸出援手,积极捐款和捐赠各类防疫物资,体现了浓浓的同胞亲情,体现了海内外中华儿女守望相助、共克时艰的凝聚力向心力。

（三）平衡疫情防控与经济社会民生

在毫不放松加强疫情防控的同时，稳妥有序放开经济和社会活动，做好"六稳"工作，落实"六保"任务，形成同疫情防控相适应的经济社会运行秩序，努力将疫情对经济社会发展的冲击和影响降到最低，为抗击疫情提供有力的物资保障和社会保障。

保持社会稳定、有序运转。 着力加强社会安全稳定工作，加强社会治安管理，强化防疫物资质量和价格监管，维护市场秩序和社会稳定。及时出台受疫情影响困难群众兜底保障政策，有效保障基本生活。将心理危机干预纳入疫情防控，妥善处理疫情防控中思想和心理问题，加强思想引导和心理疏导，培育理性平和、积极健康的心态，及时预防化解涉疫矛盾纠纷。疫情大考下，在交通管制、全民居家隔离等严格管控措施的情况下，不论是城市还是农村，水、电、燃气、通信不停，生活物资供应不断，社会秩序不乱，食品、药品、能源、基础工业品、基本公共服务等关系国计民生的重点行业有序运转，14亿人民的基本民生得到有效保障，经济社会大局保持了稳定有序。

有序推动复工复产。 密集制定出台多项政策，为企业特别是中小企业和个体工商户减负纾困，实施减费降税，增加财政补贴，加大金融支持，减负稳岗扩就业，优化政府服务。各地方及时制定实施细则，将疫情防控、公共事业运行、群众生活必需等领域的1万多家企业列为重点,通过租用专车、专列、包机等方式"点对点""一站式"帮助农民工返岗,并从个人防护物资、人流、物流等方面为企业复工提供全方位服务。针对公共交通运输、餐饮、住宿、旅游、体育、娱乐等受疫情影响较大的行业,采取免征增值税等税收优惠政策。阶段性减免企业社保费,缓缴住房公积金,免收公路通行费,降低企业用电用气价格,减轻小微企业和个体工商户房租负担。对中小微企业贷款实施临时性延期还本付息、新增优惠利率贷款。支持大学生、农民工等重点群体创业就业,扩大中小微企业稳岗返还政策受益面,发力稳就业,促进中小企业发展。用好用足出口退税、出口信用保险政策,扩大出口信贷投放,开拓多元化市场,加快压减外资准入负面清单,持续扩大外资市场准入,为企业"补血""减负""拓空间"。国有企业发挥主力军作用,带动上下游产业和中小企业全面复工复产。截至 4 月底,全国规模以上工业企业复工率超过 99%,中小微企业复工率达到 88.4%,重大项目复工率超过 95%;湖北全省规模以上工业企业复工率、员工到岗率分别达到 98.2%、92.1%,整体接近全国平均水平。一批国家重点科技专项、超级民生工程、重大标志性外资项目重现往日繁忙景象。中国经济运行加快回归常态,经济活力正在快速释放。

公众生活逐步恢复。随着疫情防控形势积极向好,公众日常生活逐步恢复。公共交通全面恢复运行,餐饮门店有序开放堂食。"五一"假期重新绽放活力,全国铁路、道路、水路、民航累计发送旅客 1.21 亿人次,全国累计接待国内游客 1.15 亿人次,实现国内旅游收入 475.6 亿元,经受住了疫情和假期的双重考验。在落实防控措施前提下,全面开放商场、超市、宾馆、餐馆等生活场所。全国分批分次复学复课,截至 5 月 31 日,各省(自治区、直辖市)和新疆生产建设兵团中小学部分学段均已开学,共有 1.63 亿学生(含幼儿园)返校。中国社会正在恢复往常热闹景象,人气日益回暖,消费逐步复苏。

(四) 14 亿中国人民坚韧奉献守望相助

国家兴亡,匹夫有责。14 亿中国人民,不分男女老幼,不论岗位分工,都自觉投入抗击疫情的人民战争,坚韧团结、和衷共济,凝聚起抗击疫情的磅礴力量。14 亿中国人民都是抗击疫情的伟大战士。

医务工作者白衣执甲、逆行出征。从年逾古稀的院士专家,到 90 后、00 后的年轻医护人员,面对疫情义无反顾、坚定前行。54 万名湖北省和武汉市医务人员冲锋在前,4 万多名军地医务人员第一时间驰援湖北省和武汉市,数百万名医务人员战斗在全国抗疫一线。他们以对人民的赤诚和对生命的敬佑,争分夺秒、舍生忘死、连续作战,挽救了一个又一个垂危生命,用血肉之躯构筑起阻击病毒的钢铁长城,为病毒肆虐的漫漫黑夜带来了光明,守护了国家和民族生生不息的希望。他们与病毒直面战斗,承受难以想象的身体和心理压力,付出巨大牺牲,2000 多人确诊感染,几十人以身殉职。没有人生而英勇,只是选择了无畏。中国医生的医者仁心和大爱无疆,永远铭刻在中华民族历史上,永远铭刻在中国人民心中。

武汉人民和湖北人民顾全大局、顽强不屈,为阻击病毒作出巨大牺牲。武汉人民、湖北人民面对离汉离鄂通道关闭后与外隔绝、交通停滞、城市"停摆",克服了近距离接触病毒、医疗资源和生活物资紧张以及长时间隔离带来的困难,忍住失去至爱亲朋的痛苦,服从大局,咬紧牙关,团结坚守。在伟大的抗疫战争中,英雄的武汉人民、湖北人民将载入史册为人们所铭记。

社区工作者、公安民警、海关关员、基层干部、下沉干部不辞辛苦、日夜值守,为保护人民生命安全牺牲奉献。400万名社区工作者奋战在全国65万个城乡社区中,监测疫情、测量体温、排查人员、站岗值守、宣传政策、防疫消杀,认真细致,尽职尽责,守好疫情防控"第一关口"。公安民警及辅警驻守医院、转运病人、街道巡逻、维护秩序,面对急难险重任务勇挑重担,130多人牺牲在工作岗位。海关关员依法履行卫生检疫职责,筑牢口岸检疫防线。社区防控一线广大党员、干部及时将党和政府的声音传导到基层,组织动员群众做好防控,积极为群众排忧解难,抓实抓细网格服务管理。

快递小哥、环卫工人、道路运输从业人员、新闻工作者、志愿者等各行各业工作者不惧风雨、敬业坚守。疫情期间,千家万户关门闭户,数百万快递员顶风冒雪、冒疫前行,在城市乡村奔波,给人们送来温暖。全国180万环卫工人起早贪黑、不辞辛劳,高标准做好卫生清扫、消毒杀菌、医疗废物集中处理、垃圾清理清运。数千万道路运输从业人员坚守岗位,许多城市出租车司机没有停工,有力保障疫情防控、生产生活物资运输和复工复产。新闻工作者不惧风险、深入一线,记录中国抗疫的点点滴滴,传递中国人民抗击疫情的温情和力量。许多普通人投入一线志愿服务,社区值守、排查患者、清洁消杀、买药送菜,缓解居民燃眉之急。据不完全统计,截至5月31日,全国参与疫情防控的注册志愿者达到881万人,志愿服务项目超过46万个,记录志愿服务时间超过2.9亿小时。

广大民众扛起责任、众志成城,自觉参与抗击疫情。危难面前,中国人民对中国共产党和中国政府高度信任,勇敢承担起社会责任,为取得抗疫胜利约束自我乃至牺牲自我。疫情暴发正值春节假期,国家一声令下,全民响应,一致行动,整个社会紧急停下脚步。人们取消了春节期间的走亲访友和各种聚会,克服困难就地隔离,外出自觉佩戴口罩、测量体温、保持社交距离。保护自己就是保护别人、就是为国家作贡献成为社会共识和每个人的自觉行动。人们长时间在家隔离,上网课、学美食、陪家人,用各种方式缓解压力,以积极乐观的态度抗击疫情。"所有好的做法如果想要奏效,必须要有公众的集体意愿。正因如此,中国有能力通过传统公共卫生干预方法应对一种新型的未知病毒"[①]。

重大危机是考验执政党执政理念、执政效能的试金石。中国在较短时间内遏制疫情蔓延,根本在于中国共产党的坚强领导。中国共产党有坚强有力的领导核心,有以人民为中心的执政理念,面对疫情危机,迅速科学作出决策,实行高效有力的危机应对。中国共产党

---

① 中国—世界卫生组织联合专家考察组新闻发布会,北京,2020年2月24日。

严密的组织体系和高效的运行机制,在短时间内建立横向到边、纵向到底的危机应对机制,有效调动各方积极性,全国上下令行禁止、统一行动。中国共产党 460 多万个基层组织,广泛动员群众、组织群众、凝聚群众、服务群众,筑起一座座抗击疫情的坚强堡垒。在疫情危及人民生命安全的危难关头,共产党员冲在最前面,全国 3900 多万名党员、干部战斗在抗疫一线,1300 多万名党员参加志愿服务,近 400 名党员、干部为保卫人民生命安全献出了宝贵生命。广大党员自觉捐款,为疫情防控斗争真情奉献。注重在疫情考验中锤炼党员干部,检验为民初心和责任担当,对湖北省委和武汉市委领导班子作出调整补充,对不担当、不作为、失职渎职的党员干部严肃问责,对敢于担当、认真负责的党员干部大力褒奖、大胆使用,立起了鲜明导向。历经疫情磨砺,中国人民更加深切地认识到,风雨来袭,中国共产党的领导是最重要的保障、最可靠的依托,对中国共产党更加拥护和信赖,对中国制度更加充满信心。

四、共同构建人类卫生健康共同体

当前,新冠肺炎疫情仍在全球肆虐,每天都有许多生命逝去。面对严重危机,人类又一次站在了何去何从的十字路口。坚持科学理性还是制造政治分歧?加强团结合作还是寻求脱钩孤立?推进多边协调还是奉行单边主义?迫切需要各个国家作出回答。中国主张,各国应为全人类前途命运和子孙后代福祉作出正确选择,秉持人类命运共同体理念,齐心协力、守望相助、携手应对,坚决遏制疫情蔓延势头,打赢疫情防控全球阻击战,护佑世界和人民康宁。

(一) 中国感谢和铭记国际社会宝贵支持和帮助

在中国疫情防控形势最艰难的时候,国际社会给予了中国和中国人民宝贵的支持和帮助。全球 170 多个国家领导人、50 个国际和地区组织负责人以及 300 多个外国政党和政治组织向中国领导人来函致电、发表声明表示慰问支持。77 个国家和 12 个国际组织为中国人民抗疫斗争提供捐赠,包括医用口罩、防护服、护目镜、呼吸机等急用医疗物资和设备。84 个国家的地方政府、企业、民间机构、人士向中国提供了物资捐赠。金砖国家新开发银行、亚洲基础设施投资银行分别向中国提供 70 亿、24.85 亿元人民币的紧急贷款,世界银行、亚洲开发银行向中国提供国家公共卫生应急管理体系建设等贷款支持。中国感谢国际社会给予的宝贵理解和支持,中国人民永远铭记在心。中华民族是懂得感恩、投桃报李的民族,中国始终在力所能及的范围内为国际社会抗击疫情提供支持。

（二）中国积极开展国际交流合作

疫情发生以来,中国始终同国际社会开展交流合作,加强高层沟通,分享疫情信息,开展科研合作,力所能及为国际组织和其他国家提供援助,为全球抗疫贡献中国智慧、中国力量。中国共产党同 110 多个国家的 240 个政党发出共同呼吁,呼吁各方以人类安全健康为重,秉持人类命运共同体理念,携手加强国际抗疫合作。

习近平主席亲自推动开展国际合作。疫情发生以来,习近平主席同近 50 位外国领导人和国际组织负责人通话或见面,介绍中国抗疫努力和成效,阐明中国始终本着公开、透明、负责任的态度,及时发布疫情信息,分享防控和救治经验,阐明中国对其他国家遭受的疫情和困难感同身受,积极提供力所能及的帮助,呼吁各方树立人类命运共同体意识,加强双多边合作,支持国际组织发挥作用,携手应对疫情挑战。习近平主席出席二十国集团领导人特别峰会并发表讲话,介绍中国抗疫经验,提出坚决打好新冠肺炎疫情防控全球阻击战、有效开展国际联防联控、积极支持国际组织发挥作用、加强国际宏观经济政策协调等 4 点主张和系列合作倡议,呼吁国际社会直面挑战、迅速行动。5 月 18 日,习近平主席在第 73 届世界卫生大会视频会议开幕式上发表致辞,呼吁各国团结合作战胜疫情,共同构建人类卫生健康共同体,提出全力搞好疫情防控、发挥世界卫生组织作用、加大对非洲国家支持、加强全球公共卫生治理、恢复经济社会发展、加强国际合作等 6 点建议,并宣布两年内提供 20 亿美元国际援助、与联合国合作在华设立全球人道主义应急仓库和枢纽、建立 30 个中非对口医院合作机制、中国新冠疫苗研发完成并投入使用后将作为全球公共产品、同二十国集团成员一道落实"暂缓最贫困国家债务偿付倡议"等中国支持全球抗疫的一系列重大举措。

同国际社会分享疫情信息和抗疫经验。 中国及时向国际社会通报疫情信息,交流防控经验,为全球防疫提供了基础性支持。疫情发生后,中国第一时间向世界卫生组织、有关国家和地区组织主动通报疫情信息,分享新冠病毒全基因组序列信息和新冠病毒核酸检测引物探针序列信息,定期向世界卫生组织和有关国家通报疫情信息。中国与东盟、欧盟、非盟、亚太经合组织、加共体、上海合作组织等国际和地区组织,以及韩国、日本、俄罗斯、美国、德国等国家,开展 70 多次疫情防控交流活动。国家卫生健康委汇编诊疗和防控方案并翻译成 3 个语种,分享给全球 180 多个国家、10 多个国际和地区组织参照使用,并与世界卫生组织联合举办"新冠肺炎防治中国经验国际通报会"。国务院新闻办公室在武汉举行两场英文专题发布会,邀请相关专家和一线医护人员介绍中国抗疫经验和做法。中国媒体开设"全球疫情会诊室""全球抗疫中国方案"等栏目,为各国开展交流搭建平台。中国智库和专家通过多种方式开展对外交流。中国—世界卫生组织联合专家考察组实地考察调研北京、成都、广州、深圳和武汉等地一线疫情防控工作,高度评价中国抗疫的努力和成效。

向国际社会提供人道主义援助。在自身疫情防控仍然面临巨大压力的情况下,中国迅速展开行动,力所能及地为国际社会提供援助。向世界卫生组织提供两批共5000万美元现汇援助,积极协助世界卫生组织在华采购个人防护用品和建立物资储备库,积极协助世界卫生组织"团结应对基金"在中国筹资,参与世界卫生组织发起的"全球合作加速开发、生产、公平获取新冠肺炎防控新工具"倡议。积极开展对外医疗援助,截至5月31日,中国共向27个国家派出29支医疗专家组,已经或正在向150个国家和4个国际组织提供抗疫援助;指导长期派驻在56个国家的援外医疗队协助驻在国开展疫情防控工作,向驻在国民众和华侨华人提供技术咨询和健康教育,举办线上线下培训400余场;地方政府、企业和民间机构、个人通过各种渠道,向150多个国家、地区和国际组织捐赠抗疫物资。中国政府始终关心在华外国人士的生命安全和身体健康,对于感染新冠肺炎的外国人士一视同仁及时进行救治。

有序开展防疫物资出口。中国在满足国内疫情防控需要的基础上,想方设法为各国采购防疫物资提供力所能及的支持和便利,打通需求对接、货源组织、物流运输、出口通关等方面堵点,畅通出口环节,有序开展防疫物资出口。采取有力措施严控质量、规范秩序,发布防疫用品国外市场准入信息指南,加强防疫物资市场和出口质量监管,保质保量向国际社会提供抗击疫情急需的防疫物资。3月1日至5月31日,中国向200个国家和地区出口防疫物资,其中,口罩706亿只,防护服3.4亿套,护目镜1.15亿个,呼吸机9.67万台,检测试剂盒2.25亿人份,红外线测温仪4029万台,出口规模呈明显增长态势,有力支持了相关国家疫情防控。1月至4月,中欧班列开行数量和发送货物量同比分别增长24%和27%,累计运送抗疫物资66万件,为维持国际产业链和供应链畅通、保障抗疫物资运输发挥了重要作用。

开展国际科研交流合作。加强同世界卫生组织沟通交流,同有关国家在溯源、药物、疫苗、检测等方面开展科研交流与合作,共享科研数据信息,共同研究防控和救治策略。科技部、国家卫生健康委、中国科协、中华医学会联合搭建"新型冠状病毒肺炎科研成果学术交流平台",供全球科研人员发布成果、参与研讨,截至5月31日,共上线104种期刊、970篇论文和报告。国家中医药管理局联合上合组织睦邻友好合作委员会召开"中国中西医结合专家组同上海合作组织国家医院新冠肺炎视频诊断会议",指导世界中医药学会联合会和世界针灸学会联合会开展"中医药抗疫全球直播""国际抗疫专家大讲堂"等活动。中国科学院发布"2019新型冠状病毒资源库",建成"新型冠状病毒国家科技资源服务系统""新型冠状病毒肺炎科研文献共享平台",截至 5 月 31 日,3 个平台为全球超过 37 万用户提供近 4800 万次下载、浏览和检索服务。建立国际合作专家库,同有关国家开展疫苗研发、药品研发等合作。充分发挥"一带一路"国际科学组织联盟作用,推动成员之间就新冠病毒研究和新冠肺炎治疗开展科技合作。中国医疗机构、疾控机构和科学家在《柳叶刀》《科学》《自然》《新英格兰医学杂志》等国际知名学术期刊上发表数十篇高水平论文,及时发布新冠肺炎首批患者临床特征描述、人际传播风险、方舱医院经验、药物研发进展、疫苗动物实验结果等研究成果。同有关国家、世界卫生组织以及流行病防范创新联盟(CEPI)、全球疫苗免疫联盟(GAVI)等开展科研合作,加快推进疫苗研发和药物临床试验。

(三) 国际社会团结合作共同抗疫

疫情在全球传播蔓延的形势令人担忧。无论是阻击病毒的传播蔓延,还是抵御不断恶化的全球经济衰退,都需要国际社会团结合作,都需要坚持多边主义、推动构建人类命运共同体。团结合作是国际社会战胜疫情最有力武器。未来的成败取决于今天的作为。中国呼吁各国紧急行动起来,更好团结起来,全面加强合作,联合抗疫,共克时艰。

有效开展联防联控国际合作。应对疫情必须各国协同作战,建立起严密的联防联控网络。疫情发生以来,世界卫生组织秉持客观公正立场,积极履行职责,采取一系列专业、科学、有效措施,为领导和推进国际抗疫合作作出了重大贡献。中国坚定支持世界卫生组织发挥全球抗疫领导作用,呼吁国际社会加大对世界卫生组织政治支持和资金投入,调动全球资源打赢疫情阻击战。中国主张,各国在世界卫生组织的指导和协调下,采取科学合理、协同联动的防控措施,科学调配医疗力量和重要物资,在防护、隔离、检测、救治、追踪等重要领域采取有力举措,同时,加强信息共享和经验交流,开展检测方法、临床救治、疫苗药物研发国际合作,继续支持各国科学家开展病毒源头和传播途径的全球科学研究。中国呼吁,二十国集团、亚太经合组织、金砖国家、上海合作组织等多边机制加大机制内对话交流与政策协调力度,二十国集团成员切实落实二十国集团领导人特别峰会达成的共识。开展联防联控国际合作,大国的负责任、担当和主动作为至关重要。中国愿同各国包括美国加强交流合作,共同应对疫情挑战,特别是在疫苗和特效药的研发、生产和分发上开展合作,为阻断病毒传播作出应有贡献。

合作应对疫情给世界经济带来的影响。疫情在全球传播蔓延,人员流动、跨境商贸活动受阻,金融市场剧烈震荡,全球产业链供应链受到双重打击,世界经济深度衰退不可避免,国际社会联手稳定和恢复世界经济势在必行。中国愿同各国一道,在加强疫情防控的同时,一齐应对日益上升的全球经济衰退,加强国际宏观经济政策协调,共同维护全球产业链供应链的稳定、安全与畅通。新冠肺炎疫情改变了经济全球化形态,但全球化发展大势没有改变,搞"脱钩""筑墙""去全球化",既割裂全球也难以自保。中国主张,各国继续推进全球化,维护以世界贸易组织为基石的多边贸易体制,减免关税、取消壁垒、畅通贸易,使全球产业链供应链安全顺畅运行,同时,实施有力有效的财政和货币政策,加强金融监管协调,维护金融市场稳定,防止引发全球性金融危机导致世界经济陷入大规模、长周期衰退。中国将继续向国际市场供应防疫物资、原料药、生活必需品等产品,坚定不移扩大改革开放,积极扩大进口,扩大对外投资,为各国抗击疫情、稳定世界经济作出更大贡献。

向应对疫情能力薄弱的国家和地区提供帮助。亚洲、非洲和拉美地区发展中国家特别是非洲国家,公共卫生体系薄弱,难以独立应对疫情带来的严峻挑战,帮助他们提升疫情防控能力和水平是全球抗疫的重中之重。中国呼吁,联合国、世界卫生组织、国际货币基金组织、世界银行等多边机构向非洲国家提供必要的紧急援助;发达国家向发展中国家特别是非洲国家提供更多物资、技术、人力支持,在全球抗疫中担负更多责任、发挥更大作用。中国积极参与并落实二十国集团缓债倡议,已宣布 77 个有关发展中国家暂停债务偿还。在向 50 多个非洲国家和非盟交付医疗援助物资、派出 7 个医疗专家组的基础上,中国将进一步加大援非抗疫力度,继续向非洲国家提供力所能及的支持,援助急需医疗物资,开展医疗技术合作,派遣更多医疗专家组和工作组,帮助非洲国家提升疫情防控能力和水平。中国将向联合国人道应对计划提供支持。

坚决反对污名化和疫情政治化。面对新冠病毒对人类生命安全和健康的严重威胁,当务之急是团结合作、战胜疫情。人类的共同敌人是病毒,而不是某个国家、某个种族。中国呼吁国际社会更加团结起来,摒弃偏见和傲慢,抵制自私自利、"甩锅"推责,反对污名化和疫情政治化,让团结、合作、担当、作为的精神引领全世界人民取得全球抗疫胜利。中国是病毒受害国,也是全球抗疫贡献国,应该得到公正对待而不是责难。中国在疫情初期就向国际社会发出清晰而明确的信息,个别国家无视这些信息耽误疫情应对和拯救生命,却反称被中国"延误",真是"欲加之罪,何患无辞"。中国始终坚持公开、透明、负责任原则及时向国际社会公布疫情信息,无端指责中国隐瞒疫情信息和死亡病例数据,是对14亿中国人民、对被病毒夺去生命的逝者、对数百万中国医护人员的极不尊重,中国对此坚决反对。新冠病毒是人类未知的新病毒,病毒溯源是科学问题,需要科学家和医学专家进行研究,基于事实和证据得出科学结论。通过转嫁责任掩盖自身问题,既不负责任也不道德,中国绝不接受任何滥诉和索赔要求。面对疫情在全球传播蔓延,中国向国际社会提供力所能及的援助,源于中国人民的古道热肠,源于对其他国家人民遭受疫情苦难的感同身受,源于面对灾难同舟共济的人道主义精神,源于大国的责任和担当,绝非输出中国模式,更不是为谋求所谓地缘政治利益。

健全完善惠及全人类、高效可持续的全球公共卫生体系。人类发展史也是同病毒的斗争史。当前,全球公共卫生治理存在诸多短板,全球传染病联防联控机制远未形成,国际公共卫生资源十分匮乏,逆全球化兴起使得全球公共卫生体系更加脆弱。人类终将战胜疫情,但重大公共卫生突发事件对人类来说不会是最后一次。中国呼吁,各国以此次疫情为鉴,反思教训,化危为机,以卓越的政治远见和高度负责的精神,坚持生命至上、全球一体、平等尊重、合作互助,建立健全全球公共卫生安全长效融资机制、威胁监测预警与联合响应机制、资源储备和资源配置体系等合作机制,建设惠及全人类、高效可持续的全球公共卫生体系,筑牢保障全人类生命安全和健康的坚固防线,构建人类卫生健康共同体。中国支持在全球疫情得到控制之后,坚持客观公正原则和科学专业态度,全面评估全球应对疫情工作,总结经验,弥补不足。中国主张,为人类发展计、为子孙后代谋,各国应立即行动起来,采取断然措施,最大限度消除病毒对人类的现实和潜在威胁。中国作为负责任大国,始终秉持人类命运共同体理念,积极推进和参与卫生健康领域国际合作,认真落实习近平主席在第 73 届世界卫生大会视频会议开幕式上提出的 6 点建议和 5 项举措,为维护地区和世界公共卫生安全,推动构建人类卫生健康共同体作出更大贡献。

结　束　语

中华民族历经磨难,但从未被压垮过,而是愈挫愈勇,不断在磨难中成长、从磨难中奋起。面对疫情,中国人民万众一心、众志成城,取得了抗击疫情重大战略成果。中国始终同各国紧紧站在一起,休戚与共,并肩战斗。

当前,新冠病毒仍在全球传播蔓延,国际社会将会面对更加严峻的困难和挑战。全球疫情防控战,已经成为维护全球公共卫生安全之战、维护人类健康福祉之战、维护世界繁荣发展之战、维护国际道义良知之战,事关人类前途命运。人类唯有战而胜之,别无他路。国际社会要坚定信心,团结合作。团结就是力量,胜利一定属于全人类!

新冠肺炎疫情深刻影响人类发展进程,但人们对美好生活的向往和追求没有改变,和平发展、合作共赢的历史车轮依然滚滚向前。阳光总在风雨后。全世界人民心怀希望和梦想,秉持人类命运共同体理念,目标一致、团结前行,就一定能够战胜各种困难和挑战,建设更加繁荣美好的世界。

新疆的劳动就业保障

（2020 年 9 月）

中华人民共和国
国务院新闻办公室

前　言

劳动是人的存在方式,也是人类的本质活动。劳动创造美好生活,促进人的全面发展和人类文明进步。《中华人民共和国宪法》赋予公民劳动的权利和义务。保障劳动权就是维护人的尊严,就是保障人权。

中国是人口大国,也是劳动力大国。做好劳动就业保障工作,关系劳动者基本权利和生活幸福,关系经济发展、社会和谐,关系国家繁荣、民族复兴。中国坚持以人民为中心的发展思想,高度重视劳动就业保障工作,大力实施就业优先战略和积极的就业政策。充分尊重劳动者意愿,依法保障公民劳动权利,积极践行国际劳工和人权标准,努力使人人都能通过辛勤劳动创造幸福生活、实现自身发展。

按照国家关于劳动就业的大政方针和打赢脱贫攻坚战的总体部署,中国新疆把促进劳动就业作为最大的民生工程、民心工程、根基工程,坚持把劳动者自主就业、市场调节就业、政府促进就业和鼓励创业相结合,多渠道增加就业,千方百计稳定就业。通过积极的劳动就业政策,新疆各族人民物质文化生活水平不断提高,各项人权得到有效保障和发展,为确保新疆各族群众同全中国人民一道迈入全面小康社会、实现新疆社会稳定和长治久安打下了坚实基础。

一、新疆劳动就业的基本状况

新疆地处中国西北边陲,长期以来,受历史和自然等因素的影响,发展相对滞后,贫困人口较多。特别是南疆四地州(和田地区、喀什地区、阿克苏地区、克孜勒苏柯尔克孜自治州)生态环境恶劣,经济基础薄弱,就业承载能力严重不足,是国家确定的深度贫困地区。加之长期以来暴力恐怖势力、民族分裂势力、宗教极端势力鼓吹"来世天定""教法大于国法",煽动广大群众抵制学习国家通用语言文字,排斥现代科学知识,拒绝学习掌握就业技能、改善经济条件、提升自我发展能力,导致一些群众思想观念落后,文化程度不高,就业能力不足,就业率较低,收入十分有限,生活陷入长期贫困。

做好劳动就业工作,对于保障各族人民劳动就业权利、发展和改善民生、促进社会和谐稳定意义重大。特别是2012年中共十八大以来,新疆大力实施就业惠民工程,持续加大就业培训力度,积极拓宽就业渠道,有效扩大就业容量,就业形势持续向好,各族群众收入水平不断提升、生活质量越来越高,获得感、幸福感、安全感显著增强。

政策体系进一步健全。 近年来,新疆贯彻落实国家稳就业促就业决策部署,顺应人民呼声并结合自身实际,制定了《新疆维吾尔自治区党委 自治区人民政府关于进一步促进就业创业工作的意见》《新疆维吾尔自治区人民政府关于做好当前和今后一段时期就业创业工作的实施意见》《新疆维吾尔自治区"十三五"促进就业规划》等文件,在经济发展、财政保障、税收优惠、金融支持和城乡、区域、群体统筹,以及支持灵活就业、帮助困难群体就业等方面,作出系统安排,为促进劳动就业、维护劳动者权益提供了坚实的制度保障。

就业规模不断扩大。聚焦劳动就业重点群体和深度贫困地区,引导各族群众就地就近就业、有序进城就业和自主创业,扎实推进贫困劳动力转移就业。2014年至2019年,新疆的劳动就业总人数从1135.24万人增加到1330.12万人,增长17.2%;年均新增城镇就业47.12万人以上,其中,南疆地区14.8万人,占比31.4%;年均农村富余劳动力转移就业276.3万人次以上,其中,南疆地区167.8万人次,占比60%以上。

就业结构更趋合理。以推进供给侧结构性改革为主线,坚持一产上水平、二产抓重点、三产大发展,培育壮大特色优势产业和劳动密集型产业,引导劳动力向第三产业有序流动。从三次产业分布看,就业人员占比2014年为45.4∶16.0∶38.6,2019年为36.4∶14.1∶49.5,其中,第三产业就业人员占比提高了10.9个百分点,成为吸纳就业最多的产业。从城乡分布看,越来越多农村富余劳动力向城镇流动,城镇吸纳就业能力进一步增强。2014年城镇就业人数535.4万人,2019年增加至734.17万人,占全部就业人员的55.2%。

劳动力素质明显提升。通过实施教育惠民工程,新疆的学前教育、九年义务教育、高中阶段教育、高等教育、职业教育均达历史最高水平。2019年,普通高等教育在校生45.38万人,比2014年增加

14.62万人；中等教育在校生184.36万人，比2014年增加14.76万人。通过开展就业技能培训，培养造就了一支新时代知识型、技能型、创新型劳动者大军。据统计，2014年至2019年，全疆年均培训城乡各类劳动者128.8万人次，其中，南疆地区年均培训45.14万人次。参训人员至少掌握1项就业技能，绝大多数取得了职业资格证书、职业技能等级证书或专项职业能力证书，实现稳定就业。

居民和职工收入稳步增长。2014年至2019年，新疆维吾尔自治区城镇居民人均可支配收入由2.32万元增至3.47万元，年均名义增长8.6%，农村居民人均可支配收入由8724元增至1.31万元，年均名义增长8.9%；新疆生产建设兵团城镇居民人均可支配收入由2.76万元增至4.07万元，年均名义增长8.5%，连队居民人均可支配收入由1.39万元增至2.2万元，年均名义增长9.9%。全疆城镇非私营单位就业人员年均工资由5.35万元增至7.94万元，年均增长8.4%；城镇私营单位就业人员年均工资由3.62万元增至4.59万元，年均增长5.4%。2018年至2019年，南疆地区及兵团四个深度贫困团场有15.5万名建档立卡贫困家庭劳动力转移就业并实现了脱贫。

事实说明，近年来新疆的劳动就业保障工作取得了显著成效，总体态势良好。但也要看到，还面临经济发展底子薄、农村富余劳动力人数多、就业技能水平低等困难和挑战。进一步优化产业结构、提升劳动力素质、转变思想观念，是解决新疆劳动就业的一项长期任务。

二、大力实施积极的就业政策

近年来，新疆更加注重制定实施有利于扩大就业的经济社会发展战略，及时健全完善各项促进就业政策，努力实现劳动者稳定就业、持续就业、长期就业。

优化产业结构扩充就业容量。紧紧抓住"一带一路"建设机遇，完善多元化产业体系，既注重发展资本、技术和知识密集的先进制造业和新兴产业，又大力发展纺织服装、消费电子、鞋帽箱包等劳动密集型产业，以及电子商务、文化创意、全域旅游、健康养老等现代服务业，着力拓展就业空间，扩大就业规模。2012年成立的新疆准东经济技术开发区，立足优势资源转换，大力发展新材料、新能源等六大产业，截至2019年底，已吸纳8万余人就业。2014年以来，国家大力支持新疆纺织业发展，仅2017年至2019年全疆纺织服装产业新增就业35万人。喀什地区重点发展农副产品加工、电子产品组装等产业，积极引进和培育相关企业入驻园区并向乡村生产车间延伸。截至2019年底，该地区有农副产品加工企业210家，吸纳就业1.67万人，各类园区落户工业企业1406家，吸纳就业8.41万人。阿克苏地区加强产教融合，推动纺织服装企业与职业院校联合办学，带动3.24万人就业。

帮助重点群体实现稳定就业。对农村富余劳动力，重点实施就地就近就业政策,因地制宜建立乡村"卫星工厂""扶贫车间"吸纳就业,扶持农村劳务合作组织带动就业,推动产业(工业)园区稳定就业,发展旅游产业促进就业。聚焦南疆地区 22 个深度贫困县和兵团四个深度贫困团场,实施就业扶贫三年规划,2018 年至 2020 年 6 月,累计帮助 22.1 万名建档立卡贫困家庭劳动力转移就业。在喀什、和田两个地区,实施城乡富余劳动力转移就业三年规划,2017 年至 2019 年,累计帮助 13.5 万人转移就业。在全疆对就业困难人员和零就业家庭,实行实名动态管理和分类精准帮扶,做到"出现一户,认定一户,帮扶一户,稳定一户"。2014 年至 2019 年,累计帮助 33.43 万名城镇就业困难人员实现就业,确保零就业家庭 24 小时动态清零。对高校毕业生,实施就业创业促进计划、基层成长计划、"三支一扶"计划、青年就业启航计划等,引导和鼓励毕业生到基层就业、到企业就业和自主创业。2019 年,新疆高校应届毕业生就业率达 90.36%,返疆内地高校新疆籍少数民族毕业生就业率达 95.08%,均创历史新高。

支持创新创业带动就业。把创新作为扩大就业的新引擎,大力推进放管服改革,降低市场准入门槛,持续完善创业扶持政策,落实创业担保贷款及贴息、自主创业补贴、税费减免,支持有意愿、有条件的创业者创业。培育创新创业载体,加强创业服务能力建设,加快发展市场化、专业化、集成化、网络化的众创空间,为创业者提供更多的创业平台和均等化服务。目前,新疆已建设国家级创业孵化示范基地 5 个,自治区级(兵团级)创业孵化示范基地 27 个,累计孵化小微企业

1412 家,带动就业 10121 人。培育支持吸纳就业能力强的创新型创业企业和带头人,鼓励发展"互联网+创业",切实发挥创业带动就业的倍增效应。2019 年,仅和田地区发放创业担保贷款 9.1 亿元,帮助高校毕业生、农村劳动力、就业困难人员等 1.25 万人创业。昌吉市萧民等 6 名妇女在当地人社部门的扶持下,创办了新疆巾帼众心人力资源服务有限公司,逐步成长为集人力资源服务、劳务派遣、后勤托管、政策咨询、信息化建设等多项业务为一体的劳务产业供应链龙头企业,有各族员工 4800 多人,为全疆 318 家企事业单位提供劳务服务,累计安置失业人员、农村富余劳动力 3 万多人次,实现总产值 1.56 亿元。

开展技能培训促进就业。根据劳动力市场需求,着眼提升劳动者就业能力、增强就业稳定性,通过发展高等职业技术学院、中等专业技术学校、技工院校、就业培训中心、企业职工培训中心、职业技能教育培训中心等职业教育和培训机构,积极开展基本劳动素质培训和订单、定岗、定向就业技能培训,构建了比较完整的职业教育和培训体系。以和田地区为例,2019 年共有 10.33 万农牧民参加就业技能培训,实现就业 9.83 万人,就业率达 95.16%。

发挥制度优势拓宽就业渠道。新疆充分发挥中华民族大家庭各民族平等互助、共同发展进步的制度优势,利用国家对口援疆机制,统筹疆内疆外就业岗位,为各族群众到内地省(市)就业积极创造条件。2014 年以来,已有 11.7 万人转移至收入更高的内地省(市)就业。新疆按照"按需培训、先培训后输出"的原则,开展以国家通用语言文字、法律知识、城市生活常识、劳动技能等为主要内容的就业培训。转移就业人员到达就业所在地后,由企业安排住宿,提供被褥、洗漱品等日常生活用品,保障务工人员的住宿条件。部分省(市)企业还为务工人员提供公租房、廉租房、夫妻房。新疆及时为转移就业人员办理异地就业备案手续,解决转移就业人员在当地看病就医问题。内地省(市)及企业及时帮助转移就业人员解决子女入托、上学等问题,推动务工人员与当地群众共事共学共享共乐。

克服疫情困难稳就业保民生。针对新冠肺炎疫情带来的不利影响,新疆统筹推进疫情防控和经济社会发展,扎实做好稳就业、稳金融、稳外贸、稳外资、稳投资、稳预期工作,全面落实保居民就业、保基本民生、保市场主体、保粮食能源安全、保产业链供应链稳定、保基层运转任务,实行减负、稳岗、扩就业等多项措施,实施阶段性、有针对性的减税降费政策,积极推动企业复工达产,有效推进复商复市,着力提升投资和产业带动就业能力。截至 2020 年 6 月底,全疆共减免企业养老、失业、工伤三项社会保险费 75.53 亿元,大型企业减半征收 18.95 亿元,中小微企业全免 56.58 亿元。核准缓缴困难企业社会保险费 7.06 亿元,惠及 1237 家企业。为 8.31 万户企业返还失业保险费 9.04 亿元,惠及职工 183.61 万人。55.24 万人享受各项就业补贴 16.95 亿元。实现城镇新增就业 33.97 万人,新增创业 4.18 万人、带动就业 6.95 万人,就业困难人员实现就业 3.16 万人。农村富余劳动力转移就业 256.5 万人次,同比增长 46.1%。通过多措并举,新疆在常态化疫情防控条件下,取得了扩大就业、保障民生的重要阶段性成果。

三、充分尊重劳动者的就业意愿

新疆始终把尊重劳动者意愿作为制定就业政策、拓宽就业渠道、开发就业岗位、开展就业培训、提供就业服务的重要依据,确保广大劳动者能够自主自愿、心情舒畅地生产生活。

全面了解劳动力资源状况。持续完善就业失业统计指标体系,实施农村劳动力资源定点监测、企业用工监测和人力资源市场供求情况监测,建立失业监测预警机制,依托乡镇(街道)劳动保障事务所、村(社区)劳动保障工作站,对辖区内劳动力数量、年龄、性别、文化程度、就业状况等基本信息进行摸底,根据监测和调查结果制定就业政策和规划。调查显示,截至 2019 年底,全疆有农村富余劳动力 259.03 万人,其中,南疆地区 165.41 万人,占比 63.86%。

及时掌握劳动者就业意愿和需求。定期开展劳动者就业意愿调查,及时掌握劳动者在就业地点、就业岗位、薪酬待遇、工作条件、生活环境、发展前景等方面的需求,以便提供更有针对性的服务,努力达到人岗精准匹配,促进长期稳定就业。据调查,2020 年初,喀什地区莎车县古勒巴格镇奥依巴格村共有 3540 人,其中,有劳动能力的 1509 人中,1288 人有转移就业意愿,占比 85%。这些人员中,有 923 人愿到工厂车间工作,平均期望月薪 5000 元左右;365 人愿到外地从事打馕、餐饮、干果经营、文艺演出等职业。2019 年,和田地区和田县巴格其镇的 3 个村共有人口 5307 人,其中,有劳动能力的 1699 人中,1493 人有转移就业意愿,占比 88%;有 180 人愿留在当地就业,希望到乡镇企业或村办工厂、扶贫合作社工作,平均期望月薪 3000 元左右;另有 26 人希望在当地创业,经营物流运输、物业家政、建筑工程、美发、餐饮、商超等。通过掌握就业意愿,满足个性化需求,有效促进了劳动力有序流动,提升了就业稳定性和满意度。

积极搭建就业信息平台。广泛联系用人单位,收集整理岗位供求信息,依托信息化技术手段,通过人力资源市场、公共就业服务机构、公共就业服务网络平台、广播、电视、村社区宣传栏等渠道及时公开发布,为劳动者自愿就业、自由择业提供信息服务。例如,阿克苏地区以公共就业服务门户网站、微信公众号等为载体,集中发布岗位信息和求职信息,为用人单位和劳动者搭建双向选择平台。2014 年以来,全地区组织各类招聘会 621 场次,吸引 4953 家企业参与,提供就业岗位 14.5 万余个,实现 3.86 万人就业。阿克苏市阿依库勒镇贫困户艾比布拉·马木提,通过招聘会了解到杭州一家电器企业的用工信息,主动应聘,录用后当年收入 5.5 万元,实现了脱贫。

不断强化公共就业服务。面向供求双方,建立覆盖全疆、层级清晰、功能互补、上下联动的五级公共就业服务体系,不断拓展政策咨询、就业失业登记、职业指导和职业介绍、技能培训、创业培训等基本公共就业服务内容。截至 2019 年底,全疆县级以上人力资源市场 144 家,团场劳动保障经办机构 149 个,基层劳动保障站所 8668 个,当年累计提供各类就业服务 2172.84 万余人次。

坚决防范打击强迫劳动行为。根据《中华人民共和国刑法》《中华人民共和国劳动法》《中华人民共和国劳动合同法》《中华人民共和国治安管理处罚法》有关规定,严厉禁止以暴力、威胁或者非法限制人身自由的手段强迫劳动,以及侮辱、体罚、殴打、非法搜查和拘禁劳动者等行为,对违法行为,依法予以行政处罚;构成犯罪的,依法追究刑事责任。新疆严格遵守国家有关法律法规,大力推进法治宣传教育,不断增强用人单位和劳动者的法治意识,深入开展常态化劳动执法检查,切实把劳动关系的建立、运行、监督、调处的全过程纳入法治化轨道,坚决防范和打击一切强迫劳动行为。

四、依法保障劳动者的基本权利

尊重公民的劳动权利,维护劳动者合法权益,实现体面劳动,是中国政府一贯坚持的理念和目标。新疆严格遵循《中华人民共和国宪法》《中华人民共和国劳动法》《中华人民共和国劳动合同法》《中华人民共和国就业促进法》《中华人民共和国社会保险法》《中华人民共和国妇女权益保障法》《中华人民共和国残疾人保障法》等法律法规精神,结合本地区实际,制定实施《新疆维吾尔自治区实施〈中华人民共和国就业促进法〉办法》《新疆维吾尔自治区实施〈劳动保障监察条例〉办法》《新疆维吾尔自治区职工劳动权益保障条例》《新疆维吾尔自治区实施〈中华人民共和国妇女权益保障法〉办法》《新疆维吾尔自治区实施〈中华人民共和国残疾人保障法〉办法》等地方性法规规章,为公民平等享有劳动就业权利提供了坚实法治保障。

切实保障劳动者平等就业权利。遵照平等保护公民权利的法治原则,确保劳动者不因民族、地域、性别、宗教信仰不同而受歧视,也不因城乡、行业、身份等而受限制。在保障妇女平等就业权利方面,新疆努力消除阻碍妇女平等就业的壁垒,制定实施扶持妇女自主创业政策。2019年,城镇新增就业48.09万人,其中,妇女22.81万人,占比47.43%。在保障残疾人劳动权利方面,不断加大职业技能培训力度,大力发展集中就业、辅助性就业、公益性岗位就业,积极推动残疾人按比例就业,鼓励支持残疾人通过个体就业、自主创业、灵活就业等多种形式就业。截至 2019 年底,全疆残疾人就业 18.37 万人,占就业年龄段有劳动能力残疾人总数的 59.37%。

切实保障劳动者获得报酬权利。全面落实国家关于建立企业职工工资正常增长机制的政策要求,完善企业工资指导线制度和劳动力市场工资指导价位制度。2014 年至 2019 年,新疆每年制订并发布企业工资指导线。建立健全最低工资标准调整机制,最低工资标准由 2013 年的 1520 元/月,提高至 2018 年的 1820 元/月,增长 19.74%,在全国处于较高水平。出台《新疆维吾尔自治区企业工资集体协商条例》等地方性法规,积极稳妥推进工资集体协商,并不断扩大覆盖面。健全工资支付保障制度,依法惩处拒不支付劳动报酬等违法犯罪行为,保障劳动者按时足额获得工资报酬。

切实保障劳动者休息休假权和职业安全权。严格贯彻落实国家有关规定,实行劳动者每日工作 8 小时、每周工作 40 小时的工时制度。用人单位因生产经营需要延长工作时间,必须依法与工会和劳动者协商,并安排补休或支付相应报酬。保障劳动者依法享有春节、肉孜节、古尔邦节等法定节假日和休息日的休息权利。严格执行国家职业安全卫生规程和标准,健全安全生产和职业病防治责任体系,不断强化安全生产、职业病预防主体责任,开展劳动安全和职业健康执法检查,最大限度预防和减少各类生产安全事故发生,从根本上控制和消除职业病危害因素。

切实保障劳动者参加社会保险的权利。全面实施全民参保计划,积极推动和引导中小微企业职工和进城务工人员、灵活就业人员、新业态就业人员等重点群体参加社会保险,努力实现应保尽保。截至 2019 年底,新疆基本养老、失业、工伤三项社会保险参保2213.33 万人次。同时,各级劳动保障监察机构持续加大执法力度,及时受理对违反劳动保障法律、法规、规章行为的举报、投诉,依法纠正和查处用人单位不参加社会保险、不缴纳社会保险费等违法行为,切实维护广大劳动者合法权益。

切实保障劳动者宗教信仰自由和使用本民族语言文字等权利。严格执行《中华人民共和国宪法》《中华人民共和国民族区域自治法》《中华人民共和国国家通用语言文字法》《宗教事务条例》等法律法规。充分尊重和保障各族劳动者宗教信仰自由权利,任何组织和个人不得干涉。在依法推广国家通用语言文字的同时,充分尊重和保障少数民族劳动者使用本民族语言文字的权利,劳动者可以自主选择使用何种语言文字进行交流。充分尊重各族劳动者风俗习惯,创造良好的工作和生活环境。克孜勒苏柯尔克孜自治州乌恰县的托克哈利·吐尔汗巴依是有清真饮食习惯的新疆籍少数民族,也是一位信教群众,现在广东一家制鞋厂工作。他曾担心饮食不习惯、没地方做礼拜,但工作后发现,工厂的生活环境很舒适、清真餐饮很可口,休息时间逛街购物,与家人视频聊天,还可以到附近清真寺参加宗教活动,于是很快适应了新环境。

切实加强劳动者权益保障和救济机制。全面推行劳动合同制度,明确用人单位和劳动者权利义务。健全政府、工会和企业组织代表协商劳动关系三方机制,研究解决劳动关系领域重大问题,积极构建和谐劳动关系。注重发挥工会在维护职工合法权益方面的作用。切实加强劳动保障监察和劳动争议调解仲裁,及时妥善处理劳动争议。对违反劳动保障法律法规的突出问题进行集中整治,对重大违法案件进行专项督办,有效保障劳动者在职业介绍、劳动合同、工作时间、休息休假、工资支付、社会保险、特殊劳动保护等方面的合法权益。

五、劳动就业创造美好生活

随着一系列就业惠民政策措施的深入实施,"家家有门路、人人有事干、月月有收入"的工作目标基本实现。新疆特别是南疆地区各族群众的生产生活、精神面貌发生了深刻变化,老百姓的"钱袋子"越来越鼓,日子越来越红火,心情越来越舒畅,笑容越来越灿烂。

家庭收入大幅增加。无论是在疆内还是在外省(市)就业,各族劳动者都获得了稳定的劳动报酬。据不完全统计,在外省(市)转移就业的新疆籍劳动者人均年收入约4万元,与就业所在地城镇常住居民人均可支配收入基本相当。在疆内转移就业的劳动者人均年收入约3万元,远高于在家务农收入。例如,和田地区洛浦县恰尔巴格乡的阿拉帕提·艾合麦提江,在家务农时全家年收入不足1万元,2017年到江西省南昌市一家电器企业务工,不到3年时间收入16万余元。喀什地区叶城县乌夏巴什镇的买买提依明·吐拉麦提,在家务农时年收入只有几千元,到昌吉州一家企业就业后,月收入4000元以上,生活大为改善,盖了新房,娶了新娘。阿克苏地区阿瓦提县乌鲁却勒镇的阿米娜·热合曼夫妇,属建档立卡贫困户,2018年3月看到乡劳动保障事务所发布的招聘信息后,主动应聘,被江西省九江市一家公司录用,两人月收入约9000元,目前不仅还清了贷款,还有了9万多元存款。

生活水平明显改善。通过辛勤劳动,各族群众从吃饱到吃好,从穿暖到穿美,从毛驴车代步到现代交通工具出行,折射出生活今非昔比的变化。克孜勒苏柯尔克孜自治州阿克陶县玉麦乡贫困户热汗古丽·依米尔到浙江省慈溪市务工后,4年时间给家里汇款十几万元,在老家盖了新房,买了新家具,家庭面貌焕然一新。和田市玉龙喀什镇的玉山·艾山,之前以打零工为生,生活拮据,经同乡介绍,2018年7月到乌鲁木齐市一家肉类加工企业工作,从杂工干起,经过勤学苦练,很快掌握了工作技能,在他的带动下,妻子来到乌鲁木齐市一家服装店打工,也有了稳定的收入,2020年在乌鲁木齐市购置了新房。

就业能力显著增强。通过各种形式的就业培训,各族群众劳动技能普遍提高,很多人成长为企业的岗位能手、技术骨干,一些人成为管理人员,一些人自主创业当了老板。和田地区于田县斯也克乡的阿米娜·吾布力,到乌鲁木齐市一家能源企业工作后,经过多个岗位锻炼,3年时间成为业务骨干,被企业评为"优秀员工"。和田地区皮山县的阿尔祖古丽·伊斯坎代尔,在安徽省巢湖市一家纺织企业工作,在老员工手把手帮带下,成长为企业的技术能手,当上了师傅。阿克苏地区库车市的阿迪莱·阿不来提,2018年从北京服装学院毕业后返乡创业,在政府帮扶下开办了一家服装公司,2019年实现产值200多万元,带动了40多名妇女就业。阿勒泰市的吉别克·努尔兰汗,是一名残疾人,大学毕业后回到家乡,当地人社部门安排她参加了创业培训班,并帮助她筹集10万元资金,注册了阿克依额克百货商店，主营哈萨克刺绣手工艺品，实现月收入 6000 多元。

思想观念不断转变。过去，一些群众不重视学习科学文化知识，重男轻女思想严重，就业观念落后，习惯于等靠要；如今，"美好生活靠劳动创造""幸福是奋斗出来的"理念深入人心，各族群众劳动意识、创业愿望、奋斗精神明显增强。例如，喀什地区麦盖提县在举办就业岗位推介会时，很多群众争先恐后咨询岗位信息，积极主动报名应聘，场面十分火爆。一些群众看到同村的人外出务工回来，实实在在赚到了钱，人也变得时尚了，纷纷表示也想出去看一看、闯一闯，改变自己并让家人过上好日子。阿克苏地区拜城县康其乡的阿不力米提·克尤木，往返于新疆和其他省（市）经商，他常说："我不会满足于现状，我要更加努力工作、学习，过上美好的现代生活。"和田市吐沙拉乡的柔孜妮萨·伊敏，2019 年 3 月报名前往福建省晋江市工作，她用赚来的钱帮助家里发展特色养殖。在她的激励下，刚从职业高中毕业的弟弟也打算到福建就业，梦想闯出一片天地。

人生理想得以实现。许多人经过自主选择，找到了适合自己的工作。他们从农村到城市，从田间地头到生产车间，由农民变为工人，不仅学到了技能，提高了收入，实现了脱贫致富，更重要的是开阔了视野，增长了知识才干，实现了人生价值。绝大多数人对当前的工作生活状况表示满意，对未来充满希望。和田地区和田县的买买提托合提·依明托合提一直渴望有一家自己的餐厅，2017 年到乌鲁木齐市一家餐厅当学徒，很快掌握了中式面点技术，在师傅帮助下开了一家餐厅，深受顾客欢迎。克孜勒苏柯尔克孜自治州乌恰县膘尔托阔依乡的帕夏古丽·克热木,热心公益,乐于助人,先后带领 500 多名同乡前往广东务工,帮助大家实现了脱贫,获得了全国脱贫攻坚奋进奖和"全国五一劳动奖章"。

交往交流交融更加密切。各族劳动者干在一起、学在一起、生活在一起,增进了相互了解,加深了彼此感情,像兄弟姐妹一样互相关心、互相帮助,结下了深厚的友谊,谱写了民族团结互助的新篇章。江苏省一家电器企业,吸纳了来自新疆各地州 16 个民族近 200 名员工,各族员工经常在一起唱歌、跳舞、聚会、购物、旅游,工作之余一起制作抓饭、烤肉等特色美食,关系融洽,亲如一家。新疆生产建设兵团女职工尤良英,开办棉花和果品种植合作社,17 次穿越数百公里的沙漠,热心帮助数千名各族群众学习先进种植技术,在实现脱贫致富的同时,增进了民族感情。十几年来,她无私帮助和田地区皮山县农民麦麦提图如普·穆萨克,麦麦提图如普·穆萨克又传递爱心、回馈社会,这一感人故事传遍天山南北。

六、积极践行国际劳工和人权标准

新疆大力实施积极的劳动就业政策,依法保障各族群众的劳动权益,努力让广大劳动者实现体面劳动,创造美好生活,体现了国际社会的共同价值追求,为维护社会公平正义,促进人的全面发展做出了不懈努力。

履行国际公约义务。中国是国际劳工组织创始成员国、常任理事国,批准了包括《男女工人同工同酬公约》《准予就业最低年龄公约》《禁止和立即行动消除最恶劣形式的童工劳动公约》《消除就业和职业歧视公约》4个核心公约在内的26个国际劳工公约,同时也是联合国《经济、社会及文化权利国际公约》《消除一切形式种族歧视国际公约》《消除对妇女一切形式歧视公约》《禁止酷刑和其他残忍、不人道或有辱人格的待遇或处罚公约》《儿童权利公约》《残疾人权利公约》《联合国打击跨国有组织犯罪公约关于预防、禁止和惩治贩运人口特别是妇女和儿童行为的补充议定书》等国际条约的缔约国。中国积极吸收和转化国际劳工和人权标准,通过立法、政策制定及实施,切实保障劳动者各项权利,严格禁止使用童工,反对强迫劳动,反对就业歧视,反对职场性骚扰,深入开展整治和打击非法用工等专项行动,预防和惩治劳动领域各种违法犯罪行为。新疆各级政府切实履行劳动就业保障责任,促进不同地区、不同民族、不同发展水平的群众实现充分就业和更高质量就业,推动各民族共同发展进步,成为国际劳工和人权标准在欠发达民族地区的成功实践。

探索消除贫困路径。消除贫困是人类梦寐以求的理想,也是保障人权的重要内容。联合国2030年可持续发展议程把"在全世界消除一切形式的贫困"确定为可持续发展的首要目标,表达了国际社会对消除贫困的迫切期待。中国积极落实联合国议程,坚持全面小康是全体中国人民的小康,一个民族都不能掉队。新疆始终坚持以发展促人权,以教育培训、能力建设、劳动就业促脱贫,在有效预防和打击恐怖主义、极端主义的同时,实现社会稳定和民生改善,贫困人口大幅减少,贫困发生率显著下降。2013年至2019年底,新疆共有25个贫困县摘帽、3107个贫困村退出,贫困发生率由19.4%降至1.24%。2014年至2019年底,累计实现73.76万户、292.32万人脱贫,2020年底可实现全部脱贫。新疆探索出了破解反恐、去极端化与人权保障,脱贫与可持续发展等世界性难题的新路子。

响应体面劳动倡议。让所有劳动者体面劳动,进而实现人的全面发展,是国际劳工组织的重要倡议,也是尊重和保障人权的应有之义,反映了国际社会的共识和追求。中国政府始终坚持以人为本,积极响应国际劳工组织倡议,认真落实《中国体面劳动国别计划(2016—2020)》,将体面劳动理念融入国家政策和发展规划。新疆严格执行国家有关政策措施,着力在尊重劳动者意愿、保护劳动者权益、改善劳动环境和条件、体现劳动者价值上下功夫,保障各族劳动者在自由、平等、安全和有尊严的条件下工作,有力促进了广大劳动者体面就业。严格依据《中华人民共和国宪法》《中华人民共和国劳动法》《中华人民共和国就业促进法》等法律规定和要求，立足本地区实际，推出了一系列有力政策措施，千方百计帮助各族劳动者实现稳定就业。近年来，新疆城镇登记失业率保持在 3.5% 以下，最大限度保障了各族群众充分享有劳动权，为在更高层次和更广泛意义上实现生存权和发展权奠定了坚实基础。

结　束　语

中共中央总书记、国家主席、中央军委主席习近平强调，"就业是最大的民生"。国际劳工组织通过的《全球就业议程》提出，"就业是消除贫困的核心"。实现体面劳动，对保障劳动者生存发展、家庭和谐幸福、社会长治久安至关重要。新疆实施积极的劳动就业保障政策，有力维护了各族群众劳动就业基本权利，显著改善了各族群众的生产生活条件，极大满足了各族群众创造美好生活的愿望。

一段时间以来，国际上一些势力出于意识形态偏见和反华需要，无视新疆为保障人权所做的巨大努力，搞人权双重标准。他们罔顾事实，颠倒黑白，肆意炒作所谓新疆"强迫劳动"问题，抹黑新疆的劳动就业保障工作，妄图剥夺新疆各族群众的劳动权，使其永远生活在自我隔绝、封闭落后的贫困状态，这是对新疆各族人民追求美好幸福生活的反动，理应遭到一切爱好正义进步的人们的坚决反对。

尊重和保障人权是中国的宪法原则，中国共产党和中国政府始终重视保障公民的劳动就业权利，坚决预防和消除任何形式的强迫劳动。新疆的劳动就业保障政策及其实践，符合中国宪法法律，符合国际劳工和人权标准，契合新疆各族人民过上美好生活的强烈愿望，惠民生，顺民意，得民心。

劳动改变生活，劳动创造幸福。展望未来，新疆将坚持以人民为中心的发展思想,坚持就业是民生之本的理念,继续实施就业优先战略和更加积极的就业政策,大力促进劳动就业,为实现更加充分、更高质量的就业,不断满足各族人民日益增长的美好生活需要而不懈努力。

中国军队参加联合国维和行动 30 年

（2020 年 9 月）

中华人民共和国
国务院新闻办公室

前　言

今年是中国人民抗日战争暨世界反法西斯战争胜利 75 周年,是联合国成立 75 周年,是中国军队参加联合国维和行动 30 周年。

和平是中国人民的永恒期望,是中国发展的鲜明特征。新中国成立以来,中国坚定不移走和平发展道路,在实现自我发展的同时,为世界和平与发展作出了重要贡献。中国始终坚定维护以联合国为核心的国际体系,坚定维护以《联合国宪章》宗旨和原则为基石的国际关系基本准则,同各国一道,坚守多边主义,维护公平正义。

中国以实际行动维护世界和平,积极参加联合国维和行动,是联合国第二大维和摊款国和会费国,是安理会常任理事国第一大出兵国。30 年来,中国军队认真践行《联合国宪章》宗旨和原则,先后参加 25 项联合国维和行动,累计派出维和官兵 4 万余人次,忠实履行维和使命,为维护世界和平、促进共同发展作出积极贡献,彰显了和平之师、正义之师、文明之师形象。

进入新时代,中国军队全面落实习近平主席出席联合国维和峰会时宣布的承诺,以服务构建人类命运共同体为目标,加大对联合国维和行动的支持和参与力度,为冲突地区实现和平发展带去更多信心和希望。新时代的中国军队,已经成为联合国维和行动的关键因素和关键力量,为世界和平与发展注入更多正能量。

当今世界正经历百年未有之大变局。和平与发展仍是时代主题,但面临着日益严峻、不断增多的风险和挑战。不管国际风云如何变幻,中国始终是世界和平的建设者、全球发展的贡献者、国际秩序的维护者,中国军队始终是世界和平与发展的正义力量。

回顾中国军队参加联合国维和行动 30 年的光辉历程,介绍新时代中国军队维护世界和平的理念与行动,中国政府特发布此白皮书。

一、中国军队为世界和平出征

联合国维和行动为和平而生,为和平而存,为维护世界和平作出了重要贡献。1971年,中国恢复在联合国的合法席位,以更加积极的姿态在国际事务中发挥作用。改革开放后,中国逐步参与联合国维和事务。1990年4月,中国军队向联合国停战监督组织派遣5名军事观察员,开启了中国军队参加联合国维和行动的历程。30年来,中国军队在联合国维和行动中,始终牢记履行大国担当、维护世界和平、服务构建人类命运共同体的初心和使命,为世界和平英勇出征、砥砺前行,中国"蓝盔"成为联合国维护和平的关键力量。

中国军队参加联合国维和行动,源于中华民族的和平基因。中华民族的"和"文化,蕴涵着天人合一的宇宙观、协和万邦的国际观、和而不同的社会观、人心和善的道德观,和平、和睦、和谐是中华民族最朴素的追求,和合共生、以和为贵、与人为善等理念在中国代代相传。几千年来,和平融入中华民族的血脉中,刻进中国人民的基因里,成为中国军队的不懈追求。

中国军队参加联合国维和行动,源于中国人民的天下情怀。中国人民历来有"世界大同,天下一家"的梦想,有"大道之行也,天下为公"的胸襟,有"先天下之忧而忧,后天下之乐而乐"的抱负,不仅希望自己过得好,也希望其他国家人民过得好。中国军队走出国门,播撒的是希望,带去的是和平。

中国军队参加联合国维和行动,源于人民军队的根本宗旨。中国军队来自于人民、植根于人民,为人民而生、为人民而战,任何时候任何情况下都坚持全心全意为人民服务的根本宗旨,与人民同呼吸、共命运、心连心,把人民的利益放在第一位。中国维和部队胸怀人间大爱,秉持人道主义精神,为当地谋和平,为当地人民谋幸福。

中国军队参加联合国维和行动,源于中国的大国担当。中国是联合国创始成员国,坚定维护联合国权威和地位,积极参加联合国维和行动,是中国作为国际社会负责任成员的应尽义务。中国是联合国安理会常任理事国,积极参加联合国维和行动,是中国履行大国责任的应有担当。世界和平不可分割,人类命运休戚与共。积极参加联合国维和行动,是中国携手各国推动构建人类命运共同体的应有之义。

中国军队参加联合国维和行动,秉持以下政策立场:

——坚持《联合国宪章》宗旨和原则。始终坚持恪守所有会员国主权平等、以和平方式解决国际争端等联合国主要原则,尊重各国自主选择的社会制度和发展道路,尊重并照顾各方合理安全关切。

——坚持联合国维和行动基本原则。始终坚持当事国同意、中立、非自卫或履行授权不使用武力的基本原则,尊重主权国家领土完整与政治独立,保持公平立场,准确执行安理会授权。

——坚持共商共建共享的全球治理观。始终坚持对话协商,建设持久和平的世界;坚持共建共享,建设普遍安全的世界;坚持合作共赢,建设共同繁荣的世界;坚持交流互鉴,建设开放包容的世界;坚持绿色低碳,建设清洁美丽的世界。

——坚持共同、综合、合作、可持续的新安全观。始终坚持尊重和保障每一个国家的安全,坚持统筹维护传统领域和非传统领域安全,坚持通过对话合作促进各国和本地区安全,坚持发展和安全并重以实现持久安全。

——坚持以和平方式解决争端。始终坚持以和平方式解决国家间和国家内部存在的分歧和争端,以对话增进互信,以对话解决纷争,以对话促进安全,坚决反对动辄诉诸武力或以武力相威胁。

——坚持筑牢维和伙伴关系。始终坚持通过维和行动改革,调动当事国、出兵国、出资国等积极性,充分发挥区域和次区域组织的作用,在维和行动领域推动构建更加紧密的伙伴关系。

二、中国军队是联合国维和行动的关键力量

30 年来,中国军队派出维和官兵的数量和类型全面发展,从最初的军事观察员,发展到工兵分队、医疗分队、运输分队、直升机分队、警卫分队、步兵营等成建制部队以及参谋军官、军事观察员、合同制军官等维和军事专业人员。中国维和官兵的足迹遍布柬埔寨、刚果(金)、利比里亚、苏丹、黎巴嫩、塞浦路斯、南苏丹、马里、中非等 20 多个国家和地区,在推进和平解决争端、维护地区安全稳定、促进驻在国经济社会发展等方面作出了重要贡献。

(一) 监督停火

监督停火旨在确保冲突各方履行停火协议,是联合国维和行动的初始职能,也是中国军队承担的首项联合国维和任务。自 1990 年起,以军事观察员、参谋军官、合同制军官等为代表的中国维和军事专业人员队伍不断发展壮大。30 年来,中国军队累计向 25 个维和特派团及联合国总部派出维和军事专业人员 2064 人次。迄今,共有 13 名中国军人担任特派团司令、副司令,战区司令、副司令等重要职务。2020 年 8 月,有 84 名维和军事专业人员正活跃在维和特派团和

联合国总部,主要担负巡逻观察、监督停火、联络谈判、行动指挥、组织计划等任务。

军事观察员部署在冲突一线,为维和行动决策提供信息,经常受到武装冲突威胁。2006年7月25日,黎以冲突期间,中国军事观察员杜照宇在炮火中坚守岗位履行职责,为和平事业献出了年轻的生命,被追记一等功,并被联合国授予哈马舍尔德勋章。

（二）稳定局势

迅速稳定局势是推进和平进程的前提条件,是联合国维和特派团的主要任务,也是近年来中国维和部队职能拓展的重要方向。部分维和任务区安全形势严峻,各类冲突不断,恐怖袭击、暴力骚乱频发。在各类维和分队中,步兵营主要执行武装巡逻、隔离冲突、止暴平暴、警戒搜查等任务,是维和行动的主力军、安全局势的"稳定器"。

2015年1月,中国军队向联合国南苏丹特派团(联南苏团)派遣1支700人规模的步兵营,这是中国军队首次成建制派遣步兵营赴海外执行维和任务。5年来,中国军队先后向南苏丹派遣6批维和步兵营。迎着朝霞出发、披着星光归营,在枪声中入睡、在炮声中惊醒,这是维和步兵营官兵工作生活的真实写照。截至2020年8月,维和步兵营累计完成长途巡逻51次、短途巡逻93次,武装护卫任务314次,武器禁区巡逻3万余小时,为稳定当地局势发挥了重要作用。2018年8月,南苏丹首都朱巴发生大规模械斗流血事件。中国维和步兵营奉命出击,果断处置,迅速平息事态。

(三) 保护平民

保护平民是联合国维和行动的重要内容,也是中国维和官兵义不容辞的责任、义无反顾的抉择。近代以来,中国人民饱受战乱之苦,中国官兵深知和平之宝贵、生命之无价。在战火频仍的维和任务区,中国维和官兵用汗水和青春浇灌美丽的和平之花,用热血和生命撑起一片片和平的蓝天。

2016 年 7 月,南苏丹首都朱巴爆发武装冲突,政府军和反政府武装持续激战,双方投入坦克、大口径火炮、武装直升机等重型武器,身处交火地域的大量平民生命安全受到严重威胁。中国维和步兵营及友邻部队共同承担辖区内朱巴城区及城郊百余村庄平民的安全保护任务。面对枪林弹雨,中国维和官兵用血肉之躯构筑"生命防线",阻止武装分子接近平民保护区,守护了 9000 多名平民的生命安全。执行任务期间,李磊、杨树朋两名战士壮烈牺牲,用生命履行使命,以英勇无畏践行了保护生命、捍卫和平的铮铮誓言,被追记一等功,并被联合国授予哈马舍尔德勋章。

(四) 安全护卫

安全护卫是确保联合国特派团设施和人员安全的重要任务。中国军队作为联合国维和行动的重要参与者,积极派出维和安全部队,为联合国维和行动提供有力的安全保障。

2013年12月,中国军队向联合国马里多层面综合稳定特派团(联马团)派遣1支170人的警卫分队,承担联马团东战区司令部安全警戒、要员护卫等任务,这是中国军队首次派遣安全部队参与维和行动。马里是联合国最危险的维和任务区之一,自杀式袭击、路边炸弹等恐袭事件屡屡发生。7年来,中国军队先后向马里维和任务区派遣8批警卫分队、官兵1440人次,在危机四伏的撒哈拉沙漠南缘,警卫分队官兵出色完成任务,累计执行武装巡逻及警戒护卫等行动3900余次,被联马团东战区誉为"战区王牌"。2016年5月31日,中国维和士兵申亮亮为阻止载有炸药的恐怖分子车辆冲入联合国维和营地壮烈牺牲,被追记一等功,并被联合国授予哈马舍尔德勋章。中华人民共和国成立70周年之际,申亮亮烈士被授予"人民英雄"国家荣誉称号。

2017年3月12日,南苏丹边境城镇耶伊爆发激烈冲突,7名联合国民事人员被困在交火区域中心,生命安全面临严重威胁。中国赴南苏丹维和步兵营火速派出12名官兵前往救援。行进途中险情不断,救援官兵临危不惧,与武装分子斗智斗勇,3次突破拦截,成功将全部被困民事人员安全转移。此次救援行动及时高效,被联南苏团作为解救行动成功范例加以推广。

（五）支援保障

工程、运输、医疗、直升机等后勤保障分队在联合国维和行动中扮演着不可或缺的重要角色,是当前中国军队向海外派遣维和部队的主体。在各维和任务区,中国后勤保障分队官兵以过硬的素质、精湛的技能和敬业的精神,创造了"中国质量""中国速度""中国标准"等一块块闪亮的中国品牌。

2020年1月,联马团北战区泰萨利特维和营地遭到恐怖袭击,造成20多人受伤。部署在东战区的中国医疗分队紧急前出,将7名乍得维和部队伤员接回至中国医疗分队。经过全力抢救,所有伤员转危为安。2020年5月,中国维和工兵分队克服新冠肺炎疫情防控压力大、安全形势严峻等不利因素,高标准、高质量完成南苏丹西部索普桥修建,打通瓦乌至拉加线路,赢得当地政府和人民的高度评价和赞誉。

30年来,中国军队先后向柬埔寨、刚果(金)、利比里亚、苏丹、黎巴嫩、苏丹达尔富尔、南苏丹、马里8个维和任务区派遣111支工兵分队25768人次,累计新建和修复道路1.7万多千米、桥梁300多座,排除地雷及未爆炸物1.4万余枚,完成大量平整场地、维修机场、搭建板房、构筑防御工事等工程保障任务;先后向利比里亚、苏丹2个任务区派遣27支运输分队5164人次,累计运送物资器材120万余吨,运输总里程1300万余千米;先后向刚果(金)、利比里亚、苏丹、黎巴嫩、南苏丹、马里6个任务区派遣85支医疗分队4259人次,累计接诊救治病人、抢救伤员24.6万余人次;向苏丹达尔富尔派遣3支直升机分队420人次,累计飞行1602架次、1951小时,运送人员10410人次、物资480余吨。

(六) 播撒希望

过上幸福美好生活,是各国人民的共同期盼。远赴海外的中国维和官兵用实际行动,为遭受战火摧残的人民带去了和平、点亮了希望。

积极协助开展人道主义救援。30年来,中国维和部队与国际人道主义机构携手,积极参与难民安置、救济粮发放、难民营修建和抢险救灾等行动,开展了大量卓有成效的工作。2020年4月,刚果(金)东部乌维拉地区暴发罕见洪灾,人民生命财产安全面临严重威胁,中国工兵分队临危受命,紧急加固堤坝、修复被毁桥梁,打通生命通道,有力保护当地人民安全。

广泛参与战后重建。战乱国家或地区签署和平协议后,帮助其恢复社会秩序、改善民生,是防止冲突再起、实现持久和平与稳定的治本之策。中国维和部队积极参与驻地战后重建进程,承担重要基础设施援建、协助监督选举、医护人员培训及环境保护等任务,得到驻在国政府和人民的积极评价。苏丹达尔富尔地区地处沙漠边缘、地质结构复杂,是世界上极度贫水地区之一,2007年至2013年期间,中国工兵分队给水官兵克服重重困难，先后在当地打井 14 口，有效缓解当地人民的饮水难题。

传递温暖和爱心。中国维和官兵不仅是和平的守护人，也是友谊的传播者。中国赴刚果（金）医疗分队与驻地布卡武市"国际儿童村"结成对子，用真情传递爱心和温暖，中国女官兵被孩子们亲切称作"中国妈妈"，这一爱心接力棒已经接续了 17 年，在当地传为佳话。中国赴南苏丹维和部队向当地人民传授农业技术、赠送农具菜种，并应邀到当地中学开设中国文化和汉语课程，深受学生们欢迎。

30 年来，中国军队先后参加 25 项联合国维和行动，累计派出维和官兵 4 万余人次，16 名中国官兵为了和平事业献出了宝贵生命。2020 年 8 月，2521 名中国官兵正在 8 个维和特派团和联合国总部执行任务。中国女性维和官兵在维和行动中发挥了越来越重要的作用，先后有 1000 余名女性官兵参与医疗保障、联络协调、扫雷排爆、巡逻观察、促进性别平等、妇女儿童保护等工作，展示了中国女性的巾帼风采。中国维和部队的出色表现，受到联合国高度认可，赢得国际社会广泛赞赏，为国家和军队赢得了荣誉。2019 年 10 月 1 日，中国维和部队方队首次在国庆阅兵中接受祖国和人民检阅。

三、中国全面落实联合国维和峰会承诺

2015年9月28日,中国国家主席习近平出席联合国维和峰会,宣布支持联合国维和行动的6项承诺。中国政府和军队坚决贯彻落实习近平主席决策部署,言必信、行必果,以实际行动履行相关承诺,取得一系列重要成果。5年来,中国维和部队构成从单一军种为主向多军兵种拓展,任务类型从支援保障向综合多能转型,行动目标从制止武装冲突向建设持久和平延伸,维和能力进一步提升。

(一) 完成维和待命部队组建

维和行动快速部署,能为和平争取机会,为生命赢得时间。中国军队大力支持联合国维和能力待命机制建设,提升维和行动快速部署能力。2017年9月,完成8000人规模维和待命部队在联合国的注册,包括步兵、工兵、运输、医疗、警卫、快反、直升机、运输机、无人机、水面舰艇等10类专业力量28支分队。2018年10月,13支维和待命分队通过联合国组织的考察评估,晋升为二级待命部队。2019年至2020年,先后有6支维和待命分队由二级晋升为三级待命部队。中国维和待命部队按照联合国标准严格施训,始终保持规定待命状态,是一支训练有素、装备精良、纪律严明的专业力量。中国已成为联合国维和待命部队数量最多、分队种类最齐全的国家。此外，中国公安部 2016 年 6 月率先组建了全球首支成建制常备维和警队，该警队 2019 年 10 月晋升为快速部署等级。

（二）派遣更多保障人员参加联合国维和行动

工程、运输、医疗等后勤保障力量是维和行动的重要支撑，既有效提高特派团履职效能，又为驻在国战后重建和改善民生发挥重要作用。中国军队具有派遣保障分队参加维和行动的传统和优势。2015 年联合国维和峰会以来，中国军队积极响应联合国维和行动在工程保障、医疗救治等方面的力量需求，先后派遣 25 批维和工兵和医疗分队共 7001 人，参加在刚果（金）、南苏丹、苏丹达尔富尔、马里、黎巴嫩的维和行动。2020 年 8 月，中国军队有 6 支工兵分队 1188 人、4 支医疗分队 199 人正在遂行联合国维和任务。他们在危险动荡和艰苦环境下修路架桥、扫雷排爆、救死扶伤、支援重建，圆满完成联合国赋予的各项任务，为当地和平进程作出积极贡献，树立了联合国维和部队的良好形象。

（三）完成为各国培训维和人员任务

中国军队秉持资源共享、合作共赢的精神，积极帮助其他出兵国提高训练水平,增强应对复杂环境能力,更好遂行联合国维和任务。5 年来,先后举办了保护平民、维和特派团高级官员、维和教官、维和军事专业人员、女性维和军官等 20 批专业培训,为 60 多个国家训练维和人员 1500 余人。中国军队开展扫雷援助项目,为柬埔寨、老挝、埃塞俄比亚、苏丹、赞比亚、津巴布韦等国培训扫雷人员 300 余人。此外,中国公安部培训多国维和警务人员 1000 余人。

(四) 向非盟提供无偿军事援助

维和行动的主要需求在非洲。为支持非洲国家提高自身维和维稳能力,以非洲方式解决非洲问题,中国军队积极落实对非盟 1 亿美元无偿军事援助,支持非洲常备军和危机应对快速反应部队建设。迄今为止,中国军队已向非盟交付首批军援装备和物资,派遣军事专家组对非方人员进行交装培训,并与非盟就下阶段军援安排达成一致。

(五) 派出首支维和直升机分队遂行任务

中国战鹰为和平翱翔。2017 年 8 月,中国军队向非盟—联合国达尔富尔混合行动(联非达团)派出 140 人的首支直升机分队部署到位,编配 4 架中型多用途直升机,主要承担部队投送、行动支援、人员搜救后送、后勤补给等任务。中国维和直升机分队在海外陌生复杂环境下完成多个高风险任务，成为联非达团重要的军事航空力量，为联合国在苏丹达尔富尔地区的维和行动提供了重要支撑。

（六）设立中国—联合国和平与发展 基金支持联合国维和行动

为更好支持联合国和平事业，促进多边合作，中国设立了中国—联合国和平与发展基金。2016 年至 2019 年，中国—联合国和平与发展基金在和平安全领域共开展 52 个项目，使用资金约 3362 万美元。其中 23 个项目涉及支持联合国维和行动，使用资金约 1038 万美元，包括联合国维和行动统筹规划、非洲维和能力建设、维和人员安保、在苏丹达尔富尔与马里等维和行动中的民生项目等。

四、中国军队积极推动维和国际合作

世界和平需要各国共同维护,维和行动需要多方加强合作。中国军队先后与 90 多个国家、10 多个国际和地区组织开展维和交流与合作,通过团组互访、专家交流、联演联训、人员培训等形式增进相互了解,交流经验做法,加强务实合作,密切双多边关系,不断提升维和能力。

(一) 加强战略沟通,凝聚维和共识

加强与联合国高层的战略沟通,是联合国维和行动向前发展的重要途径。2012 年以来,习近平主席 11 次会见联合国秘书长,在多个国际场合就世界和平与发展提出中国主张、中国方案,表达支持联合国维和行动的立场。2015 年,习近平主席出席联合国维和峰会,提出恪守维和基本原则、完善维和行动体系、提高快速反应水平、加大对非洲的帮扶等主张。中国军队坚决贯彻落实领导人达成的共识,加强与联合国相关机构密切沟通,多次参加联合国维和部长级会议、联合国维和出兵国参谋长会议,积极推动维和领域合作。

加强双多边沟通交流,增进理解互信。中国军队与俄罗斯、巴基

斯坦、柬埔寨、印尼、越南、法国、德国、英国、美国等国军队在维和领域积极开展互访,加强政策沟通,规划维和合作,助推两国两军友好关系发展。2010年5月,首次中美维和事务磋商在北京举行。2015年4月,中国与越南两国国防部长在北京签署两国国防部维和领域合作备忘录;同年,中国同巴西、俄罗斯、印度、南非首次举行金砖国家维和事务磋商。2017年2月,首次中英维和事务磋商在英国举行。2018年4月,联合国军事参谋团的俄、法、英、美军事代表访华,同中方就维和行动进行广泛交流;5月,中国与巴基斯坦签署维和行动政策合作议定书;10月,德国国防部长参访中国国防部维和事务中心培训基地,中国国防部维和代表团参访德国国防军联合国中心。

(二)分享经验做法,贡献中国智慧

相互学习借鉴,开展经验交流,是改进联合国维和行动的有效方式。中国军队积极开展维和领域国际交流,派出维和专业团组访问阿根廷、芬兰、德国等国军队维和培训机构。180余次接待各国和联合国、非盟等国际组织代表团参观访问。举办"中英维和研讨会""21世纪和平行动面临的挑战国际研讨会""中国—东盟维和研讨会""2009北京国际维和研讨会"等10多项大型维和国际研讨活动。在马里、苏丹、南苏丹、刚果(金)、利比里亚、黎巴嫩的中国维和部队与法国、塞内加尔、西班牙等国维和部队交流分享经验做法。

中国军队广泛参与联合国维和专题审议和政策制定,为维和行动发展贡献智慧。积极参加联大维和特委会、出兵国自携装备会议，邀请联合国维和行动高级别评审专家组、安理会代表团访华，就联合国维和行动改革、提高维和行动效能、保障维和人员安全等建言献策；组织《联合国维和工兵分队手册》《联合国维和军事情报手册》等专家编审国际会议，派专家参加联合国维和步兵、警卫、航空、运输、卫勤、军民合作等指导手册编写修订。

（三）深化联演联训，共同提升能力

开展维和领域联演联训，是提升遂行联合国维和行动任务能力，培养储备维和人才的重要举措。中国军队通过多种形式，与联合国、有关国家和地区组织开展维和演训活动，相互借鉴，共同提高。2009年6月至7月，中国与蒙古国在北京举办"维和使命—2009"联合训练；2014年2月，派员赴菲律宾参加东盟10+8多国维和桌面推演；2015年至2019年，每年派实兵赴蒙古国参加"可汗探索"多国维和演习；2016年3月、2019年9月，分别派实兵赴印度、印尼参加东盟10+8维和与人道主义扫雷行动联合演习；2016年5月、2018年5月，两次派员赴泰国参加多国维和桌面推演；2018年4月派员赴巴西参加"维京"多国模拟指挥所推演。

2009年6月中国军队组建维和专业培训机构以来，举办联合国军事观察员、联合国维和参谋军官、联合国非洲法语区维和教官、联合国维和行动规划管理等各类国际培训班20余期。积极邀请联合国专家和有关国家资深教官来华授课交流,强化维和部队和维和军事专业人员部署前培训。先后派维和教官赴澳大利亚、德国、荷兰、瑞士、泰国、越南等国维和培训机构施训,派出100多名军官参加联合国及各出兵国举办的维和培训或观摩。

五、中国军队服务构建人类命运共同体

当今世界正经历百年未有之大变局,新冠肺炎疫情全球大流行使这个大变局加速变化,国际安全形势不稳定性不确定性增加,世界和平面临多元威胁。联合国维和行动受制因素日趋增多,职能任务日趋繁重,安全环境日趋复杂,面临多重挑战和考验。中国将继续发挥安理会常任理事国作用,坚定支持和参与联合国维和行动,积极响应联合国"为维和而行动"倡议,支持对联合国维和行动进行合理必要改革,为建设持久和平、普遍安全、共同繁荣、开放包容、清洁美丽的世界作出应有贡献。

(一)秉持人类命运共同体理念,
携手维护世界和平

当今世界,冲突地区人民依然饱受战乱之苦,对和平的渴望更加强烈,对联合国的期待更加殷切,对维和行动的期盼更加迫切。各国应相互尊重、平等相待,以最大诚意和耐心,坚持通过对话协商解决矛盾和问题,不能动辄诉诸武力或以武力相威胁,破坏世界和平、损害主权国家利益。各国应增强人类命运共同体意识,弘扬人道主义精神,更加坚定支持和积极参加联合国维和行动。中国将继续履行大国责任,加大对联合国维和行动的支持力度,同其他国家一道,推动联合国维和行动改革朝着健康合理方向发展。中国军队将继续加大联合国维和行动参与力度,全面提升维和能力,忠实履行使命任务,为维护世界和平作出更大贡献。

（二）推动完善维和行动体系，
标本兼治解决冲突根源

发展和安全并重,标本兼治解决冲突根源,和平才可持续。维和行动既要同预防外交、维护和平纵向衔接,也要同政治斡旋、推进法治、民族和解、民生改善等横向配合。中国支持联合国构建更加完善的维和行动体系,在聚焦维和行动根本任务的同时,将有限的资源更多投入发展领域,充分尊重当事国政府根据国情自主选择社会制度和发展道路的权利,尊重当事国人民的生存权和发展权,使当事国能够集中力量进行发展重建,巩固和平成果,实现可持续和平。中国军队在维和行动中,将一如既往为冲突国家和地区创造安全稳定环境,积极参与医疗卫生、人道救援、环境保护、民生发展、社会重建等工作,提供更多公共服务产品,努力使当地人民享受和平发展的红利。

（三）坚持共商共建优势互补，
构筑新型维和伙伴关系

出兵国和出资国都是维和行动的重要贡献者。各国在维和领域应承担起各自应有责任,按照共商共建原则,优势互补,形成合力。中国支持联合国积极构筑维和伙伴关系,加强安理会、秘书处同出兵国和当事国在维和行动方面的协调,加强与区域和次区域组织在维和方面的分工协作。中国军队将积极响应联合国倡导的三方合作机制,在技术、装备、人员、资金等方面为其他出兵国以及区域或次区域组织维和行动提供力所能及的支持。

(四)支持改进安理会维和授权,全面提升维和行动效能

安理会授权是维和特派团开展行动的依据和指南,是决定维和行动合法性和有效性的关键因素。制定和更新维和行动授权,要综合考虑当事国国情和实际需求,以及出兵国能力等各方面因素,并根据需求变化,不断调整各阶段优先任务和工作重点。中国支持联合国设立绩效问责机制,节约使用资源,加强高新技术运用,提高维和行动效能,确保维和行动发挥应有作用。中国支持联合国采取多种措施,帮助发展中国家加强维和维稳能力建设、提升人员素质和装备水平、增强维和部队履职能力。中国军队将继续为各国培训更多的优秀专业人才。

(五)充分发挥能力待命机制作用,提高快速反应水平

联合国维和能力待命机制是快速应对危机冲突的重要保障。中

国支持联合国推动维和能力待命机制建设,优先选择和部署符合联合国标准的待命部队。中国军队将按照相关机制建设要求,继续加强 8000 人规模维和待命部队建设,保持高水平待命状态,可根据需要派遣水面舰艇、快反等多种类型部队参加维和行动。

（六）积极应对多种风险威胁，
切实保障维和人员安全

维和行动环境日益恶化和复杂,只有确保维和人员自身安全,才能更有效地执行联合国安理会授权。中国主张维和行动应系统性应对日益增长的传统及非传统安全威胁,支持联合国综合施策,加强信息搜集和分享,提高预警和威胁感知能力,改善安防装备和设施,提升医疗救护水平,加强传染病防治应对,全方位保障维和人员的安全与健康。

结　束　语

75年前,世界人民经过浴血奋战,付出巨大代价和牺牲,取得了反法西斯战争胜利,建立了以联合国为核心的国际体系。回顾历史,更加感受到和平的来之不易和守护和平的艰难。当前,人类正站在何去何从的十字路口,和平还是战争,合作还是对抗,进步还是倒退,是各国需要面对的重大课题。

和平需要争取,和平需要维护。中国坚定不移走和平发展道路,也希望各国都走和平发展道路。只有各国都走和平发展道路,才能共同发展、和平相处,世界才能真正实现和平。中国军队将一如既往支持联合国维和行动,履行守护和平的庄严承诺,给冲突地区带去更多信心,让当地人民看到更大希望。中国愿同所有爱好和平的国家一道,坚定捍卫和践行多边主义,坚定维护以联合国为核心的国际体系,坚定维护以《联合国宪章》宗旨和原则为基石的国际关系基本准则,推动构建人类命运共同体,携手建设更加美好的世界。

附录1 中国军队参加联合国维和行动大事记

1990年4月,中国军队向联合国停战监督组织派遣5名军事观察员,开启中国军队参加联合国维和行动的序幕。

1992年4月,中国军队向联合国柬埔寨临时权力机构派出由400名官兵组成的维和工程兵大队,首次成建制参加联合国维和行动。

2000年9月,中国国家主席江泽民出席联合国安理会首脑会议,就安理会的作用、联合国维和行动及非洲问题等发表讲话。

2001年12月,中国国防部维和事务办公室成立,负责协调和管理军队维和工作,开展对外维和事务交流等任务。

2002年2月,中国正式加入联合国一级维和待命安排机制,指定1个工程建筑营、1个二级医院和2个运输连为联合国待命安排部队,承诺在接到联合国派兵请求后90天内部署到维和任务区。

2003年4月,中国军队向联合国刚果民主共和国特派团派出维和分队,包括1支175人工兵分队和1支43人医疗分队。

2003年12月,中国军队向联合国利比里亚特派团派出维和部队,包括1支275人工兵分队、1支240人运输分队和1支43人医疗分队。

2006 年 4 月，中国军队向联合国驻黎巴嫩临时部队派出 1 支 182 人工兵分队。

2006 年 5 月，中国军队向联合国苏丹特派团派出维和部队，包括 1 支 275 人工兵分队、1 支 100 人运输分队和 1 支 60 人医疗分队。

2007 年 1 月，中国军队向联合国驻黎巴嫩临时部队增派 1 支 60 人医疗分队，并将工兵分队扩编至 275 人。

2007 年 2 月，中国国家主席胡锦涛在对利比里亚进行国事访问期间，视察慰问在当地执行维和任务的中国官兵，并题词："忠实履行使命，维护世界和平"。

2007 年 9 月，赵京民少将就任联合国西撒哈拉全民投票特派团司令，成为首位担任联合国维和部队高级指挥官的中国军人。

2007 年 11 月，中国军队向非盟—联合国达尔富尔混合行动派出 1 支 315 人多功能工兵分队，成为第一支进驻该地区的联合国维和部队。

2009 年 6 月，中国国防部维和中心成立，担负中国军队维和培训、理论研究、国际合作与交流等任务。

2009 年 6 月至 7 月，中国军队与蒙古国军队首次举行代号为"维和使命—2009"的维和联合训练，这是中国军队首次与外军开展维和联合训练。

2010 年 9 月，中国国防部维和事务办公室与联合国维和行动部在中国北京共同举办"联合国维和特派团高级官员国际培训班"，这是中国军队首次举办维和高级培训。

2011 年 3 月,中国国防部维和事务办公室与联合国维和行动部首次共同举办"联合国维和教官国际培训班"。

2011 年 7 月,中国赴联合国苏丹特派团维和工兵分队和维和医疗分队转隶新成立的联合国南苏丹特派团,维和运输分队完成任务回撤归国。

2013 年 6 月,联合国秘书长潘基文访华期间参观访问中国国防部维和中心。

2013 年 12 月,中国军队向联合国马里多层面综合稳定特派团派遣维和部队,包括 1 支 155 人工兵分队、1 支 170 人警卫分队和 1 支 70 人医疗分队。

2014 年 10 月,中国国防部维和事务办公室、中国国际战略学会、瑞典伯纳德特学院在北京举办"和平行动挑战论坛"2014 年年会,联合国和 19 个国家共 86 名代表参加。

2015 年 1 月,中国军队首次向联合国南苏丹特派团派遣 1 支 700 人维和步兵营。

2015 年 4 月,中国与越南两国国防部长在北京签署两国国防部维和领域合作备忘录。

2015 年 5 月,中国军队向联合国驻黎巴嫩临时部队增派 1 支 200 人建筑工兵分队。

2015 年 6 月,中国军队首次派实兵赴蒙古国参加"可汗探索"多国维和演习。

2015 年 6 月,中国国防部维和事务办公室与联合国妇女署共同举办保护平民国际培训班。

2015年9月，中国国家主席习近平出席联合国维和峰会并发表讲话，提出中国支持和改进联合国维和行动的4点主张和6项承诺。

2015年11月，中国军队在联合国总部举办"为和平而来——中国军队参加联合国维和行动25周年图片展"。

2016年7月，联合国秘书长潘基文访华期间，参观访问中国军队首批赴苏丹达尔富尔维和直升机分队。

2017年1月，中国国家主席习近平在联合国日内瓦总部出席"共商共筑人类命运共同体"高级别会议，发表题为《共同构建人类命运共同体》的主旨演讲，深刻、全面、系统阐述人类命运共同体理念。

2017年6月，中国军队首次向非盟—联合国达尔富尔混合行动派遣1支140人维和直升机分队。

2017年9月，中国军队8000人规模维和待命部队完成在联合国注册。

2017年12月，中国以副主席国身份主持《联合国维和军事情报手册》编写工作。

2018年5月，中国与巴基斯坦在伊斯兰堡签署维和行动政策合作议定书。

2018年6月，中国国防部维和事务办公室改编为中国国防部维和事务中心，中国国防部维和中心改编为中国国防部维和事务中心培训基地。

2018 年 9 月,中国维和部队官兵代表应邀出席中非合作论坛北京峰会。

2018 年 10 月,中国 13 支维和待命分队通过联合国考察评估晋升至二级待命等级。

2018 年 12 月,中国以副主席国身份主持《联合国维和工兵分队手册》修订工作。

2019 年至 2020 年,中国先后有 6 支二级维和待命分队通过联合国审核晋升至三级待命等级。

2019 年 10 月,庆祝中华人民共和国成立 70 周年大会在北京隆重举行,维和部队方队首次在国庆阅兵中接受检阅。

附录2 中国军队参加的 联合国维和行动

序号	联合国维和行动名称	中国军队参加时间
1	联合国停战监督组织	1990 年 4 月至今
2	联合国伊拉克—科威特观察团	1991 年 4 月—2003 年 1 月
3	联合国西撒哈拉全民投票特派团	1991 年 9 月至今
4	联合国柬埔寨先遣特派团	1991 年 12 月—1992 年 3 月
5	联合国柬埔寨临时权力机构	1992 年 3 月—1993 年 9 月
6	联合国莫桑比克行动	1993 年 6 月—1994 年 12 月
7	联合国利比里亚观察团	1993 年 11 月—1997 年 9 月
8	联合国塞拉利昂观察团	1998 年 8 月—1999 年 10 月
9	联合国塞拉利昂特派团	1999 年 10 月—2005 年 12 月
10	联合国埃塞俄比亚—厄立特里亚特派团	2000 年 10 月—2008 年 8 月
11	联合国刚果民主共和国特派团	2001 年 4 月—2010 年 6 月
12	联合国利比里亚特派团	2003 年 10 月—2017 年 12 月
13	联合国科特迪瓦行动	2004 年 4 月—2017 年 2 月
14	联合国布隆迪行动	2004 年 6 月—2006 年 9 月
15	联合国苏丹特派团	2005 年 4 月—2011 年 7 月
16	联合国驻黎巴嫩临时部队	2006 年 3 月至今
17	联合国东帝汶综合特派团	2006 年 10 月—2012 年 11 月
18	非盟—联合国达尔富尔混合行动	2007 年 11 月至今
19	联合国刚果民主共和国稳定特派团	2010 年 7 月至今
20	联合国驻塞浦路斯维持和平部队	2011 年 2 月—2014 年 8 月
21	联合国南苏丹特派团	2011 年 7 月至今
22	联合国阿卜耶伊临时安全部队	2011 年 7 月—2011 年 10 月
23	联合国叙利亚监督团	2012 年 4 月—2012 年 8 月
24	联合国马里多层面综合稳定特派团	2013 年 10 月至今
25	联合国中非共和国多层面综合稳定特派团	2020 年 1 月至今

附录 3　中国军队在联合国维和行动中牺牲的官兵

序号	姓名	联合国维和行动名称	牺牲时间
1	刘鸣放	联合国柬埔寨临时权力机构	1993 年 1 月 21 日
2	陈知国	联合国柬埔寨临时权力机构	1993 年 5 月 21 日
3	余仕利	联合国柬埔寨临时权力机构	1993 年 5 月 21 日
4	雷润民	联合国伊拉克—科威特观察团	1994 年 5 月 7 日
5	付清礼	联合国刚果民主共和国特派团	2003 年 5 月 3 日
6	李　涛	联合国利比里亚特派团	2004 年 8 月 11 日
7	张　明	联合国利比里亚特派团	2005 年 10 月 24 日
8	杜照宇	联合国停战监督组织	2006 年 7 月 25 日
9	谢保军	联合国苏丹特派团	2010 年 5 月 28 日
10	张海波	联合国利比里亚特派团	2014 年 9 月 11 日
11	申亮亮	联合国马里多层面综合稳定特派团	2016 年 5 月 31 日
12	李　磊	联合国南苏丹特派团	2016 年 7 月 10 日
13	杨树朋	联合国南苏丹特派团	2016 年 7 月 11 日
14	付　森	联合国南苏丹特派团	2019 年 11 月 26 日
15	王旭东	联合国南苏丹特派团	2020 年 2 月 15 日
16	陈　顺	非盟—联合国达尔富尔混合行动	2020 年 8 月 6 日

新时代的中国能源发展

（2020 年 12 月）

中华人民共和国
国务院新闻办公室

前　言

能源是人类文明进步的基础和动力,攸关国计民生和国家安全,关系人类生存和发展,对于促进经济社会发展、增进人民福祉至关重要。

新中国成立以来,在中国共产党领导下,中国自力更生、艰苦奋斗,逐步建成较为完备的能源工业体系。改革开放以来,中国适应经济社会快速发展需要,推进能源全面、协调、可持续发展,成为世界上最大的能源生产消费国和能源利用效率提升最快的国家。

中共十八大以来,中国发展进入新时代,中国的能源发展也进入新时代。习近平主席提出"四个革命、一个合作"能源安全新战略,为新时代中国能源发展指明了方向,开辟了中国特色能源发展新道路。中国坚持创新、协调、绿色、开放、共享的新发展理念,以推动高质量发展为主题,以深化供给侧结构性改革为主线,全面推进能源消费方式变革,构建多元清洁的能源供应体系,实施创新驱动发展战略,不断深化能源体制改革,持续推进能源领域国际合作,中国能源进入高质量发展新阶段。

生态兴则文明兴。面对气候变化、环境风险挑战、能源资源约束等日益严峻的全球问题,中国树立人类命运共同体理念,促进经济社会发展全面绿色转型,在努力推动本国能源清洁低碳发展的同时,积极参与全球能源治理,与各国一道寻求加快推进全球能源可持续发展新道路。习近平主席在第七十五届联合国大会一般性辩论上宣布,中国将提高国家自主贡献力度,采取更加有力的政策和措施,二氧化碳排放力争于 2030 年前达到峰值,努力争取 2060 年前实现碳中和。新时代中国的能源发展,为中国经济社会持续健康发展提供有力支撑,也为维护世界能源安全、应对全球气候变化、促进世界经济增长作出积极贡献。

为介绍新时代中国能源发展成就,全面阐述中国推进能源革命的主要政策和重大举措,特发布本白皮书。

一、走新时代能源高质量发展之路

新时代的中国能源发展,积极适应国内国际形势的新发展新要求,坚定不移走高质量发展新道路,更好服务经济社会发展,更好服务美丽中国、健康中国建设,更好推动建设清洁美丽世界。

(一) 能源安全新战略

新时代的中国能源发展,贯彻"四个革命、一个合作"能源安全新战略。

——推动能源消费革命,抑制不合理能源消费。坚持节能优先方针,完善能源消费总量管理,强化能耗强度控制,把节能贯穿于经济社会发展全过程和各领域。坚定调整产业结构,高度重视城镇化节能,推动形成绿色低碳交通运输体系。在全社会倡导勤俭节约的消费观,培育节约能源和使用绿色能源的生产生活方式,加快形成能源节约型社会。

——推动能源供给革命,建立多元供应体系。坚持绿色发展导向,大力推进化石能源清洁高效利用,优先发展可再生能源,安全有序发展核电,加快提升非化石能源在能源供应中的比重。大力提升油气勘探开发力度,推动油气增储上产。推进煤电油气产供储销体系建设,完善能源输送网络和储存设施,健全能源储运和调峰应急体系,不断提升能源供应的质量和安全保障能力。

——推动能源技术革命,带动产业升级。深入实施创新驱动发展战略,构建绿色能源技术创新体系,全面提升能源科技和装备水平。加强能源领域基础研究以及共性技术、颠覆性技术创新,强化原始创新和集成创新。着力推动数字化、大数据、人工智能技术与能源清洁高效开发利用技术的融合创新,大力发展智慧能源技术,把能源技术及其关联产业培育成带动产业升级的新增长点。

——推动能源体制革命,打通能源发展快车道。坚定不移推进能源领域市场化改革,还原能源商品属性,形成统一开放、竞争有序的能源市场。推进能源价格改革,形成主要由市场决定能源价格的机制。健全能源法治体系,创新能源科学管理模式,推进"放管服"改革,加强规划和政策引导,健全行业监管体系。

——全方位加强国际合作,实现开放条件下能源安全。坚持互利共赢、平等互惠原则,全面扩大开放,积极融入世界。推动共建"一带一路"能源绿色可持续发展,促进能源基础设施互联互通。积极参与全球能源治理,加强能源领域国际交流合作,畅通能源国际贸易、促进能源投资便利化,共同构建能源国际合作新格局,维护全球能源市场稳定和共同安全。

（二）新时代能源政策理念

——坚持以人民为中心。牢固树立能源发展为了人民、依靠人民、服务人民的理念，把保障和改善民生用能、贫困人口用能作为能源发展的优先目标，加强能源民生基础设施和公共服务能力建设，提高能源普遍服务水平。把推动能源发展和脱贫攻坚有机结合，实施能源扶贫工程，发挥能源基础设施和能源供应服务在扶贫中的基础性作用。

——坚持清洁低碳导向。树立人与自然和谐共生理念，把清洁低碳作为能源发展的主导方向，推动能源绿色生产和消费，优化能源生产布局和消费结构，加快提高清洁能源和非化石能源消费比重，大幅降低二氧化碳排放强度和污染物排放水平，加快能源绿色低碳转型，建设美丽中国。

——坚持创新核心地位。把提升能源科技水平作为能源转型发展的突破口，加快能源科技自主创新步伐，加强国家能源战略科技力量，发挥企业技术创新主体作用，推进产学研深度融合，推动能源技术从引进跟随向自主创新转变，形成能源科技创新上下游联动的一体化创新和全产业链协同技术发展模式。

——坚持以改革促发展。充分发挥市场在资源配置中的决定性作用，更好发挥政府作用，深入推进能源行业竞争性环节市场化改革，发挥市场机制作用，建设高标准能源市场体系。加强能源发展战略和规划的导向作用,健全能源法治体系和全行业监管体系,进一步完善支持能源绿色低碳转型的财税金融体制,释放能源发展活力,为能源高质量发展提供支撑。

——坚持推动构建人类命运共同体。面对日趋严峻的全球气候变化形势,树立人类命运共同体意识,深化全球能源治理合作,加快推动以清洁低碳为导向的新一轮能源变革,共同促进全球能源可持续发展,共建清洁美丽世界。

二、能源发展取得历史性成就

中国坚定不移推进能源革命,能源生产和利用方式发生重大变革,能源发展取得历史性成就。能源生产和消费结构不断优化,能源利用效率显著提高,生产生活用能条件明显改善,能源安全保障能力持续增强,为服务经济高质量发展、打赢脱贫攻坚战和全面建成小康社会提供了重要支撑。

(一) 能源供应保障能力不断增强

基本形成了煤、油、气、电、核、新能源和可再生能源多轮驱动的能源生产体系。初步核算,2019 年中国一次能源生产总量达 39.7 亿吨标准煤,为世界能源生产第一大国。煤炭仍是保障能源供应的基础能源,2012 年以来原煤年产量保持在 34.1 亿—39.7 亿吨。努力保持原油生产稳定,2012 年以来原油年产量保持在 1.9 亿—2.1亿吨。天然气产量明显提升,从 2012 年的 1106 亿立方米增长到2019 年的 1762 亿立方米。电力供应能力持续增强,累计发电装机容量 20.1 亿千瓦,2019 年发电量 7.5 万亿千瓦时,较 2012 年分别增长 75%、50%。可再生能源开发利用规模快速扩大,水电、风电、光伏发电累计装机容量均居世界首位。截至 2019 年底,在运在建核电装机容量 6593 万千瓦,居世界第二,在建核电装机容量世界第一。

能源输送能力显著提高。建成天然气主干管道超过 8.7 万公里、石油主干管道 5.5 万公里、330 千伏及以上输电线路长度 30.2 万公里。

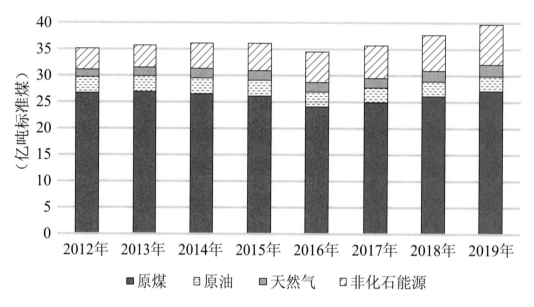

图1 中国能源生产情况(2012—2019年)

数据来源:国家统计局

能源储备体系不断健全。建成 9 个国家石油储备基地,天然气产供储销体系建设取得初步成效,煤炭生产运输协同保障体系逐步完善,电力安全稳定运行达到世界先进水平,能源综合应急保障能力显著增强。

截至 2019 年底,中国可再生能源发电总装机容量 7.9 亿千瓦,约占全球可再生能源发电总装机的 30%。其中,水电、风电、光伏发电、生物质发电装机容量分别达 3.56 亿千瓦、2.1 亿千瓦、2.04 亿千瓦、2369 万千瓦,均位居世界首位。2010 年以来中国在新能源发电领域累计投资约 8180 亿美元,占同期全球新能源发电建设投资的 30%。

可再生能源供热广泛应用。截至 2019 年底,太阳能热水器集热面积累计达 5 亿平方米,浅层和中深层地热能供暖建筑面积超过 11 亿平方米。

风电、光伏发电设备制造形成了完整的产业链,技术水平和制造规模处于世界前列。2019 年多晶硅、光伏电池、光伏组件的产量分别约占全球总产量份额的 67%、79%、71%,光伏产品出口到 200 多个国家及地区。风电整机制造占全球总产量的 41%,已成为全球风电设备制造产业链的重要地区。

(二) 能源节约和消费结构优化成效显著

能源利用效率显著提高。2012 年以来单位国内生产总值能耗累计降低 24.4%,相当于减少能源消费 12.7 亿吨标准煤。2012 年至 2019 年,以能源消费年均 2.8% 的增长支撑了国民经济年均 7% 的增长。

能源消费结构向清洁低碳加快转变。初步核算,2019 年煤炭消费占能源消费总量比重为 57.7%,比 2012 年降低 10.8 个百分点;天然气、水电、核电、风电等清洁能源消费量占能源消费总量比重为 23.4%,比 2012 年提高 8.9 个百分点;非化石能源占能源消费总量比重达 15.3%,比 2012 年提高 5.6 个百分点,已提前完成到 2020 年非

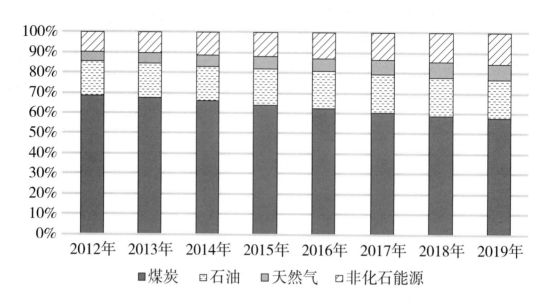

图 2　中国能源消费结构（2012—2019 年）

数据来源：国家统计局

化石能源消费比重达到 15% 左右的目标。新能源汽车快速发展，2019 年新增量和保有量分别达 120 万辆和 380 万辆，均占全球总量一半以上；截至 2019 年底，全国电动汽车充电基础设施达 120 万处，建成世界最大规模充电网络，有效促进了交通领域能效提高和能源消费结构优化。

（三）能源科技水平快速提升

持续推进能源科技创新，能源技术水平不断提高，技术进步成为推动能源发展动力变革的基本力量。建立完备的水电、核电、风电、太阳能发电等清洁能源装备制造产业链，成功研发制造全球最大单机容量 100 万千瓦水电机组，具备最大单机容量达 10 兆瓦的全系列风电机组制造能力，不断刷新光伏电池转换效率世界纪录。建成若干应用先进三代技术的核电站,新一代核电、小型堆等多项核能利用技术取得明显突破。油气勘探开发技术能力持续提高,低渗原油及稠油高效开发、新一代复合化学驱等技术世界领先,页岩油气勘探开发技术和装备水平大幅提升,天然气水合物试采取得成功。发展煤炭绿色高效智能开采技术,大型煤矿采煤机械化程度达98%,掌握煤制油气产业化技术。建成规模最大、安全可靠、全球领先的电网,供电可靠性位居世界前列。"互联网+"智慧能源、储能、区块链、综合能源服务等一大批能源新技术、新模式、新业态正在蓬勃兴起。

(四) 能源与生态环境友好性明显改善

中国把推进能源绿色发展作为促进生态文明建设的重要举措,坚决打好污染防治攻坚战、打赢蓝天保卫战。煤炭清洁开采和利用水平大幅提升,采煤沉陷区治理、绿色矿山建设取得显著成效。落实修订后的《大气污染防治法》,加大燃煤和其他能源污染防治力度。推动国家大气污染防治重点区域内新建、改建、扩建用煤项目实施煤炭等量或减量替代。能源绿色发展显著推动空气质量改善,二氧化硫、氮氧化物和烟尘排放量大幅下降。能源绿色发展对碳排放强度下降起到重要作用,2019年碳排放强度比2005年下降48.1%,超过了2020年碳排放强度比2005年下降40%—45%的目标,扭转了二氧化碳排放快速增长的局面。

　　煤炭清洁开采水平大幅提升。积极推广充填开采、保水开采等煤炭清洁开采技术,加强煤矿资源综合利用。2019 年原煤入选率达 73.2%,矿井水综合利用率达 75.8%,土地复垦率达 52%。

　　建成全球最大的清洁煤电供应体系。全面开展燃煤电厂超低排放改造。截至 2019 年底,实现超低排放煤电机组达 8.9 亿千瓦,占煤电总装机容量 86%。超过 7.5 亿千瓦煤电机组实施节能改造,供电煤耗率逐年降低。

　　燃煤锅炉(窑炉)替代和改造成效显著。淘汰燃煤小锅炉 20 余万台,重点区域 35 蒸吨/时以下燃煤锅炉基本清零。有序推进对以煤、石油焦、重油等为燃料的工业窑炉实行燃料清洁化替代。

　　车用燃油环保标准大幅提升。实施成品油质量升级专项行动,快速提升车用汽柴油标准,从 2012 年的国三标准提升到 2019 年的国六标准,大幅减少了车辆尾气排放污染。

（五）能源治理机制持续完善

　　全面提升能源领域市场化水平,营商环境不断优化,市场活力明显增强,市场主体和人民群众办事创业更加便利。进一步放宽能源领域外资市场准入,民间投资持续壮大,投资主体更加多元。发用电计划有序放开、交易机构独立规范运行、电力市场建设深入推进。加快推进油气勘查开采市场放开与矿业权流转、管网运营机制改革、原油进口动态管理等改革,完善油气交易中心建设。推进能源价格市场化,进一步放开竞争性环节价格,初步建立电力、油气网络环节科学定价制度。协同推进能源改革和法治建设,能源法律体系不断完善。覆盖战略、规划、政策、标准、监管、服务的能源治理机制基本形成。

（六） 能源惠民利民成果丰硕

把保障和改善民生作为能源发展的根本出发点,保障城乡居民获得基本能源供应和服务,在全面建成小康社会和乡村振兴中发挥能源供应的基础保障作用。2016 年至 2019 年,农网改造升级总投资达 8300 亿元,农村平均停电时间降低至 15 小时左右,农村居民用电条件明显改善。2013 年至 2015 年,实施解决无电人口用电行动计划,2015 年底完成全部人口都用上电的历史性任务。实施光伏扶贫工程等能源扶贫工程建设,优先在贫困地区进行能源开发项目布局,实施能源惠民工程,促进了贫困地区经济发展和贫困人口收入增加。完善天然气利用基础设施建设,扩大天然气供应区域,提高民生用气

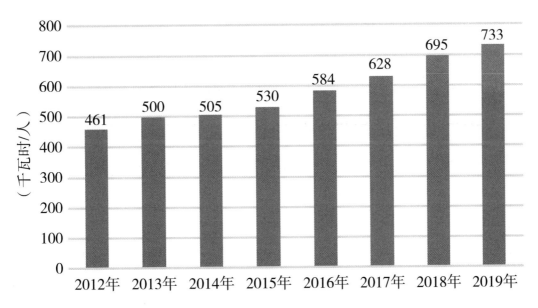

图 3　中国人均生活用电量（2012—2019 年）

数据来源：中国电力企业联合会

保障能力。北方地区清洁取暖取得明显进展,改善了城乡居民用能条件和居住环境。截至 2019 年底,北方地区清洁取暖面积达 116 亿平方米,比 2016 年增加 51 亿平方米。

三、全面推进能源消费方式变革

坚持节约资源和保护环境的基本国策,坚持节能优先方针,树立节能就是增加资源、减少污染、造福人类的理念,把节能贯穿于经济社会发展全过程和各领域。

(一) 实行能耗双控制度

实行能源消费总量和强度双控制度,按省、自治区、直辖市行政区域设定能源消费总量和强度控制目标,对各级地方政府进行监督考核。把节能指标纳入生态文明、绿色发展等绩效评价指标体系,引导转变发展理念。对重点用能单位分解能耗双控目标,开展目标责任评价考核,推动重点用能单位加强节能管理。

(二) 健全节能法律法规和标准体系

修订实施《节约能源法》,建立完善工业、建筑、交通等重点领域和公共机构节能制度,健全节能监察、能源效率标识、固定资产投资项目节能审查、重点用能单位节能管理等配套法律制度。强化标准引领约束作用,健全节能标准体系,实施百项能效标准推进工程,发布实施 340 多项国家节能标准,其中近 200 项强制性标准,实现主要高耗能行业和终端用能产品全覆盖。加强节能执法监督,强化事中事后监管,严格执法问责,确保节能法律法规和强制性标准有效落实。

(三) 完善节能低碳激励政策

实行促进节能的企业所得税、增值税优惠政策。鼓励进口先进节能技术、设备,控制出口耗能高、污染重的产品。健全绿色金融体系,利用能效信贷、绿色债券等支持节能项目。创新完善促进绿色发展的价格机制,实施差别电价、峰谷分时电价、阶梯电价、阶梯气价等,完善环保电价政策,调动市场主体和居民节能的积极性。在浙江等 4 省市开展用能权有偿使用和交易试点,在北京等 7 省市开展碳排放权交易试点。大力推行合同能源管理,鼓励节能技术和经营模式创新,发展综合能源服务。加强电力需求侧管理,推行电力需求侧响应的市场化机制,引导节约、有序、合理用电。建立能效"领跑者"制度,推动终端用能产品、高耗能行业、公共机构提升能效水平。

(四) 提升重点领域能效水平

积极优化产业结构,大力发展低能耗的先进制造业、高新技术产业、现代服务业,推动传统产业智能化、清洁化改造。推动工业绿色循环低碳转型升级,全面实施绿色制造,建立健全节能监察执法和节能诊断服务机制,开展能效对标达标。提升新建建筑节能标准,深化既有建筑节能改造,优化建筑用能结构。构建节能高效的综合交通运输体系,推进交通运输用能清洁化,提高交通运输工具能效水平。全面建设节约型公共机构,促进公共机构为全社会节能工作作出表率。构建市场导向的绿色技术创新体系,促进绿色技术研发、转化与推广。推广国家重点节能低碳技术、工业节能技术装备、交通运输行业重点节能低碳技术等。推动全民节能,引导树立勤俭节约的消费观,倡导简约适度、绿色低碳的生活方式,反对奢侈浪费和不合理消费。

专栏3　重点领域节能持续加强

加强工业领域节能。实施国家重大工业专项节能监察、工业节能诊断行动、工业节能与绿色标准化行动,在钢铁、电解铝等12个重点行业遴选能效"领跑者"企业。开展工业领域电力需求侧管理专项行动,发布《工业领域电力需求侧管理工作指南》,遴选153家工业领域示范企业(园区)。培育能源服务集成商,促进现代能源服务业与工业制造有机融合。

强化建筑领域节能。新建建筑全面执行建筑节能标准,开展超低能耗、近零能耗建筑示范,推动既有居住建筑节能改造,提升公共建筑能效水平,加强可再生能源建筑应用。截至2019年底,累计建成节能建筑面积198亿平方米,占城镇既有建筑面积比例超过56%,2019年城镇新增节能建筑面积超过20亿平方米。

促进交通运输节能。完善公共交通服务体系,推广多式联运。提升铁路电气化水平,推广天然气车船,发展节能与新能源汽车,完善充换电和加氢基础设施,鼓励靠港船舶和民航飞机停靠期间使用岸电,建设天然气加气站、加注站。淘汰老旧高能耗车辆、船舶等。截至2019年底,建成港口岸电设施5400余套、液化天然气动力船舶280余艘。

加强公共机构节能。实行能源定额管理,遴选发布政府机关、学校、医院等公共机构能效领跑者,实施绿色建筑、绿色办公、绿色出行、绿色食堂、绿色信息、绿色文化行动,开展3600余个节约型公共机构示范单位创建活动。

（五）推动终端用能清洁化

以京津冀及周边地区、长三角、珠三角、汾渭平原等地区为重点，实施煤炭消费减量替代和散煤综合治理，推广清洁高效燃煤锅炉，推行天然气、电力和可再生能源等替代低效和高污染煤炭的使用。制定财政、价格等支持政策，积极推进北方地区冬季清洁取暖，促进大气环境质量改善。推进终端用能领域以电代煤、以电代油，推广新能源汽车、热泵、电窑炉等新型用能方式。加强天然气基础设施建设与互联互通，在城镇燃气、工业燃料、燃气发电、交通运输等领域推进天然气高效利用。大力推进天然气热电冷联供的供能方式，推进分布式可再生能源发展，推行终端用能领域多能协同和能源综合梯级利用。

专栏4　能源绿色低碳消费水平不断提升

推进终端领域电能替代。制定《关于推进电能替代的指导意见》，在居民采暖、生产制造、交通运输等领域推行以电代煤、以电代油，稳步提升全社会电气化水平。2019年完成电能替代电量2065亿千瓦时，比上年增长32.6%。

加强分散燃煤治理。制定《燃煤锅炉节能环保综合提升工程实施方案》，提高锅炉系统高效运行水平，因地制宜推广燃气锅炉、电锅炉、生物质成型燃料锅炉。大气污染防治重点区域加快淘汰燃煤小锅炉，根据大气环境质量改善要求，划定高污染燃料禁燃区。

推进北方地区清洁取暖。制定《北方地区冬季清洁取暖规划（2017—2021年）》，将改善民生与环境治理相结合，坚持宜气则气、宜电则电、宜煤则煤、宜热则热，大力推进清洁取暖。截至2019年底，北方地区清洁取暖率达55%，比2016年提高21个百分点。

四、建设多元清洁的能源供应体系

立足基本国情和发展阶段,确立生态优先、绿色发展的导向,坚持在保护中发展、在发展中保护,深化能源供给侧结构性改革,优先发展非化石能源,推进化石能源清洁高效开发利用,健全能源储运调峰体系,促进区域多能互补协调发展。

(一) 优先发展非化石能源

开发利用非化石能源是推进能源绿色低碳转型的主要途径。中国把非化石能源放在能源发展优先位置,大力推进低碳能源替代高碳能源、可再生能源替代化石能源。

推动太阳能多元化利用。按照技术进步、成本降低、扩大市场、完善体系的原则,全面推进太阳能多方式、多元化利用。统筹光伏发电的布局与市场消纳,集中式与分布式并举开展光伏发电建设,实施光伏发电"领跑者"计划,采用市场竞争方式配置项目,加快推动光伏发电技术进步和成本降低,光伏产业已成为具有国际竞争力的优势产业。完善光伏发电分布式应用的电网接入等服务机制,推动光伏与农业、养殖、治沙等综合发展,形成多元化光伏发电发展模式。通过示范项目建设推进太阳能热发电产业化发展,为相关产业链的发展提供市场支撑。推动太阳能热利用不断拓展市场领域和利用方式,在工业、商业、公共服务等领域推广集中热水工程,开展太阳能供暖试点。

全面协调推进风电开发。按照统筹规划、集散并举、陆海齐进、有效利用的原则,在做好风电开发与电力送出和市场消纳衔接的前提下,有序推进风电开发利用和大型风电基地建设。积极开发中东部分散风能资源。积极稳妥发展海上风电。优先发展平价风电项目,推行市场化竞争方式配置风电项目。以风电的规模化开发利用促进风电制造产业发展,风电制造产业的创新能力和国际竞争力不断提升,产业服务体系逐步完善。

推进水电绿色发展。坚持生态优先、绿色发展,在做好生态环境保护和移民安置的前提下,科学有序推进水电开发,做到开发与保护并重、建设与管理并重。以西南地区主要河流为重点,有序推进流域大型水电基地建设,合理控制中小水电开发。推进小水电绿色发展,加大对实施河流生态修复的财政投入,促进河流生态健康。完善水电开发移民利益共享政策,坚持水电开发促进地方经济社会发展和移民脱贫致富,努力做到"开发一方资源、发展一方经济、改善一方环境、造福一方百姓"。

安全有序发展核电。中国将核安全作为核电发展的生命线,坚持发展与安全并重,实行安全有序发展核电的方针,加强核电规划、选址、设计、建造、运行和退役等全生命周期管理和监督,坚持采用最先进的技术、最严格的标准发展核电。完善多层次核能、核安全法规标准体系,加强核应急预案和法制、体制、机制建设,形成有效应对核事故的国家核应急能力体系。强化核安保与核材料管制,严格履行核安保与核不扩散国际义务,始终保持着良好的核安保记录。迄今为止在运核电机组总体安全状况良好,未发生国际核事件分级 2 级及以上的事件或事故。

因地制宜发展生物质能、地热能和海洋能。采用符合环保标准的先进技术发展城镇生活垃圾焚烧发电,推动生物质发电向热电联产转型升级。积极推进生物天然气产业化发展和农村沼气转型升级。坚持不与人争粮、不与粮争地的原则,严格控制燃料乙醇加工产能扩张,重点提升生物柴油产品品质,推进非粮生物液体燃料技术产业化发展。创新地热能开发利用模式,开展地热能城镇集中供暖,建设地热能高效开发利用示范区,有序开展地热能发电。积极推进潮流能、波浪能等海洋能技术研发和示范应用。

全面提升可再生能源利用率。完善可再生能源发电全额保障性收购制度。实施清洁能源消纳行动计划,多措并举促进清洁能源利用。提高电力规划整体协调性,优化电源结构和布局,充分发挥市场调节功能,形成有利于可再生能源利用的体制机制,全面提升电力系统灵活性和调节能力。实行可再生能源电力消纳保障机制,对各省、自治区、直辖市行政区域按年度确定电力消费中可再生能源应达到的最低比重指标,要求电力销售企业和电力用户共同履行可再生能源电力消纳责任。发挥电网优化资源配置平台作用,促进源网荷储互动协调,完善可再生能源电力消纳考核和监管机制。可再生能源电力利用率显著提升,2019年全国平均风电利用率达96%、光伏发电利用率达98%、主要流域水能利用率达96%。

专栏5　张家口可再生能源示范区加快建设

2015年国家批准张家口可再生能源示范区规划。规划提出,推进"三大创新":体制机制创新、商业模式创新、技术创新;实施"四大工程":规模化可再生能源开发工程、大容量储能应用工程、智能化输电工程、多元化应用示范工程;打造"五大功能区":低碳奥运专区、可再生能源科技创业城、可再生能源综合商务区、高端装备制造聚集区、农业可再生能源循环利用示范区。

截至2019年底,张家口市可再生能源发电总装机容量达1500万千瓦,占区域内全部发电装机容量的70%以上。风电供暖面积超过800万平方米,绿色数据中心消纳可再生能源电力2.85亿千瓦时,可再生能源占区域能源消费比重达27%。新能源汽车推广量约3000辆,一批氢燃料电池公交车投入运营。张北±500千伏柔性直流电网试验示范工程和张北—雄安1000千伏特高压交流工程的建设,促进形成京津冀绿色能源协同发展新模式。

到2030年,张家口市80%的电力消费以及全部城镇公共交通、城乡居民生活用能、商业及公共建筑用能将来自可再生能源,全部工业企业实现零碳排放,形成以可再生能源为主的能源供应体系。

（二）清洁高效开发利用化石能源

根据国内资源禀赋,以资源环境承载力为基础,统筹化石能源开发利用与生态环境保护,有序发展先进产能,加快淘汰落后产能,推进煤炭清洁高效利用,提升油气勘探开发力度,促进增储上产,提高油气自给能力。

推进煤炭安全智能绿色开发利用。努力建设集约、安全、高效、清洁的煤炭工业体系。推进煤炭供给侧结构性改革,完善煤炭产能置换政策,加快淘汰落后产能,有序释放优质产能,煤炭开发布局和产能结构大幅优化,大型现代化煤矿成为煤炭生产主体。2016年至2019年,累计退出煤炭落后产能9亿吨/年以上。加大安全生产投入,健全安全生产长效机制,加快煤矿机械化、自动化、信息化、智能化建设,全面提升煤矿安全生产效率和安全保障水平。推进大型煤炭基地绿色化开采和改造,发展煤炭洗选加工,发展矿区循环经济,加强矿区生态环境治理,建成一批绿色矿山,资源综合利用水平全面提升。实施煤炭清洁高效利用行动,煤炭消费中发电用途占比进一步提升。煤制油气、低阶煤分质利用等煤炭深加工产业化示范取得积极进展。

清洁高效发展火电。坚持清洁高效原则发展火电。推进煤电布局优化和技术升级,积极稳妥化解煤电过剩产能。建立并完善煤电规划建设风险预警机制,严控煤电规划建设,加快淘汰落后产能。截至2019年底,累计淘汰煤电落后产能超过1亿千瓦,煤电装机占总发电装机比重从2012年的65.7%下降至2019年的52%。实施煤电节能减排升级与改造行动,执行更严格能效环保标准。煤电机组发电效率、污染物排放控制达到世界先进水平。合理布局适度发展天然气发电,鼓励在电力负荷中心建设天然气调峰电站,提升电力系统安全保障水平。

提高天然气生产能力。加强基础地质调查和资源评价,加强科技创新、产业扶持,促进常规天然气增产,重点突破页岩气、煤层气等非常规天然气勘探开发,推动页岩气规模化开发,增加国内天然气供应。完善非常规天然气产业政策体系,促进页岩气、煤层气开发利用。以四川盆地、鄂尔多斯盆地、塔里木盆地为重点,建成多个百亿立方米级天然气生产基地。2017 年以来,每年新增天然气产量超过100 亿立方米。

专栏 6　非常规天然气勘探开发取得突破

页岩气。海相页岩气勘探开发取得重大突破,建设了四川长宁—威远、昭通、重庆涪陵等国家级页岩气示范区,推动页岩气规模化开发,2019 年产量突破 150 亿立方米。

煤层气。初步建成沁水和鄂东两大煤层气产业化基地,为富煤地区发展绿色低碳经济作出重要贡献。2019 年全国煤层气(煤矿瓦斯)抽采量超过 180 亿立方米。

致密气。致密砂岩气勘探开发取得重要进展,直接促进了鄂尔多斯盆地和川中地区致密气产量的快速增长。

提升石油勘探开发与加工水平。加强国内勘探开发,深化体制机制改革、促进科技研发和新技术应用,加大低品位资源勘探开发力度,推进原油增储上产。发展先进采油技术,提高原油采收率,稳定松辽盆地、渤海湾盆地等东部老油田产量。以新疆地区、鄂尔多斯盆地等为重点,推进西部新油田增储上产。加强渤海、东海和南海等海域近海油气勘探开发,推进深海对外合作,2019 年海上油田产量约4000 万吨。推进炼油行业转型升级。实施成品油质量升级,提升燃油品质,促进减少机动车尾气污染物排放。

（三）加强能源储运调峰体系建设

统筹发展煤电油气多种能源输运方式,构建互联互通输配网络,打造稳定可靠的储运调峰体系,提升应急保障能力。

加强能源输配网络建设。持续加强跨省跨区骨干能源输送通道建设,提升能源主要产地与主要消费区域间通达能力,促进区域优势互补、协调发展。提升既有铁路煤炭运输专线的输送能力,持续提升铁路运输比例和煤炭运输效率。推进天然气主干管道与省级管网、液化天然气接收站、储气库间互联互通,加快建设"全国一张网",初步形成调度灵活、安全可靠的天然气输运体系。稳步推进跨省跨区输电通道建设,扩大西北、华北、东北和西南等区域清洁能源配置范围。完善区域电网主网架,加强省级区域内部电网建设。开展柔性直流输电示范工程建设,积极建设能源互联网,推动构建规模合理、分层分区、安全可靠的电力系统。

健全能源储备应急体系。建立国家储备与企业储备相结合、战略储备与商业储备并举的能源储备体系,提高石油、天然气和煤炭等储备能力。完善国家石油储备体系,加快石油储备基地建设。建立健全地方政府、供气企业、管输企业、城镇燃气企业各负其责的多层次天然气储气调峰体系。完善以企业社会责任储备为主体、地方政府储备为补充的煤炭储备体系。健全国家大面积停电事件应急机制,全面提升电力供应可靠性和应急保障能力。建立健全与能源储备能力相匹配的输配保障体系,构建规范化的收储、轮换、动用体系,完善决策执行的监管机制。

完善能源调峰体系。坚持供给侧与需求侧并重,完善市场机制,加强技术支撑,增强调峰能力,提升能源系统综合利用效率。加快抽水蓄能电站建设,合理布局天然气调峰电站,实施既有燃煤热电联产机组、燃煤发电机组灵活性改造,改善电力系统调峰性能,促进清洁能源消纳。推动储能与新能源发电、电力系统协调优化运行,开展电化学储能等调峰试点。推进天然气储气调峰设施建设,完善天然气储气调峰辅助服务市场化机制,提升天然气调峰能力。完善电价、气价政策,引导电力、天然气用户自主参与调峰、错峰,提升需求侧响应能力。健全电力和天然气负荷可中断、可调节管理体系,挖掘需求侧潜力。

（四）支持农村及贫困地区能源发展

落实乡村振兴战略,提高农村生活用能保障水平,让农村居民有更多实实在在的获得感、幸福感、安全感。

加快完善农村能源基础设施。让所有人都能用上电,是全面建成小康社会的基本条件。实施全面解决无电人口问题三年行动计划,2015 年底全面解决了无电人口用电问题。中国高度重视农村电网改造升级,着力补齐农村电网发展短板。实施小城镇中心村农网改造升级、平原农村地区机井通电和贫困村通动力电专项工程。

2018年起,重点推进深度贫困地区和抵边村寨农网改造升级攻坚。加快天然气支线管网和基础设施建设,扩大管网覆盖范围。在天然气管网未覆盖的地区推进液化天然气、压缩天然气、液化石油气供应网点建设,因地制宜开发利用可再生能源,改善农村供能条件。

精准实施能源扶贫工程。能源不仅是经济发展的动力,也是扶贫的重要支撑。中国合理开发利用贫困地区能源资源,积极推进贫困地区重大能源项目建设,提升贫困地区自身"造血"能力,为贫困地区经济发展增添新动能。在革命老区、民族地区、边疆地区、贫困地区优先布局能源开发项目,建设清洁电力外送基地,为所在地区经济增长作出重要贡献。在水电开发建设中,形成了水库移民"搬得出、稳得住、能致富"的可持续发展模式,让贫困人口更多分享资源开发收益。加强财政投入和政策扶持,支持贫困地区发展生物质能、风能、太阳能、小水电等清洁能源。推行多种形式的光伏与农业融合发展模式,实施光伏扶贫工程,建成了成千上万座遍布贫困农村地区的"阳光银行"。

推进北方农村地区冬季清洁取暖。北方地区冬季清洁取暖关系广大人民群众生活,是重大民生工程、民心工程。以保障北方地区广大群众温暖过冬、减少大气污染为立足点,在北方农村地区因地制宜开展清洁取暖。按照企业为主、政府推动、居民可承受的方针,稳妥推进"煤改气""煤改电",支持利用清洁生物质燃料、地热能、太阳能供暖以及热泵技术应用。截至2019年底,北方农村地区清洁取暖率约31%,比2016年提高21.6个百分点;北方农村地区累计完成散煤替代约 2300 万户,其中京津冀及周边地区、汾渭平原累计完成散煤清洁化替代约 1800 万户。

专栏 7　农村能源建设和扶贫取得显著成就

实施新一轮农网改造升级。2017 年,小城镇中心村农网改造升级、农村机井通电和贫困村通动力电全面完成,惠及 7.8 万个村、1.6 亿农村居民;为 160 万口机井通了电,惠及 1 万多个乡镇、1.5 亿亩农田;为 3.3 万个自然村通了动力电。2019 年完成新一轮农网改造升级目标,实现农村电网供电可靠率 99.8%,综合电压合格率 97.9%。全国农村地区基本实现稳定可靠的供电服务全覆盖。

全面解决无电人口用电。2013 年至 2015 年,国家安排投资 247.8 亿元,实施无电地区电网延伸工程建设,为 154.5 万无电人口通电。实施光伏独立供电工程建设,为 118.5 万无电人口通电。2015 年底全面解决无电人口用电问题,实现用电人口全覆盖。

实施光伏发电扶贫。光伏扶贫是精准扶贫十大工程之一。2014 年以来,国家组织编制光伏扶贫规划,出台财政、金融、价格等政策,加强电网建设和运行服务,按照政府出资、企业实施方式,推动多种形式光伏扶贫工程。累计建成 2636 万千瓦光伏扶贫电站,惠及近 6 万个贫困村、415 万贫困户,每年可产生发电收益约 180 亿元,相应安置公益岗位 125 万个。

五、发挥科技创新第一动力作用

抓住全球新一轮科技革命与产业变革的机遇,在能源领域大力实施创新驱动发展战略,增强能源科技创新能力,通过技术进步解决能源资源约束、生态环境保护、应对气候变化等重大问题和挑战。

(一) 完善能源科技创新政策顶层设计

中国将能源作为国家创新驱动发展战略的重要组成部分,把能源科技创新摆在更加突出的地位。《国家创新驱动发展战略纲要》将安全清洁高效现代能源技术作为重要战略方向和重点领域。制定能源资源科技创新规划和面向 2035 年的能源、资源科技发展战略规划,部署了能源科技创新重大举措和重大任务,努力提升科技创新引领和支撑作用。制定能源技术创新规划和《能源技术革命创新行动计划(2016—2030 年)》,提出能源技术创新的重点方向和技术路线图。深化能源科技体制改革,形成政府引导、市场主导、企业为主体、社会参与、多方协同的能源技术创新体系。加大重要能源领域和新兴能源产业科技创新投入,加强人才队伍建设,提升各类主体创新能力。

（二）建设多元化多层次能源科技创新平台

依托骨干企业、科研院所和高校，建成一批高水平能源技术创新平台，有效激发了各类主体的创新活力。布局建设 40 多个国家重点实验室和一批国家工程研究中心，重点围绕煤炭安全绿色智能开采、可再生能源高效利用、储能与分布式能源等技术方向开展相关研究，促进能源科技进步。布局建设 80 余个国家能源研发中心和国家能源重点实验室，围绕煤炭、石油、天然气、火电、核电、可再生能源、能源装备重点领域和关键环节开展研究，覆盖当前能源技术创新的重点领域和前沿方向。大型能源企业适应自身发展和行业需要，不断加强科技能力建设，形成若干专业领域、有影响力的研究机构。地方政府结合本地产业优势，采取多种方式加强科研能力建设。在"大众创业、万众创新"政策支持下，各类社会主体积极开展科技创新，形成了众多能源科技创新型企业。

（三）开展能源重大领域协同科技创新

实施重大科技项目和工程，实现能源领域关键技术跨越式发展。聚焦国家重大战略产业化目标，实施油气科技重大专项，重点突破油气地质新理论与高效勘探开发关键技术，开展页岩油、页岩气、天然气水合物等非常规资源经济高效开发技术攻关。实施核电科技重大专项,围绕三代压水堆和四代高温气冷堆技术,开展关键核心技术攻关,持续推进核电自主创新。面向重大共性关键技术,部署开展新能源汽车、智能电网技术与装备、煤矿智能化开采技术与装备、煤炭清洁高效利用与新型节能技术、可再生能源与氢能技术等方面研究。面向国家重大战略任务,重点部署能源高效洁净利用与转化的物理化学基础研究,推动以基础研究带动应用技术突破。

专栏 8　重大能源技术装备取得新突破

可再生能源技术装备。掌握水能、风能、太阳能等能源系统关键技术。大型水电机组成套设计制造能力世界领先。风电、光伏发电全产业链技术快速迭代,成本大幅下降,形成一批世界级龙头企业。生物质能、地热能、海洋能等技术取得长足进步。

电网技术装备。全面掌握特高压输变电技术,柔性直流、多端直流等先进电网技术开展示范应用,智能电网、大电网控制等技术取得显著进步,输变电技术装备处于国际领先水平。

核电技术装备。掌握百万千瓦级压水堆核电站设计和建造技术。自主研发三代核电技术装备达到世界先进水平。具有自主知识产权的首个"华龙一号"示范工程——福清 5 号核电机组取得重要进展。"国和一号"(CAP1400)示范工程和高温气冷堆示范工程建设稳步推进,快堆、小型堆等多项前沿技术研究取得突破。

油气勘探开发技术装备。形成先进的低渗透和稠油油田开采技术,实现特大型超深高含硫气田安全高效开发技术等工业化应用,开发了超高破裂压力地层压裂技术,海洋深水勘探开发关键技术与装备取得重大进展,自主研发了以"海洋石油 981"为代表的 3000 米深水半潜式钻井平台。自主研制"蓝鲸 1 号""蓝鲸 2 号",助力海域天然气水合物开采技术获得突破。

清洁高效煤电技术装备。具备超超临界煤电机组自主研发和制造能力,发电煤耗下降至 256 克标准煤/千瓦时。燃煤发电空冷、二次再热、循环流化床、超低排放等技术领域处于世界领先水平。建成 10 万吨级碳捕集利用和封存示范装备。

煤炭安全绿色智能开发利用技术装备。煤炭安全绿色开采技术达到国际先进水平,煤炭生产实现向自动化、机械化、智能化转变。形成具有自主知识产权的煤制油气等煤炭深加工成套工艺技术。

（四）依托重大能源工程提升能源技术装备水平

在全球能源绿色低碳转型发展趋势下，加快传统能源技术装备升级换代，加强新兴能源技术装备自主创新，清洁低碳能源技术水平显著提升。依托重大装备制造和重大示范工程，推动关键能源装备技术攻关、试验示范和推广应用。完善能源装备计量、标准、检测和认证体系，提高重大能源装备研发、设计、制造和成套能力。围绕能源安全供应、清洁能源发展和化石能源清洁高效利用三大方向，着力突破能源装备制造关键技术、材料和零部件等瓶颈，推动全产业链技术创新。开展先进能源技术装备的重大能源示范工程建设，提升煤炭清洁智能采掘洗选、深水和非常规油气勘探开发、油气储运和输送、清洁高效燃煤发电、先进核电、可再生能源发电、燃气轮机、储能、先进电网、煤炭深加工等领域装备的技术水平。

（五）支持新技术新模式新业态发展

当前，世界正处在新科技革命和产业革命交汇点，新技术突破加速带动产业变革，促进能源新模式新业态不断涌现。大力推动能源技术与现代信息、材料和先进制造技术深度融合，依托"互联网＋"智慧能源建设，探索能源生产和消费新模式。加快智能光伏创新升级，推动光伏发电与农业、渔业、牧业、建筑等融合发展,拓展光伏发电互补应用新空间,形成广泛开发利用新能源的新模式。加速发展绿氢制取、储运和应用等氢能产业链技术装备,促进氢能燃料电池技术链、氢燃料电池汽车产业链发展。支持能源各环节各场景储能应用,着力推进储能与可再生能源互补发展。支持新能源微电网建设,形成发储用一体化局域清洁供能系统。推动综合能源服务新模式,实现终端能源多能互补、协同高效。在试点示范项目引领和带动下,各类能源新技术、新模式、新业态持续涌现,形成能源创新发展的"聚变效应"。

六、全面深化能源体制改革

充分发挥市场在能源资源配置中的决定性作用,更好发挥政府作用,深化重点领域和关键环节市场化改革,破除妨碍发展的体制机制障碍,着力解决市场体系不完善等问题,为维护国家能源安全、推进能源高质量发展提供制度保障。

(一) 构建有效竞争的能源市场

大力培育多元市场主体,打破垄断、放宽准入、鼓励竞争,构建统一开放、竞争有序的能源市场体系,着力清除市场壁垒,提高能源资源配置效率和公平性。

培育多元能源市场主体。支持各类市场主体依法平等进入负面清单以外的能源领域,形成多元市场主体共同参与的格局。深化油气勘查开采体制改革,开放油气勘查开采市场,实行勘查区块竞争出让和更加严格的区块退出机制。支持符合条件的企业进口原油。改革油气管网运营机制,实现管输和销售业务分离。稳步推进售电侧改革,有序向社会资本开放配售电业务,深化电网企业主辅分离。积极培育配售电、储能、综合能源服务等新兴市场主体。深化国有能源企业改革,支持非公有制发展,积极稳妥开展能源领域混合所有制改革,激发企业活力动力。

建设统一开放、竞争有序的能源市场体系。根据不同能源品种特点,搭建煤炭、电力、石油和天然气交易平台,促进供需互动。推动建设现代化煤炭市场体系,发展动力煤、炼焦煤、原油期货交易和天然气现货交易。全面放开经营性电力用户发用电计划,建设中长期交易、现货交易等电能量交易和辅助服务交易相结合的电力市场。积极推进全国统一电力市场和全国碳排放权交易市场建设。

专栏 9　电力领域市场化改革取得重要突破

健全输配电价监管体系。基本确立以"准许成本+合理收益"为核心的输配电价监管制度框架,改变电网企业盈利模式,为加快推进电力市场化改革奠定基础。

推进交易机构独立规范运行。组建北京、广州两家区域交易机构和 33 家省(自治区、直辖市)交易机构。实施交易机构股份制改造,完善治理结构。

放开配售电业务。鼓励社会资本参与增量配电业务。鼓励符合条件的企业从事售电业务,赋予用户更多自主选择权。截至 2019 年底,推出 380 个增量配电改革试点项目,在电力交易机构注册的售电公司近 4500 家。

推进电力市场建设。有序放开发用电计划,全面推广中长期交易,在 8 个地区开展电力现货试点,在 5 个区域电网、27 个省级电网推进电力辅助服务市场建设。2019 年,全国市场化交易电量约 2.71 万亿千瓦时,约占全社会用电量 37.5%。

(二) 完善主要由市场决定能源价格的机制

按照"管住中间、放开两头"总体思路,稳步放开竞争性领域和竞争性环节价格,促进价格反映市场供求、引导资源配置;严格政府定价成本监审,推进科学合理定价。

有序放开竞争性环节价格。推动分步实现公益性以外的发售电价格由市场形成,电力用户或售电主体可与发电企业通过市场化方式确定交易价格。进一步深化燃煤发电上网电价机制改革,实行"基准价+上下浮动"的市场化价格机制。稳步推进以竞争性招标方式确定新建风电、光伏发电项目上网电价。推动按照"风险共担、利益共享"原则协商或通过市场化方式形成跨省跨区送电价格。完善成品油价格形成机制,推进天然气价格市场化改革。坚持保基本、促节约原则,全面推行居民阶梯电价、阶梯气价制度。

科学核定自然垄断环节价格。按照"准许成本+合理收益"原则,合理制定电网、天然气管网输配价格。开展两个监管周期输配电定价成本监审和电价核定。强化输配气价格监管,开展成本监审,构建天然气输配领域全环节价格监管体系。

专栏10　油气领域市场化改革取得积极进展

推进油气勘查开采体制改革。推进矿产资源管理改革,实行探采合一制度,允许符合准入要求的市场主体参与常规油气勘查开采。已开展多轮油气探矿权竞争出让活动,竞争出让油气勘查区块,引入国有石油公司之外的多家市场主体。实行更加严格的区块退出机制,加大区块退出力度。

推进油气管网运营机制改革。2019年,组建国有资本控股、投资主体多元化的国家石油天然气管网集团有限公司,促进上下游市场公平竞争。推动油气管网设施公平开放,支持油气管网设施互联互通和公平接入。

改革油气产品定价机制。缩短成品油调价周期。逐步放开非常规天然气价格。理顺居民用气门站价格,促进更好反映供气成本和供需变化。加强天然气输配环节价格监管,减少中间供气环节,2017年核定长输管道运输价格。

完善油气进出口管理体制。完善成品油进出口政策。支持符合条件的企业开展原油非国营贸易进口业务,形成了多元、有序、有活力的原油进口队伍。

（三）创新能源科学管理和优化服务

进一步转变政府职能，简政放权、放管结合、优化服务，着力打造服务型政府。发挥能源战略规划和宏观政策导向作用，集中力量办大事。强化能源市场监管，提升监管效能，促进各类市场主体公平竞争。坚持人民至上、生命至上理念，牢牢守住能源安全生产底线。

激发市场主体活力。深化能源"放管服"改革，减少中央政府层面能源项目核准，将部分能源项目审批核准权限下放地方，取消可由市场主体自主决策的能源项目审批。减少前置审批事项，降低市场准入门槛，加强和规范事中事后监管。提升"获得电力"服务水平，压减办电时间、环节和成本。推行"互联网+政务"服务，推进能源政务服务事项"一窗受理""应进必进"，提升"一站式"服务水平。

专栏 11　用电营商环境显著改善

优化用电营商环境是提升市场主体和人民群众"获得电力"的获得感和满意度的重要内容。在全国范围内推行低压小微企业用电报装"零上门、零审批、零投资"服务。2019年底，各直辖市、省会城市实现低压小微企业用电报装"三零"服务，办电时间压缩至30个工作日以内。世界银行报告显示，2017至2019年，企业办电环节平均由5.5个压减至2个，办电时间和办电成本大幅降低，"获得电力"指标排名从第98位提升至第12位。

引导资源配置方向。制定实施《能源生产和消费革命战略

（2016—2030）》以及能源发展规划和系列专项规划、行动计划，明确能源发展的总体目标和重点任务，引导社会主体的投资方向。完善能源领域财政、税收、产业和投融资政策，全面实施原油、天然气、煤炭资源税从价计征，提高成品油消费税，引导市场主体合理开发利用能源资源。构建绿色金融正向激励体系，推广新能源汽车，发展清洁能源。支持大宗能源商品贸易人民币计价结算。

促进市场公平竞争。理顺能源监管职责关系，逐步实现电力监管向综合能源监管转型。严格电力交易、调度、供电服务和市场秩序监管，强化电网公平接入、电网投资行为、成本及投资运行效率监管。加强油气管网设施公平开放监管，推进油气管网设施企业信息公开，提高油气管网设施利用率。全面推行"双随机、一公开"监管，提高监管公平公正性。加强能源行业信用体系建设，依法依规建立严重失信主体名单制度，实施失信惩戒，提升信用监管效能。包容审慎监管新兴业态，促进新动能发展壮大。畅通能源监管热线，发挥社会监督作用。

筑牢安全生产底线。健全煤矿安全生产责任体系，提高煤矿安全监管监察执法效能，建设煤矿安全生产标准化管理体系，增强防灾治灾能力，煤矿安全生产形势总体好转。落实电力安全企业主体责任、行业监管责任和属地管理责任，提升电力系统网络安全监督管理，加强电力建设工程施工安全监管和质量监督，电力系统安全风险总体可控，未发生大面积停电事故。加强油气全产业链安全监管，油气安全生产形势保持稳定。持续强化核安全监管体系建设，提高核安全监管能力,核电厂和研究堆总体安全状况良好,在建工程建造质量整体受控。

（四）健全能源法治体系

发挥法治固根本、稳预期、利长远的保障作用,坚持能源立法同改革发展相衔接,及时修改和废止不适应改革发展要求的法律法规;坚持法定职责必须为、法无授权不可为,依法全面履行政府职能。

完善能源法律体系。推进能源领域法律及行政法规制修订工作,加强能源领域法律法规实施监督检查,加快电力、煤炭、石油、天然气、核电、新能源等领域规章规范性文件的"立改废"进程,将改革成果体现在法律法规和重大政策中。

推进能源依法治理。推进法治政府建设,推动将法治贯穿于能源战略、规划、政策、标准的制定、实施和监督管理全过程。构建政企联动、互为支撑的能源普法新格局,形成尊法、学法、守法、用法良好氛围。创新行政执法方式,全面推行行政执法公示制度、行政执法全过程记录制度、重大执法决定法制审核制度,全面落实行政执法责任制。畅通行政复议和行政诉讼渠道,确保案件依法依规办理,依法保护行政相对人合法权益,让人民在每一个案件中切实感受到公平正义。

七、全方位加强能源国际合作

中国践行绿色发展理念,遵循互利共赢原则开展国际合作,努力实现开放条件下能源安全,扩大能源领域对外开放,推动高质量共建"一带一路",积极参与全球能源治理,引导应对气候变化国际合作,推动构建人类命运共同体。

(一)持续深化能源领域对外开放

中国坚定不移维护全球能源市场稳定,扩大能源领域对外开放。大幅度放宽外商投资准入,打造市场化法治化国际化营商环境,促进贸易和投资自由化便利化。全面实行准入前国民待遇加负面清单管理制度,能源领域外商投资准入限制持续减少。全面取消煤炭、油气、电力(除核电外)、新能源等领域外资准入限制。推动广东、湖北、重庆、海南等自由贸易试验区能源产业发展,支持浙江自由贸易试验区油气全产业链开放发展。埃克森美孚、通用电气、碧辟、法国电力、西门子等国际能源公司在中国投资规模稳步增加,上海特斯拉电动汽车等重大外资项目相继在中国落地,外资加油站数量快速增长。

2017 年,修订发布《外商投资产业指导目录》,首次提出全国范围实施的外商投资准入负面清单。2018 年起,《外商投资准入特别管理措施(负面清单)》从目录中独立出来发布,负面清单之外的领域按照内外资一致原则实施管理。

2018 年《外商投资准入特别管理措施(负面清单)》取消了以下准入限制:

- 电网的建设、经营(中方控股)。
- 特殊和稀缺煤类勘查、开采(中方控股)。
- 新能源汽车整车制造的中方股比不低于 50%。
- 加油站(同一外国投资者设立超过 30 家分店、销售来自多个供应商的不同种类和品牌成品油的连锁加油站,由中方控股)建设、经营。

2019 年《外商投资准入特别管理措施(负面清单)》取消了以下准入限制:

- 石油、天然气(含煤层气,油页岩、油砂、页岩气等除外)的勘探、开发限于合资、合作。
- 城市人口 50 万以上城市燃气和热力管网建设、经营须由中方控股。

(二) 着力推进共建"一带一路"能源合作

中国秉持共商共建共享原则,坚持开放、绿色、廉洁理念,努力实现高标准、惠民生、可持续的目标,同各国在共建"一带一路"框架下加强能源合作,在实现自身发展的同时更多惠及其他国家和人民,为推动共同发展创造有利条件。

推动互利共赢的能源务实合作。中国与全球 100 多个国家、地区开展广泛的能源贸易、投资、产能、装备、技术、标准等领域合作。中国企业高标准建设适应合作国迫切需求的能源项目,帮助当地把资源优势转化为发展优势,促进当地技术进步、就业扩大、经济增长和民生改善,实现优势互补、共同发展。通过第三方市场合作,与一些国家和大型跨国公司开展清洁能源领域合作,推动形成开放透明、普惠共享、互利共赢的能源合作格局。2019年,中国等30个国家共同建立了"一带一路"能源合作伙伴关系。

建设绿色丝绸之路。中国是全球最大的可再生能源市场,也是全球最大的清洁能源设备制造国。积极推动全球能源绿色低碳转型,广泛开展可再生能源合作,如几内亚卡雷塔水电项目、匈牙利考波什堡光伏电站项目、黑山莫茹拉风电项目、阿联酋迪拜光热光伏混合发电项目、巴基斯坦卡洛特水电站和真纳光伏园一期光伏项目等。可再生能源技术在中国市场的广泛应用,促进了全世界范围可再生能源成本的下降,加速了全球能源转型进程。

加强能源基础设施互联互通。积极推动跨国、跨区域能源基础设施联通,为能源资源互补协作和互惠贸易创造条件。中俄、中国—中亚、中缅油气管道等一批标志性的能源重大项目建成投运,中国与周边7个国家实现电力联网,能源基础设施互联互通水平显著提升,在更大范围内促进能源资源优化配置,促进区域国家经济合作。

提高全球能源可及性。积极推动"确保人人获得负担得起的、可靠和可持续的现代能源"可持续发展目标的国内落实,积极参与能源可及性国际合作,采用多种融资模式为无电地区因地制宜开发并网、微网和离网电力项目,为使用传统炊事燃料的地区捐赠清洁炉灶,提高合作国能源普及水平,惠及当地民生。

（三）积极参与全球能源治理

中国坚定支持多边主义，按照互利共赢原则开展双多边能源合作，积极支持国际能源组织和合作机制在全球能源治理中发挥作用，在国际多边合作框架下积极推动全球能源市场稳定与供应安全、能源绿色转型发展，为促进全球能源可持续发展贡献中国智慧、中国力量。

融入多边能源治理。积极参与联合国、二十国集团、亚太经合组织、金砖国家等多边机制下的能源国际合作，在联合研究发布报告、成立机构等方面取得积极进展。中国与 90 多个国家和地区建立了政府间能源合作机制，与 30 多个能源领域国际组织和多边机制建立了合作关系。2012 年以来，中国先后成为国际可再生能源署成员国、国际能源宪章签约观察国、国际能源署联盟国等。

倡导区域能源合作。搭建中国与东盟、阿盟、非盟、中东欧等区域能源合作平台，建立东亚峰会清洁能源论坛，中国推动能力建设与技术创新合作，为 18 个国家提供了清洁能源利用、能效等领域的培训。

专栏 13　中国推动完善全球能源治理体系的努力
在国际多边合作框架下，中国积极推动全球能源市场稳定与供应安全、能源绿色低碳转型发展、能源可及性、能效提升等倡议的制定和实施。

- 倡议探讨构建全球能源互联网,推动以清洁和绿色方式满足全球电力需求。
- 推动在二十国集团(G20)框架下发布《G20能效引领计划》《加强亚太地区能源可及性:关键挑战与G20自愿合作行动计划》《G20可再生能源自愿行动计划》。
- 与国际可再生能源署等国际组织创设国际能源变革论坛。
- 推动成立上海合作组织能源俱乐部。
- 在中国设立亚太经合组织可持续能源中心。
- 推动设立金砖国家能源研究平台。
- 作为创始成员,加入国际能效中心。

（四） 携手应对全球气候变化

中国秉持人类命运共同体理念,与其他国家团结合作、共同应对全球气候变化,积极推动能源绿色低碳转型。

加强应对气候变化国际合作。在联合国、世界银行、全球环境基金、亚洲开发银行等机构和德国等国家支持下,中国着眼能源绿色低碳转型,通过经验分享、技术交流、项目对接等方式,同相关国家在可再生能源开发利用、低碳城市示范等领域开展广泛而持续的双多边合作。

支持发展中国家提升应对气候变化能力。深化气候变化领域南南合作,支持最不发达国家、小岛屿国家、非洲国家和其他发展中国家应对气候变化挑战。从2016年起,中国在发展中国家启动10个低碳示范区、100个减缓和适应气候变化项目和1000个应对气候变化培训名额的合作项目,帮助发展中国家能源清洁低碳发展,共同应对全球气候变化。

（五）共同促进全球能源可持续发展的中国主张

人类已进入互联互通的时代,维护能源安全、应对全球气候变化已成为全世界面临的重大挑战。当前持续蔓延的新冠肺炎疫情,更加凸显各国利益休戚相关、命运紧密相连。中国倡议国际社会共同努力,促进全球能源可持续发展,应对气候变化挑战,建设清洁美丽世界。

协同推进能源绿色低碳转型,促进清洁美丽世界建设。应对气候变化挑战,改善全球生态环境,需要各国的共同努力。各国应选择绿色发展道路,采取绿色低碳循环可持续的生产生活方式,推动能源转型,协同应对和解决能源发展中的问题,携手应对全球气候变化,为建设清洁美丽世界作出积极贡献。

协同巩固能源领域多边合作,加速经济绿色复苏增长。完善国际能源治理机制,维护开放、包容、普惠、平衡、共赢的多边国际能源合作格局。深化能源领域对话沟通与务实合作,推动经济复苏和融合发展。加强跨国、跨地区能源清洁低碳技术创新和标准合作,促进能源技术转移和推广普及,完善国际协同的知识产权保护。

协同畅通国际能源贸易投资,维护全球能源市场稳定。消除能源贸易和投资壁垒,促进贸易投资便利化,开展能源资源和产能合作,深化能源基础设施合作,提升互联互通水平,促进资源高效配置和市场深度融合。秉持共商共建共享原则,积极寻求发展利益最大公约数,促进全球能源可持续发展,共同维护全球能源安全。

协同促进欠发达地区能源可及性,努力解决能源贫困问题。共同推动实现能源领域可持续发展目标,支持欠发达国家和地区缺乏现代能源供应的人口获得电力等基本的能源服务。帮助欠发达国家和地区推广应用先进绿色能源技术,培训能源专业人才,完善能源服务体系,形成绿色能源开发与消除能源贫困相融合的新模式。

结　束　语

中国即将开启全面建设社会主义现代化国家的新征程。进入新的发展阶段，中国将继续坚定不移推进能源革命，加快构建清洁低碳、安全高效的能源体系，为 2035 年基本实现社会主义现代化、本世纪中叶全面建成社会主义现代化强国提供坚强的能源保障。

当今世界正经历百年未有之大变局。生态环境事关人类生存和永续发展，需要各国团结合作，共同应对挑战。中国将秉持人类命运共同体理念，继续与各国一道，深化全球能源治理合作，推动全球能源可持续发展，维护全球能源安全，努力实现更加普惠、包容、均衡、平等的发展，建设更加清洁、美丽、繁荣、宜居的世界。

中国交通的可持续发展

（2020 年 12 月）

中华人民共和国
国务院新闻办公室

前　言

交通运输是国民经济中基础性、先导性、战略性产业和重要的服务性行业，是可持续发展的重要支撑。

新中国成立以来特别是改革开放以来，在中国共产党领导下，中国的交通运输秉持与经济社会协调发展、与自然生态和谐共生的理念，以建设人民满意交通为目标，自立自强，艰苦奋斗，取得了举世瞩目的发展成就，从根本上改变了基础薄弱、整体落后的面貌，为经济社会发展提供了有力保障，走出了一条中国特色交通发展之路。

中共十八大以来，在习近平新时代中国特色社会主义思想指引下，中国交通发展取得历史性成就、发生历史性变革，进入基础设施发展、服务水平提高和转型发展的黄金时期，进入高质量发展的新时代。基础设施网络规模居世界前列，运输服务保障能力不断提升，科技创新能力显著增强，行业治理现代化水平大幅跃升，人民高品质出行需求得到更好满足，中国加快向交通强国迈进。

当今世界正经历百年未有之大变局，各国的前途命运从未像现在这样紧密相连，交通对于加强互联互通、促进民心相通日益重要。作为负责任大国，中国认真落实联合国2030年可持续发展议程，积极参与全球交通治理，加强国际交流与合作，为促进全球可持续发展、推动构建人类命运共同体贡献中国智慧、中国力量。

为全面介绍新时代中国交通发展成就，分享中国交通可持续发展的理念和实践，增进国际社会认识和了解，特发布本白皮书。

一、走新时代交通发展之路

中国交通积极适应新的形势要求,坚持对内服务高质量发展、对外服务高水平开放,把握基础设施发展、服务水平提高和转型发展的黄金时期,着力推进综合交通、智慧交通、平安交通、绿色交通建设,走新时代交通发展之路。

(一) 以建设人民满意交通为目标

为了人民、依靠人民、服务人民,是中国交通发展的初心和使命。新时代的中国交通,秉持人民至上、以人为本的发展理念,坚持人民共建共治共享,建设人民满意交通。

——人民交通靠人民。坚持人民主体地位,着力解决人民最关心、最直接、最现实的交通发展问题,充分调动人民的积极性主动性创造性,鼓励社会公众参与交通治理,依靠人民办好交通。

——人民交通由人民共享。统筹公平和效率,坚持普惠性、保基本、均等化、可持续方向,大力推进城乡基本公共服务均等化,保障城乡居民行有所乘,让人民共享交通发展成果。

——人民交通让人民满意。以人民满意为根本评判标准,聚焦新时代人民对交通的新期待,深化供给侧结构性改革,推动交通运输高质量发展,不断满足不同群体的交通运输需求,不断提升人民的获得感、幸福感、安全感。

（二）以当好发展"先行官"为定位

经济要发展,国家要强大,交通要先强起来。把交通运输作为经济社会发展的"先行官",坚持先行引导、适度超前原则,保持一定发展速度,为经济社会发展提供坚实基础和有力保障。

——措施上优先部署。实施京津冀协同发展、长江经济带发展、长三角一体化发展、粤港澳大湾区建设等区域协调发展战略,推进脱贫攻坚、乡村振兴、新型城镇化等重大决策部署,把交通运输作为先行领域重点部署、优先保障。

——能力上适度超前。适应新型工业化、信息化、城镇化和农业现代化发展要求,以加快建设综合立体交通网络为目标,以综合交通运输规划编制为抓手,适度超前布局交通基础设施建设,支撑经济社会发展,为未来发展留足空间。

——作用上先行引领。充分发挥交通运输在国土空间开发、产业梯度转移、城镇布局优化、经济贸易交流中的先导作用,发挥互联网新业态在培育经济发展新动能中的引领作用,促进新经济形态加速崛起。

（三）以新发展理念为引领

贯彻创新、协调、绿色、开放、共享的新发展理念,是新时代中国交通发展的关键。以新发展理念引领交通高质量发展,更新观念,转变方式,破解难题,厚植优势。

——建设安全、便捷、高效、绿色、经济的现代化综合交通运输体系。打造高品质的快速交通网、高效率的普通干线网、广覆盖的基础服务网,加快形成立体互联的综合交通网络化格局和横贯东西、纵贯南北、内畅外通的综合交通主骨架。

——推动交通运输供给侧结构性改革。降低交通运输结构性、制度性、技术性、管理性、服务性成本,促进物流业"降本增效",更好发挥交通运输在物流业发展中的基础和主体作用。

——优化营商环境。加强法治政府建设,合理划分交通运输领域中央与地方财政事权和支出责任,推进简政放权、加强管理、优化服务,健全完善以信用为基础的新型监管机制,提升营商环境的国际化、法治化、市场化水平。

——增强发展动能。鼓励和规范交通新业态发展,加快推动新旧动能转换,建立多层次、可选择、多元化的运输服务体系,提高交通服务水平。

（四）以改革开放为动力

深化改革、扩大开放是交通运输发展行稳致远的强大动力。坚持社会主义市场经济改革方向，把"有效市场"和"有为政府"更好结合起来，进一步解放和发展交通运输生产力。

——坚持市场化改革。充分发挥市场在资源配置中的决定性作用，更好发挥政府作用，放开交通运输市场，推进质量变革、效率变革、动力变革，着力依靠市场解决发展不充分的问题，更好发挥政府作用解决发展不平衡的问题，不断完善交通运输市场体系，释放交通运输活力。

——坚持高水平开放。打开国门搞建设，积极推进交通运输"走出去""请进来"，以服务共建"一带一路"为重点，着力推动陆上、海上、天上、网上"四位一体"联通和政策、规则、标准"三位一体"联通，提升与其他国家互联互通水平和国际运输便利化水平。

（五）以创新驱动为支撑

创新是交通运输发展的动力源泉。把创新作为推动发展的第一动力，以科技创新为牵引，大力推进管理创新、制度创新、文化创新，完善创新体系，优化创新环境，强化人才支撑。

——以基础设施建养技术迭代升级增强交通运输系统韧性，增强交通基础设施抵御灾害与预警监测能力,提升高速铁路、高速公路、特大桥隧、深水筑港、大型机场工程等建造技术水平。

——以智慧交通建设推进数字经济、共享型经济产业发展,推动模式、业态、产品、服务等联动创新,提高综合交通运输网络效率,构筑新型交通生态系统。

——以数字化、网络化、智能化、绿色化技术的发展,拓展交通运输高质量发展空间,抓住全球新一轮科技革命和产业变革催生新技术新模式新业态的历史机遇,推动交通运输可持续发展。

二、从交通大国向交通强国迈进

进入新时代,中国交通驶入高质量发展的快车道,基础设施建设日新月异,运输服务能力、品质和效率大幅提升,科技支撑更加有力,人民出行更加便捷,货物运输更加高效,中国正在从交通大国向交通强国迈进。

(一) 基础设施从"连线成片"到"基本成网"

牢牢把握交通基础设施优化布局、加速成网的重要机遇期,深入推进交通供给侧结构性改革,一大批综合客运、货运枢纽投入运营,综合交通网络规模和质量实现跃升,覆盖广度和通达深度不断提升。

综合交通基础设施基本实现网络化。截至 2019 年底,全国铁路营业里程达到 13.9 万公里,其中高速铁路营业里程超过 3.5 万公里;全国公路里程达到 501.3 万公里,其中高速公路里程 15 万公里;拥有生产性码头泊位 2.3 万个,其中万吨级及以上泊位数量 2520 个;内河航道通航里程 12.7 万公里;民用航空颁证运输机场 238 个;全国油气长输管道总里程达到 15.6 万公里,互联互通程度明显加强;邮路和快递服务网络总长度(单程)4085.9 万公里,实现乡乡设所、村村通邮。综合立体交通网络初步形成,有力支撑了经济社会持续快速健康发展。

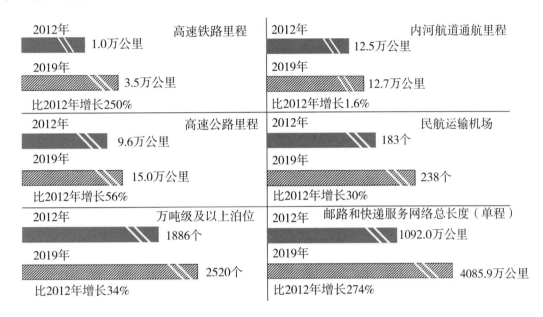

图1 交通基础设施快速发展

综合运输大通道基本贯通。着力加强综合运输大通道建设,进一步打通国家运输大动脉,有力保障国土和能源安全,强化区域间政治经济联系。加快建设"十纵十横"综合运输大通道,依托京沪、京广、沿海、沿江等综合运输大通道,长三角、珠三角、环渤海等港口群和长江沿线港口形成的经济带、城市群成为中国经济最具活力、人口最为密集的区域。上海到南京、上海到杭州高速通道沿线集聚了长三角三分之二的城市和约80%的经济总量。粤港澳大湾区形成了以高速铁路、城际铁路和高等级公路为主体的城际快速交通网络。西气东输、川气东送、海气登陆以及陕京线等天然气干线管输系统不断完善。煤炭物流通道布局更加合理,形成纵贯南北、东西的铁路能源运输大通道;粮食物流骨干通道全部打通,原粮散粮运输、成品粮集装化运输比重大幅提高,粮食物流效率稳步提升。区域间人员交流、物资流通日益便捷,横贯东西、纵贯南北、内畅外通的综合交通主骨架逐步形成。

综合交通枢纽建设步伐加快。深入推进交通、物流、信息与经济社会深度融合,大力发展枢纽经济,积极培育经济发展新动能。结合全国城镇体系布局,打造北京、上海、广州等国际性综合交通枢纽,加快建设全国性、区域性综合交通枢纽。通过规划引领,强化一体化综合客运枢纽站建设,北京大兴、上海虹桥等一批综合交通枢纽建成,实现了高铁、城市客运、轨道交通、民航等交通方式的无缝对接。优化货运枢纽布局,推进多式联运型和干支衔接型货运枢纽(物流园区)建设,上海洋山港、郑州铁路港等一批现代物流枢纽建成,提高了换装水平,加快了多式联运发展,有力推动了综合交通运输体系建设。不同运输方式通过枢纽实现有机衔接,为优化国家经济空间布局和构建现代化经济体系提供了有力支撑。

专栏 1　北京大兴国际机场

2019 年 9 月 25 日,北京大兴国际机场正式通航。机场规划占地面积 45 平方公里,规划建设 6 条跑道,满足年旅客吞吐量 1 亿人次以上需求。机场可再生能源利用率达到 16%,机场控制区内运行新能源车辆设备占比超过 60%。全机场均为绿色建筑,70% 以上达到中国最高等级绿色建筑标准。机场航站楼兼具功能性和艺术性,是现阶段世界上建设规模最大的国际航空枢纽。北京大兴国际机场在不到 5 年时间里完成预定建设任务,顺利投入运营,充分展现了中国工程建筑的雄厚实力,充分体现了中国精神、中国力量,诠释了中国基建实力的新高度,是中国面向世界的新国门,是国家发展新的动力源。

城市交通基础设施体系化建设稳步推进。截至 2019 年年底,全国城市道路总长度 45.9 万公里,人均道路面积 17.36 平方米,建成

区路网密度达到 6.65 公里/平方公里,道路面积率达到 13.19%。强化城市综合交通体系规划引领,加强内部交通与对外交通有效衔接。树立"窄马路、密路网"的城市道路布局理念,建设快速路、主干路和次支路级配合理、适宜绿色出行的城市道路网络。完善道路空间分配,充分保障绿色交通出行需求,规范设置道路交通安全设施和交通管理设施。开展人行道净化专项行动,推动自行车专用道建设,切实改善绿色出行环境。

(二) 运输服务从"走得了"到"走得好"

全面提升交通运输服务质量,"互联网+交通"等新模式快速发展,多样化、品质化、均等化水平大幅提升,运输服务实现"人便其行、货畅其流",通达性和保障性显著增强。交通运输对国家经济社会发展的支撑显著增强,促投资、促消费、稳增长作用明显。

货物运输服务保障能力不断提升。中国是世界上运输最繁忙的国家。面对日益增长的货物运输需求,加快多式联运发展,创新公铁联运、空铁联运、铁水联运、江海联运、水水中转、滚装联运等高效运输组织模式,开展铁路运能提升、水运系统升级、公路货运治理等专项行动,货物运输结构持续优化,综合运输效率不断提高,物流成本逐步降低,交通运输环境污染明显减少,原油、成品油、天然气管道建设不断提速。铁路运量占社会运输总量比例不断提升,"公转铁"行动取得突出成效。港口货物吞吐量和集装箱吞吐量均居世界第一。

快递业务量保持强劲增长态势,连续 6 年位居世界第一。运输服务能力大幅提升,推进物流降本增效取得积极成效,促进了物流业转型升级。

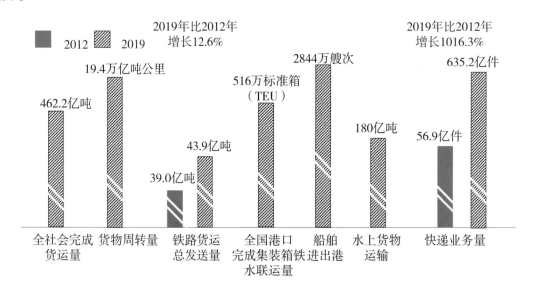

图 2　货物运输服务现状

专栏 2　中国的邮政快递

　　中国建成了惠及 14 亿人口、全球最大的邮政普遍服务体系,基本建成了连接城乡、覆盖全国、通达世界的快递服务网络,快递"三向"(面向西部地区完善服务网络,面向农村推动"工业品下乡"和"农产品进城",面向国际鼓励快递企业发展跨境快递业务)成效显著。全国邮政营业网点达到 5.4 万处,快递乡镇网点覆盖率达到 96.6%,全面实现建制村直接通邮。涌现出一批实力强大、充满活力的市场主体,形成了 1 家年营业收入超 1000 亿元、5 家超 500 亿元的企业集群。中国已成为世界上发展最快、最具活力的新兴寄递市场,包裹快递量超过美、日、欧等发达经济体总和,快递业务量连续 6 年稳居世界第一,创造了中国服务业和世界邮政业发展的奇迹。

公众高品质出行需求逐步满足。旅客运输专业化、个性化服务品质不断提升,人们对"美好出行"的需求得到更好满足,出行体验更加方便、快捷、舒适、温暖。以道路运输为基础,高铁、民航为主要

发展方向的出行服务体系更加完善,客运结构持续优化,中长距离客流逐步从公路转向高铁和民航。截至 2019 年底,动车组列车累计发送旅客 120 亿人次,占铁路旅客发送量的比重由 2007 年的 4.5% 增长到 65.4%。春节、国庆等重要节庆日大规模客流的服务保障能力显著提升,人们不仅能够"说走就走",而且走得"舒适、优雅、惬意","人享其行"的期盼逐步成为现实。

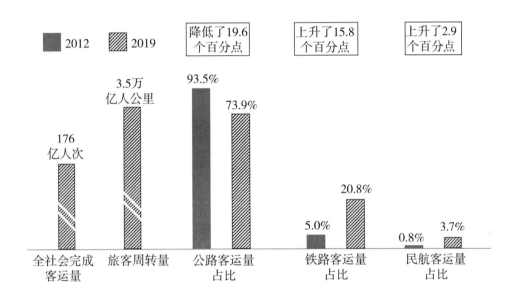

图 3　旅客运输服务现状

城市公共交通持续优先发展。发展公共交通是现代城市发展的方向,是加强城市交通治理、提升城市居民生活品质的有效措施。大力加强城市轨道交通建设,截至 2019 年底,全国共有 40 个城市开通运营城市轨道交通线路,运营里程达 6172.2 公里,城市轨道交通的骨干作用日益凸显,城市公交出行分担率稳步提高,舒适度不断提升。城市慢行交通系统较快发展,70 余个城市发布共享单车管理实施细则,360 余个城市提供了共享单车服务。城市公共交通的发展为人们出行提供了便利,满足了多样化出行需求。

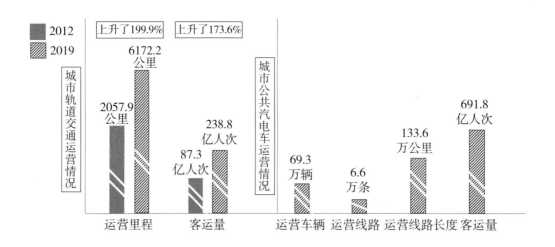

图4 城市公共交通发展现状

<table>
<tr><td style="background:#888">专栏3 公交都市建设</td></tr>
<tr><td>

公共交通发展是城市交通发展的首要任务。2012年,中国启动公交都市创建示范工程,先后分三批确定87个城市开展公交都市建设。截至2019年底,14个城市成为"国家公交都市建设示范城市"。以公交都市为标杆的城市交通出行服务系统,对城市经济产生了全局性、先导性影响,促进了城市交通健康可持续发展。

</td></tr>
</table>

基本公共服务均等化水平不断提升。努力保障公众公平享有交通服务权利,以交通和谐促进社会和谐。僻远地区开行的公益性"慢火车",站站停、低票价、公交化,架起了山村与城市的沟通桥梁,成为沿线人民的"公交车""致富车"。公路客运普及和农村物流发展有力促进了城乡一体化,截至2019年底,已开展52个城乡交通运输一体化示范县建设,全国城乡交通运输一体化发展水平达到 AAA 级、AAAA 级以上的区县比例分别超过 95% 和 79%。在铁路、公路、水运、民航、邮政等重要枢纽设置无障碍设施,推广无障碍化交通工具,为特殊群

体提供了周到的出行服务。不断加大旅客运输及出行服务普惠力度，让人民共享交通发展成果。

专栏4 交通领域无障碍建设

　　无障碍环境是保障残疾人平等参与社会生活的必要条件，也是社会文明程度的重要标志之一。中国持续加强交通基础设施的无障碍环境建设与改造，全力打造"覆盖全面、无缝衔接、安全舒适"的无障碍交通出行环境。在全国推广应用无障碍化客运车辆，多个省份客运设施无障碍建设率达到100%。3400余辆动车组列车设置了残疾人专座；公共交通工具设置"老弱病残"专座，使用低地板公交车和无障碍出租汽车；城市公交车配备车载屏幕、语音报站系统。邮政快递为重度残疾人提供上门服务，为聋人客户提供短信服务，对盲人读物免费寄送。交通领域无障碍建设为残疾人走出家门、充分参与社会生活创造了条件。

　　交通运输新业态新模式不断涌现。"互联网+"交通运输正在深刻改变着人们的出行方式。截至2019年底，网约车覆盖全国400多个城市，平台日均使用量达到2000万人次。共享单车有效解决了出行"最后一公里"难题，日均使用量约4570万人次。货运物流融入"互联网+"进程加快，推动了货运物流组织方式创新，95306铁路货运服务系统全面建成，2019年铁路网上货运业务办理比例达到85%，229家无车承运人试点企业整合货运车辆211万辆，车辆利用率提高约50.0%，较传统货运交易成本降低了6至8个百分点。"高铁网+互联网"双网融合取得突出成效，2019年12306互联网售票系统售票超过35.7亿张；电子客票基本实现全覆盖；高铁站车正逐步实现WIFI信号全覆盖，创新推出网上订餐、无线充电、智能交互等服务。截至2019年底，超过98%的二级以上汽车客运站提供省域联网

售票服务。网约车、共享单车、共享汽车等线上线下新消费模式,刷脸进站、"无纸化"登机、无人机投递、无接触配送、智慧停车、道路客运定制服务等新业态,让人们享受到了便利,为经济发展注入了新动能。

支撑区域重大战略实施。服务京津冀协同发展、长江经济带发展、粤港澳大湾区建设等区域协调发展战略,加强交通运输布局,提供基础支撑。加快构建以首都为核心的多节点、网格状世界级城市群交通体系,加快建设雄安新区一流的综合交通运输体系。强化干线铁路、城际铁路、市域(郊)铁路、城市轨道交通的高效衔接,推动"四网融合",着力打造"轨道上的京津冀"。全面推进干线航道系统化治理,提升长江黄金水道功能,疏解三峡运输"瓶颈"制约,建设长江经济带综合立体交通走廊。畅通大湾区经粤东西北至周边省区的综合运输通道,构建连接泛珠三角区域和东盟国家的陆路国际大通道,推动粤港澳大湾区现代化综合交通运输体系建设。以"海澄文(海口、澄迈、文昌)"一体化经济圈、大三亚旅游经济圈为重点,打造多节点、网格状、全覆盖的铁路、城际轨道和骨架公路网,全面支撑海南自由贸易港建设。以上海、南京、杭州、合肥、苏锡常、宁波等为节点,构建对外高效联通、内部有机衔接的多层次综合交通网络,推进长三角区域交通运输更高质量一体化发展。契合全流域生态保护和国土空间开发,加快形成黄河流域"通道+枢纽+网络"联动发展格局。差异化完善区域各板块交通网络,增强了对区域战略的交通支撑。

（三）交通科技从"跟跑为主"到
"跟跑并跑领跑"并行

经过不懈努力,交通运输科技创新能力大幅跃升,核心技术逐步自主可控,基础设施、运输装备取得标志性重大科技创新成果,可持续发展能力显著提升。中国的交通科技从跟跑世界一流水平为主,进入到跟跑、并跑、领跑并行的新阶段。

交通超级工程举世瞩目。高速铁路、高寒铁路、高原铁路、重载铁路技术达到世界领先水平,高原冻土、膨胀土、沙漠等特殊地质公路建设技术攻克世界级难题。离岸深水港建设关键技术、巨型河口航道整治技术、长河段航道系统治理技术以及大型机场工程建设技术世界领先。世界单条运营里程最长的京广高铁全线贯通,一次性建成里程最长的兰新高铁,世界首条高寒地区高铁哈大高铁开通运营,大秦重载铁路年运量世界第一,世界上海拔最高的青海果洛藏族自治州雪山一号隧道通车。川藏铁路雅安至林芝段开工建设。港珠澳大桥、西成高铁秦岭隧道群、洋山港集装箱码头、青岛港全自动化集装箱码头、长江口深水航道治理等系列重大工程举世瞩目。中国在建和在役公路桥梁、隧道总规模世界第一,世界主跨径前十位的斜拉桥、悬索桥、跨海大桥,中国分别有 7 座、6 座、6 座,世界最高的 10 座大桥中有 8 座在中国。

港珠澳大桥跨越伶仃洋,东接香港特别行政区,西接广东省珠海市和澳门特别行政区,总长约55公里,是粤港澳三地合作共建的超大型跨海交通工程。2018年10月23日,大桥开通。港珠澳大桥的建设,有力促进了三地交通连接,对于推进粤港澳大湾区建设具有重大意义。大桥建设过程中,先后攻克了人工岛快速成岛、深埋沉管结构设计、隧道复合基础等多个世界级技术难题。港珠澳大桥是中国公路建设史上技术最复杂、施工难度最高、工程规模最大的交通工程,创下多项世界之最,体现了中国的综合国力、自主创新能力,展现了勇创世界一流的民族志气,是一座圆梦桥、同心桥、自信桥、复兴桥。

交通装备技术取得重大突破。瞄准世界科技前沿发展"国之重器",交通运输关键装备技术自主研发水平大幅提升。具有完全自主知识产权的"复兴号"中国标准动车组实现世界上首次时速420公里交会和重联运行,在京沪高铁、京津城际铁路、京张高铁实现世界最高时速350公里持续商业运营,智能型动车组首次实现时速350公里自动驾驶功能;时速600公里高速磁浮试验样车、具备跨国互联互通能力的时速400公里可变轨距高速动车组下线。盾构机等特种工程机械研发实现巨大突破,最大直径土压平衡盾构机、最大直径硬岩盾构机、最大直径泥水平衡盾构机等相继研制成功。节能与新能源汽车产业蓬勃发展,与国际先进水平基本保持同步。海工机械特种船舶、大型自动化专业化集装箱成套设备制造技术领先世界,300米饱和潜水取得创新性突破。C919大型客机成功首飞。支线客机ARJ21开始商业运营。快递分拣技术快速发展。远洋船舶、高速动车组、铁路大功率机车、海工机械等领跑全球,大型飞机、新一代智联网汽车等装备技术方兴未艾,成为中国制造业走向世界的"金名片"。

专栏6　中国的高速铁路

中国构建了完备的高速铁路技术体系,总体技术水平迈入世界先进行列,部分领域达到世界领先水平。截至2019年底,全国高铁运营里程超过3.5万公里,占全球高铁运营里程的三分之二以上,初步实现了相邻大中城市间1小时至4小时交通圈、城市群内半小时至2小时工作生活圈。以"八纵八横"高速铁路为主通道,建成了北京到天津、上海到南京、北京到上海、北京到广州、哈尔滨到大连等一批设计时速350公里、具有世界先进水平的高速铁路,累计安全运行里程超过75亿公里。2019年动车组发送旅客23.6亿人次,中国高铁不仅代表了"中国速度",更续写了经济高质量发展的新篇章,为经济社会发展注入了磅礴活力,铺平了人民的幸福路。

智慧交通发展步伐加快。推进"互联网+"交通发展,推动现代信息技术与交通运输管理和服务全面融合,提升交通运输服务水平。充分运用5G通信、大数据、人工智能等新兴技术,交通运输基础设施和装备领域智能化不断取得突破。铁路、公路、水运、民航客运电子客票、联网售票日益普及,运输生产调度指挥信息化水平显著提升,截至2019年底,229个机场和主要航空公司实现"无纸化"出行。全面取消全国高速公路省界收费站,高速公路电子不停车收费系统(ETC)等新技术应用成效显著,截至2019年底,全国ETC客户累计超过2亿,全路网、全时段、全天候监测以及信息发布能力不断增强。北斗系统在交通运输全领域广泛应用,全国已有760万道路营运车辆、3.33万邮政快递干线车辆、1369艘部系统公务船舶、10863座水上助导航设施、109座沿海地基增强站、352架通用航空器应用

北斗系统,并在3架运输航空器上应用北斗系统,京张高铁成为世界首条采用北斗卫星导航系统并实现自动驾驶等功能的智能高铁。智慧公路应用逐步深入,智慧港口、智能航运等技术广泛应用。智能投递设施遍布全国主要城市,自动化分拣覆盖主要快递企业骨干分拨中心。出台自动驾驶道路测试管理规范和封闭测试场地建设指南,颁布智能船舶规范,建立无人船海上测试场,推动无人机在快递等领域示范应用。

专栏7　上海洋山港自动化码头
上海洋山港四期码头是全球最大的单体自动化智能码头和全球综合自动化程度最高的码头,是中国经济融入全球经济的重要象征。上海洋山港四期码头总用地面积223万平方米,共建设7个集装箱泊位,集装箱码头岸线总长2350米。洋山港采用中国自主研发的自动化作业系统,衔接上海港的各大数据信息平台,实现了码头主要业务环节生产调度自动化。洋山港的开港,标志着中国港口行业在运营模式、技术应用以及装备制造上实现了里程碑式的跨越升级。

三、服务决战脱贫攻坚和
决胜全面小康

全面奔小康,关键在农村;农村奔小康,交通要先行。中国将交通扶贫作为服务全面建成小康社会、推进农业农村现代化、人民共享改革发展成果的重要支撑,全力消除制约农村发展的交通瓶颈,为广大农民脱贫致富奔小康提供坚实保障。

(一) 坚决打赢交通扶贫脱贫攻坚战

把扶贫作为新时代交通运输发展的重要使命,完善扶贫规划政策体系,创新扶贫工作模式,做到"扶贫项目优先安排、扶贫资金优先保障、扶贫工作优先对接、扶贫措施优先落实",以超常规的举措和力度,助力打赢脱贫攻坚战。

加强交通扶贫规划设计。完善交通扶贫顶层设计和政策体系,制定交通扶贫规划、实施方案、行动计划,实施《集中连片特困地区交通建设扶贫规划纲要(2011—2020)》《"十三五"交通扶贫规划》《关于进一步发挥交通扶贫脱贫攻坚基础支撑作用的实施意见》等规划和政策文件,将革命老区、民族地区、边疆地区、贫困地区 1177

个县（市、区）全部纳入支持范围。以深度贫困地区为重点，加快国家高速公路、普通国省道改造建设，打造"康庄大道路""幸福小康路""平安放心路""特色致富路"，推动交通建设项目尽量向进村入户倾斜。

创新精准交通脱贫模式。加强统筹设计，建立健全五年规划、三年行动计划、年度计划相互衔接的规划计划体系，分省细化年度计划，建立台账，压茬推进。加大"扶志""扶智"工作力度，做好对贫困地区干部群众的宣传、教育、培训、科技推广，动员鼓励贫困群众参与农村公路建设，吸纳贫困家庭劳动力参与护路等工作。

持续加大交通扶贫资金投入。大幅提高贫困地区交通建设中央投资补助标准，2012年至2020年安排贫困地区公路建设的车购税资金超过1.46万亿元，占同期全国公路建设车购税资金的61.3%，带动全社会投入超过5.13万亿元。国家高速公路、普通国道补助标准分别由"十二五"时期平均占项目总投资的15%、30%，提高到"十三五"时期的30%、50%左右。乡镇、建制村通硬化路补助标准提高到平均工程造价的70%以上。通过优化中央预算内投资、车购税等资金支出结构，统筹加大各级各类资金倾斜力度，确保政策落地、资金到位、项目实施。

重点攻克深度贫困堡垒。全面建成小康社会最艰巨最繁重的任务在农村，特别是深度贫困地区。发挥交通在脱贫攻坚中的基础性、先导性作用，为深度贫困地区脱贫摘帽当好先行、做好支撑。加大对深度贫困地区支持力度，新增资金、新增项目、新增举措进一步向

"三区三州"①等深度贫困地区倾斜。2016年至2020年,安排车购税资金2746亿元支持"三区三州"交通项目建设,其中农村公路资金781亿元。

（二）"四好农村路"建设推动贫困 地区交通高质量发展

道路通,百业兴。以建好、管好、护好、运营好农村公路(简称"四好农村路")为牵引,积极推进贫困地区建设外通内联、通村畅乡、客车到村、安全便捷的交通运输网络,大力提升城乡客货运输服务水平,贫困地区交通落后面貌发生根本改变。

贫困地区综合交通网络加快形成。缺少足够的交通基础设施是贫困地区面临的最大挑战之一。2016年至2019年,国家支持贫困地区改造建设了国家高速公路1.7万公里、普通国道5.3万公里,建成内河航道约2365公里。贫困地区县城基本实现了二级及以上公路覆盖,许多贫困县通了高速公路,不少地方还通了铁路、建了机场,干支衔接的高等级内河航道网络不断完善。贫困地区综合交通运输网络加快形成,曾经"山里山外两重天"的局面彻底改变。

"四好农村路"建设成效显著。以200个"四好农村路"全国示

---

① "三区三州"是中国国家层面的深度贫困地区,自然条件和经济条件都较差。其中:"三区"是指西藏自治区和青海、四川、甘肃、云南四省涉藏州县及南疆的和田地区、阿克苏地区、喀什地区、克孜勒苏柯尔克孜自治州四地区;"三州"是指四川省凉山彝族自治州、云南省怒江傈僳族自治州、甘肃省临夏回族自治州。

范县为引领,推动农村公路高质量发展。落实农村公路建设"七公开"①制度,强化贫困地区交通建设管理和质量控制,优化农村公路路网结构,大力推进"路长制",健全"四好农村路"建设长效机制。完善和落实省、市、县、乡镇、村五级责任,清晰界定工作职责,结合事业单位和乡镇机构改革,完善县乡农村公路管理体制。推动农村公路"满意工程"建设,推广建养一体化等建设养护模式。结合美丽乡村建设开展路域环境整治。统筹城乡客运资源,创新农村客运发展模式,整合交通、邮政、供销、电商等资源,推进了贫困地区农村物流发展。"四好农村路"建设取得了实实在在的成效,为农村特别是贫困地区带去了人气、财气。

专栏8 "四好农村路"

"四好农村路"是新时代中国农村变化和社会变迁的重要标志。截至2019年底,农村公路总里程占全国公路总里程的83.8%,其中等级公路比例达到93.2%。2019年,农村公路列养率达到98.8%,优、良、中路率达到83.0%,建制村通客车率达到99.8%。支持贫困地区改造建设约5.9万公里资源路、旅游路、产业路,出行难等长期没有解决的老大难问题普遍得到解决。"四好农村路"连片成网,极大地缩短了往返城乡的时空距离,深刻改变了农村的生产生活条件和社会面貌,为偏远闭塞的乡村开辟了一条通往现代文明的大道。人流、物流带动了知识流、信息流、资金流,促进了贫困地区知识的传播、思想的开化、文化的交流、风俗的改进,真正使扶贫与扶志、扶智相结合,为广大农民通过知识文化致富提供了坚实保障。

"出行难"得到有效解决。农村公路建设实现跨越式发展,"晴

---

① "七公开"为:建设计划公开、补助政策公开、招标过程公开、施工管理公开、质量监管公开、资金使用公开和竣(交)工验收公开。

天一身土,雨天一身泥"成为历史。截至 2019 年底,全国实现了具备条件的乡镇和建制村 100%通硬化路;截至 2020 年 9 月,实现了具备条件的乡镇和建制村 100%通客车。城乡道路客运一体化发展水平持续提升,以县城为中心、乡镇为节点、建制村为网点的交通网络初步形成,乡村之间、城乡之间连接更加紧密,6 亿农民"出门水泥路,抬脚上客车"的梦想变成了现实。

(三) 交通助推广大农民脱贫致富奔小康

交通运输的快速发展,破解了长期以来制约贫困地区经济社会发展的瓶颈,为广大农民脱贫致富奔小康、加快推进农业农村现代化提供了有力支撑,为谱写新时代乡村振兴新篇章奠定了坚实基础。

农村公路助力广大农民奔小康。农村公路发展,重点在"建",目标在"通"。2012 年至 2019 年,中国新改建农村公路 208.6 万公里(其中贫困地区约 110 万公里),农村公路总里程达到 420.1 万公里,贫困地区新增 5.1 万个建制村通硬化路。2016 年至 2019 年,贫困地区建设约 9.6 万公里通较大人口规模自然村的硬化路,建设 45.8 万公里农村公路安全生命防护工程,农村公路运行安全条件全面改善。出台《农村公路建设管理办法》《农村公路建设质量管理办法》《农村公路养护管理办法》,加快推进相关技术标准和规范制修订工作。出台《关于深化农村公路管理养护体制改革的意见》及相关配套制度,推进农村公路管理养护体制改革,建立健全农村公路管理养护长效机制。2012年至2019年,通行客车的建制村新增5.4万个。加快建设县乡村三级农村物流节点体系建设,推进农村物流发展,2019年农村地区收投快件超150亿件,工业品下乡、农产品出村、快递服务入户等运输服务能力不断提升。

铁路扶贫助力全面小康。持续提升贫困地区铁路网覆盖通达水平,加快连接贫困地区铁路规划建设,完善贫困地区铁路网络。截至2019年底,国家向14个集中连片特困地区、革命老区、少数民族地区、边疆地区累计投入3.3万亿元,占铁路基建总投资的78%。新投产铁路覆盖了274个国家级贫困县,助力融入"高铁经济圈"。运用大数据分析,优化贫困地区旅客列车开行方案,2019年日均开行途经贫困地区的旅客列车2328列,开行旅游扶贫专列594列,带动了沿线旅游、商贸、餐饮等产业发展和消费升级。精准开行农产品"点对点"运输专列、集装箱快运班列和高铁快运等,2018年以来累计运送贫困地区货物17.1亿吨。

"交通+"产业发展成效显著。积极推动"交通+'旅游''产业''扶贫'"等发展新模式,推动贫困地区交通与产业深度融合。2012年至2019年,贫困地区新改建资源路、旅游路、产业路约5.9万公里。大力推进"交通+快递"扶贫工程,整合交通运输、供销、商贸、电商、邮政快递等资源,开展无人机物流配送应用试点,2018年全国邮政企业累计实现农村电商交易额1.4万亿元。"交通+特色农业+电商""交通+文化+旅游""交通+就业+公益岗"等扶贫模式不断创新发展。特色产业因路而起、因路而兴,为广大农民打开一扇脱贫致富的大门。

农村交通有力促进美丽乡村建设。将农村公路建设作为社会主义新农村"村容整洁"和"乡风文明"建设的重要切入点,同步开展公路沿线绿化以及沿途村镇的美化建设,将农村公路打造成一道道靓丽的乡村风景线。农村公路的畅达,带动了农村人居环境同步改善和教育、医疗、文化等公共服务水平同步提升,推动了城乡经济一体化加快发展,广大农村因路而富、因路而美。

四、推进交通治理现代化

　　中国是世界上最大的发展中国家,交通运输体量庞大、情况复杂且处于快速发展当中,交通治理难度大。中国立足本国国情,借鉴国际经验,大力推进交通治理现代化,通过改革创新释放技术和市场活力、提升治理效能,促进了交通高质量发展。

(一) 推进交通治理体系改革

　　立足当前、着眼长远,积极推进综合交通体制机制改革,不断完善法律法规,统一开放、竞争有序的交通运输市场基本形成,适应新时代国家发展的交通运输治理体系逐步健全。

　　综合交通运输管理体制机制不断完善。以深化供给侧结构性改革为主线,以提升行业治理能力为重点,持续深化交通运输体制机制改革。2013 年形成由交通运输部管理国家铁路局、中国民用航空局、国家邮政局的大部门管理体制架构,交通运输大部门制主体组织架构基本建立。深入推进中国铁路总公司、中国邮政集团公司的公司制改革工作,两家公司分别更名为中国国家铁路集团有限公司、中国邮政集团有限公司,建立健全现代法人治理结构和中国特色现代国有企业制度。省级综合交通运输体制改革加快推进,大部分省份基本建立综合交通运输管理体制或运行协调机制。组建国家铁路局、中国国家铁路集团有限公司,实现铁路政企分开。民航体制机制改革持续深化,机场公安体制、运输价格、民航业投资准入机制、空管系统体制机制等改革有序推进。邮政体制改革有序推进,邮政改革配套措施不断完善。交通运输综合行政执法改革稳步推进,整合执法队伍,理顺职能配置,减少执法层级,权责统一、权威高效、监管有力、服务优质的交通运输综合行政执法体制逐步形成。综合交通运输发展规划协调机制初步建立,铁路、公路、水运、民航、邮政等专项规划之间的衔接平衡不断加强。通过改革,综合交通运输发展的体制机制进一步优化,各种运输方式进一步融合,交通运输发展内生动力进一步增强,行业现代化治理水平进一步提升。

交通运输法治政府部门建设持续深化。贯彻落实习近平法治思想,以"法治政府部门"建设工程为载体,把法治贯穿交通运输规划、建设、运营、管理和安全生产全过程各方面,为加快建设交通强国提供坚实保障。依法行政制度基本确立,行业立法、执法监督、行政复议与应诉、法治宣传教育和普法等工作机制逐步健全。加快推进铁路、公路、水运、民航、邮政等行业立法,综合交通运输法规体系已基本建成。聚焦国家重大战略实施和行业发展改革领域,制定和修订铁路法、公路法、海上交通安全法、港口法、航道法、民用航空法、邮政法等行业龙头法。出台和制修订水上水下活动通航安全管理规定、交通运输标准化管理办法等行业急需的规章,稳步开展规章规范性文件清理。

深化"放管服"改革优化营商环境。坚持问题导向,加快转变政府职能,深化"放管服"改革,持续优化营商环境。逐步放宽市场准入门槛,持续清理交通运输领域各类不合理和非必要罚款及检查,建立涉企收费目录清单制度。深入落实交通运输领域各项减税降费政策,降低物流税费成本。强化事中事后监管,取消中介服务等行政审批事项,推进商事制度改革。推行"双随机、一公开"①监管工作,运用大数据、云计算、物联网等信息技术,推动跨省大件运输等并联许可系统全国联网。加快构建以信用为核心的新型市场监管机制。推进新业态协同监管,线上线下一体化监管模式进一步创新,市场环境更加公平有序。优化行政审批服务方式,推广交通运输政务服务"一网通办",企业群众办事"只进一扇门""最多跑一次"服务,办事效率显著提升。交通运输"放管服"改革,推动了优化营商环境向纵深发展,激发了交通发展活力,提高了政府服务效能,促进了交通运输行业健康发展。

(二) 推进交通运输绿色发展

树立和践行绿水青山就是金山银山的理念,交通运输生态文明制度体系日益完善,节能降碳取得实效,环境友好程度不断增加。

全面推进节能减排和低碳发展。坚定不移推进节能减排,努力建设低碳交通,走出一条能耗排放做"减法"、经济发展做"加法"的

---

① "双随机、一公开"是指随机抽取检查对象、随机选派执法检查人员,抽查情况及查处结果及时向社会公开。

新路子。严格实施能源消费总量和强度双控制度,着力提升交通运输综合效能,全国铁路电气化比例达到 71.9%,新能源公交车超过 40 万辆,新能源货车超过 43 万辆,天然气运营车辆超过 18 万辆,液化天然气(LNG)动力船舶建成 290 余艘,机场新能源车辆设备占比约 14%,飞机辅助动力装置(APU)替代设施全面使用,邮政快递车辆中新能源和清洁能源车辆的保有量及在重点区域的使用比例稳步提升。全国 942 处高速公路服务区(停车区)内建成运营充电桩超过 7400 个,港口岸电设施建成 5800 多套,覆盖泊位 7200 余个,沿江沿海主要港口集装箱码头全面完成"油改电"。绿色交通省(城市)、绿色公路、绿色港口等示范工程,年节能量超过 63 万吨标准煤。通过中央车购税资金,支持建设综合客运枢纽、货运枢纽、疏港铁路,统筹推进公铁联运、海铁联运等多式联运发展,推进运输结构调整。

强化资源集约节约利用。牢固树立为国家长远发展负责、为子孙后代负责的理念,着力推动交通资源利用方式由粗放型向集约型、节约型转变。结合国土空间规划编制和三条控制线①划定落实,统筹铁路、公路、水运、民航、邮政等交通运输各领域融合发展,推动铁路、公路、水路、空域等通道资源集约利用,提高线位资源利用效率。因地制宜采用低路基、以桥(隧)代路等,加强公路、铁路沿线土地资源保护和综合利用,减少对周边环境的影响。加强航道建设的生态保护和绿色建养,推进航道疏浚土综合利用,严格港口岸

---

① "三条控制线"是指生态保护红线、永久基本农田、城镇开发边界三条控制线。

线使用审批管理与监督,提高岸线使用效率,探索建立岸线资源有偿使用制度。推动废旧路面、沥青、废旧轮胎、建筑废料等材料资源化利用。高度重视和推进快递包装的绿色化、减量化、可循环,大力推进可循环中转袋全面替代一次性塑料编织袋,电子面单①使用率达98%。

强化大气与水污染防治。坚决打好交通运输领域污染防治攻坚战,用最严格的制度、最严密的法治治理环境污染。在沿海和长江干线等水域设立船舶大气污染物排放控制区,按照国际公约要求对进入中国水域的国际航行船舶实施船用燃油硫含量限制措施,推动船舶使用清洁能源和加装尾气污染治理装备,建立船用低硫燃油供应保障和联合监管机制。执行船舶水污染物排放控制国家强制性标准,推动港口船舶含油污水、化学品洗舱水、生活污水和垃圾等接收处置设施建设,开展港口粉尘污染控制。在全国沿海实施"碧海行动"②计划,打捞存在污染环境风险和影响海上交通运输安全的沉船沉物。加快老旧和高能耗、高排放营运车辆、施工机械治理和淘汰更新,推进实施机动车排放检测与强制维护制度(I/M制度)。中央财政采取"以奖代补"方式支持京津冀及周边地区、汾渭平原淘汰国Ⅲ及以下排放标准营运柴油货车。全面开展运输结构调整三年行动,2012年至2019年全国机动车污染物排放量下降65.2%。

---

① 电子面单,是向商家提供的一种使用不干胶热敏纸打印客户收派件信息的面单,也被称为热敏纸快递标签、经济型面单、二维码面单等。
② "碧海行动"是经国务院批准的公益性民生工程,是推动生态文明建设和国家战略实施,建设绿色交通、平安交通所采取的一项重大举措。2014年起,交通救捞系统连续6年执行了"碧海行动"沉船打捞任务,累计打捞沉船79艘。

　　中国高度重视交通运输污染防治,印发《珠三角、长三角、环渤海(京津冀)水域船舶排放控制区实施方案》《船舶大气污染物排放控制区实施方案》《2020年全球船用燃油限硫令实施方案》等一系列政策文件。先期重点针对珠三角、长三角、环渤海(京津冀)三大重点区域,提出了着力降低船舶硫氧化物、氮氧化物、颗粒物和挥发性有机物等大气污染物的排放,持续改善沿海和内河港口城市空气质量的目标。《方案》实施以来污染物减排效果显著。目前,船舶大气污染物排放控制区进一步扩大地理范围至沿海和长江干线、西江干线等水域,并对海南水域提出了更为严格的控制要求。推进实施船舶大气污染物排放控制区,是实现空气质量持续改善、满足人民对美好生活的期望、落实"打好污染防治攻坚战、打赢蓝天保卫战"总体要求的重要抓手,是中国参与全球环境治理的重要行动。

　　加大生态保护与修复力度。严守生态保护红线,严格落实生态保护和修复制度。交通基础设施建设全面实行"避让—保护—修复"模式,推进生态选线选址,强化生态环保设计,避让耕地、林地、湿地等具有重要生态功能的国土空间。在铁路、公路、航道沿江沿线开展绿化行动,提升生态功能和景观品质。铁路、公路建设工程注重动物通道建设,青藏铁路建设的动物通道有效保障了藏羚羊的顺利迁徙及其他高原动物的自由活动。港口码头建设和航道整治注重减少对水生态和水生生物的影响,建设过鱼通道,促进鱼类洄游。组织实施公路港口生态修复总面积超过5000万平方米。推进长江非法码头、非法采砂整治,截至2019年底,完成1361座非法码头整改,改善了生态环境条件,更好保障了长江防洪、供水和航运安全。

（三）加强安全防控和应急保障能力建设

坚持人民至上、生命至上，不断提升交通运输业应对突发公共事件的能力，特别是突发重大公共卫生事件的能力，加强安全治理和应急保障能力建设，统筹发展和安全，全力推进建设更高水平平安交通，为经济社会发展和群众出行提供安全运输保障。

交通安全防控能力显著提升。坚持预防为主、综合施策，深化和完善交通运输平安体系，持续完善安全生产风险管控和隐患排查治理双重预防控制机制，下大力气减少重特大交通运输安全事故，牢牢守住交通安全生产底线。2012年以来，未发生重大铁路交通事故，2019年铁路运输事故死亡人数和10亿吨公里死亡率与2012年相比分别下降46.1%和53.8%。普通公路较大、重特大道路交通事故起数连续下降，发生较大以上等级事故和死亡人数与2012年相比分别下降55.9%和60%。2019年，未发生重大等级水上交通事故，较大等级以上事故和死亡人数与2012年相比分别下降68.5%和69.4%。民航实现运输航空持续安全飞行112个月、8068万小时的安全新纪录。

交通应急保障能力显著提升。加强交通应急保障能力建设，及时防范化解交通重大安全风险，有效应对处置各类灾害事故。实施高铁安全防护工程，推进人防、物防、技防"三位一体"安全保障体系建设，集中开展高铁沿线环境综合整治，消除高铁沿线环境安全隐患

6.4 万处,深入推进普速铁路安全环境整治。实施乡道及以上公路安全保障工程和安全生命防护工程,累计实施 88.9 万公里,改造危桥 4.7 万座,车辆运输车治理取得决定性成效。加强海上搜救和重大海上溢油应急处置,建立政府领导、统一指挥、属地为主、专群结合、就近就便、快速高效的海上搜救工作格局,配备 70 余艘专业救助船舶、120 多艘打捞船舶、20 余架专业救助航空器,建立 20 余支应急救助队,基本建成以专业救捞力量、军队和国家公务力量、社会力量等为主要力量的海上搜救队伍。2012 年至 2019 年,全国组织协调海上搜救行动 1.6 万次,派出搜救船舶 7.2 万艘次、飞机 2780 架次,成功救助遇险船舶 1.1 万艘、遇险人员 12.2 万人,搜救成功率达 96.2%。

应对突发公共事件处置能力显著提升。科学高效应对各类突发公共事件,健全工作体系,提升应急能力。新冠肺炎疫情发生后,中国果断做出"一断三不断"[①]部署,适时推出铁路"七快速"[②],公路"三不一优先"[③],水运"四优先"[④],民航客运"五个一"[⑤]、货运"运贸对接"[⑥]以及邮政"绿色通道"等政策措施,一方面全力阻断病毒通过交通工具传播,另一方面保障全国各地应急物资运输和人民生活需求,为打赢疫情防控人民战争、总体战、阻击战提供了有力支撑。

---

① "一断三不断"是指坚决阻断病毒传播渠道,保障交通网络不断、应急运输绿色通道不断、必要的群众生产生活物资运输通道不断。
② "七快速"是指应急运输物资快速受理、快速配空、快速装车、快速挂运、快速输送、快速卸车、快速交付。
③ "三不一优先"是指对应急运输车辆做到不停车、不检查、不收费、优先通行。
④ "四优先"是指应急运输船舶优先过闸、优先引航、优先锚泊、优先靠离泊。
⑤ "五个一"是指一个航司一个国家只保留一条航线,一周最多执行一班。
⑥ "运贸对接"是指外贸外资企业与航空运输企业供需精准对接。

专栏 10　交通运输为抗击新冠肺炎疫情发挥重要作用

　　抗击新冠肺炎疫情斗争中,交通运输在传染病防控、保障医疗物资及时供应、维持人民正常生活等方面发挥了重要作用。疫情发生后,全国通过铁路、公路、水运、民航、邮政快递等运输方式向湖北地区运送防疫物资和生活物资 158.9 万吨,运送电煤、燃油等生产物资 579.6 万吨,4000 多万交通从业人员日夜奋战在抗疫一线,数百万快递员顶风冒雪、冒疫前行。分区分级精准有序恢复运输服务,免收全国收费公路车辆通行费,铁路、公路、水路交通以及城市公交、地铁、出租车在做好疫情防控前提下正常运营,有力保障了生产生活物资运输和复工复产。

五、推动构建全球交通命运共同体

中国坚持互利共赢的开放战略,深化与各国在交通领域合作,积极推进全球互联互通,积极参与全球交通治理,认真履行交通发展的国际责任与义务,在更多领域、更高层面上实现合作共赢、共同发展,推动构建全球交通命运共同体,服务构建人类命运共同体。

(一) 助力共建"一带一路"

共建"一带一路"承载着人们的美好梦想。中国秉持共商共建共享理念,与有关国家加快推进基础设施互联互通合作,共同打造开放包容、互利共赢的高质量发展之路,共同打造和平之路、合作之路、幸福之路。

推动交通基础设施互联互通。注重发挥交通运输对于推进全球连通、促进共同繁荣的基础性先导性作用,加强与各国在交通互联互通领域互利合作。扎实推进巴基斯坦1号铁路干线升级改造项目(ML1)、中尼(泊尔)跨境铁路合作项目以及中老铁路、中泰铁路、雅万高铁建设。中国企业参与建成蒙内铁路、亚吉铁路、巴基斯坦拉哈尔"橙线"轨道交通项目等铁路。中欧班列累计开行突破3.1万列、通达21个欧洲国家的92个城市。合作建成白沙瓦——卡拉奇高速公路（苏库尔——木尔坦）、喀喇昆仑公路二期（赫韦利扬——塔科特）、昆曼公路、中俄黑河公路大桥、同江铁路大桥等公路、桥梁项目。参与希腊比雷埃夫斯港、斯里兰卡科伦坡港、巴基斯坦瓜达尔港等海外港口的建设和运营。在有关国家积极参与和共同努力下，"六廊六路多国多港"的互联互通架构基本形成。以铁路、公路、航运、航空为重点的全方位、多层次基础设施网络正在加快形成，区域间商品交易、流动成本逐渐降低，促进了跨区域资源要素的有序流动和优化配置。

推进国际运输便利化。积极推进政策、规则、标准"三位一体"联通，为互联互通提供机制保障。以共建"一带一路"为合作平台，与19个国家签署22项国际道路运输便利化协定；分别与比利时、阿联酋、法国签署机动车驾驶证互认换领双边协议；与66个国家和地区签署70个双边和区域海运协定，海运服务覆盖沿线所有沿海国家；与26个国家（地区）签署单边或者双边承认船员证书协议，与新加坡签署电子证书谅解备忘录，便利船舶通关，引领和推进电子证书在全球航运业的应用进程；建立中欧班列国际铁路合作机制，与22个国家签署邮政合作文件，实现中欧班列出口运邮常态化运作；与100个国家签订双边政府间航空运输协定，截至2019年底，中外航空公司在中国通航54个合作国家，每周运行6846个往返航班，与东盟、欧盟签订了区域性航空运输协定。建立中日韩俄四国海上搜救合作机制，与印尼国家搜救局签订部门间海上搜救合作备忘录。国际运输便利化推动了中国与沿线国家合作更加紧密、往来更加便利、利益更加融合。

（二）积极推动全球交通治理体系变革

当前,全球交通治理体系面临一系列新课题,迫切需要变革创新,为全球发展提供更好助力和支撑。中国坚定支持多边主义,积极推动全球交通治理体系建设与变革,努力为全球交通治理提供中国智慧、中国方案。

共谋全球交通治理。中国作为负责任大国,认真履行国际责任和义务。加入近 120 项交通运输领域多边条约,积极参与联合国亚洲及太平洋经济社会委员会、铁路合作组织、国际铁路联盟、世界道路协会、国际运输论坛、国际海事组织、国际民航组织、万国邮政联盟等国际组织事务,多次当选或连任国际海事组织 A 类理事国、万国邮政联盟相关理事会理事国,积极主办世界交通运输大会等国际会议。推动实现联合国 2030 年可持续发展议程框架下的交通领域可持续发展目标,携手其他发展中国家推动交通可持续发展全球治理改革,为发展中国家发展营造良好的国际环境。

推动全球气候治理。中国高度重视应对气候变化,积极承担符合自身发展阶段和国情的国际责任,实施积极应对气候变化国家战略。积极引导全球海运温室气体减排战略的制定和实施,在全球航空减排市场机制制定和实施进程中努力维护发展中国家权益,推动和引导建立公平合理、合作共赢的全球气候治理体系,为全球生态文明建设和可持续发展贡献力量。

（三）加强国际交流与合作

中国遵循平等互利、合作共赢的原则，与各国深入开展交通领域交流合作，不断拓展广度深度，推动构建开放型世界经济。

扩大开放合作"朋友圈"。依托中俄总理定期会晤委员会运输合作分委会、中美交通论坛、中国—中东欧国家交通部长会议等平台，深化交通可持续发展合作，为构建新型国际关系发挥积极作用。秉持亲诚惠容周边外交理念，加强与周边国家交通合作，推动建立中日韩运输与物流部长会议、上海合作组织交通部长会议、中国—东盟（10+1）交通部长会议、中老缅泰澜沧江—湄公河商船通航联合协调委员会等合作机制，以及中俄、中朝界河航道航行管理机制。推动建立并参与亚太海事局长会议、中国—东盟海事磋商机制会议等区域合作机制。参与大湄公河次区域（GMS）、中亚区域经济合作（CAREC）等机制下的交通合作，为促进地区经济发展作出积极贡献。秉持正确义利观，积极开展与相关国家的海事能力建设和技术合作项目，向其他发展中国家提供基础设施建设、规划编制、能力建设等方面支持和援助。通过广泛深入的交流合作，推动形成市场合作互利共赢、成果经验互鉴共享的开放新格局。

开展国际抗疫合作。新冠病毒是人类共同的敌人。中国加强与其他国家交通领域抗疫合作，推动构建人类卫生健康共同体。推动国际海事组织向 174 个成员国、有关国际组织转发《船舶船员新冠肺炎疫情防控操作指南》《港口及其一线人员新冠肺炎疫情防控工作指南》等多份文件。中国民用航空局向 40 多个重点通航国家民航部门分享《运输航空公司、机场疫情防控技术指南》。国家邮政局通过万国邮政联盟向其 192 个成员国分享《中国邮政新型冠状病毒防控指导手册》。以视频会议形式举办"中日韩运输与物流部长会议特别会议""中国—东盟交通部长应对新冠疫情特别会议""第 19 次中国—东盟交通部长会议",发布部长联合声明。建立抗疫援助物资国内绿色运输通道,成立国际物流工作专班,实施包机串飞、商业航班、海陆联运、中欧班列等多式联运方式,全力支持做好抗疫援助物资运输保障工作。截至目前,已向 150 个国家和 7 个国际组织提供了 294 批次抗疫物资援助和支持,向 33 个国家派出援外医疗专家组 35 队 262 人。

六、中国交通的未来展望

中共十九大提出到 2035 年基本实现社会主义现代化、到本世纪中叶建成社会主义现代化强国的宏伟目标,中共十九届五中全会提出"加快建设交通强国",中国的交通运输迎来更加宝贵的"黄金时期"。

交通高质量发展更加紧迫。中国决胜全面建成小康社会取得决定性成就。进入新发展阶段,贯彻新发展理念、构建新发展格局对交通发展提出了更高要求,也提供了更大空间。人民对美好生活的向往呈现多样化、多层次、多方面特点,对交通运输服务需求更加旺盛、更加多元。新一轮科技革命和产业变革加速推进,给交通运输带来革命性变化。同时,国际环境日趋复杂,不稳定性不确定性明显增加,新冠肺炎疫情在全球传播推动世界百年未有之大变局加速演进,单边主义、保护主义、霸权主义使国际产业链供应链运转严重受阻,气候变化给生态系统安全及经济社会发展带来现实和潜在威胁。

面对国际国内形势的发展变化,加快构建国家综合立体交通网,建设人民满意、保障有力、世界前列交通强国,既面临机遇,也面临挑战。适应新的生产生活方式变化,建设人民满意交通,全面提升综合交通运输网络效率和服务品质的要求更高;服务国土空间开发保护和城乡区域协调发展,全方位提升交通保障能力,保持交通基础设施适度超前发展、充分发挥交通先行作用的要求更高;服务经济高质量发展,转变交通发展方式,提高安全智慧绿色发展水平,提升安全防控、应急处置和救援保障能力,推进治理现代化的要求更高;支撑全方位对外开放,强化交通基础设施互联互通,完善面向全球的运输服务网络的要求更高。

加快建设交通强国。进入新的发展阶段,中国交通坚持以人民为中心的发展思想,以高质量发展为主题,以供给侧结构性改革为主线,牢牢把握"先行官"定位,适度超前,推动交通发展由追求速度规模向更加注重质量效益转变,由各种交通方式相对独立发展向更加注重一体化融合发展转变,由依靠传统要素驱动向更加注重创新驱动转变,构建安全、便捷、高效、绿色、经济的现代化综合交通体系,打造一流设施、一流技术、一流管理、一流服务,努力建设人民满意、保障有力、世界前列的交通强国。

到 2035 年,基本建成交通强国。现代化综合交通体系基本形成,人民满意度明显提高,支撑国家现代化建设能力显著增强。拥有发达的快速网、完善的干线网、广泛的基础网,城乡区域交通协调发展达到新高度。基本形成都市区 1 小时通勤、城市群 2 小时通达、全国主要城市 3 小时覆盖的"全国 123 出行交通圈"和国内 1 天送达、周边国家 2 天送达、全球主要城市 3 天送达的"全球 123 快货物流圈",旅客联程运输便捷顺畅,货物多式联运高效经济。智能、平安、绿色、共享交通发展水平明显提高,城市交通拥堵基本缓解,无障碍出行服务体系基本完善。交通科技创新体系基本建成,交通关键装备先进安全,人才队伍精良,市场环境优良。基本实现交通治理现代化。交通国际竞争力和影响力显著提升。交通运输全面适应人民日益增长的美好生活需要,为基本实现社会主义现代化提供有力支撑。

结 束 语

中国即将开启全面建设社会主义现代化国家的新征程。进入新的发展阶段，中国交通将更好履行经济社会发展"先行官"使命，践行新发展理念，服务新发展格局，让交通更加安全、便捷、高效、绿色、经济，为 2035 年基本实现社会主义现代化、本世纪中叶全面建成社会主义现代化强国提供坚实基础。

当前，新冠肺炎疫情仍在全球蔓延，各国面临疫情冲击和经济衰退双重挑战，交通运输对于全球团结抗疫、推动经济增长十分重要。中国将秉持人类命运共同体理念，落实联合国 2030 年可持续发展议程，加强交通国际交流合作，与世界各国一道，更好推进全球互联互通、民心相通，为建设繁荣美好世界作出更大贡献。

第二部分　英文版

Fighting Covid-19
China in Action

The State Council Information Office of
the People's Republic of China

June 2020

Foreword

The Covid-19 global pandemic is the most extensive to afflict humanity in a century. A serious crisis for the entire world, and a daunting challenge, it poses a grave threat to human life and health.

This is a war that humanity has to fight and win. Facing this unknown, unexpected, and devastating disease, China launched a resolute battle to prevent and control its spread. Making people's lives and health its first priority, China adopted extensive, stringent, and thorough containment measures, and has for now succeeded in cutting all channels for the transmission of the virus. 1.4 billion Chinese people have exhibited enormous tenacity and solidarity in erecting a defensive rampart that demonstrates their power in the face of such natural disasters.

Having forged the idea that the world is a global community of shared future, and believing that it must act as a responsible member, China has fought shoulder to shoulder with the rest of the world. In an open, transparent, and responsible manner and in accordance with the law, China gave timely notification to the international community of the onset of a new coronavirus, and shared without reserve its experience in containing the spread of the virus and treating the infected. China has great empathy with victims all over the world, and has done all it can to provide humanitarian aid in support of the international community's endeavors to stem the pandemic.

The virus is currently wreaking havoc throughout the world. China grieves for those who have been killed and those who have sacrificed their lives in the fight, extends the greatest respect to those who are struggling to save lives, and offers true moral support to those who are infected and receiving treatment. China firmly believes that as long as all countries unite and cooperate to mount a collective response, the international community will succeed in overcoming the pandemic, and will emerge from this dark moment in human history into a brighter future.

To keep a record of China's efforts in its own fight against the virus, to share its experience with the rest of the world, and to clarify its ideas on the global battle, the Chinese government now releases this white paper.

I. China's Fight against the Epidemic: A Test of Fire

The Covid-19 epidemic is a major public health emergency. The virus has spread faster and wider than any other since the founding of the People's Republic in 1949, and has proven to be the most difficult to contain. It is both a crisis and a major test for China. The Communist Party of China (CPC) and the Chinese government have addressed the epidemic as a top priority, and taken swift action. General Secretary Xi Jinping has taken personal command, planned the response, overseen the general situation and acted decisively, pointing the way forward in the fight against the epidemic. This has bolstered the Chinese people's confidence and rallied their strength. Under the leadership of the CPC, the whole nation has followed the general principle of "remaining confident, coming together in solidarity, adopting a science-based approach, and taking targeted measures", and waged an all-out people's war on the virus.

Through painstaking efforts and tremendous sacrifice, and having paid a heavy price, China has succeeded in turning the situation around. In little more than a single month, the rising spread of the virus was contained; in around two months, the daily increase in domestic coronavirus cases had fallen to single digits; and in approximately three months, a decisive victory was secured in the battle to defend Hubei Province and its capital city of Wuhan. With these strategic achievements, China has protected its people's lives, safety and health, and made a significant contribution to safeguarding regional and global public health.

As of 24:00 of May 31, 2020, a cumulative total of 83,017 confirmed cases had been reported on the Chinese mainland, 78,307 infected had been cured and discharged from hospital, and 4,634 people had died. This demonstrates a cure rate of 94.3 percent and a fatality rate of 5.6 percent (see charts 1, 2, 3 and 4).

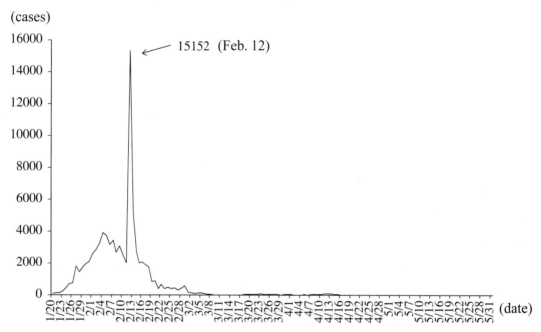

Note: On February 12, newly confirmed cases reached 15,152 (including 13,332 cumulative clinically diagnosed cases in Hubei).

Chart 1. Daily Figure for Newly Confirmed Cases on the Chinese Mainland

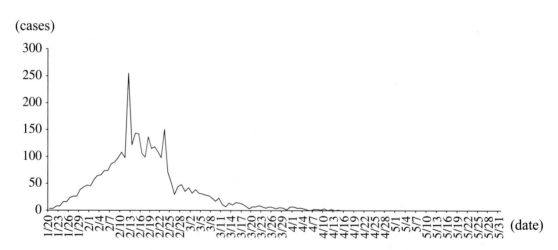

Chart 2. Daily Figure for New Fatalities on the Chinese Mainland

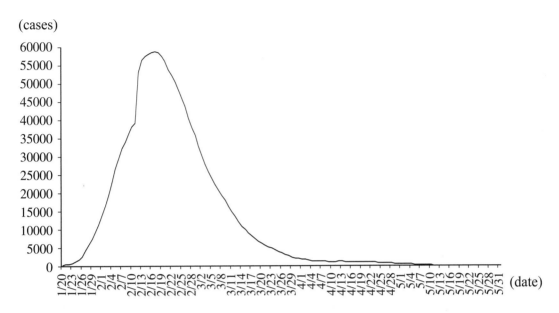

**Chart 3. Cumulative Total of Outstanding Cases on the
Chinese Mainland**

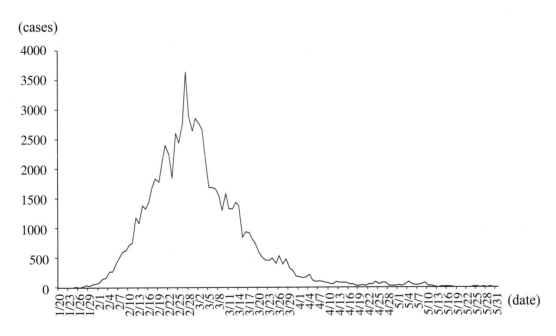

Chart 4. Daily Figure for Cured Cases on the Chinese Mainland

China's fight against the epidemic can be divided into five stages.

Stage I: Swift Response to the Public Health Emergency (December 27, 2019-January 19, 2020)

As soon as cases of pneumonia of unknown cause were identified in Wuhan City, Hubei Province, China acted immediately to conduct etiological and epidemiological investigations and to stop the spread of the disease, and promptly reported the situation. In a timely manner, China informed the WHO and other countries, including the US, of the developing situation, and released the genome sequence of the novel coronavirus. After community spread and clusters of cases emerged in Wuhan, and confirmed cases were reported in other Chinese regions, which were due to virus carriers traveling from the city, a nationwide program of epidemic prevention and control was launched.

(1) December 27, 2019: Hubei Provincial Hospital of Integrated Chinese and Western Medicine reported cases of pneumonia of unknown cause to the Wuhan Jianghan Center for Disease Prevention and Control. The Wuhan city government arranged for experts to look into these cases through an analysis of the patients' condition and clinical outcome, the findings of epidemiological investigations, and preliminary laboratory testing results. The conclusion was that they were cases of a viral pneumonia.

(2) December 30: The Wuhan City Health Commission (WCHC) issued Urgent Notice on Treatment of Patients with Pneumonia of Unknown Cause. Upon learning of developments, the National Health Commission (NHC) acted immediately to organize research into the disease.

(3) December 31: The NHC made arrangements in the small hours to send a working group and an expert team to Wuhan to guide its response to the situation and conduct on-site investigations.

The WCHC website carried its Information Circular on the Pneumonia Cases in Wuhan, confirming 27 cases and urging the public to stay away from enclosed public places with poor ventilation and venues where large crowds gathered. The commission also suggested the use of face masks when going out. From that day on, the WCHC began to release updates on the disease in accordance with the law.

(4) January 1, 2020: The NHC set up a leading group on the disease response. The next day, it formulated Guidelines on Early Detection, Early Diagnosis and Early Quarantine for Prevention and Control of Viral Pneumonia of Unknown Cause. The Chinese Center for Disease Control and Prevention (China CDC) and the Chinese Academy of Medical Sciences (CAMS) received the first batch of samples of four cases discovered in Hubei and began the pathogen identification process.

(5) January 3: The WCHC issued Information Circular on Viral Pneumonia of Unknown Cause, reporting a total of 44 cases.

Under the direction of the NHC, China CDC and three other institutions carried out parallel laboratory testing of the samples to identify the pathogen. The NHC and the Health Commission of Hubei Province jointly formulated nine documents, including Diagnosis and Treatment Protocol for Viral Pneumonia of Unknown Cause (for Trial Implementation).

From that day on, on a regular basis, China began to update the WHO, relevant countries, and regional organizations, as well as its own regions of Hong Kong, Macao and Taiwan, on the development of the disease.

(6) January 4: The head of China CDC held a telephone conversation with the director of the US CDC, briefing him about the new pneumonia. The two sides agreed to keep in close contact on information sharing and cooperation on technical matters.

The NHC and related health departments in Hubei Province produced Treatment Manual for Viral Pneumonia of Unknown Cause.

(7) January 5: The WCHC updated information on its website, reporting a total of 59 cases of the viral pneumonia of unknown cause. Laboratory tests ruled out respiratory pathogens as the cause, such as influenza, avian influenza, adenovirus, the Severe Acute Respiratory Syndrome coronavirus, and the Middle East Respiratory Syndrome coronavirus.

China sent a situation update to the WHO. The WHO released its first briefing on cases of pneumonia of unknown cause in Wuhan.

(8) January 6: The NHC gave a briefing on cases of pneumonia of unknown cause in Wuhan at a national health conference, calling for greater efforts to monitor, analyze and study them, and prepare for a timely response.

(9) January 7: Xi Jinping, general secretary of the CPC Central Committee, presided over a meeting of the Standing Committee of the Political Bureau of the CPC Central Committee and issued instructions on the prevention and control of a possible epidemic of the pneumonia of unknown cause in Wuhan.

(10) January 7: China CDC succeeded in isolating the first novel coronavirus strain.

(11) January 8: An expert evaluation team designated by the NHC initially identified a new coronavirus as the cause of the disease. The heads of the China and US CDCs held a telephone discussion on technical exchanges and cooperation.

(12) January 9: The NHC expert evaluation team released information on the pathogen of the viral pneumonia of unknown cause, and made a preliminary judgment that a new coronavirus was the cause.

China informed the WHO of developments and the initial progress that had been made in determining the cause of the viral pneumonia. The WHO released on its website a statement regarding a cluster of pneumonia cases in Wuhan, indicating that the preliminary identification of a novel coronavirus in such a short period of time was a notable achievement.

(13) January 10: Research institutions including China CDC and the Wuhan Institute of Virology (WIV) under the Chinese Academy of Sciences (CAS) came up with an initial version of test kits. Wuhan immediately began to test all relevant cases admitted to local hospitals to screen for the new coronavirus.

The heads of the NHC and China CDC held separate telephone conversations with the head of the WHO about China's response to the disease, and exchanged information.

(14) January 11: China started to update the WHO and other parties concerned on a daily basis.

(15) January 12: The WCHC changed "viral pneumonia of unknown cause" to "pneumonia caused by the novel coronavirus" in an information circular on its website.

China CDC, the CAMS and the WIV, as designated agencies of the NHC, submitted to the WHO the genome sequence of the novel coronavirus (2019-nCoV), which was published by the Global Initiative on Sharing All Influenza Data to be shared globally.

(16) January 13: Premier Li Keqiang chaired a State Council meeting and announced requirements for epidemic prevention and control.

(17) January 13: The NHC held a meeting to provide guidance to Hubei and Wuhan authorities, advising them to further strengthen management, step up body temperature monitoring at ports and stations, and reduce crowded gatherings.

The WHO issued on its website a statement on the discovery of novel coronavirus cases in Thailand, recognizing that China's sharing of the genome sequence of the virus had enabled more countries to rapidly diagnose cases.

An inspection team from Hong Kong, Macao and Taiwan visited Wuhan to learn about the prevention and control of the disease.

(18) January 14: The NHC held a national teleconference, specifying arrangements for epidemic prevention and control in Hubei and Wuhan, and for emergency preparations and response across the country. The NHC cautioned that there was great uncertainty about the new disease, and that more research was needed to understand its mode of transmission and the risk of human-to-human transmissibility. Further spread could not be ruled out.

(19) January 15: The NHC unveiled the first versions of Diagnosis and Treatment Protocol for Novel Coronavirus Pneumonia, and Protocol on Prevention and Control of Novel Coronavirus Pneumonia.

(20) January 16: As the optimization of the Polymerase Chain Reac-

tion (PCR) diagnostic reagents was completed, Wuhan began to screen all patients treated in fever clinics or under medical observation in the 69 hospitals at or above the level of grade two in the city.

(21) January 17: The NHC sent seven inspection teams to different provincial-level health agencies to guide local epidemic prevention and control.

(22) January 18: The NHC released the second version of Diagnosis and Treatment Protocol for Novel Coronavirus Pneumonia.

(23) January 18-19: The NHC assembled a high-level national team of senior medical and disease control experts and sent them to Wuhan to study the local response to the epidemic. In the middle of the night of January 19, after careful examination and deliberation, the team determined that the new coronavirus was spreading between humans.

Stage II: Initial Progress in Containing the Virus (January 20-February 20, 2020)

The situation became most pressing with the rapid increase in newly confirmed cases in China. As a crucial step to stem the spread of the virus, the Chinese government took the decisive measure to close outbound traffic from Wuhan. This marked the beginning of an all-out battle to protect Wuhan and Hubei from the epidemic.

The CPC Central Committee set up a leading group for novel coronavirus prevention and control and sent the Central Steering Group to Hubei. A joint epidemic prevention and control mechanism and in due course a mechanism to facilitate resumption of work were set up under the State Council. Resources were mobilized nationwide to assist Hubei and Wuhan. Major public health emergency responses were activated across China.

The most comprehensive, stringent and thorough epidemic prevention and control campaign was launched nationwide, and initial progress was made in curbing the spread of the virus (see Chart 5).

(1) January 20: President Xi Jinping, also general secretary of the

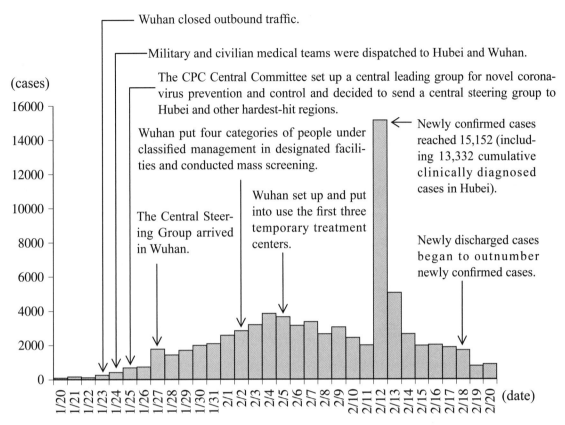

Wuhan closed outbound traffic.

Military and civilian medical teams were dispatched to Hubei and Wuhan.

The CPC Central Committee set up a central leading group for novel coronavirus prevention and control and decided to send a central steering group to Hubei and other hardest-hit regions.

Wuhan put four categories of people under classified management in designated facilities and conducted mass screening.

The Central Steering Group arrived in Wuhan.

Wuhan set up and put into use the first three temporary treatment centers.

Newly confirmed cases reached 15,152 (including 13,332 cumulative clinically diagnosed cases in Hubei).

Newly discharged cases began to outnumber newly confirmed cases.

Chart 5. Daily Figure for Newly Confirmed Cases on the Chinese Mainland (January 20-February 20)

CPC Central Committee and chairman of the Central Military Commission, gave important instructions on fighting the novel coronavirus. He emphasized that people's lives and health must come first and resolute efforts should be taken to stem the spread of the virus. He called for prompt release of information on the epidemic and enhanced international cooperation.

(2) January 20: During an executive meeting of the State Council, Premier Li Keqiang decided to take more steps for epidemic prevention and control. A decision was taken to classify the novel coronavirus pneumonia as a Class B infectious disease in compliance with the Law

of the People's Republic of China on Prevention and Treatment of Infectious Diseases, but to apply to it the preventive and control measures for a Class A infectious disease.

(3) January 20: The State Council convened a teleconference to plan for nationwide prevention and control of the disease.

(4) January 20: The NHC held a press conference for the high-level expert team, at which it was confirmed that the virus could transmit from human to human.

(5) January 20: The NHC made a statement on implementing the above State Council decision and bringing the pneumonia under quarantinable infectious disease management in accordance with the Frontier Health and Quarantine Law of the People's Republic of China. The NHC also released Protocol on Prevention and Control of Novel Coronavirus Pneumonia (Edition 2).

(6) January 22: Xi Jinping ordered the immediate imposition of tight restrictions on the movement of people and channels of exit in Hubei and Wuhan.

(7) January 22: The NHC issued Diagnosis and Treatment Protocol for Novel Coronavirus Pneumonia (Trial Version 3). The State Council Information Office held its first press conference on the novel coronavirus.

The NHC was notified by the United States about its first confirmed case.

The 2019 Novel Coronavirus Resource database was officially launched by the China National Center for Bioinformation, which released the novel coronavirus genome and provided information on variation analysis to the international community.

(8) January 23: At around 2 a.m. Wuhan City Novel Coronavirus Prevention and Control Command Center issued the No. 1 public notice declaring temporary closure of the city's outbound routes at its airports and railway stations at 10 a.m. the same day. The Ministry of Transport issued an emergency circular suspending passenger traffic into Wuhan from

other parts of the country by road or waterway. The NHC and five other government departments also issued Notice on Preventing the Transmission of Novel Coronavirus Pneumonia via Means of Transport. From January 23 to January 29, all provinces and equivalent administrative units on the Chinese mainland (hereafter all provinces) activated Level 1 public health emergency response.

(9) January 23: Researchers of the WIV, Wuhan Jinyintan Hospital and the Hubei Provincial CDC discovered that the whole genome sequence of the 2019-nCoV shares 79.5 percent of the SARS-CoV sequence.

The Novel Coronavirus National Science and Technology Resource Service System, jointly set up by the National Microbiology Data Center and the National Pathogen Resource Collection Center, released the first electron microscope image of the virus and its strain information.

(10) January 24: Dispatch of national medical teams to Hubei and Wuhan began. In the ensuing period, a total of 346 medical teams composed of 42,600 medical workers and 965 public health workers from across the country and the armed forces were dispatched.

(11) January 25: Xi Jinping chaired a meeting of the Standing Committee of the Political Bureau of the CPC Central Committee. He called for resolute efforts to win the battle to contain the virus with "confidence and solidarity, a science-based approach and targeted measures". He urged Hubei to make epidemic control its top priority and apply more rigorous measures to stem the spread of the virus within the province and beyond. All confirmed patients, he said, must be hospitalized without delay, and severe cases must be sent to designated hospitals with sufficient medical resources so that they could be treated by medical experts. A decision was taken at the meeting that the central Party leadership would set up a leading group for novel coronavirus prevention and control under the Standing Committee of the Political Bureau. It was also decided that the central Party leadership would send a steering group to Hubei to oversee epidemic control on the ground.

(12) January 25: The NHC released six sets of guidelines on disease

prevention: for general use, tourism, households, public places, public transport and home observation.

(13) January 26: Premier Li Keqiang, also member of the Standing Committee of the Political Bureau of the CPC Central Committee and head of the Central Leading Group for Novel Coronavirus Prevention and Control, chaired the group's first meeting.

The General Office of the State Council issued the decision to extend the Chinese New Year holiday of 2020 and postpone the opening of all universities, colleges, secondary schools, elementary schools and kindergartens.

The National Medical Products Administration fast-tracked approval of four novel coronavirus test kits made by four companies to boost capacity for producing virus nucleic acid test kits.

(14) January 27: Xi Jinping issued an instruction calling on all CPC organizations and members to bear in mind the supremacy of the people's interests and the Party's founding mission, strengthen confidence and solidarity, take a science-based approach and targeted measures, and lead the people in implementing the decisions made by the central Party leadership.

(15) January 27: Li Keqiang paid an inspection visit to Wuhan on behalf of Xi Jinping, where he gave guidance on virus control and expressed appreciation to frontline health workers. The Central Steering Group arrived in Wuhan on the same day to strengthen overall guidance of and supervision over the prevention and control of the disease at the front line.

(16) January 27: The NHC released Diagnosis and Treatment Protocol for Novel Coronavirus Pneumonia (Trial Version 4).

The head of the NHC discussed epidemic prevention and control with the head of the US Department of Health and Human Services (US HHS) in a telephone call.

(17) January 28: Xi Jinping met with WHO Director General Tedros Adhanom Ghebreyesus in Beijing. He said, "The virus is a devil, and we must hunt it down. The Chinese government has been providing timely updates on the epidemic in an open, transparent and responsible way. We

have responded to the concerns of various parties and enhanced cooperation with the international community." He expressed China's readiness to work with the WHO and the international community to safeguard public health both in the region and globally.

(18) January 28: The NHC released Protocol on Prevention and Control of Novel Coronavirus Pneumonia (Edition 3).

(19) January 30: The NHC notified the US through the official channel that American experts were welcome to join the WHO-China Joint Mission on Coronavirus Disease. The US replied and expressed its appreciation on the same day.

(20) January 31: The WHO declared the novel coronavirus outbreak a public health emergency of international concern. The NHC released Guidelines on Treating Novel Coronavirus Patients with Severe Symptoms in Designated Hospitals.

(21) February 2: Under the guidance of the Central Steering Group, Wuhan began to adopt measures to put four categories of people – confirmed cases, suspected cases, febrile patients who might be carriers, and close contacts – under classified management in designated facilities. The policy of ensuring that all those in need are tested, isolated, hospitalized or treated was implemented. Actions were taken to conduct mass screenings to identify people with infections, hospitalize them, and collect accurate data on case numbers.

(22) February 2: The head of the NHC sent a letter to the head of the US HHS to further exchange views on bilateral cooperation on public health and epidemic prevention and control.

(23) February 3: Xi Jinping chaired a meeting of the Standing Committee of the Political Bureau of the CPC Central Committee. He required that epidemic control measures be improved and strengthened and that the principle of early detection, reporting, quarantine and treatment be strictly observed. He called for saving lives by raising admission and cure rates and lowering infection and fatality rates.

(24) February 3: The Central Steering Group sent to Wuhan 22 na-

tional emergency medical teams from all over China, and gave the order to construct temporary treatment centers.

(25) February 4: The head of China CDC took a telephone call from the head of the US National Institute of Allergy and Infectious Diseases in which they exchanged views on the novel coronavirus.

(26) February 5: Xi Jinping chaired the third meeting of the Commission for Law-based Governance under the CPC Central Committee. He stressed the importance of putting the people's lives and health first, and the need to raise China's overall capacity of law-based disease prevention and control through the joint efforts of the legislature, law enforcement agencies, the judiciary and the public. This would ensure that epidemic prevention and control is conducted in compliance with the law.

(27) February 5: The State Council through its Joint Prevention and Control Mechanism strengthened coordination, which made it possible for the supply of medical N95 masks to exceed Hubei's requirement.

(28) February 5: The NHC released Diagnosis and Treatment Protocol for Novel Coronavirus Pneumonia (Trial Version 5).

(29) February 7: Through its Joint Prevention and Control Mechanism, the State Council issued Notice on Delivery of Duties for Effective Prevention and Control of the Disease.

The NHC released Protocol on Prevention and Control of Novel Coronavirus Pneumonia (Edition 4).

(30) February 8: The NHC gave briefings on China's epidemic control efforts and measures at a meeting of the APEC health working group. It also gave briefings to Chinese diplomatic missions overseas on the guidelines for prevention and control, diagnosis and treatment, monitoring, epidemiological investigation and laboratory testing of the novel coronavirus.

Heads of Chinese and US health authorities further exchanged views on arrangements for American experts to join the WHO-China Joint Mission on Coronavirus Disease.

(31) February 10: Xi Jinping inspected prevention and control work

in Beijing. He also talked by video link to doctors from Wuhan Jinyintan Hospital, Wuhan Union Hospital and Huoshenshan Hospital where novel coronavirus patients were being treated. He called for strengthening confidence and taking more decisive measures to stem the spread of and win the people's all-out war against the virus. He emphasized that top priority must be given to Hubei and Wuhan, as they were the decisive battlegrounds. Victory in Wuhan would ensure victory in Hubei, and ultimately victory across the country. No effort would be spared in saving lives. The infected should be treated in designated hospitals by top-level doctors and with all necessary resources guaranteed. Strict measures must be taken to forestall inbound and intra-city transmissions, neutralize all sources of infection and stem the spread of the virus to the greatest extent possible.

(32) February 10: A mechanism was established to organize pairing assistance from other provinces to Hubei's cities other than Wuhan for treatment of the infected. Assistance from 19 provinces was rendered to 16 cities in Hubei.

(33) February 11: Thanks to strengthened coordination under the State Council Joint Prevention and Control Mechanism, the supply of medical protective suits to Hubei exceeded its needs.

(34) February 11: China CDC experts had a teleconference at the request of flu experts from the US CDC, during which they shared information on novel coronavirus prevention and control.

(35) February 12: At a meeting of the Standing Committee of the Political Bureau of the CPC Central Committee, Xi Jinping noted that China's novel coronavirus prevention and control had reached the most crucial stage. Key epidemic control tasks must be fulfilled, and greater attention must be given to the hardest-hit and high-risk areas. He called for improvements in key links in disease control to raise the admission and cure rates and lower the infection and fatality rates. Hospital capacity must be boosted to ensure admission and treatment for all patients. The best medical resources and technologies should be pooled to treat all infections, particularly the most severe cases. He urged those provinces and

cities with large population inflows to strengthen cross-region joint prevention and control and society-wide efforts to contain the virus.

(36) February 13: The head of the NHC received a letter from the head of the US HHS on arrangements concerning bilateral cooperation on public health and novel coronavirus prevention and control.

(37) February 14: Xi Jinping chaired the 12th meeting of the Commission for Further Reform under the CPC Central Committee. He emphasized that protecting people's lives and health is a high priority on the CPC's governance agenda. Immediate, science-based and targeted measures must be taken to stamp out the virus. Experience and lessons must be drawn to enhance preparedness in the future. Swift actions must be taken to address problems, plug loopholes, and reinforce weak links. He also emphasized the need to improve both the mechanism for preventing and controlling major epidemics and the national public health emergency response system.

(38) February 14: All provinces and equivalent administrative units other than Hubei saw a continuous drop in newly confirmed cases for the 10th consecutive day.

(39) February 15: The State Council Information Office held its first press conference on novel coronavirus prevention and control in Wuhan. By that day, seven types of test reagents had been approved for market launch, and progress had been made in drug screening, development of therapeutic regimens and vaccines, and animal model construction.

(40) February 16: The WHO-China Joint Mission on Covid-19, consisting of 25 experts from China, Germany, Japan, ROK, Nigeria, Russia, Singapore, the US and the WHO, started its nine-day field visit to Beijing, Chengdu, Guangzhou, Shenzhen and Wuhan.

(41) February 17: Through its Joint Prevention and Control Mechanism, the State Council issued Guidelines on Taking Science-based, Targeted, Region-specific, and Tiered Measures for Covid-19 Prevention and Control. Local authorities and government departments were required to take measures matching the corresponding levels of emergency response

and ensure an orderly return to work and normal life.

(42) February 18: Nationwide, the daily number of newly cured and discharged coronavirus patients exceeded that of newly confirmed cases, and the number of confirmed cases began to drop.

The NHC sent a reply to the US HHS on further arrangements concerning bilateral health and anti-virus cooperation.

(43) February 19: Xi Jinping chaired a meeting of the Standing Committee of the Political Bureau of the CPC Central Committee. The meeting heard reports on coronavirus prevention and control, and studied plans on strengthening virus control while promoting economic and social development.

(44) February 19: The NHC released Diagnosis and Treatment Protocol for Covid-19 (Trial Version 6).

(45) February 19: For the first time in Wuhan, newly cured and discharged cases outnumbered newly confirmed ones.

Stage III: Newly Confirmed Domestic Cases on the Chinese Mainland Drop to Single Digits
(February 21-March 17, 2020)

China had made significant progress: The rapid spread of the virus had been contained in Wuhan and the rest of Hubei Province, the situation in other parts on the mainland had stabilized, and the daily figure for new cases had remained in single digits since mid-March. As the situation evolved, the CPC Central Committee decided to coordinate epidemic control with economic and social development, and organize an orderly return to normal work and daily life (see Chart 6).

(1) February 21: Xi Jinping chaired a meeting of the Political Bureau of the CPC Central Committee. He pointed out that while significant progress had been made in containing the epidemic, the turning point had not yet arrived at the national level. Wuhan and the entire province of Hubei still faced a grave and complex threat. He instructed that differentiated control measures be adopted to address the problems in different regions,

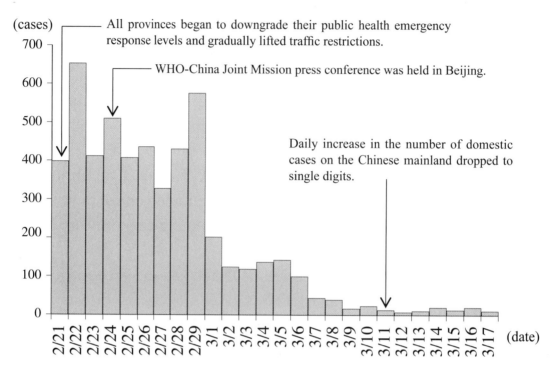

Chart 6. Daily Figure for Newly Confirmed Cases on the Chinese Mainland
(February 21-March 17)

to defend Hubei and its capital city, to step up support to regions with insufficient capacity, and to make an all-out effort to ensure the safety of Beijing, the national capital. He required that the economic and social order be managed in parallel with the anti-epidemic endeavor, and called for an orderly return to normal work and daily life.

(2) February 21: Through its Joint Prevention and Control Mechanism, the State Council issued Guidelines on Covid-19 Prevention and Control Measures for Resumption of Work.

The NHC released Protocol on Prevention and Control of Novel Coronavirus Pneumonia (Edition 5).

(3) February 21: Most provinces and equivalent administrative units started to downgrade their public health emergency response level in light of the local situation, and gradually lifted traffic restrictions. By February

24, all provincial trunk highways had reopened, and order was restored to the transport networks with the exception of those in Hubei and Beijing.

(4) February 23: President Xi spoke to 170,000 officials nationwide by video link, at a meeting on coordinating epidemic control with economic and social development. He emphasized that this epidemic, given the speed and scope of its spread, represented the most challenging public health emergency in China since the founding of the People's Republic, and that it was both a serious crisis and a major test.

He acknowledged the arduous efforts of all involved, welcoming the fact that control measures were producing increasingly positive results, but noting that the overall situation remained complex and serious, and this stage would be crucial in curbing the spread. The people must maintain their faith in ultimate victory and make unremitting efforts in all of their prevention and control work. He encouraged the nation to turn pressure into strength and adversity into opportunities, and steadily resume normal work and daily life. He demanded a redoubled effort to stabilize the six fronts – employment, finance, foreign trade, inbound investment, domestic investment, and market expectations, called for stronger policies to unleash the full potential and maintain the strong momentum of China's development, and urged the nation to achieve the goals and tasks set for this year's economic and social development.

(5) February 24: The WHO-China Joint Mission on Covid-19 held a press conference in Beijing, during which team members agreed that China had achieved notable success in slowing the spread of the virus and blocking human-to-human transmission, at least delaying and possibly preventing hundreds of thousands of infections. "This approach, what we call an 'all-of-government, all-of-society' approach, very old-fashioned, too old in some ways, has probably, definitely reverted, and probably prevented at least tens of thousands, but probably hundreds of thousands of cases of Covid-19 in China".

By February 24, the daily number of new infections on the Chinese mainland had remained below 1,000 for five consecutive days, the number of existing confirmed cases had kept dropping for almost a week, and the daily figure for discharged patients was now equal to or had surpassed that of new infections in all provincial-level administrative units.

(6) February 25: China started to tighten up border quarantine, conducting a strict check of health and body temperature, and carrying out medical inspection, epidemiological investigation, medical screening, and sample monitoring of all inbound and outbound travelers, in order to minimize the cross-border spread of the epidemic.

(7) February 26: Xi Jinping chaired a meeting of the Standing Committee of the Political Bureau of the CPC Central Committee. He told the meeting that the national situation in epidemic control was turning for the better and economic and social development was quickly returning to normal, while Wuhan and Hubei as a whole still faced a grave and complex situation, and the possibility of an epidemic resurgence must not be overlooked in other regions.

He called for a greater effort to marshal the resources of the whole country to reinforce Wuhan and Hubei. He emphasized the need to make an accurate assessment of the epidemic dynamics and the conditions facing economic and social development, and focus on the main problems and the key elements of these problems, so as to ensure an overall victory in the battle against the virus, and achieve the goals of building a moderately prosperous society in all respects and of the country's poverty alleviation.

(8) February 27: The daily figure for new cases in Hubei other than Wuhan, and in other places on the mainland outside Hubei, both dropped to single digits for the first time.

(9) February 28: Through its Joint Prevention and Control Mechanism, the State Council released Notice on Furthering Differentiated, Region-specific and Tiered Prevention and Control Measures.

(10) February 29: The WHO-China Joint Mission on Covid-19 released a report about its field study trip in China. The report described China's control efforts. It said, "In the face of a previously unknown

virus, China has rolled out perhaps the most ambitious, agile and aggressive disease containment effort in history... As striking, has been the uncompromising rigor of strategy application that proved to be a hallmark in every setting and context where it was examined... Achieving China's exceptional coverage with and adherence to these containment measures has only been possible due to the deep commitment of the Chinese people to collective action in the face of this common threat. At a community level this is reflected in the remarkable solidarity of provinces and cities in support of the most vulnerable populations and communities."

(11) March 2: President Xi inspected several scientific institutions in Beijing, observing their research and development on Covid-19 prevention and control. He said that this work must be taken as a major and pressing task and proceed as speedily as possible, while abiding by the rules of science and ensuring safety, so as to provide strong scientific and technological support for overcoming the epidemic.

Xi Jinping pointed out that saving as many lives as possible, by every possible means, was the number one priority. Research on and development of medicines and medical equipment should be integrated with clinical treatment, with the twin goals of raising the cure rate and lowering the fatality rate. Development of vaccines should be expedited through multiple approaches, so as to make them available for clinical trial and application as quickly as possible.

The president said that biosecurity should be an important part of the holistic approach to national security, and he called for efforts to enhance China's scientific research capacity regarding epidemic prevention and control and public health.

(12) March 3: The NHC released Diagnosis and Treatment Protocol for Covid-19 (Trial Version 7), which made modifications in the determination of transmission routes and clinical symptoms, updated diagnostic criteria, and emphasized the integration of traditional Chinese medicine and Western medicine in treating the disease.

(13) March 4: Xi Jinping chaired a meeting of the Standing Commit-

tee of the Political Bureau of the CPC Central Committee. He emphasized the need to quickly bring order to economic and social development in the context of epidemic control, improve relevant measures, and consolidate and extend the country's hard-won progress. Wuhan and Hubei must continue their epidemic control, and continue the measures for preventing the virus from spreading within their local area or beyond.

(14) March 6: Xi Jinping attended a symposium on securing a decisive victory in poverty alleviation. He pointed out that the solemn pledge to lift all rural people living below current poverty line out of poverty by 2020 had been made by the CPC Central Committee to the whole nation, and it must be fulfilled on schedule. He called for greater determination and intensity in advancing poverty alleviation, and highlighted the need to offset the impact of the epidemic in order to clinch a complete victory over poverty – a cause of such tremendous importance to China and all of humanity.

(15) March 6: The daily increase in the number of domestic cases on the Chinese mainland dropped below 100, and fell further to single digits on March 11.

(16) March 7: The NHC released Protocol on Prevention and Control of Covid-19 (Edition 6).

(17) March 10: Xi Jinping went to Wuhan to inspect work on epidemic control. He acknowledged that the situation in Hubei and Wuhan was improving and that hard work had delivered important results, and pointed out that the task remained arduous. He encouraged the people to persevere in their efforts and win the battles against the virus in Hubei and Wuhan. He praised residents in Wuhan for considering the national interest and the general situation. They had proved themselves indomitable and resilient, and they had consciously subordinated their needs to the overall interests of epidemic control, joined the battle against the epidemic, and made a huge contribution.

He pointed out that there were two fronts in the battle against the epidemic: the hospital and the community – the life-saving front and the epidemic prevention and control front. Communities should play their key role in epidemic prevention and control, and every community should serve as a bastion of defense against the virus. He called for a general mobilization, putting in place a defense line across the whole of society and relying on the people to win the battle.

(18) March 11: WHO Director General Tedros Adhanom Ghebreyesus announced, "We have therefore made the assessment that Covid-19 can be characterized as a pandemic."

(19) March 11-17: The daily increase in the number of domestic cases on the Chinese mainland remained in single digits. The epidemic peak had passed in China as a whole, with the number of new cases steadily declining and the epidemic comfortably under control.

(20) March 17: Forty-two medical teams from around the country left Wuhan, having completed their mission there.

Stage IV: Wuhan and Hubei – An Initial Victory in a Critical Battle
(March 18-April 28, 2020)

By making critical advances in the city of Wuhan, the main battleground against the virus, China initially halted the spread of Covid-19 on the mainland. Restrictions on outbound traffic from Wuhan City and Hubei Province were lifted, and all Covid-19 patients in Wuhan hospitals were discharged. China won a critical battle in defending Wuhan and Hubei against Covid-19, which was a major step forward in the nation-wide virus control effort.

During this period, sporadic cases were reported, and more infections were caused by inbound arrivals carrying the virus which continued to spread overseas. In response to the evolving Covid-19 dynamics, the CPC Central Committee adopted an approach to prevent the coronavirus from entering the country and stem its domestic resurgence. Efforts were made to consolidate gains in virus control, promptly treat cluster cases, and get the country back to work sector by sector. Care and support were given to Chinese citizens abroad (see Chart 7).

(1) March 18: Xi Jinping chaired a meeting of the Standing Committee of the Political Bureau of the CPC Central Committee. He emphasized the need to take rigorous steps to stop inbound cases, so that hard-won gains in virus control would not be lost. He urged stronger measures to protect the health of Chinese citizens overseas.

(2) March 18: The State Council issued Decision on Implementation of Measures to Stabilize Employment by Offsetting the Impact of Covid-19.

(3) March 18: For the first time, no new domestic cases were confirmed on the Chinese mainland. By March 19, no new cases had been confirmed for seven days outside of Hubei Province.

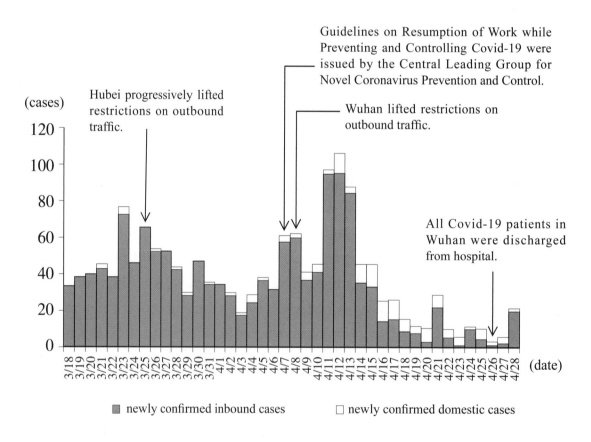

Chart 7. Daily Figure for Newly Confirmed Cases on the Chinese Mainland (March 18-April 28)

(4) March 25: Xi Jinping chaired a meeting of the Standing Committee of the Political Bureau of the CPC Central Committee to hear briefings about virus control and current economic conditions and discuss virus control measures and ways to sustain economic growth.

(5) March 25: Hubei lifted outbound traffic restrictions and removed all health checkpoints on highways across the province except in Wuhan. With the exception of Wuhan, work and life gradually returned to normal in the whole province, and people could now leave Hubei if they had a "green" health code to show that they were not infected.

(6) March 25: Confirmed inbound cases were reported in 23 provinces, signaling the need to curb the spread of the virus.

(7) March 26: President Xi attended the G20 Extraordinary Leaders' Summit on Covid-19 and delivered a speech titled "Working Together to Defeat the Covid-19 Outbreak".

(8) March 27: Xi Jinping chaired a meeting of the Political Bureau of the CPC Central Committee. He called for a timely improvement in China's Covid-19 control measures in response to changing Covid-19 dynamics, both domestic and globally, with a shift in focus to preventing inbound cases and domestic resurgence, so as to sustain the positive momentum in virus control.

He stressed the need to speedily resume work and normal life while continuing Covid-19 prevention and control, in order to minimize the losses caused by Covid-19 and fulfill the goals of economic and social development set for the year. Provided that prevention and control protocols were duly observed, support should be given to get Hubei back to work in an orderly manner, and help enterprises create jobs, keep their employees, and ensure their livelihoods.

(9) March 29-April 1: Xi Jinping made an inspection tour to Zhejiang Province to review its Covid-19 control and economic and social development.

He stressed that guarding against inbound infections should be the top priority for the country both now and in the foreseeable future and that control must be targeted and effective so as to build a strong line of defense against inbound cases.

He emphasized the need to remain sensitive to changes, respond to them with well-judged actions, be ready to adjust the approach when necessary, and identify and seize opportunities in the current crisis.

He urged a steady return to work in more sectors while strictly continuing virus control measures and resolving problems hindering the return to work, so as to restore the operation of complete industrial chains.

(10) April 1: Chinese customs began nucleic acid testing (NAT) on inbound arrivals at all points of entry – air, water and land.

(11) April 4: A nationwide ceremony was held on the traditional Tomb-sweeping Day to pay tribute to all those who had given their lives in fighting Covid-19, and others who had died of the novel coronavirus.

(12) April 6: Through its Joint Prevention and Control Mechanism, the State Council issued Notice on Prevention and Control Measures for Key Locations, Organizations and Population Groups, and Manual for Management of Asymptomatic Virus Carriers.

(13) April 7: The Central Leading Group for Novel Coronavirus Prevention and Control issued Guidelines on Resumption of Work while Preventing and Controlling Covid-19; and the State Council released Guidelines on Covid-19 Prevention and Control Measures for Localities at Different Risk Levels to Resume Work. Region-specific and tiered measures for Covid-19 control were adopted to pave the way for a return to normal work in different locations.

(14) April 8: Xi Jinping chaired a meeting of the Standing Committee of the Political Bureau of the CPC Central Committee. He reiterated the need to stay alert against potential risks and be prepared, both in thinking and action, to respond to long-term changes in the external environment.

He warned against any relaxation of the efforts to both stop inbound cases and forestall domestic resurgence of cases. Targeted measures should be taken to manage asymptomatic cases, build a strong line of defense and plug any loopholes that might cause a resurgence of the virus. Control at land and sea points of entry should be tightened to minimize domestic cases caused by inbound arrivals carrying the virus.

(15) April 8: Wuhan lifted its 76-day outbound traffic restrictions; and local work and daily life began to return to normal.

(16) April 10: The number of patients in severe or critical condition in Hubei dropped to double digits for the first time.

(17) April 14: Premier Li Keqiang delivered a speech at a special meeting attended by leaders of ASEAN nations, China, Japan, the Republic of Korea on fight against the novel coronavirus. He shared with these leaders China's experience in coordinating the fight against the virus with its efforts to continue economic and social development. He proposed to strengthen cooperation on the fight against the virus, on efforts to resume economic development, and on policy coordination among the participating countries.

(18) April 15: Xi Jinping chaired a meeting of the Standing Committee of the Political Bureau of the CPC Central Committee to hear briefings on virus control and current economic conditions, and discuss virus response measures and ways to sustain economic growth.

(19) April 17: Xi Jinping chaired a meeting of the Political Bureau of the CPC Central Committee. He called for full implementation of virus control measures to prevent both inbound cases and domestic resurgence and to build positive momentum in Covid-19 control.

He emphasized the need to follow the general principles of pursuing stable performance and making new progress, returning to work while continuing Covid-19 control, restoring economic and social order, fostering new growth areas, and actively promoting development.

(20) April 17: Wuhan City Novel Coronavirus Prevention and Control Command Center released Briefing on Modifying the Figures of Confirmed Covid-19 Cases and Fatalities in Wuhan. By midnight on April 16, the total number of confirmed cases in the city had been revised up by 325 to 50,333, and the number of deaths up by 1,290 to 3,869.

(21) April 20-23: Xi Jinping made an inspection tour to Shaanxi Province. He urged local officials to pursue steady performance, make new progress, and act according to the new development philosophy. He called on them to carry out the following tasks: stabilizing employment, finance, foreign trade, inbound investment, domestic investment, and market expectations, and guaranteeing jobs, daily living needs, food and energy, industrial and supply chains, the interests of market players, and the smooth functioning of grassroots government. By so doing, China could offset the adverse impact of Covid-19 and fulfill the goals of eliminating poverty and achieving moderate prosperity.

(22) April 23: Premier Li Keqiang chaired a video conference on the economic situation in some provinces and cities in order to promote economic and social development in these regions.

(23) April 26: The last hospitalized Covid-19 patient in Wuhan was discharged.

(24) April 27: Xi Jinping chaired the 13th meeting of the Commission for Further Reform under the CPC Central Committee. He pointed out that the CPC leadership and China's socialist system had played a critical role in Covid-19 control and the resumption of business activities in China. As the environment for development became more complicated, China should be more resolute in furthering reform and improving its governing systems, and it should fully leverage its strengths to deal with risks and challenges.

(25) April 27: The Central Steering Group returned to Beijing from Hubei.

Stage V: Ongoing Prevention and Control
(Since April 29, 2020)

Sporadic cases have been reported on the mainland, resulting in case clusters in some locations. Inbound cases are generally under control. The positive momentum in Covid-19 control has thus been locked in, and nationwide virus control is now being conducted on an ongoing basis. China has made vigorous efforts to resume work and reopen schools. The ongoing control measures passed the test of the travel peak during the May Day holiday.

With the approval of the CPC Central Committee, an inter-departmental contact group under the Joint Prevention and Control Mechanism of the State Council was dispatched to Hubei to oversee local virus control.

(1) April 29: Xi Jinping chaired a meeting of the Standing Committee of the Political Bureau of the CPC Central Committee. He concluded that thanks to arduous efforts, China had won a vital battle in defending Wuhan and Hubei against the novel coronavirus, and achieved a major strategic success in the nationwide control efforts. At the same time, he emphasized that virus control should continue in key regions and target key groups, with a focus on inbound cases.

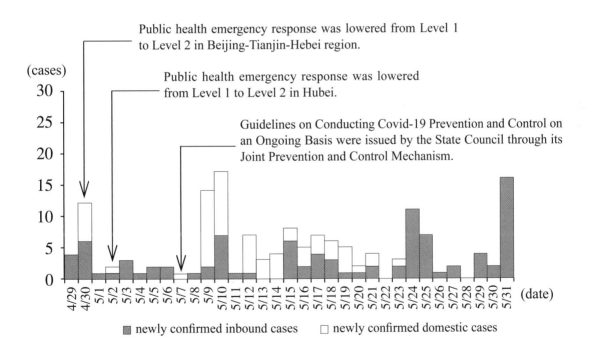

Chart 8. Daily Figure for Newly Confirmed Cases on the Chinese Mainland (April 29-May 31)

(2) April 30: The public health emergency response was lowered to Level 2 in the Beijing-Tianjin-Hebei region.

(3) May 1: The WHO announced that given the current international Covid-19 dynamics, the novel coronavirus still remained a "public health emergency of international concern".

(4) May 2: The public health emergency response was lowered to Level 2 in Hubei.

(5) May 4: An inter-departmental contact group under the Joint Prevention and Control Mechanism of the State Council was dispatched to Wuhan with the approval of the CPC Central Committee.

(6) May 6: Xi Jinping chaired a meeting of the Standing Committee of the Political Bureau of the CPC Central Committee. He pointed out that under the strong leadership of the Central Committee and with the support of all the people, the Central Steering Group had been working with the people of Wuhan and other parts of Hubei Province. They had done their utmost in the fight to curb the spread of the virus and erected a first line of defense for the nation, making a significant contribution to beating the virus.

He said the contact group should guide and support follow-up work in Wuhan and other parts of Hubei and advise on the rehabilitation and psychological counseling of patients in recovery, to ensure that the gains would be consolidated.

(7) May 7: Through the Joint Prevention and Control Mechanism, the State Council released Guidelines on Conducting Covid-19 Prevention and Control on an Ongoing Basis.

(8) May 8: The CPC Central Committee held a meeting to hear the views and proposals from the central committees of China's eight other political parties, representatives of the All-China Federation of Industry and Commerce, and prominent figures without party affiliation. General Secretary Xi chaired and addressed the meeting.

He said that when the novel coronavirus struck, catching the country unawares, the CPC Central Committee gave its full attention to the matter. Putting people's lives and health first, it swiftly adopted a series of policies on prevention and control of the virus and treatment of the infected. It took the country over a month to achieve initial success in curbing the spread of the virus, about two months to bring the daily figure of new domestic cases on the mainland down to single digits, and three months to win a decisive victory in defending Wuhan City and Hubei Province. For China, with a large population of 1.4 billion, this achievement did not come easily.

(9) May 11-12: Xi Jinping made an inspection tour to Shanxi Province to be briefed on what had been done in the province to conduct Covid-19 prevention and control on an ongoing basis while promoting economic and social development, and to consolidate gains in poverty alleviation.

He urged local officials to act according to the new development philosophy for making steady progress, and carry out supply-side structural reform. They were required to stabilize the six fronts (employment, finance, foreign trade, inbound investment, domestic investment, and market expectations), and guarantee the six priorities (jobs, daily living needs, food and energy, industrial and supply chains, the interests of market players, and the smooth functioning of grassroots government).

He called on local officials to overcome the adverse impact of the virus, accelerate high-quality economic transformation, and meet the goals of eliminating poverty and achieving moderate prosperity in all respects.

(10) May 14: Xi Jinping chaired a meeting of the Standing Committee of the Political Bureau of the CPC Central Committee. He urged that Covid-19 control be strengthened in key areas and key places to prevent its resurgence, and that targeted measures be taken where case clusters had recently occurred. Flexible and effective measures should be adopted to respond to evolving Covid-19 dynamics overseas, and key sectors and weak links in the prevention of inbound infection should be shored up.

(11) May 15: Xi Jinping chaired a meeting of the Political Bureau of the CPC Central Committee to discuss the draft Report on the Work of the

Government, which the State Council would submit to the forthcoming Third Session of the 13th National People's Congress for deliberation.

He pointed out that to fulfill the tasks of the year, the nation must carry out Covid-19 prevention and control as well as promoting economic and social development to reach the goal of achieving moderate prosperity in all respects.

He said that while conducting control on an ongoing basis, the country should continue to deliver steady performance, act according to the new development philosophy, conduct supply-side structural reform, promote high-quality development through further reform and opening up, and continue the three critical battles against poverty, pollution and major risks. There should be solid progress in stabilizing the six fronts and guaranteeing the six priorities. Domestic consumption must be expanded, and economic development and social stability must be maintained, so as to fulfill the goals of eliminating poverty and achieving moderate prosperity in all respects.

(12) May 18: President Xi delivered a speech titled "Fighting Covid-19 through Solidarity and Cooperation, Building a Global Community of Health for All" at the opening of the 73rd World Health Assembly.

(13) May 21-27: The Third Session of the 13th National Committee of the Chinese People's Political Consultative Conference was held in Beijing. May 22-28: The Third Session of the 13th National People's Congress was held in Beijing.

II. Well-Coordinated Prevention, Control and Treatment

The coronavirus caught China unawares. Putting people's lives and health first, the Chinese government has acted swiftly to fight the virus and provide medical treatment for patients. It has adopted the most thorough, rigorous and comprehensive prevention and control measures, enforced quarantine and isolation on a scale never seen before, and mobilized medical resources across the country. It has ensured that all those in need have been tested, quarantined, hospitalized or treated. With these measures in place, China has prevented a wider spread and further development of the virus. "The time that can be gained through the full application of these measures [in China] – even if just days or weeks – can be invaluable in ultimately reducing Covid-19 illness and deaths," says Report of the WHO-China Joint Mission on Coronavirus Disease 2019 (Covid-19) published on February 28, 2020.[1]

1. Centralized and Efficient Command

Under the strong leadership of the CPC Central Committee with Xi Jinping at its core, China has put in place an efficient system under which the central authorities exercise overall command, while local authorities and all sectors follow the leadership and instructions of the cen-

---

[1] Report of the WHO-China Joint Mission on Coronavirus Disease 2019 (Covid-19), February 28, 2020.
http://www.who.int/publications-detail/report-of-the-who-china-joint-mission-on-coronavirus-disease-2019-(covid-19).

tral authorities, perform their respective duties, and cooperate with each other. This highly efficient system has made it possible for China to win its all-out people's war against the virus.

General Secretary Xi Jinping takes charge of Covid-19 response. Attaching high importance to Covid-19 prevention and control, Xi Jinping assumed full command over the control efforts from the very beginning. He highlighted the need to put people's lives and health first, to firm up confidence, strengthen solidarity, adopt a science-based approach, and take targeted measures. He called for a nationwide effort to block the spread of the virus and defeat it.

Xi Jinping has chaired 14 meetings of the Standing Committee of the Political Bureau of the CPC Central Committee, 4 meetings of the Political Bureau, meetings of the Central Commission for Law-based Governance, Central Cyberspace Affairs Commission, Central Commission for Further Reform, and Central Commission for Foreign Affairs, and a meeting with prominent non-CPC figures. At these meetings, he heard briefings from the Central Leading Group for Novel Coronavirus Prevention and Control and the Central Steering Group, adjusted response measures in view of the evolving Covid-19 dynamics, and made decisions on overall plans for strengthening control efforts and international cooperation.

He inspected community response and Covid-19 research in Beijing, and visited Wuhan to guide frontline response. He made inspection tours to Zhejiang, Shaanxi and Shanxi provinces where he was briefed on progress in coordinating epidemic prevention and control with economic and social development, and in poverty alleviation. He has closely followed developments in China's virus control and made timely decisions accordingly.

Government departments have made well-coordinated control efforts. Premier Li Keqiang, as head of the Central Leading Group for Novel Coronavirus Prevention and Control, has chaired more than 30 meetings of the leading group to discuss key issues concerning Covid-19 control and economic and social development, and important decisions were made at the meetings. He visited Wuhan and inspected China CDC, the Institute of Pathogen Biology CAMS & PUMC, Beijing West Railway Station, Beijing Capital International Airport, and the National Distribution Center for Major Anti-epidemic Medical Supplies.

The Central Steering Group responded swiftly to guide Hubei Province and Wuhan City to intensify their control efforts. It thus helped contain the virus and hold a strong first line of defense against the virus.

The Joint Prevention and Control Mechanism of the State Council has played the coordinating role and held regular meetings to keep abreast of the situation, dispatch medical teams, and allocate supplies, and it has made timely adjustments to control policies and priorities in response to new developments. Through its mechanism for promoting the return to work, the State Council has strengthened guidance and coordination, removed barriers in the industrial and supply chains, and ensured the resumption of normal daily life.

Local authorities and other stakeholders have lived up to their responsibilities. Emergency command mechanisms headed by leading Party and government officials were established in provinces, cities and counties across the country, forming a top-down system with unified command, frontline guidance, and coordination between departments and among provinces. Local authorities and other stakeholders have implemented each and every one of the decisions, plans and prohibitions of the central authorities, and strictly and effectively enforced all response measures. Thus, an effective and well-functioning whole-of-the-nation control mechanism is in place.

2. A Tight Prevention and Control System Involving All Sectors of Society

The Chinese New Year is marked by enormous population flows in dense groups. In view of this fact, the Chinese government quickly mobilized the whole of society and galvanized the people into a nationwide response. A targeted, law- and science-based approach was adopted, and public health emergency response measures were rolled out on an unprecedented and extensive scale across the country. Through the strictest social distancing and flexible, people-centered social management, China put in place a prevention and control system involving governments at all levels and the whole of society, and launched a people's war on the virus applying non-medical means that has effectively blocked its transmission routes.

Strong measures were taken to control sources of infection. The Chinese government defined a set of requirements: early detection, reporting, quarantine and treatment with a focus on the four categories of vulnerable people (confirmed cases, suspected cases, febrile patients who might be carriers, and close contacts). It had also taken measures to ensure that they were hospitalized, treated, tested or quarantined as appropriate. It has done everything in its power to reduce infections to the minimum.

While keeping all its outbound routes closed, Wuhan carried out two rounds of community-based mass screening of its 4.21 million households, leaving no person or household unchecked and ruling out all potential sources of infection.

The Chinese government redoubled efforts to increase the capacity of nucleic acid testing, supply more test kits, and approve more testing institutions. As a result, the testing period was shortened and the quality enhanced, ensuring that all those in need could be tested immediately and as appropriate. In Hubei Province, the testing period was shortened from 2 days to 4-6 hours, and the daily capacity expanded from 300 samples in the early stage of the epidemic to more than 50,000 in mid-April. Such advances made early detection and confirmation of infection possible and reduced the risk of transmission.

To identify the four categories of vulnerable people, community grid-based screening was carried out across the country. All residents were requested to report their health condition on a daily basis. Community workers for their part visited households door-to-door to collect and verify this information. Temperature checking was made a routine at all places. Work was done to strengthen the monitoring and online reporting of cases identified at fever clinics of medical facilities – all such cases had to be reported online to higher authorities within 2 hours; their test results sent back to the reporting clinics within 12 hours; and on-site epidemiological investigation completed within 24 hours – so that confirmed cases and asymptomatic carriers would be identified and reported without delay. Epidemiological tracing and investigation was enhanced to precisely detect and cut off virus transmission routes. As of May 31, a total of more than 740,000 close contacts had been traced and handled as appropriate.

Breaking the chains of transmission through early intervention. The strictest closure and traffic restrictions were enforced on all outbound routes from Wuhan and Hubei. International passenger flights, and ferries and long-distance passenger transport services in many parts of the province were suspended, as were road and waterway passenger services bound for Wuhan from other places of the country. Airports and railway stations were closed and intra-city public transport halted in Wuhan and many other parts of Hubei. All these restrictions effectively stopped the virus from spreading nationwide, especially in rural Hubei where public health infrastructure was relatively weak.

Areas outside Hubei took a differentiated approach to traffic control. The provinces abutting Hubei built traffic control "isolation zones" around the province, preventing the virus from spreading beyond Hubei. Other parts of China adopted a targeted, tiered, and region-specific approach. They exercised a dynamic control over urban and rural road transport services and strengthened health and quarantine measures for domestic routes.

Rigorous measures were taken to prevent public gatherings and cross-infection. The Chinese New Year holiday was extended, public gatherings were canceled or postponed, and the spring semester was postponed in schools. Cinemas, theaters, internet cafés, and gyms were all closed. Strict procedures had to be followed in essential public facilities, including bus stations, airports, ports, farmers markets, shopping malls, supermarkets, restaurants and hotels, and in enclosed transport vehicles such as buses, trains and planes. All persons were required to wear masks and undergo temperature monitoring when accessing these venues or vehicles. In addition, all such facilities had to be disinfected, meet certain hygiene standards, ensure good ventilation, monitor visitors' temperature, and control the number of passengers or visitors at a given period of time.

Government services were provided online and through prior reservation, non-physical-contact delivery or services were extended, people were encouraged to stay at home and work from home, and businesses were encouraged to telecommute – all these measures effectively reduced population flows and public gatherings. Clear signs urging people to maintain at least one meter of distance and avoid close contact could be seen in all public places.

Strict health and quarantine measures were enforced at points of entry and exit across China to prevent inbound and outbound spread of the virus. The strictest-ever measures were applied at border control to suspend non-urgent and nonessential outbound travel by Chinese citizens.

The community-based line of defense was well guarded. Communities and villages made up the first line of defense in epidemic prevention and control, a major barrier to inbound cases and local transmission. They served as the mainstay in China's Covid-19 response. Residents and villagers were mobilized to help manage communities. Strict access control and grid-based management were exercised in communities, and human and material resources were channeled down to the community level to reinforce implementation of targeted measures. Task forces comprising both full-time and part-time community workers were set up, while officials at the sub-district/township and community/village levels, health workers of community medical facilities, and family doctors all performed their duties as a team. Through all these efforts, communities and villages were turned into strongholds, securing full implementation of response measures down to the lowest level.

To deal with the four categories of vulnerable people, a number of measures were taken in accordance with the law, such as tracing, registering, and visiting each individual, placing them under community management, and transferring them, if necessary, to designated medical facilities for quarantine or treatment as per due procedures. Community actions were taken to keep local areas in good condition and promote health education.

In Wuhan, rigorous 24-hour access control was enforced in all residential communities. No residents were allowed to leave and no non-residents allowed to access the community area other than for essential medical needs or epidemic control operations. Community workers were responsible for the purchase and delivery of daily necessities according to residents' needs. This approach was also applied in communities and villages in other parts of China, where all residents had to register and undergo temperature checking when leaving or entering the residential area or village.

Education programs were conducted to raise public awareness of the need for personal protection and enhance the sense of social responsibility. People observed self-quarantine at home and 14-day self-isolation after cross-region travel. They strictly followed personal protection measures such as wearing a mask when going out, maintaining proper social distancing, avoiding crowds, frequent handwashing, and regular ventilation. The tradition of the Patriotic Public Health Campaign which was initiated in the 1950s, with an emphasis on sanitation and personal hygiene, was also encouraged, along with a healthy, environment-friendly lifestyle .

A multi-level, category-specific, dynamic and targeted approach was adopted. China also applied a region-specific, multi-level approach to epidemic prevention and control. To better prevent and control the epidemic, each region at or above the county level was classified by risk level on the basis of a comprehensive evaluation of factors such as population and number of infections in a given period of time. There are three levels of risk: low, medium, and high. Regions could take measures according to the risk level, which was dynamic and adjusted in light of the evolving situation.

In response to Covid-19, a low-risk region was requested to remain vigilant against any potential inbound transmission while fully restoring normal order in work and daily life; a medium-risk region had to prevent inbound and local transmission while restoring normal work and daily life as soon as possible; and a region classified as high-risk was obliged to prevent any spread in its jurisdiction or beyond, enforce strict control measures, and focus on containment. Once the situation stabilized, provincial-level authorities could step up efforts to restore order in work and daily life in areas under their jurisdiction, while adapting to the new normal of Covid-19 control by establishing a sound long-term epidemic response system that ensures early detection, quick response, targeted prevention and control, and effective treatment. Every effort has been made to stem the virus spread in the capital of Beijing to safeguard public health.

Appropriate measures were implemented to prevent any cluster outbreaks in key locations, major organizations, and priority population groups, and manage the aftermath of any such outbreaks. The elderly, children, pregnant women, students, and health workers were to be well protected as a priority.

Health management of priority population groups was enhanced. Protective measures were intensified in medical facilities, communities, office buildings, shopping malls and supermarkets, passenger terminals, transport vehicles, child-care centers and kindergartens, elementary and secondary schools, colleges and universities, nursing homes, charity houses, mental health institutions, and first-aid stations. These measures were implemented nationwide, covering all population groups, locations, and communities, and leaving no areas unattended and no hidden dangers unaddressed.

To control any inbound infections from overseas, China has strictly enforced its border health and quarantine rules to ensure a full, closed cycle of management of all arrivals, from their entry at the border to the doorstep of where they would stay. Sustained, meticulous efforts have been made to prevent both inbound cases and a recurrence in domestic cases.

Legal safeguards for epidemic prevention and control were strengthened. China listed Covid-19 as a Class B infectious disease, but addressed it with measures applicable to a Class A infectious disease under the Law of the People's Republic of China on Prevention and Treatment of Infectious Diseases. It also applied control and quarantine measures under the Frontier Health and Quarantine Law of the People's Republic of China consistent with relevant provisions of international law and other domestic laws. Standing committees of some sub-national people's congresses launched emergency legislation procedures as per the national legal framework, empowering local governments to introduce interim emergency administrative rules relating to healthcare and epidemic control.

The Law on Prevention and Treatment of Infectious Diseases and measures for its implementation have been strictly enforced, and guidelines have been promulgated on controlling the disease, combating epidemic-related crimes in accordance with the law, and protecting people's lives and health. Law and order, and market supervision have been strengthened. Price gouging, hoarding and profiteering, production and sales of counterfeit or sub-standard products, and any other crimes impeding response efforts have been punished by law. Quality and price control of anti-epidemic supplies has been reinforced, and stronger measures have been taken against deceptive and illegal advertising, ensuring social order and stability. Supervision on administrative law enforcement has been intensified during epidemic control to ensure that the law is enforced in a strict, impartial, procedure-based, and non-abusive way. Legal disputes associated with the epidemic have been resolved in accordance with the law, and legal guarantees and services have been provided for Covid-19 response and for businesses returning to work. The government has also made greater efforts to raise public legal awareness and guide people to act within the parameters of the law.

Prevention and control efforts have been based on science. Covid-19 is a new virus and it will take time for humanity to understand it completely. In its quest for victory over the coronavirus, China has been mapping its own route to success – one based on reliable experience, tailored to its national conditions, and rooted in sound epidemiological practice.

China values the role of experts in virology, epidemiology, clinical medicine and related fields. China's response has been professional because its response measures were based on timely analyses and assessments by scientists and public health experts, whose views and proposals were fully respected.

China has given full support to factual and scientific research on virus infection, pathogenesis, transmission routes and transmissibility while maintaining exchanges and communication with the WHO and other countries and regions.

With a growing body of knowledge of the virus, China has modified and optimized its response measures in a timely manner to make them more effective. It has developed a Covid-19 prevention and control protocol and updated it five times based on assessments of the evolving epidemic dynamics. The protocol provides a set of reliable standards for case monitoring, epidemiological investigation, management of close contacts and of those suspected of exposure to infection, and procedure-based tests in laboratories. China has also published 15 technical manuals on epidemic prevention and control for key population groups, locations and organizations, 6 work plans on psychological counseling for people affected by Covid-19, and 50 specific technical guidelines. All of this has ensured that China's prevention and control efforts are more targeted and science-based.

3. An All-Out Effort to Treat Patients and Save Lives

From the outset, China's goal in its medical response to Covid-19 has been to improve the patient admission and cure rates and reduce the infection and fatality rates. The infected were treated in dedicated medical facilities where medical specialists from all over the country and all the necessary medical resources were concentrated. Both traditional Chinese medicine and Western medicine were applied. A condition-specific and category-based approach was applied to medical treatment of patients. Severe cases were treated by the best doctors using the most advanced equipment, and critical supplies were pooled to save lives at all costs. It is through such efforts that the Covid-19 fatality rate in China has dropped sharply. Early medical intervention has made it possible to have patients with mild symptoms cured without delay, thus significantly reducing the risk that their condition might worsen.

Pooling premium resources to treat severe cases. The sudden appearance of Covid-19 in Wuhan put an overwhelming strain on its medical resources. There was a severe shortage of hospital beds in the early stage as the number of infections surged. By directing resources to Wuhan, China expanded the capacity of designated hospitals to deal with severe cases and increased the number of beds. Patients in severe and critical condition were gathered for treatment and intensive care at the best hospitals with the greatest capacity for accommodating patients with infectious respiratory diseases. Two hospitals with 1,000-plus beds each – Huoshenshan and Leishenshan – were built as specialist hospitals for treating infectious diseases, and a number of designated and general hospitals were expanded or remodeled. The number of beds for severe cases quickly increased from around 1,000 to more than 9,100. Hospitals were able to admit large numbers of patients who were seriously ill.

The treatment strategy for severe cases was improved, and tailored treatment provided to individual patients. Inspection teams consisting of top experts were organized to regularly inspect Wuhan's designated hospitals and evaluate patients in critical condition and their therapeutic regimen. For those with serious underlying medical conditions, who accounted for more than 80 percent of all severe cases, case-by-case treatment was prescribed after consultation with a multidisciplinary team consisting of experts on infection, respiratory diseases, heart and kidney diseases, and intensive care. In addition, a set of standards were formulated for nursing patients in severe and critical condition, and such measures as high-flow nasal cannula oxygen therapy, non-invasive and invasive mechanical ventilation, and ventilation in a prone position were adopted. Expert consultation on complex, severe and critical cases, and fatal cases, and other core medical security systems were strictly implemented. Those who have been cured and discharged from hospital have received rigorous health monitoring, and patients in severe condition have been given quality medical treatment.

The plasma of convalescent Covid-19 patients has been collected to set up an emergency plasma reserve, and convalescent plasma therapy has been applied in clinical treatment. As of May 31, convalescent plasma had been collected from 2,765 recovered patients, and 1,689 patients had been treated with the therapy, with positive results.

Early intervention for patients with mild symptoms. China has been quick to have patients with mild symptoms admitted to designated medical facilities for early medical intervention, and has done its best to prevent mild cases from worsening. The national clinical treatment network has been expanded to include more than 10,000 hospitals dedicated to the treatment of Covid-19 patients. A national network of medical treatment coordination has also been formed to provide technical support through online consultation.

In Wuhan, faced with surging infections and considering that 80 percent of cases were mild, the city government mobilized resources to repurpose stadiums and exhibition centers into 16 temporary treatment centers. With some 14,000 beds, these centers were able to admit all confirmed mild cases for treatment. This helped to reduce infections and virus transmission in communities and prevent mild cases from worsening. The

16 treatment centers received a total of more than 12,000 patients; 8,000 and more were cured and discharged; and more than 3,500 were transferred to hospitals. While in service, these facilities had zero cases of infection, death, or relapse.

Temporary treatment centers, or Fangcang shelter hospitals, are a major innovative solution that provided enough beds to admit all confirmed cases, thus turning the tide in the battle against Covid-19. An article in *The Lancet* wrote, "To relieve the huge pressure on the healthcare system, Fangcang shelter hospitals have also been crucial."[1]

Reviewing diagnostic and therapeutic plans and applying effective ones on a broad scale. China's diagnostic and therapeutic plans for Covid-19 have been developed and improved through clinical practice, medical research, experimentation and regular reviews. Based on scientific knowledge and accumulated evidence, R&D results and the diagnostic and therapeutic regimens that proved effective were incorporated in the national diagnosis and treatment plans. These include seven versions of the diagnosis and treatment protocol, three editions of the protocol for severe and critical cases, two editions of the manual for mild case management, two editions of convalescent plasma therapy treatment protocol, and one rehabilitation treatment program for patients discharged from hospitals. All these protocols and plans have contributed to science-based treatment of patients and the establishment of standards for medical treatment.

In Diagnosis and Treatment Protocol for Covid-19 (Trial Version 7), information on pathological changes, clinical symptoms, criteria for diagnosis, therapies, and criteria for patient discharge was added or updated. The protocol states that asymptomatic cases may be contagious. It also notes that plasma from convalescent cases may work in treating the infected. This edition has been adopted or used for reference in a number of countries.

---

[1] *The Lancet*: "Sustaining Containment of COVID-19 in China", April 18, 2020.
https://www.thelancet.com/journals/lancet/article/PIIS0140-6736(20)30864-3/fulltext.

Concerning discharged patients, quarantining, monitoring of their health and rehabilitation, and reexamination and re-testing have all been strengthened. Integrated medical services covering treatment, rehabilitation and health monitoring have been put in place. Differentiated treatment approaches have been adopted for children and pregnant women, among other groups.

Leveraging the unique strength of traditional Chinese medicine (TCM). Both TCM and Western medicine were used and traditional Chinese and Western drugs administered. China has leveraged the unique strength of TCM in preemptive prevention, differentiated medication, and multi-targeted intervention, and at every step of Covid-19 treatment and control. The etiology and pathogen of the disease were analyzed and confirmed through TCM methodology, as were the principles and methods of treatment. A set of TCM diagnosis and treatment protocols were developed to cover the entire process of medical observation, treatment of mild, moderate, severe, and critical cases, and recovery, and they have been applied nationwide.

TCM hospitals were used in the treatment of Covid-19 patients, and TCM teams took charge of and ran some wards for patients in severe condition at designated hospitals and some treatment centers. All the other shelter hospitals had resident TCM experts. TCM has played its part in the entire process of Covid-19 response, from early intervention to administering case-specific treatment. TCM drugs and treatment methods were used for early intervention and treatment of patients with mild symptoms; for patients with severe symptoms they were used in combination with Western medicine; for those under medical observation for fever and those who had been in close contact with confirmed cases they served to improve immunity; they helped to strengthen the constitution of those who had recovered. A national TCM coordination network was formed to offer guidance to patients recovering from the disease.

Chinese herbal formulas and drugs were administered to 92 percent of all confirmed cases. In Hubei Province, more than 90 percent of confirmed cases received TCM treatment that proved effective. Jinhua Qing-gan Granules, Lianhua Qingwen Capsules/Granules, Xuebijing Injection, Lung Cleansing and Detoxifying Preparation, Dampness Resolving and Detoxifying Preparation, Lung Diffusing and Detoxifying Preparation, and other TCM drugs and herbal formulas have proved effective in treating different types of Covid-19 patients. They have significantly reduced the incidence rate, prevented cases with mild symptoms from worsening, increased the cure rate, lowered the fatality rate, helped nucleic acid turn negative, and sped up the rehabilitation of recovered Covid-19 patients.

Providing free treatment for patients. Government funds for Covid-19 control were made available in advance to ensure that patients could receive timely treatment and local authorities could proceed smoothly with measures for medical treatment and epidemic control. As of May 31, a total of RMB162.4 billion had been allocated by governments of all levels to fight the virus.

Policies for medical insurance were quickly adjusted, with clear provisions for confirmed or suspected Covid-19 patients. They could get treatment with delayed settlement of accounts. All Covid-19 patients, confirmed or suspected, received subsidies from state finance for any medical bills not covered by basic medical insurance, serious disease insurance, or the medical assistance fund. In the case of patients receiving treatment in places where they were not registered for basic medical insurance, their medical bills related to Covid-19 were paid by the local insurance fund first and settled later.

As of May 31, the medical bills of 58,000 inpatients with confirmed infections had been settled by basic medical insurance, with a total expenditure of RMB1.35 billion, or RMB23,000 per person. The average cost for treating Covid-19 patients in severe condition surpassed RMB150,000, and in some critical cases the individual cost exceeded RMB1 million, all covered by the state.

Strengthening infection control at medical institutions and ensuring personal protection for health workers. A set of technical manuals and normative documents on infection control were developed to regulate the layout of key areas in medical institutions and the consultation and treatment process, including clean zones, partially contaminated zones, contaminated zones, and separate passages for medical staff and patients. Health workers received training in workplace infection control, and nationwide supervision was strengthened to ensure control measures were implemented to the letter. Targeted guidance was given to the hardest-hit areas, hospitals at a higher risk of infection among staff, and areas and hospitals under the greatest pressure in treating patients. A major effort was put into the sorting, collection, storage and removal of medical waste, and the treatment of the remains of the deceased.

All emergency medical teams coming to Wuhan and Hubei from other parts of China had at least one infection control expert. Thanks to this arrangement, there have been no cases of infection in the teams. Since February there has been a sharp drop in the number of reported infections among medical staff nationwide. Health workers have been cared for and their needs attended to. A series of policies and measures have been introduced to ensure their wellbeing, such as psychological counseling and staff rotation, to ease their physical and psychological stress, help them stay healthy, and allow them to continue the fight on the front line.

4. China Has Released Information in an Open and Transparent Manner as Required by Law

While making an all-out effort to contain the virus, China has also acted with a keen sense of responsibility to humanity, its people, posterity, and the international community. It has provided information on Covid-19 in a thoroughly professional and efficient way. It has released authoritative and detailed information as early as possible on a regular basis, thus effectively responding to public concern and building public consensus. Its experience is something other countries can draw on in their fight against the virus.

A strict system of information release has been established. China has released information on Covid-19 in a timely, open and transparent manner as required by law. Strict regulations are in place to see there is no withholding of information, underreporting, or delay in reporting cases of infection. On December 31, 2019, the Wuhan government began to release coronavirus information in accordance with the law, and gradually increased the frequency of release. Since January 21, 2020, the NHC has provided daily updates on nationwide cases on its official website and social media platform, and provincial health departments have done the same on local cases. Starting from February 3, the NHC has released the information simultaneously on its English-language website.

A tiered news release mechanism has been formed. At both national and local levels, a tiered information release mechanism has been formed to circulate authoritative information through various channels and platforms, both onsite and online, in order to address domestic and international concerns on virus control, medical treatment, and scientific research. By May 31, the Joint Prevention and Control Mechanism and the Information Office of the State Council had held 161 press conferences during which officials from more than 50 government departments appeared over 490 times and answered more than 1,400 questions from Chinese and foreign media. One hundred and three press conferences had been held in Hubei and 1,050 in the other provinces.

Covid-19 statistics have been updated in accordance with the law. In the early stage of Covid-19 control, there were late, incomplete and erroneous reports of Covid-19 cases in Wuhan due to unverified deaths at home, inadequate hospital capacity, hospitals being overwhelmed, and incomplete recording of deaths. After the domestic spread of Covid-19 had been brought under control, the city updated the number of confirmed cases and deaths based on big data application and an epidemiological investigation to ensure accuracy of the data, and released the results in an open and transparent manner in accordance with the law.

Covid-19-related information is provided through various channels and platforms. The NHC's official Chinese and English websites and its social media platform have special sections where Covid-19-related information is released on a daily basis, including information on relevant policies, progress in China's containment efforts, updates on disease prevention and control, and clarifications that refute rumors. Information on local Covid-19 control has been promptly released on government websites and social media platforms of all provinces. To disseminate knowledge about its Covid-19 response, China has released relevant information through platforms for popularizing science, and through the media and the internet. Leading medical experts have offered advice on routine self-protection to help the public see Covid-19 in a rational way and forestall panic. The media has expanded public outreach and sent a positive message in combating the virus, and public opinion has played its role of oversight to help solve problems affecting virus control.

5. Science and Technology Underpin China's Efforts

Science and technology are the sharp blade that humanity wields in the battle against disease. Such battles could not have been won without scientific advances and technological innovation. Confronted by Covid-19, a previously unknown virus, China has exploited the pioneering role of science and technology and fully applied the results of scientific and technical innovation in recent years. Top scientific research resources have gathered from around the nation to support virus control. Focusing on the main battlefield of Wuhan and coordinating efforts in the most severely-affected areas and across the rest of the country, China pinpointed key R&D areas for different stages of virus control. The close coordination between scientific research, clinical application, and frontline virus control, and between enterprises, universities, and research institutes, has given powerful support for the war against the virus.

Key progress has been made in scientific research. Following the principles of safety, effectiveness and availability, China has accelerated the R&D and application of medicines, vaccines, and new test kits. To meet the urgent needs of frontline virus control, and to ensure traceability of infection sources, diagnosis and treatment of patients, and prevention and control of infections, China has pooled resources from enterprises, universities, and research institutes, directing them to focus on five areas – clinical treatment, new medicines and vaccines, testing techniques and products, viral etiology and epidemiology, and animal model construction. Top research resources from around the nation have been galvanized to work on these tasks in pursuit of early results and application. A total of 83 emergency R&D programs have been initiated. Vaccines are being developed in five categories – inactivated vaccines, recombinant protein vaccines, live attenuated influenza vaccines, adenovirus vaccines, and nucleic acid-based vaccines. To date, four inactivated vaccines and one adenovirus vaccine have been approved for clinical trials. While scientists in China and abroad have kept up with mutual developments, China leads the world in the development of certain types of vaccines. Research teams have also been assembled to trace the origin of Covid-19.

Scientific R&D has been integrated with clinical treatment and epidemic control. Having promptly developed nucleic acid test kits, China has also introduced a range of high-sensitivity, easy-to-use test equipment and reagents. Its R&D of reagents covers nucleic acid testing, gene testing, and immunological testing.

Putting existing medicines to new use, China has searched for effective medicines and new therapies, and summarized clinical experience based on rigorous in vitro experiments and pathogenic research. Ten types of medicine, including chloroquine phosphate, tocilizumab, finished TCM drugs, and herbal preparations, as well as convalescent plasma therapy, have been adopted in treatment plans. Approval for clinical trial has been given to four medicines, and guidelines formed or expert consensus reached in five areas. Clinical treatments have been trialed, and diagnosis and treatment methods and medicines that have proven clinically effective have been rolled out at a faster pace. Biosecurity has been strengthened at laboratories, as has the management of blood samples for Covid-19 testing and biological samples for laboratory testing.

Big data and artificial intelligence have been used in epidemic control. China has fully utilized big data, artificial intelligence, and other new technologies in research and analysis to forecast the trend of Covid-19 developments. These tools have also been exhaustively applied in epidemiological investigations to find every infected person and track every close contact for quarantine. A database has been set up in accordance with the law to provide data services for virus risk control, precisely identify different groups at risk, predict risk factors in different areas, and facilitate the orderly flow of people and the resumption of business operations. Via online platforms based on 5G technology, epidemiological teams in remote mountainous areas have been able to engage in real-time discussion with top experts thousands of miles away. With authorization from the public, health QR codes and digital travel records have been employed as permits for making trips, going to school or work, and accessing certain public venues, and for other daily errands. The results shown on the codes and records provide a base for travel control and differentiated response measures, which has made risk identification and targeted control possible in different areas and at different levels. Applying big data technology, an "epidemic map" has been created to display the specific names and locations of the communities where cases have been reported and the number of infections that has been ascertained. The map has made it easier for the public to guard against infection.

Through the battle against Covid-19, China has accumulated valuable experience in responding to major public health emergencies, and deficiencies in the national response system have been exposed. Summarizing this experience and learning from lessons, China will adopt a series of important measures to reinforce weak links. China will:
  • reform and improve the disease prevention and control system;
  • establish a major epidemic prevention, control and treatment system adapted to both times of peace and times of crisis;
  • improve the emergency supply system;

- strengthen the new strategy of pooling nationwide resources for breakthroughs in core technologies;
- continue to implement initiatives to improve public sanitation; and
- improve the public health system.

China will make solid efforts to build capacity and improve its response to major public health emergencies, and better safeguard people's lives and health.

III. Assembling a Powerful Force to Beat the Virus

Facing the sudden onslaught of a previously unknown virus, China has put the people's interests first – nothing is more precious than people's lives. It has rapidly mobilized the manpower and resources of the whole nation and done everything possible to protect the lives and health of its people. A powerful synergy has been formed thanks to the following factors: observing the people-centered governance philosophy of the CPC; China's ability to mobilize resources to accomplish major initiatives; its composite national strength built up during more than four decades of reform and opening up, particularly since the 18th CPC National Congress held in November 2012; remarkable achievements in modernizing governance; two defining values of Chinese culture – solidarity and mutual assistance; and the profound love of the Chinese people for their family and their country.

1. Lives Are Precious

At a critical time when people's lives and health were endangered, the CPC and the Chinese government acted with a keen sense of responsibility and swiftly identified the problem. The central authorities took multiple factors into consideration, made timely and resolute decisions, employed extraordinary measures to deal with an extraordinary emergency, and made every effort to safeguard people's lives and health.

Placing people's lives above economic growth. When the novel coronavirus struck, China decided that it would protect the lives and health of its people even at the cost of a short-term economic downturn and even a temporary shutdown. The government took strict and comprehensive control measures, never tried before, in the city of Wuhan and Hubei Province. To stem the spread of the virus, the movement of people across the country was tightly restricted, the Chinese New Year holiday was extended, gatherings were stopped, and the spring semester and business operations were postponed. In an editorial, *The Lancet* stated: "China's success has come with huge social and economic costs, and China must make difficult decisions to achieve an optimal balance between health and economic protection."[1]

At the critical juncture of the fight against the virus, based on a precise understanding of the evolving situation, China took the major decision to continue Covid-19 prevention and control while resuming economic and social development. While restarting normal work in an orderly manner, it took targeted measures in different regions based on local conditions, so as to ensure people's daily life and wellbeing to the greatest possible extent. Having succeeded in containing the spread of the virus on the mainland, the Chinese government adopted a strategy of preventing inbound infections and domestic resurgence, to ensure its hard-won progress would not be lost.

Saving lives at all costs. In the early stage of the epidemic, as the cases of infection soared, China made raising the cure rate and lowering the fatality rate its top priority. The best doctors and nurses were rapidly dispatched to the front line of the fight against the virus. Employing proactive, science-based, and flexible ways of treatment, they did everything possible to treat each and every patient, from an infant only 30 hours old to a centenarian. The goal was to save every single patient whatever the cost.

Medical workers braved the threat of infection to collect virus speci-

---

[1] *The Lancet*: "Sustaining containment of COVID-19 in China", April 18, 2020.
https://www.thelancet.com/journals/lancet/article/PIIS0140-6736(20)30864-3/fulltext.

mens. No one flinched, however daunting their task. To treat seriously ill patients, local governments and hospitals tried every means to acquire and reallocate ECMO equipment. Since the virus struck, hospitals in Wuhan designated for treating severe cases have treated more than 9,600 such cases. The recovery rate has risen from 14 percent to 89 percent, higher than the average rate for normal viral pneumonia. Tailored treatment was given to elderly patients with underlying medical conditions. As long as there was the slightest hope, doctors would never give up, and the need for personnel, medicines, equipment, or funds was met. To date, more than 3,000 patients over the age of 80, including 7 centenarians, have been cured, with many of them brought back to life from the verge of death. For example, a 70-year-old patient was saved thanks to intensive treatment and care by more than 10 medical workers over a period of several weeks. The cost of his treatment, nearly RMB1.5 million, was fully covered by the government.

Care and compassion for Chinese citizens overseas. China takes the safety of its citizens abroad very seriously. It has urged the governments of other countries to take effective measures to ensure the safety of Chinese students, the personnel of Chinese-funded institutions, and other Chinese nationals in their countries, and has supported them in doing so. Medical expert teams and work groups have been dispatched overseas and telemedicine service platforms set up, which provide scientific and professional guidance on Covid-19 prevention and control for Chinese citizens in other countries. Chinese medical teams have worked with host countries to ensure the best possible treatment for Chinese citizens diagnosed with infection. China has fully mobilized experts at home, medical teams on foreign aid missions, and other resources to assist foreign countries to provide treatment to these patients.

Performing their consular protection duties, Chinese embassies and consulates abroad have disseminated information on Covid-19 prevention and self-protection through all channels, and have provided more than 1 million "health kits" to overseas Chinese students. They have also helped overseas Chinese citizens in difficulty to return home.

National tribute to the deceased. On April 4, the Chinese traditional Tomb-sweeping Day, China paid tribute to all those who had given their lives in the fight against Covid-19, and those who had died of the disease. People throughout the country observed a silence to mourn the loss of lives and pay tribute to heroes who had protected others' lives at the cost of their own. From the top leader to ordinary people, 1.4 billion Chinese bade farewell to their dear departed. This solemn national ceremony demonstrates that the country respects and holds in awe the dignity and lives of people as individuals. It signifies the solidarity and strength of 1.4 billion Chinese.

2. Mobilizing the Whole Country to Fight the Epidemic

When a disaster strikes in one location, help comes from all quarters. After the outbreak, the entire country acted promptly. Relying on its overall national strength, China mobilized the people, enhanced R&D, procured supplies, and brought them to those in need rapidly. It mustered the support of the whole country to assist Hubei, and particularly Wuhan, to combat the disease. It pooled all its strength in the shortest period of time, and halted the spread of the epidemic. Hailing the speed and scale of China's response, WHO Director General Tedros Adhanom Ghebreyesus described it as unprecedented, and said it showed the efficiency and the strength of China's system.[1]

Launching the largest medical assistance operation since the founding of the PRC. China mobilized all its medical resources to support the efforts in Wuhan and other locations in Hubei. From January 24, Chinese New Year's Eve, to March 8, it rallied 346 national medical

---

[1] "China Focus: Xi Voices Full Confidence in Winning Battle against Novel Coronavirus", Xinhuanet.com, January 28, 2020.
http://www.xinhuanet.com/english/2020-01/28/c_138739962.htm.

teams, consisting of 42,600 medical workers and more than 900 public health professionals to the immediate aid of Hubei and the city of Wuhan. Nineteen provinces and equivalent administrative units assisted 16 other cities in Hubei in the form of paired assistance. While burdened with the heavy responsibility of coronavirus prevention and control and treatment of patients in their home cities, they still pooled together quality medical resources to assist Hubei and Wuhan.

The People's Liberation Army (PLA) dispatched over 4,000 medical personnel to Hubei to work in epidemic control. They took on medical work in three designated medical institutions, including Huoshenshan Hospital in Wuhan. The PLA Air Force dispatched aircraft to transport emergency medical supplies. Medical teams were formed within two hours of receiving the order, and they arrived at their destinations within 24 hours, carrying a seven-day stock of protective materials. On arrival, they started to treat patients right away.

The government urgently solicited automatic temperature measuring equipment, negative pressure ambulances, ventilators, electrocardiogram monitors, and other key medical supplies from across the country for Wuhan and other locations in Hubei (see Table 1). It mobilized 40,000 construction workers and several thousand sets of machinery and equipment to build two hospitals. The construction of the 1,000-bed Huoshenshan Hospital was completed in just 10 days, and that of the 1,600-bed Leishenshan Hospital in just 12 days. In 10 short days, 16 temporary treatment centers providing over 14,000 beds were built. To increase blood supply for clinical use in surgery, 10 provinces donated to Hubei 45,000 units of red blood cells, 1,762 therapeutic doses of platelets, and 1,370 liters of fresh frozen plasma (not including convalescent plasma). These massive and powerful medical assistance actions have guaranteed Covid-19 treatment in Hubei and Wuhan, greatly relieving the pressure on the hardest-hit areas caused by severe shortages of medical resources.

**Table 1. Medical Supplies Sent to Hubei since the Onset of the Epidemic
(As of April 30)**

Serial number	Category	Product	Unit	Quantity
1	Medical equipment	Automatic temperature measuring equipment	set	20,033
2		Negative pressure ambulance	unit	1,065
3		Ventilator	set	17,655
4		Electrocardiogram monitor	set	15,746
5	Disinfectant products	84 antiseptic solution	tonne	1,874
6		Hand sanitizer	1,000 bottles	714
7	Personal protective equipment	Medical gloves	million pairs	1.99
8		Protective suit	million suits	7.73
9		Medical N95 mask	million pieces	4.98
10		Medical non-N95 mask	million pieces	27.2
11	Medicines for Covid-19 prevention and control	Chloroquine phosphate	1,000 tablets	400
12		Arbidol	million tablets	3.6

Increasing the production and supply of medical supplies and medical support services. Victory in the battle against Covid-19 depends on logistical support. In view of the extreme scarcity of medical protective materials in Wuhan during the early stage of the epidemic, medical workers on the front line overcame difficulties and used every item for the longest possible time, so as to conserve them in the race to save lives. To address the shortfall in medical resources while patient numbers surged, China exploited the full strength of its comprehensive and resilient manufacturing sector and its complete industrial chain.

To overcome the unfavorable combination of a pause in work and the resultant decline in manufacturing output during the Chinese New Year holiday, the Chinese government mobilized factories across the country to operate at full capacity and tap into their full potential. With all its strength, it supported raw materials supplies and transport facilities throughout the industrial chain, so as to ensure large-scale production and distribution of materials for epidemic prevention and control. Medical manufacturers overcame such difficulties as labor shortages caused by workers not having returned to their posts. They resumed production as quickly as possible, and expanded capacity to the maximum.

Enterprises in other industries made rapid adjustments to their manufacturing facilities and turned to producing masks, protective suits, disinfectants, temperature measuring devices, and other products for the fight against the epidemic, thereby effectively expanding the overall output of such materials and equipment. The Chinese government quickly started procedures to review applications for producing medical supplies in times of emergency, and imposed stricter quality and safety supervision across the board, so as to facilitate production, ensure the quickest approval for sale, and guarantee supplies.

As of May 31, relevant authorities had approved 19 applications for clinical trials of 17 medicines and vaccines for coronavirus prevention and control, and conditionally approved the applications for sale of two medicines. Thanks to the joint efforts of many parties, manufacturing capacity for medical supplies increased steadily, and efforts to ensure the supply of medical materials and equipment achieved rapid progress: from acute shortage to borderline sufficiency, then from demand-supply balance to timely and sufficient supplies (see Table 2). The daily output of medical N95 masks and medical non-N95 masks increased from 130,000 and 5.86 million in early February to over 5 million and 200 million by the end of April. These efforts opened up unimpeded supply chains and logistics channels, gave birth to a coordination mechanism ensuring material supply, and allowed continuous transport of materials from across the country to the hardest-hit areas.

Table 2. Production of Key Medical Supplies
(As of April 30)

	Category	Product \ Unit	Daily production capacity	Daily production	Multiple of the daily production in the early stage of the epidemic (late January)
1	Personal protective equipment	Medical protective suit (million suits)	1.89	0.8	90.6
2	Disinfectant products	Hand sanitizer (tonne)	409	308	2.6
		84 antiseptic solution (1,000 packs)	366	117	1.6
3	Medical equipment	Automatic infrared temperature measuring device (1,000 sets)	10.7	3.4	23.3
4	Test materials	Virus testing reagent (million kits)	10.2	7.6	58

Coordinating and ensuring the supply of daily necessities. Once outbound traffic from Wuhan had been halted, nearly 10 million people were under home isolation in the city, requiring a huge amount of grain, vegetables, meat, eggs, and milk every day. A coordination mechanism was established to ensure supply of such products, which involved nine provinces, and 500 enterprises for prioritizing the shipment of supplies in times of emergency. The mechanism involved coordination between central and local governments, and joint actions by government and enterprises. It boosted the supply of grain and cooking oil, released central government reserves of frozen pork, and raised the supply capacity of provinces which are major vegetable bases. Transport teams were organized for emergency supplies, and forceful measures were taken to ensure the production, stocks, supply, and price stability of daily necessities for residents in Hubei, and particularly in Wuhan.

From January 27 to March 19, 928,800 tonnes of epidemic prevention and control materials and daily necessities were transported from across the country to Hubei via railway, highway, waterway, civil aviation, and express postal services. Bulk goods such as thermal coal and fuel totaling 1.49 million tonnes were also shipped. Sufficient supplies of coal, electricity, fuel, gas, and heat ensured the normal functioning of society and the smooth implementation of quarantine measures in Hubei and particularly in Wuhan. In Wuhan, delivery of daily necessities was included in community services, thus the last link of daily distribution – from supermarkets to communities – was assured. Through contactless delivery, vegetables that had gone through quarantine and met the standards were delivered directly to communities, meeting residents' needs and ensuring safety in terms of epidemic prevention.

Public participation in virus control. Trade unions, Communist Youth League organizations, women's federations, and other mass organizations organized and mobilized their contacts among the general public to get involved in Covid-19 prevention and control. Urban and rural residents, enterprises, and social organizations donated money and materials. Charities and the Red Cross Society of China improved the allocation of donated funds and materials, with a focus on Wuhan and other severely affected areas inside Hubei Province and elsewhere. As of May 31, they had received donations totaling about RMB38.93 billion and 990 million items of different materials. Of these, RMB32.83 billion and 940 million items had been disbursed.

Since the onset of the epidemic, fellow countrymen and women in Hong Kong, Macao, and Taiwan, and overseas Chinese have given a helping hand through various means and channels. They have actively donated money and materials for epidemic prevention and control. This shows how much we Chinese at home and abroad are committed to each other and demonstrates the unity and cohesion of the Chinese nation in times of difficulty.

3. Coordinating Prevention and Control with Social and Economic Development

Without compromising Covid-19 control, China has steadily resumed social and economic activities in an orderly way, so as to stabilize the six fronts (employment, finance, foreign trade, inbound investment, domestic investment, and market expectations), and guarantee the six priorities (jobs, daily living needs, food and energy, industrial and supply chains, the interests of market players, and the smooth functioning of grassroots government).

It has fostered a social and economic order under the conditions imposed by Covid-19 control and striven to minimize their impact on social and economic development, thus providing a strong material and social buttress for the fight against the epidemic.

Maintaining social order and stability. China has made every effort to ensure social order and stability, market order, public security, and supervision over the quality and pricing of epidemic-control supplies. It has adopted timely policies to ensure the basic livelihood of people in difficulties caused by Covid-19. Psychological counseling is provided to ease distress, nurture a healthy mindset, prevent and resolve potential problems, and defuse local disputes.

Despite strict measures such as traffic control and home-based quarantine, the economy and society have remained resilient. The supply of water, electricity, natural gas and telecommunication services continues, as does the supply of daily necessities in urban and rural areas. Key sectors providing food, pharmaceuticals, energy, basic industrial products, and public services that are essential to social stability and people's wellbeing are in normal operation, meeting the basic needs of 1.4 billion people.

Orderly resumption of work. The central government has quickly adopted a host of policies to reduce the burdens of businesses, particularly small and medium enterprises and self-employed people. These include measures such as reducing fees and lowering taxes, increasing government subsidies, strengthening financial support, stabilizing and expanding employment, and improving government services.

Local governments have issued detailed rules to implement these policies, especially to help the 10,000 plus key enterprises essential to Covid-19 control, public services, and daily necessities. Comprehensive services are being provided to help enterprises to resume operation, including providing personal protective gear and facilitating the flow of labor and materials. Point-to-point buses, trains and planes were chartered to send migrant workers back to their work posts. Preferential tax treatments such as exemption from value-added tax are available to businesses in transport, catering, hospitality, tourism, sport, entertainment and other sectors hit hard by the epidemic. Businesses also enjoy a temporary reduction in or exemption from social security contributions, a waiver of highway tolls, and reduced electricity and gas prices, and they are allowed to postpone their housing provident fund payments. Rent is being reduced for small and micro enterprises and the self-employed. The principal and interest repayment periods on loans to micro, small and medium enterprises are being extended, and more concessional loans are being provided.

Key groups such as college graduates and migrant workers are receiving support in finding jobs or starting businesses. Subsidies given to micro, small and medium enterprises to reduce layoffs are being extended to more businesses so as to stabilize employment and help them survive.

Policies on export tax rebates and export credit insurance are being put to good use, export credits expanded and new export markets explored. The negative list of market access for foreign investment has been cut to attract foreign investment. All these efforts will cut burdens on enterprises and stimulate their growth.

State-owned enterprises have taken the lead in resuming operations, providing impetus for upstream and downstream industries, including small and medium enterprises. By the end of April, 99 percent of companies of designated size – with a revenue of more than RMB20 million per annum – had resumed operations, as had 88.4 percent of micro, small and medium enterprises. Construction of over 95 percent of major projects across the country had resumed. In Hubei Province, more than 98.2 percent of enterprises of designated size had resumed operations, and 92.1 percent of their employees had returned to their jobs, and both these figures were close to the national average. Now, work on some key national science and technology projects, major national projects related to people's daily lives, and landmark foreign-funded projects has resumed. The Chinese economy is accelerating its return to normal operation, and it is becoming increasingly robust.

Gradual return to normal life. With steady progress made in Covid-19 control, public life is gradually returning to normal. Public transport services have fully resumed. More restaurants are reopening to the public. The May Day holiday in China saw a bustle of activity. During the five-day holiday, 121 million trips were made via railways, highways, waterways and air; and 115 million visits were paid to domestic tourist attractions, generating revenue of RMB47.56 billion.

Services such as shops, supermarkets, hotels, and restaurants have reopened their doors under Covid-19 control conditions. Students across the country have resumed their studies, and some have now returned to school. As of May 31, 163 million students and children in some grades of kindergarten, elementary and secondary schools across the country had returned to school or kindergarten. Public life is returning to normal in China, with people resuming their daily routines and consumption gradually picking up.

4. Uniting as One – China's Billion People

All citizens share a responsibility for the fate of their country. The 1.4 billion Chinese people, irrespective of their gender, age, and occupation, have plunged themselves into the battle against the epidemic. Resilient and united, they represent a formidable force.

Medical workers rose to the challenge. Medical workers, from the very young to the very old, showed no hesitation in confronting the epidemic. At the outset, some 540,000 medical workers from Wuhan and other parts of Hubei plunged into the fray, joined soon by more than 40,000 civilian and military medical workers who rushed from other parts of the country. Millions of medical workers grappled with the epidemic at the front line across the country. Showing professional devotion and a deep respect for life, many of them risked their own lives, racing against time and working round the clock to try to save every patient. They built a Great Wall against the virus, bringing light and hope to the nation at a dark time. They endured tremendous fatigue and stress, and paid a heavy price. More than 2,000 medical workers were infected, and scores died in the line of duty. No one is born a hero, yet their selflessness made them fearless. These people, with the nobility, kindness, and devotion that are intrinsic to their profession, have etched an unforgettable chapter in the history of the Chinese nation and in the hearts of the Chinese people.

People in Wuhan and other parts of Hubei fought with resolve against the novel coronavirus and made sacrifices to contain its spread. The people of Wuhan and Hubei were confronted with many challenges. All channels of exit from the city and the province were temporarily closed, intra-city public transport was suspended, and the capital city came to a standstill. The high risk of infection, tight supply of medical and daily necessities, and extended period of isolation were compounded by the trauma of bereavement for those who lost friends or family members to the virus. However, with grit in their hearts and the wider interests of others in their minds, they united to stop the transmission of the virus. In this great war, their heroism will be remembered and will go down in history.

Community workers, primary and community-level officials, officials sent to work in communities, police, and customs officers worked day and night to protect lives and public safety. Some 4 million community workers are working in around 650,000 urban and rural communities, monitoring the situation, taking body temperatures, screening for infection, disseminating government policies, and sanitizing neighborhoods. Dedicated and responsible, they have meticulously protected their communities from the virus. CPC members working in communities quickly communicated the policies of the Party and the government, mobilized residents to engage in epidemic prevention and control, and actively helped them solve their daily difficulties. They divided communities into sub-units called grids to improve services and management.

Police and auxiliary police officers handled emergent, dangerous, difficult, and burdensome tasks such as guarding hospitals, transporting patients, and patrolling the streets to maintain order. More than 130 have died in the line of duty.

Customs officers have applied the law and carried out quarantine and other health-related duties, preventing the virus from entering the country.

Couriers, sanitation workers, transport employees, media workers, volunteers, and many people from other sectors of society also devoted themselves to the fight against the epidemic. When things were at their most serious, while people kept their doors closed, millions of couriers braved the virus and the cold, delivering warmth and comfort to people in cities and rural areas.

China's 1.8 million sanitation workers worked from dawn to dusk to clean and disinfect public spaces, and collect and transport medical and other wastes to centralized treatment facilities.

Tens of millions of transport employees, including taxi drivers in many cities, remained at their posts, providing a vital support to epidemic prevention and control, carrying supplies for work and daily life, and helping to get the country back to work.

Some media workers also worked at the front line, recording the battle against the epidemic, spreading warmth, and evoking strength.

Many ordinary people volunteered at the front line, standing guard in communities, screening for infection, carrying out cleaning and disinfection work, and buying medicines and delivering groceries for other residents' pressing needs. Preliminary statistics show that as of May 31, 8.81 million registered volunteers across the country had participated in more than 460,000 volunteer projects, rendering a total of more than 290 million hours of voluntary service.

The general public shouldered their responsibilities, united as one, and proactively participated in epidemic prevention and control. In the face of adversity, Chinese people have great faith in the Party and the government. They courageously shouldered their social responsibilities, and on this occasion made great sacrifices to win the battle against the epidemic.

The Chinese New Year holiday arrived amid the epidemic. Following government orders to contain the virus, the whole population acted in concert, and social exchanges shrank to a minimum. Visits to friends and relatives were canceled and so were other gatherings; people quarantined themselves, wore masks, began to take their body temperature regularly, and practiced other social distancing measures. The consensus was that protecting oneself was protecting others and making contribution to the country, so everyone took voluntary actions against the virus. People stayed at home for extended periods of time, taking online courses, honing culinary skills, and spending time with their families. Many found creative ways to keep themselves occupied, and confronted the epidemic with a positive attitude.

Speaking of the general public in China, Dr. Bruce Aylward, former assistant director general of the WHO and senior advisor to WHO director general, said at the press conference of WHO-China Joint Mission on Covid-19 held on February 24 in Beijing, "And that's because we want to emphasize this can't work without the collective will of the population contributing to it. And that's what really distinguishes this country, this response and the ability to take these old-fashioned strategies, some of the earliest ones we had in public health, apply them to the most modern virus and somehow do that."[1]

---

[1] Press Conference of WHO-China Joint Mission on Covid-19, Beijing, February 24, 2020. https://www.who.int/docs/default-source/coronaviruse/transcripts/joint-mission-press-conference-script-english-final.pdf?sfvrsn=51c90b9e_10.

A major crisis is a litmus test of the ruling Party's governance philosophy and effectiveness. The strong leadership of the CPC has been fundamental to China's rapid containment of the virus. The CPC has a strong leadership core, a people-oriented governance philosophy, and well-established organization and operation mechanisms. It quickly made the right decisions in response to the crisis. Under its leadership, efficient and powerful response measures were implemented. Within a short time, across-the-board crisis-response mechanisms were established down to the community level, motivating all those involved across the country to follow instructions and act as one.

The CPC has more than 4.6 million primary-level organizations, which have served as strongholds against the epidemic, rallying and serving the general public. With the epidemic putting people's lives and safety in danger, CPC members have acted as the vanguard. More than 39 million CPC members fought the virus at the front line, and more than 13 million CPC members volunteered their services. Nearly 400 CPC members have defended others' lives and safety at the cost of their own. Party members have also voluntarily donated money for epidemic prevention and control.

The CPC attaches great importance to tempering its members in times of trial, to gauge their commitment to serving the people and their sense of responsibility. The leadership of Wuhan City and Hubei Province was reshuffled, with some officials sanctioned for irresponsibility and dereliction of duty while others have been honored and promoted for their dedication and sense of responsibility.

After weathering the epidemic, the Chinese people have keenly realized that the CPC leadership is the most reliable shelter against storms. Their trust in and support for the Party have increased, along with their confidence in China's political system.

IV. Building a Global Community of Health for All

Coronavirus is raging all over the world, and lives are being lost every day. In the face of this serious crisis humanity once again stands at a crossroads. Which route shall we take? Shall we uphold science and rationality, or shall we manufacture political disputes? Strengthen unity and cooperation, or seek isolation? Promote multilateral coordination, or pursue unilateralism? Every country has a choice to make. China believes that all countries should make the choice that is right for the interests of all humanity and the wellbeing of our future generations. Upholding the vision of a global community of shared future, we should support each other and join hands to contain the spread of the virus, and protect the health and wellbeing of people across the globe.

1. China Appreciates Support from the International Community

At the time when the situation in China was at its most difficult, the international community provided valuable support and assistance to our country and our people. Leaders of more than 170 countries, heads of 50 international and regional organizations, and more than 300 foreign political parties and organizations expressed solidarity and support for China through phone calls, letters, and statements. Seventy-seven countries and 12 international organizations donated emergency medical supplies, including masks, protective suits, goggles, and ventilators. Donations of materials were also made by local governments, enterprises, non-governmental organizations and people from 84 countries. The BRICS New Development Bank and the Asian Infrastructure Investment Bank provided emergency loans of RMB7 billion and RMB2.485 billion, while the World Bank and the Asian Development Bank offered loans for the building of China's public health emergency management system. China appreciates the understanding and support of the international community, which our people will always cherish. The Chinese nation never forgets the help and generosity it receives, and always reciprocates with the same goodwill. We are now doing all we can to support the international community in the fight against the coronavirus.

2. China Conducts Active International Exchanges and Cooperation

China has been carrying out exchanges and cooperation with the international community from the outset. It has strengthened high-level communication, shared information, and cooperated in scientific research with international organizations and other countries, and done all it can to provide assistance, contributing ingenuity and strength to the global fight against the coronavirus. The CPC has issued a joint appeal with 240 political parties in more than 110 countries, calling on all stakeholders to put people's lives and health first, uphold the vision of a global community of shared future, and pull together to combat the virus.

President Xi has personally promoted international cooperation. In phone calls or meetings with nearly 50 foreign leaders and heads of international organizations, President Xi explained China's tactics and achievements in fighting the virus, and emphasized China's open, transparent and responsible approach towards releasing information and sharing its experience in virus control and the treatment of infected cases. He expressed empathy for the difficulties faced by other countries, saying that China would do all it can to help them. He called on all parties to build a global community of shared future, strengthen bilateral and multilateral cooperation, and support international organizations in order to work together to meet the challenge.

President Xi delivered a speech at the G20 Extraordinary Leaders'

Summit on Covid-19 on China's experience. In a call on the international community to rise to the challenge and act swiftly, he put forward a series of cooperation initiatives and four key proposals – launch an all-out global war against Covid-19, establish a collective response for control and treatment at the international level, support international organizations in playing their roles, and strengthen coordination of international macroeconomic policies.

On May 18, he addressed the opening of the 73rd World Health Assembly, calling for a joint effort on the part of all countries to overcome the virus and build a global community of health for all. Six proposals were put forward: to do everything we can for Covid-19 control and treatment, to support the WHO in leading the global response, to provide greater support for Africa, to strengthen global governance in public health, to restore economic and social development, and to strengthen international cooperation. He also announced a series of major measures that China would take in supporting the global fight, including US$2 billion of international aid over two years, the establishment of a global humanitarian response depot and hub in China in cooperation with the United Nations, the establishment of a cooperation mechanism for Chinese hospitals to pair up with 30 African hospitals, the Covid-19 vaccine to be used as a global public product once it is developed and deployed in China, and the implementation of the Debt Service Suspension Initiative for the poorest countries together with other G20 members.

China has shared information and experience with the international community. China has provided support for global virus prevention and control by promptly sharing information and experience with the international community. It wasted no time in releasing information such as the whole coronavirus genome sequence and the specific primers and probes for detecting the coronavirus to the WHO and other relevant countries and regional organizations, and has kept them informed with regular updates. China has conducted more than 70 exchanges with international and regional organizations including ASEAN, the European Union, the

African Union (AU), APEC, the Caribbean Community, and the Shanghai Cooperation Organization (SCO), as well as the ROK, Japan, Russia, the United States, Germany, and other countries. The National Health Commission (NHC) has worked out diagnosis, treatment, prevention and control solutions, had them translated into three languages, and shared them with over 180 countries and more than 10 international and regional organizations. Together with the WHO it held an international briefing via video link on China's experience in Covid-19 control. The Information Office of the State Council held two special English-language press conferences in Wuhan, inviting experts and frontline health workers to talk about China's experience and practices. To build platforms for exchanges between countries, the Chinese media has designed a TV program *Covid-19 Frontline* and a newspaper column *Fighting Covid-19 the Chinese Way*, among others. Chinese think tanks and experts have communicated with their counterparts around the world in a variety of ways. The WHO-China Joint Mission on Covid-19 made site visits to Beijing, Chengdu, Guangzhou, Shenzhen, and Wuhan, and spoke highly of China's efforts and success in prevention and control.

China has provided humanitarian assistance to the international community. Even while under the tremendous pressure of coronavirus control, China has moved quickly to provide as much assistance to the international community as it can. It has provided two batches of cash support totaling US$50 million to the WHO, assisted the organization in purchasing personal protective equipment and establishing reserve centers of supplies in China, and helped its Covid-19 Solidarity Response Fund to raise funds in China. It has also participated in the WHO's "Access to Covid-19 Tools (act) Accelerator" initiative, aiming to speed up the development, production and equitable distribution of new tools.

China has been active in providing medical aid to other countries. As of May 31, China had sent 29 medical expert teams to 27 countries, and offered assistance to 150 countries and 4 international organizations. It has instructed its medical teams stationed in 56 countries to support the local fight, and provide counseling and health information to local people and overseas Chinese. They have so far organized over 400 online and offline training sessions in this regard. Local governments, enterprises, non-governmental organizations and individuals in China have donated materials to more than 150 countries and regions, and international organizations through various channels. The Chinese government has always had at heart the lives and health of foreigners in China, and it has provided undifferentiated and timely treatment to those infected with the disease.

China has made arrangements for orderly exports of protective materials. While ensuring domestic needs, China has tried every possible means to provide support to all countries in purchasing protective materials. It has smoothed the channels for supply-demand docking, organized logistics, transport, and the supply of goods, and accelerated export customs clearance. It has taken effective measures to control product quality, regulate export procedures, issue guidelines on foreign market access, and strengthen market and export quality supervision, so as to provide other countries with goods of the highest quality. From March 1 to May 31, China exported protective materials to 200 countries and regions, among which there were more than 70.6 billion masks, 340 million protective suits, 115 million pairs of goggles, 96,700 ventilators, 225 million test kits, and 40.29 million infrared thermometers.

China's growing exports provide strong support for the prevention and control efforts of affected countries. From January to April, the number of China-Europe freight trains and the volume of goods delivered increased by 24 percent and 27 percent compared with the same period last year, and a total of 660,000 packages were transported. This has played an important role in maintaining a smooth flow of international industrial and supply chains, and in ensuring the delivery of protective supplies to relevant countries.

China has carried out international exchanges and cooperation on scientific research. China has strengthened communication and exchanges with the WHO, conducted exchanges and cooperation with other countries on research in virus traceability, medicines, vaccines, and testing, shared scientific research data and information, and jointly studied prevention, control and treatment strategies. The Ministry of Science and Technology, the NHC, the China Association for Science and Technology, and the Chinese Medical Association have jointly put in place a Covid-19 Academic Research Communication Platform for worldwide researchers to release results and participate in discussion. By May 31, a total of 104 journals and 970 papers and reports had been posted. The National Administration of Traditional Chinese Medicine and the SCO Committee on Good-Neighborliness, Friendship and Cooperation held a video conference on the diagnosis and treatment of Covid-19 between a group of Chinese experts on integrating traditional Chinese medicine and Western medicine, and hospitals from SCO countries. It also guided the World Federation of Chinese Medicine Societies and the World Federation of Acupuncture-Moxibustion Societies in organizing such events as Expert Dialogue on Covid-19 Prevention and Control with Traditional Chinese Medicine and International Lectures on Covid-19.

The Chinese Academy of Sciences has released the 2019 Novel Coronavirus Resource database, and built the Novel Coronavirus National Science and Technology Resource Service System and the Covid-19 Pneumonia Scientific Literature Sharing Platform. As of May 31, the three platforms had provided nearly 48 million download, browsing and retrieval services to more than 370,000 users worldwide. China has established an international pool of experts and has cooperated with other countries in vaccine and medicine research and development. It has encouraged the Alliance of International Science Organizations in the framework of the Belt and Road Initiative to promote cooperation among its members in Covid-19 treatment and research. Chinese scientists, medical institutions, and disease control centers have published dozens of well-researched papers in some of the world's leading academic journals such as *The Lancet*, *Science*, *Nature* and *The New England Journal of Medicine*, releasing timely results of tests on the first patients, including the clinical characteristics of the virus, the risk of human-to-human transmission, China's experience of temporary treatment centers, medicine research and development, and experimental results of vaccines on animals. To accelerate the development of vaccines and the clinical trials of medicines, China has also carried out cooperation in scientific research with other countries, and with such organizations as the WHO, the Coalition for Epidemic Preparedness and Innovation and the Global Alliance for Vaccines and Immunisation.

3. International Solidarity and Cooperation in Fighting the Pandemic

The global spread of Covid-19 is causing great concern. Both the fight to rein in the virus and the endeavor to fend off a deepening global recession call for the international community to stand in unity and engage in cooperation. They also call for multilateralism, and commitment to building a global community of shared future. Solidarity and cooperation are the most powerful weapons available to the international community in the war against the pandemic. What we do today determines how we will fare in the future. China calls on all countries to act promptly, demonstrate solidarity, strengthen cooperation on all fronts, and fight the pandemic together.

Conducting effective international cooperation on joint prevention and control. In responding to a pandemic, all countries must act in coordination to establish an impermeable network for joint prevention and control. Since Covid-19 struck, the WHO has diligently performed its duties, adopted an objective and impartial stance, and taken a slew of professional, science-based, and effective measures. It has made a significant contribution to the fight against the pandemic by leading and advancing global cooperation. China firmly supports the WHO in playing the leading role in this global battle, and calls on the international community to give it more political and financial support, so that we can mobilize the necessary resources worldwide to defeat this virus.

China maintains that all countries should implement their response under the guidance and coordination of the WHO. This includes adopting science-based, rational, and well-coordinated prevention and control measures, appropriately allocating medical resources and key supplies, adopting effective methods in key areas such as prevention, isolation, testing, treatment and case tracing, stepping up information sharing and experience exchanges, engaging in international cooperation on the research and development of testing methods, clinical treatments, drugs and vaccines, and supporting scientists around the world in studying the origin and transmission routes of the virus.

China calls on multilateral organizations, including the G20, APEC, BRICS, and SCO, to increase dialogue, exchanges and policy coordination within their respective frameworks. G20 members should act on the consensus reached at the G20 Extraordinary Leaders' Summit on Covid-19 held in late March 2020.

In international cooperation on joint prevention and control, it is essential that major countries take the initiative, fulfill their responsibilities and do their share of the work. China is ready to strengthen exchanges and cooperation with other countries including the US to jointly tackle this pandemic, especially in the fields of research, development, production and distribution of vaccines and drugs.

Managing the pandemic's impact on the world economy through cooperation. The global spread of the pandemic has impeded the flow of people, cross-border trade, and other economic activities, triggered fluctuations on the financial market, and delivered a blow to both the industrial and supply chains, making a severe global economic recession unavoidable. It is imperative that the international community work together to stabilize and rehabilitate the world economy. While continuing to heighten epidemic control, China is ready to join forces with other countries to address the deepening global recession, stepping up international coordination on macroeconomic policies, and jointly safeguarding the stable, secure and smooth operation of international industrial and supply chains.

Covid-19 is changing the form but not the general trend of economic globalization. Decoupling, erecting walls and deglobalization may divide the world, but will not do any good to those who themselves are engaged in these acts. China believes that the international community should proceed with globalization, safeguard the multilateral trading system based on the WTO, cut tariffs, remove barriers, facilitate the flow of trade, and keep international industrial and supply chains secure and smooth. Countries also need to implement strong and effective fiscal and monetary policies, better coordinate financial regulation to keep global financial markets stable, and thus prevent a global financial crisis that may consequently plunge the world economy into a massive, protracted recession. China will continue to supply the international market with anti-epidemic materials, pharmaceutical ingredients, daily necessities, and other supplies. At the same time, China will continue to advance reform and opening up, expand imports and outbound investment, and thereby contribute further to other countries' fight against the virus and to a stable world economy.

Assisting weaker countries and regions. Without assistance, developing countries with weaker public health systems in Asia, Africa and Latin America – especially Africa – will struggle to handle the daunting challenges posed by this pandemic. Helping them improve their capacity and performance in epidemic prevention and control should be a top priority in the global response. China calls on multilateral organizations including the UN, the WHO, the IMF and the World Bank to provide emergency aid to African countries, and calls on developed countries to take on more responsibilities, to play a bigger role in the global battle, and to provide more material, technological and personnel support to their developing counterparts, especially those in Africa.

China has actively participated in and acted upon the Debt Service Suspension Initiative of the G20. It has so far announced the suspension of debt repayments from 77 developing countries. In addition to the medical supplies sent to over 50 African countries and the AU, and the seven medical expert teams dispatched to the continent, China will offer more assistance to African countries, and continue to do all in its power to offer support. This includes sending the most urgent medical supplies, conducting cooperation on medical technologies, and dispatching more medical expert teams and task forces. China will also provide support to the Covid-19 Global Humanitarian Response Plan of the UN.

Firmly opposing stigmatization and politicization of the virus. In the face of a novel coronavirus that poses a worldwide threat to human lives and health, the most urgent task is to defeat it through solidarity and cooperation. The common enemy of humanity is this virus, not any particular country or any particular race. China calls on the international community to come together, abandon prejudice and arrogance, resist scapegoating and other such self-serving artifices, and stand against stigmatization and politicization of the virus. In doing so we will see that the spirit of solidarity, cooperation, responsibility and dedication leads people around the world towards victory in our fight against the pandemic.

China has suffered tremendously but has contributed generously to the global efforts to combat the virus. Its efforts should be duly recognized, and it should not be criticized groundlessly. Since the early days of the outbreak China has informed the rest of the world of every development in clear and unambiguous terms. Certain countries ignored this information, and now blame China for their own failure to respond to the epidemic and protect their people's lives. Those who are intent on maligning others will easily find a pretext. China has always acted with openness, transparency and responsibility, and informed the international community of developments of the epidemic in a timely manner. The baseless accusation that China concealed epidemic information and death figures is a calculated slur on the 1.4 billion Chinese people, including those killed by the virus, and on millions of Chinese medical workers. China categorically rejects any such accusation.

The novel coronavirus is a previously unknown virus. Determining its origin is a scientific issue that requires research by scientists and doctors. The conclusion must be based on facts and evidence. It is both irresponsible and immoral to play the blame game in an attempt to cover up one's own shortcomings. China will never accept any frivolous lawsuits or compensation claims.

In the face of a virus that is spreading worldwide, China has offered help to other countries to the best of its ability. It is doing so out of the kindness of its people, the empathy they have with people of other countries suffering from the pandemic, the humanitarian spirit of helping each other amid disasters, and its sense of responsibility as a major country. China is not exporting its model, nor is it pursuing selfish geopolitical interests.

Building an efficient and sustainable global public health system for the benefit of all humanity. Human history is a history of grappling with viruses. There are multiple deficiencies in current global health governance, including the absence of an international mechanism for joint prevention and control of infectious diseases and a dire shortage of international public health resources. On top of these, the upsurge in deglobalization has rendered the global public health system even more vulnerable.

Humanity will prevail over the pandemic, but it will certainly not be the last major public health emergency we will encounter. China therefore calls on the international community to draw lessons from this pandemic, reflect carefully, and turn crises into opportunities. Countries should show extraordinary political vision and a strong sense of responsibility by doing the following:

- embrace a philosophy that puts life above everything else, regards the world as a whole, and stresses equality, mutual respect, cooperation and mutual assistance;
- establish sound mechanisms for international cooperation, including a long-term financing mechanism, a monitoring, early warning and joint response mechanism for threats to public health, and a

mechanism for reserving and allocating resources;
- create an efficient, sustainable global public health system for all;
- fortify defenses for the lives and health of all; and
- build a global community of health for all.

China supports efforts to make a full, objective, impartial, scientific, and professional assessment of the global response once the pandemic has been brought under control. This will enable us to learn lessons and remedy weaknesses. China proposes that countries take immediate action and adopt decisive measures to minimize both the imminent and potential threats of the virus. This is in the interest of future generations and the wellbeing of all humanity.

As a responsible country, China stands for the vision of a global community of shared future, and has actively participated in and advanced international cooperation in public health. It will put into action the six proposals and five measures put forward by President Xi Jinping in his speech at the opening of the 73rd World Health Assembly, and contribute more to securing regional and international public health and building a global community of health for all.

Afterword

The Chinese nation has never been driven down by adversity. The more daunting the challenge, the greater the courage it has mustered. Overcoming difficulties has helped China to grow stronger. Confronted by this virus, the Chinese people have joined together as one and united their efforts. They have succeeded in containing the spread of the virus. In this battle, China will always stand together with other countries.

Now, when the coronavirus is still spreading and causing devastation all over the world, the international community will have to face even greater difficulties and challenges. Preventing and controlling the spread of the virus has become a fight to safeguard global public health, to secure the wellbeing of humanity, to maintain world prosperity, and to enforce morality and conscience on the international community. It is a fight that will determine the future of the human race. We have no other choice but to overcome the pandemic. The international community must find resolve and forge unity. Solidarity means strength. The world will win this battle.

The pandemic will have a significant impact on the development of humanity, but the people's longing for a happy life will remain unchanged. Peace, development, and win-win cooperation will prevail. The sun will always shine again after a storm. As long as the world's peoples can cherish hopes and dreams, can embrace the idea of a global community of shared future, and can unite in pursuit of a common goal, we will be able to overcome all our current difficulties and challenges, and build a better world for all.

Employment and Labor Rights in Xinjiang

The State Council Information Office of
the People's Republic of China

September 2020

Preface

Work creates the means of existence and is an essential human activity. It creates a better life and enables all-round human development and the progress of civilization. The *Constitution of the People's Republic of China* provides that all citizens have the right and obligation to work. To protect the right to work is to safeguard human dignity and human rights.

China has a large population and workforce. Employment and job security are key to guaranteeing workers' basic rights and wellbeing, and have a significant impact on economic development, social harmony, national prosperity, and the nation's rejuvenation. China is committed to the people-centered philosophy of development, attaches great importance to job security, gives high priority to employment, and pursues a proactive set of policies on employment. It fully respects the wishes of workers, protects citizens' right to work in accordance with the law, applies international labor and human rights standards, and strives to enable everyone to create a happy life and achieve their own development through hard work.

In accordance with the country's major policies on employment and the overall plan for eliminating poverty, the Xinjiang Uygur Autonomous Region takes the facilitation of employment as the most fundamental project for ensuring and improving people's wellbeing. It has made every effort to increase and stabilize employment through various channels: encouraging individual initiative, regulatory role of the market, and government policies facilitating employment, entrepreneurship, and business startups. Through its proactive labor and employment policies, Xinjiang has continuously improved the people's material and cultural lives, and guaranteed and developed their human rights in every field. This has laid a solid foundation for ensuring that the people of all ethnic groups in Xinjiang have the opportunity to enjoy moderate prosperity in all respects and achieve long-term social stability together with their fellow countrymen and countrywomen in other parts of China.

I. Employment in Xinjiang

Xinjiang is located in the northwest of China. For historical and a range of natural reasons, it has long lagged behind other parts of the country in development, and there is a large impoverished population. Four prefectures in southern Xinjiang – Hotan, Kashgar, Aksu and Kizilsu Kirgiz – have a particularly poor eco-environment, weak economic foundations, and a serious shortfall in employment carrying capacity. They are identified as areas of extreme poverty. In addition, terrorists, separatists and religious extremists have long preached that "the afterlife is fated" and that "religious teachings are superior to state laws", inciting the public to resist learning the standard spoken and written Chinese language, reject modern science, and refuse to improve their vocational skills, economic conditions, and the ability to better their own lives. As a result, some local people have outdated ideas; they suffer from poor education and employability, low employment rates and incomes, and have fallen into long-term poverty.

Employment and job security carries great significance for ensuring people's right to work, improving their living standards, and promoting social harmony and stability. Especially since the 18th National Congress of the Communist Party of China (CPC) in 2012, Xinjiang has vigorously implemented employment projects, enhanced vocational training, and expanded employment channels and capacity. Thanks to these efforts, the employment situation in Xinjiang has continued to improve, people's incomes and quality of life are rising, and their sense of gain, happiness and security has significantly increased.

Policies have further improved. In recent years, to implement the national policies and strategies for stabilizing and facilitating employment and respond to calls from the public and local conditions, Xinjiang has formulated the *Opinions of the CPC Committee and the People's Government of the Xinjiang Uygur Autonomous Region on Further Facilitating Employment and Business Startups,* the *Opinions of the People's Government of the Xinjiang Uygur Autonomous Region on Facilitating Employment and Business Startups Now and in the Future,* and the *13th Five-Year Plan of the Xinjiang Uygur Autonomous Region for Facilitating Employment.* Systematic arrangements have been made in the areas of economic development, governmental financial guarantees, tax incentives, support from the financial sector, and overall planning of urban and rural areas, different regions, and diverse groups, as well as in supporting flexible employment and helping groups in need to find jobs. All these provide a solid institutional guarantee for facilitating employment and safeguarding the rights and interests of workers.

The scale of employment has expanded continuously. Xinjiang focuses on areas of extreme poverty and key groups with difficulty finding work. It guides people of all ethnic groups to find work nearby, or to locate jobs or start their own businesses in cities, and encourages the impoverished workforce to seek employment outside their hometowns. From 2014 to 2019, the total number of people employed in Xinjiang rose from 11.35 million to 13.3 million, an increase of 17.2 percent. The average annual increase in urban employment was more than 471,200 people (148,000 in southern Xinjiang, accounting for 31.4 percent); and the average annual relocation of surplus rural labor was more than 2.76 million people, of whom nearly 1.68 million, or over 60 percent, were in southern Xinjiang.

The employment structure has become more rational. Xinjiang considers supply-side structural reform as a key priority, and endeavors to raise the level of the primary industry, focus on key projects in the secondary industry, and boost the tertiary industry. It nurtures and strengthens industries with distinctive strengths and labor-intensive industries, and guides the orderly flow of labor to the tertiary industry. In terms of workforce distribution across the three industries, the ratio in 2014 was 45.4 : 16.0 : 38.6, which evolved to 36.4 : 14.1 : 49.5 in 2019. The tertiary industry saw an increase of 10.9 percentage points, making it the most job-intensive sector. In terms of workforce distribution in urban and rural areas, surplus rural labor is increasingly moving to cities and towns, and the ability of these places to absorb workforce has been strengthened. The number of people employed in cities and towns increased from 5.35 million in 2014 to 7.34 million in 2019, accounting for 55.2 percent of the total number of people employed in the region.

The quality of the workforce has improved significantly. Thanks to the government's education projects, enrollments in preschool education, nine-year compulsory education, senior high school education, higher education and vocational education in Xinjiang have all reached the highest level in history. In 2019, there were 453,800 full-time students studying at universities and colleges (an increase of 146,200 over 2014), and 1.84 million students studying at secondary schools (an increase of 147,600 over 2014). Through vocational training, Xinjiang has built a large knowledge-based, skilled and innovative workforce that meets the requirements of the new era. Every year from 2014 to 2019 Xinjiang provided training sessions to an average of 1.29 million urban and rural workers, of which 451,400 were in southern Xinjiang. The trainees mastered at least one skill with employment potential, and the vast majority of them obtained vocational qualifications, skill level certificates, or specialized skill certificates, allowing them to go on to find stable employment.

The income of residents and workers has increased steadily. From 2014 to 2019, the per capita disposable income of residents in Xinjiang increased as follows:

• urban residents: from RMB23,200 to RMB34,700 (an average annual nominal growth of 8.6 percent);

• rural residents: from RMB8,724 to RMB13,100 (an average annual nominal growth of 8.9 percent);

• urban residents in areas under the administration of Xinjiang

Production and Construction Corps (a special entity entrusted by the state to cultivate and guard China's border areas in Xinjiang): from RMB27,600 to RMB40,700 (an average annual nominal growth of 8.5 percent);

• residents of the company residence areas of the Corps: from RMB13,900 to RMB22,000 (an average annual nominal growth of 9.9 percent);

• average annual salary of employees in non-private sectors in cities and towns: from RMB53,500 to RMB79,400 (an annual growth of 8.4 percent);

• average annual salary of employees in private sectors in cities and towns: from RMB36,200 to RMB45,900 (an annual growth of 5.4 percent).

From 2018 to 2019, 155,000 people from registered poor households in southern Xinjiang and in four impoverished regimental farms of the Xinjiang Production and Construction Corps found employment outside their hometowns and subsequently emerged from poverty.

The above statistics show that, in recent years Xinjiang has achieved remarkable results in providing employment services and job security to the residents, and the overall situation is good. However, it should be noted that Xinjiang is still faced with difficulties and challenges including a weak foundation for economic development, a large labor surplus in rural areas, and a low level of vocational skills. To solve its problem of employment in the long term, Xinjiang must further optimize the industrial structure, improve the quality of the workforce, and change people's outdated mindset.

II. Implementation of Proactive Policies on Employment

In recent years, Xinjiang has formulated and put in place economic and social development strategies conducive to expanding employment, and has improved various policies to facilitate employment, with the goal of helping local people achieve stable, continuous, and long-term employment.

Upgrading the industrial structure to increase employment. Xinjiang has seized the development opportunities brought by the Belt and Road Initiative to diversify its industrial structure, promoting capital-, technology- and knowledge-intensive advanced manufacturing industries and emerging industries, boosting labor-intensive industries such as textiles and garments, shoes and accessories, and consumer electronics, and encouraging modern service industries such as e-commerce, cultural and creative businesses, regional tourism, health care, and elderly care, all with a view to expanding the capacity and scale of employment.

In 2012, Xinjiang Zhundong Economic and Technological Development Zone was established, utilizing competitive resources to develop six pillar industries, including new materials and new energy. By the end of 2019, the development zone was providing employment for more than 80,000 people. Since 2014, the state has given strong support to Xinjiang's textiles industry, which created 350,000 new jobs from 2017 to 2019.

Prioritizing the development of agro-product processing and electronics assembly, Kashgar Prefecture has attracted related enterprises to its industrial development zones (IDZs) and helped them expand their production to rural areas. By the end of 2019, the prefecture had 210 agro-product processing enterprises providing 16,700 jobs, and 1,406 industrial enterprises located in the various IDZs providing 84,100 jobs.

Aksu Prefecture has been integrating industry and vocational education, offering joint education programs by textile and garment enterprises and vocational schools, and has facilitated employment for 32,400 people.

Assisting key groups to obtain stable employment. Xinjiang has adopted a policy to encourage surplus rural labor to work in or near their hometowns, developing "satellite factories" and "poverty alleviation workshops" in light of local conditions to create jobs, supporting rural organizations for labor service cooperation to facilitate employment, promoting IDZs to stabilize employment, and developing tourism to boost employment.

Xinjiang has launched a three-year program to intensify its poverty alleviation efforts in 22 extremely poor counties in its south and 4 extremely poor regimental farms under the Xinjiang Production and Construction Corps. From 2018 to June 2020, the local government helped 221,000 people from registered poor households in southern Xinjiang to find work outside their hometowns. In Kashgar and Hotan prefectures, a three-year relocation assistance program from 2017 to 2019 for both urban and rural surplus labor helped 135,000 people to find jobs outside their hometowns.

Xinjiang has provided dynamic, categorized and targeted assistance to people having difficulty finding work and to zero-employment households in the entire autonomous region – having each and every one of them identified, registered, assisted, and ensured stable employment. From 2014 to 2019, Xinjiang provided jobs for 334,300 urban residents having difficulty finding work, and ensured that zero-employment households found jobs within 24 hours once they were identified.

For university graduates, Xinjiang has implemented a number of plans to facilitate employment and the creation of new businesses, to guide them to work and grow at primary-level organizations, to encourage them to take up primary-level posts in education, agriculture, health care, and poverty alleviation in rural areas, and to help long-term unemployed youth find jobs. In 2019, the employment rate of university graduates in Xinjiang reached 90.4 percent, and the employment rate of ethnic minorities who graduated from universities in other parts of China and returned to Xinjiang reached 95.1 percent, both figures representing record highs.

Encouraging innovation and entrepreneurship to generate employment. Xinjiang promotes innovation as a new engine for creating jobs, and advances reform to streamline administration, delegate power, improve regulation and upgrade services. To encourage people who are eager and eligible to start their own businesses, the local government eases market access, improves policies in support of business startups, and sees to it that guaranteed loans, interest subsidies, allowances and tax breaks for startups are implemented. Xinjiang fosters platforms for innovation and entrepreneurship, improves capacity building for startups, and develops makerspaces which are market-oriented, professional, integrated and networked, to provide young entrepreneurs with more platforms and equal access to services.

Currently, Xinjiang has 5 business incubation demonstration bases at national level and 27 at provincial and equivalent level, which have fostered 1,412 micro and small businesses and created more than 10,000 jobs. Xinjiang supports innovation-driven startups and entrepreneurs as capable job creators, and encourages Internet plus entrepreneurship to multiply employment opportunities.

In 2019, Hotan Prefecture alone issued RMB910 million guaranteed loans for business startups, which helped 12,500 people to start businesses, including university graduates, rural workers and people having difficulty finding work. Xiao Min and five other women from Changji City, Changji Hui Autonomous Prefecture founded a human resources service company. It has become a leader of the local labor supply chain, integrating human resource services, dispatch of labor, logistics outsourcing, policy consultancy, and IT application. It has more than 4,800 employees from various ethnic groups and serves 318 enterprises and public institutions across the whole of Xinjiang. It has provided jobs for more than 30,000 unemployed and surplus rural laborers, and has created a total output value of RMB156 million.

Providing vocational training to facilitate employment. Based on the market demand for labor, Xinjiang focuses on improving employability of workers and promoting stable employment. It has developed a complete system of vocational education and training, including colleges for higher vocational and technical education, secondary technical schools, technical institutes, job placement training centers, employee training centers, and vocational education and training centers, with the goal of raising the basic quality of trainees and organizing training oriented to specific demands, jobs and employers. In 2019, Hotan Prefecture alone provided vocational training for 103,300 farmers and herders, of whom 98,300 found work, with an employment rate of over 95 percent.

Leveraging institutional strengths to expand employment channels. China has institutional strengths that promote equality and mutual assistance among all ethnic groups towards common development and progress. It has also formed a mechanism in which better-developed provinces pair up with and provide assistance for various parts of Xinjiang. Fully leveraging these strengths and this mechanism, Xinjiang coordinates jobs in and outside the autonomous region, to create favorable conditions for its local residents to work in other parts of China.

Since 2014, 117,000 people in Xinjiang have achieved employment with higher income in other parts of the country. Following the principle of "providing training according to market demand and before dispatching workers", Xinjiang has organized employment-oriented training on standard spoken and written Chinese, relevant legal knowledge, general knowhow of urban life, and labor skills. Recipients of relocation assistance are provided by their employers with daily necessities and proper accommodation. In some provinces, enterprises provide them with public rental housing, low-rent housing, or housing for couples. Xinjiang provides timely registration and certification services for those who find employment through relocation assistance, to facilitate their medical care in their host provinces. Employers and host provinces help guarantee their children's access to kindergartens and schools, and help them integrate into local life and share local resources.

Securing employment and public wellbeing in the face of Covid-19. In response to the impact of Covid-19, Xinjiang has coordinated epidemic prevention and control with social and economic development. It has worked hard to stabilize employment, finance, foreign trade, inbound investment, domestic investment, and market expectations, and has put in place measures to guarantee jobs, daily living needs, food and energy, industrial and supply chains, the interests of market players, and the smooth functioning of grassroots government. The local government has taken multiple measures to alleviate economic difficulties and stabilize and boost employment, and adopted policies offering periodical and targeted cuts in taxes and other employer contributions, aiming to facilitate the resumption of production and business activities, and increase employment generated by investment and industries.

Through all these measures, Xinjiang has achieved significant progress in increasing employment and ensuring public wellbeing while implementing Covid-19 control on an ongoing basis. This can be exemplified by the following statistics as of the end of June 2020:

• cuts of some RMB7.6 billion to old-age insurance, unemployment insurance, and work-related injury compensation insurance paid by enterprises, which represents a 50 percent reduction of RMB1.9 billion for large enterprises, and a complete exemption of RMB5.7 billion for micro, small and medium enterprises.

• approval to 1,237 enterprises in difficulties to postpone the payment of their social insurance premiums, totaling RMB706 million.

• reimbursement of unemployment insurance premiums of RMB904 million to 83,100 enterprises, benefiting 1.8 million employees.

• provision of various employment subsidies totaling about RMB1.7

billion to 552,400 people.

• creation of 339,700 new jobs in cities and towns, 41,800 new businesses hiring 69,500 employees, and jobs for 31,600 people with difficulty finding work.

• placement of 2.6 million surplus rural workers through relocation, a year-on-year increase of 46.1 percent.

III. Full Respect for Workers' Job Preferences

Workers' job preferences have always served as an important reference for the local government of Xinjiang in designing its employment policies, expanding employment channels, creating jobs, organizing vocational training sessions, and providing placement services. This ensures that the people can make their own choices about work and enjoy a happy life.

Forming a comprehensive picture of the local labor resources. The local government has constantly improved the statistical indicators for measuring employment and unemployment. It has put in place systems for monitoring labor resources in rural areas, employment in enterprises, and supply and demand on the human resource market, and has set up an unemployment monitoring and alert mechanism accordingly. Based on the labor offices at township/sub-district and village/community levels, local authorities have established basic information on the number, age, gender, education level, and employment status of the workforce in their respective jurisdiction. The monitoring and survey results serve as reference for formulating employment policies and plans. Surveys show that by the end of 2019, Xinjiang had a surplus rural workforce of 2.59 million people, among whom 1.65 million were in southern Xinjiang, accounting for almost two-thirds of the total.

Keeping track of the job preferences and needs of workers. The local government conducts regular surveys of the job preferences of workers, to keep track of their expectations in terms of location, position, salary, future prospects, and working and living environment. This allows the provision of more targeted services, aiming for the best possible match between employees and positions and promoting long-term stable employment. According to a survey in early 2020, with a population of 3,540, the Aybagh Village in Gulbagh Town, Shache (Yarkant) County, Kashgar Prefecture, had a workforce of 1,509 people, of whom 1,288, or 85 percent, were interested in working outside their county. Among these people, 923 wished to do factory work in the expectation of an average salary of about RMB5,000; 365 preferred to make a living by making naan bread, engage in catering or the dried fruit business, or pursue a career in the performing arts.

In 2019, a survey in three villages of Baghchi Town, Hotan County, Hotan Prefecture counted a total population of 5,307, with 1,699 people capable of work, of whom, 1,493, or 88 percent, were keen to work outside their home villages. Of the remainder, 180 preferred to work locally in township enterprises, village factories, or poverty-relief cooperatives offering an average monthly salary of RMB3,000; the other 26 wished to start businesses locally, engaging in transport and logistics, property management and household services, construction, hairdressing, catering or retail stores. These indicators give the government a clearer understanding of the job preferences of workers so it can better satisfy their individual needs, effectively promote the orderly flow of the workforce, and improve employment stability and job satisfaction.

Building employment information platforms. The local government has built an extensive contact network with employers to collect and collate job information, which is released timely, with the help of information technology, through the human resource market, public placement agencies, online service platforms, radio, TV, village and community bulletin boards, enabling people to look for the jobs that suit them best.

For example, the Aksu Prefecture has released job and candidate information on its public placement service portal and its WeChat account, to build two-way selection platforms for employers and employees. Since 2014, it has organized 621 job fairs, attracting 4,953 companies, providing over 145,000 job opportunities, and helping 38,600 people to find work. A poor villager named Habibulla Mamut from Aykol Town of Aksu City applied for a position with an electrical appliance company in Hangzhou at a local job fair, was offered the post, and earned RMB55,000 that year, raising himself and his family out of poverty.

Bolstering public employment services. The local government has built a well-defined, dynamic, five-tiered public employment service system for employers and employees, which is well-coordinated at all levels and covers every part of Xinjiang. It has also expanded its services in areas such as policy advice, employment and unemployment registration, career guidance and recommendation, and skills and business startup training. By the end of 2019, there were 144 human resource markets at the county level or above, 149 job placement agencies on the farms of the Xinjiang Production and Construction Corps, and 8,668 primary-level labor offices across Xinjiang, providing employment services to more than 21.73 million people that year.

Preventing and punishing any incidents of forced labor. China's *Criminal Law, Labor Law, Labor Contract Law,* and *Public Security Administrative Punishment Law* all stipulate that the following actions are strictly forbidden and will lead to administrative punishments: forcing a person to work by means of violence, threat, or illegal limitation of personal freedom; or affronting, physically punishing, beating, illegally searching or detaining an employee. Should it be established that a crime has taken place, the perpetrator will be subjected to a criminal investigation. Xinjiang strictly observes the relevant laws and regulations of the state, providing information on the law through education campaigns, strengthening the legal awareness of employers and employees, and conducting routine inspections to ensure that labor laws are enforced. The goal is to bring the establishment, management, supervision and arbitration of labor relations under legal scrutiny, and take resolute action to prevent or punish any incidents of forced labor.

IV. Labor Rights Protection

The Chinese government is committed to respecting citizens' right to work, safeguarding their legitimate labor rights and interests, and ensuring them a decent job. Strictly following the above principles as embodied in the *Constitution of the People's Republic of China* and relevant national laws, including the *Labor Law, Labor Contract Law, Employment Promotion Law, Social Insurance Law, Law on the Protection of Women's Rights and Interests*, and *Law on the Protection of Persons with Disabilities,* Xinjiang has formulated and implemented a series of autonomous regional regulations based on local conditions, including measures for implementing the national *Employment Promotion Law, Regulations on Labor and Social Security Supervision, Law on the Protection of Women's Rights and Interests*, and *Law on the Protection of Persons with Disabilities*, as well as the *Regulations of the Xinjiang Uygur Autonomous Region on the Protection of Labor Rights and Interests*. These laws and regulations provide a solid legal guarantee for citizens in Xinjiang to enjoy equal rights to work.

Guaranteeing workers' equal right to employment. In accordance with the principle of equal protection of civil rights, Xinjiang ensures that there is no discrimination against workers on the basis of ethnicity, region, gender, and religious belief, and that no individuals' rights are restricted because of their urban or rural status, profession or position. In ensuring women's rights, Xinjiang strives to remove barriers to employment and formulates policies to support women in starting their own businesses. In 2019, 480,900 new jobs were created in cities and towns; 228,100 of these were for women, accounting for 47 percent of the total. To protect the labor rights of persons with disabilities, Xinjiang puts in more efforts on their vocational training, promotes their employment at public welfare enterprises and institutions, offers them flexible and less demanding jobs and public service positions, and advances their proportional employment. It also supports them in finding work through self-employment, starting new businesses or other flexible ways of employment. By the end of 2019, 183,700 of them were employed – almost 60 percent of the total workforce of persons with disabilities in Xinjiang.

Guaranteeing workers' right to remuneration. Xinjiang fully applies the country's policy requirements on establishing a dynamic salary growth mechanism for enterprise employees, and improves the salary guidance systems for enterprises and for the labor market respectively. Each year from 2014 to 2019, it released a salary growth guideline for enterprises. It established and improved the minimum salary adjustment mechanism, raising the minimum salary by almost 20 percent from RMB1,520 per month in 2013 to RMB1,820 per month in 2018, which was at a high level in the country. Xinjiang has issued the *Regulations of Xinjiang Uygur Autonomous Region on Collective Salary Negotiation in Enterprises* and other regulations to promote and steadily expand the coverage of collective salary negotiation. The local government has also improved the system for guaranteeing salary payments. It punishes illegal and criminal acts of withholding labor remuneration, and thus ensures that workers receive their salaries in full and on time.

Guaranteeing workers' right to rest and leisure and to occupational safety. Xinjiang strictly applies relevant state regulations and adopts the system of the eight-hour workday and 40-hour workweek. If an employer wishes to extend working hours for operational reasons, it must consult with the trade union and the employees in accordance with the law, and arrange for compensation in the form of additional time off or remuneration. Workers are guaranteed the right to time off on weekends and statutory holidays including the Spring Festival, Roza Festival (Eid al-Fitr) and Corban Festival (Eid al-Adha). Xinjiang also strictly applies the national occupational safety and health regulations and standards, consistently improves the responsibility system for workplace safety and occupational disease prevention, and carries out inspections over occupational health law enforcement. As a result, the autonomous region has succeeded in preventing or reducing to a minimum all kinds of workplace safety incidents, and established fundamental control over or eliminated occupational disease hazards.

Guaranteeing workers' right to participate in social insurance. Xinjiang has fully implemented the national plan to ensure that everyone has access to social security and all those in need are covered. Workers in micro, small and medium-sized enterprises, and key groups including migrant workers, the self-employed, and people engaged in new forms of business are encouraged to participate in social insurance. By the end of 2019, more than 22 million people were participating in basic pension, unemployment, and work-related injury insurance. Labor and social security supervision bodies at all levels continue to step up law enforcement, address reports and complaints about violations of relevant laws, regulations, and rules in a timely manner, and investigate and correct in accordance with the law illegal acts where employers fail to register for or contribute to social insurance, resolutely safeguarding the legitimate rights and interests of workers.

Guaranteeing workers' freedom of religious belief and the right to use their own spoken and written languages. Xinjiang strictly applies the *Constitution* and relevant national laws and regulations, including the *Law on Regional Ethnic Autonomy*, the *Law on the Standard Spoken and Written Chinese Language*, and the *Regulations on Religious Affairs*. The local government fully respects and guarantees the right of workers of all ethnic groups to freedom of religious belief, and ensures that no organization or individual interferes with this freedom. While promoting standard spoken and written Chinese in accordance with the law, Xinjiang fully respects and protects the rights of ethnic minority workers to use their own spoken and written languages, and ensures that workers can choose which languages to use for communication. The customs of workers of all ethnic groups are fully respected and guaranteed and efforts are made to create a good working and living environment for them. Tokhali Turhanbay from Wuqia (Ulughchat) County, Kizilsu Kirgiz Autonomous Prefecture, now works in a shoe factory in Guangdong Province. He belongs to an ethnic minority and is a religious believer who follows halal diet. Before going to work at the factory, he was concerned that he would have difficulty maintaining his eating practices, and that there would be no place to worship. But when he arrived, he found that the living environment in the factory was comfortable, and the halal food was excellent. He also found that it was convenient to go shopping and video chat with his family during his spare time, and he was able to attend religious activities at a nearby mosque. Therefore, he quickly adapted to the new environment.

Protecting workers' rights and interests and strengthening the relief mechanism. Xinjiang fully implements the labor contract system, which clarifies the rights and obligations of employers and workers. The autonomous region keeps improving the tripartite mechanism of consultation among representatives of the government, trade unions, and business organizations, investigates and solves major problems involving labor relations, and seeks to build harmony in the workplace. Xinjiang also encourages trade unions to play an active role in safeguarding the legitimate rights and interests of workers. It reinforces labor and social security supervision as well as mediation and arbitration of labor disputes, and handles labor disputes in a timely and appropriate manner. It has taken targeted actions to rectify major violations of labor laws and regulations, and carried out special supervision over the handling of major cases. As a result it is able to effectively protect the legitimate rights and interests of workers concerning job intermediation, labor contracts, working hours, time off and leave, salary payment, social insurance, and special labor protection.

V. Better Jobs for Better Lives

With the implementation of a series of employment policies and measures, the goal that "each household has access to job opportunities, each person has work to do, and each month goes with an income" has been largely achieved. Profound changes have taken place in the life, work and mentality of the people of all the ethnic groups in Xinjiang and particularly in southern Xinjiang – their pockets are better filled, their lives are better, and they are happier.

A marked increase in family incomes. People working either within or outside of Xinjiang all have stable incomes. The annual per capita income of workers from Xinjiang who are working in other provinces is about RMB40,000, roughly equal to the per capita disposable income of permanent urban residents in the places where they work. The local people who left their home to work elsewhere in Xinjiang have an annual per capita income of RMB30,000, much higher than earnings from farming. For example, a villager named Arapat Ahmatjan from Charbagh Township, Lop County, Hotan Prefecture earned less than RMB10,000 per year as a farmer; but when he found work in an electric appliance company in Nanchang City, Jiangxi Province in 2017, he earned more than RMB160,000 in less than three years.

Likewise, another villager named Mamtimin Turamat from Ushshar-bash Town, Yecheng (Qaghilik) County, Kashgar Prefecture earned only a few thousand yuan annually as a farmer, but his monthly income rose to more than RMB4,000 after he began to work for a company in Changji Hui Autonomous Prefecture. His life was much better – he built a new house and got married.

Amina Rahman and her husband from a registered poor household in Ghoruchol Town, Awat County, Aksu Prefecture, applied for jobs after seeing the information released by the township's labor and social security office in March 2018, and were then both hired by a company in Jiujiang City, Jiangxi Province. They now have a monthly income of about RMB9,000, paying off their loans and saving over RMB90,000 yuan.

Notable improvement in living standards. From having their basic needs met to enjoying decent lives, and from traveling by a donkey cart to traveling in modern vehicles, the people in Xinjiang have witnessed tremendous changes in their lives.

A villager called Reyhangul Imir from a poor household in Ojma Township, Akto County, Kizilsu Kirgiz Autonomous Prefecture sent back more than RMB100,000 to her family in the four years she spent working in Cixi City, Zhejiang Province. With the money, her family upgraded their lives by building a new house equipped with new furniture in her hometown.

Yusan Hasan from Yurungqash Town, Hotan City used to make a living by taking odd jobs, and struggled to make ends meet. In July 2018, thanks to helpful acquaintances, he found a job at a meat-packing plant in Urumqi, the capital city of Xinjiang. Starting as a handyman, his hard work paid off and he soon picked up new skills. He then persuaded his wife to join him, and she found a stable job in a clothing store in Urumqi. They soon settled in the city, buying an apartment in 2020.

Enhanced employability. Through various pre-employment training programs, the local people have greatly improved their employment skills; many have grown into master hands and technical experts, and some have become managers and even started up their own businesses.

After three years of rotating in various positions, Amina Obul from Siyak Township, Yutian (Keriya) County, Hotan Prefecture has become one of the best employees of an energy company. Arzugul Iskandar from Pishan (Guma) County, Hotan Prefecture works at a textile company in Chaohu City, Anhui Province. She has become a technical expert and a master for young workers with the help of senior colleagues.

After graduating from Beijing Institute of Fashion Technology, Adila Ablat from Kucha City, Aksu Prefecture started a garment company in 2018 in his hometown with the help of the local government. In 2019 his company achieved an output value of over RMB2 million, and created jobs for over 40 women.

A college graduate with disabilities, Jibek Nurlanhan from Altay City, Altay Prefecture, Ili Kazak Autonomous Prefecture returned to her hometown after graduation. The local human resources and social security department arranged for her to take a startup training class, and helped her to raise RMB100,000 to create a store selling Kazak embroidery handicrafts. She now has a monthly income of over RMB6,000.

A change in mindset. In the past, some local people undervalued education, and valued men over women. With outdated employment ideas, some used to rely on government aid and relief for a living. But today, the belief that "only hard work can bring a better life" is widespread, and all ethnic groups here are eager to rely on their own efforts to improve their lives – full of drive, and ready to start up their own businesses. For example, at a job fair held in Makit County, Kashgar Prefecture, many candidates hurried around gathering information on available opportunities and applying for positions. It was an inspiring scene. Some villagers were motivated to find opportunities outside their villages and give their families a better life after seeing their peers had made some money and were looking more prosperous.

Ablimit Keyum from Kanchi Township, Baicheng (Bay) County, Aksu Prefecture, who is doing business in Xinjiang and other provinces, said, "I'm not satisfied with the status quo, and I want to study and work harder to make my life better."

Rozinisa Imin from Tusalla Township, Hotan City signed up for work in Jinjiang City, Fujian Province in March 2019. The money she earned helped to support her family's animal farming. Her brother, who has just graduated from vocational high school, sees her as his inspiration. He plans to seek work in Fujian as well, and dreams of a bright future.

Life dreams realized. Many people find the right jobs through their own initiative. They move from rural to urban areas, and turn from farmers to workers. In this process, they learn skills, increase their incomes, and achieve prosperity; more importantly, they have broadened their horizons, acquired knowledge and greater abilities, and achieved their potential. Most people are satisfied with their current life and are optimistic about the future.

Mamattohti Imintohti from Hotan County, Hotan Prefecture longed to own his own restaurant. He began to work as an apprentice at a restaurant in Urumqi in 2017 and soon mastered the skills of a pastry cook. With the help of his teacher, he opened a restaurant which has become very popular.

Pashagul Keram from Boritokay Township, Wuqia (Ulughchat) County, Kizilsu Kirgiz Autonomous Prefecture is public-spirited and ready to help – she has led more than 500 local residents to find work in Guangdong, and thereby helped them escape from poverty. She was awarded the national May 1st Labor Medal and the National Award for Efforts in Poverty Alleviation.

Closer communication and bonds between all ethnic groups. Workers of all ethnic groups in Xinjiang have forged profound friendships while working, studying and living together. They care for and help each other like family, demonstrating ethnic unity and mutual assistance built on a close bond towards each other.

An electrical appliance company in Jiangsu Province took on about 200 employees from 16 ethnic groups from Xinjiang. The workers often gather together to enjoy themselves, singing, dancing, having parties, shopping, traveling, and cooking pilaf and kebabs like a family.

You Liangying, an employee of Xinjiang Production and Construction Corps who set up a cotton and fruit planting cooperative, helped thousands of people from different ethnic groups to learn advanced planting skills in her 17 trips crossing deserts stretching hundreds of miles. Her efforts not only helped them out of poverty, but also fostered closer ethnic ties. Over the past decade and more, she has selflessly helped Mamatturup Musak from Pishan (Guma) County, Hotan Prefecture, who chose to repay the favor by giving back to society. Their story is well-known across Xinjiang.

VI. Application of International Labor and Human Rights Standards

Xinjiang implements a proactive employment policy, protects the lawful labor rights and interests of people of all ethnic groups, and strives to provide decent work and a better life for all. This embodies the common values that are championed by the international community, and contributes to safeguarding social fairness and justice and promoting the all-round development of humanity.

Fulfilling international convention obligations. China is a founding and permanent member state of the International Labour Organization (ILO). China has ratified 26 international labor conventions, including four of the ILO's fundamental conventions – *Equal Remuneration Convention, Minimum Age Convention, Worst Forms of Child Labour Convention,* and *Discrimination (Employment and Occupation) Convention.*

China is also a signatory state to a host of UN conventions, including the *International Covenant on Economic, Social and Cultural Rights,* the *International Convention on the Elimination of All Forms of Racial Discrimination,* the *Convention on the Elimination of All Forms of Discrimination against Women,* the *Convention against Torture and Other Cruel, Inhuman or Degrading Treatment or Punishment,* the *Convention on the Rights of the Child,* the *Convention on the Rights of Persons with Disabilities,* and the *Protocol to Prevent, Suppress and Punish Trafficking in Persons, Especially Women and Children, Supplementing the United Nations Convention against Transnational Organized Crime.*

China applies international labor and human rights standards in its legislation, policymaking and policy implementation, to effectively safeguard workers' rights. China prohibits child labor, opposes forced labor, employment discrimination, and workplace sexual harassment, takes targeted actions to combat illegal employment, and prevents and punishes all kinds of violations and crimes concerning employment. In fulfilling their responsibilities to secure employment, local governments at all levels in Xinjiang promote full and high-quality employment for people in different areas, of different ethnic groups, and with different economic conditions, to achieve common development and progress among all ethnic groups. Xinjiang has thus become a successful example of practicing international labor and human rights standards in underdeveloped areas with large populations of ethnic minorities.

Finding new approaches to eradicating poverty. Ending poverty has been a lasting goal of humanity and a major component of human rights protection. In the *UN 2030 Agenda for Sustainable Development*, "ending poverty in all its forms everywhere" tops all other development goals, expressing a pressing demand by the international community to this end. In implementing the 2030 Agenda, China makes it clear that the goal of achieving moderate prosperity in all respects is for its entire people, and that not a single ethnic group is allowed to be lagged behind. Xinjiang protects human rights through development, and strives to eradicate poverty through education and training, capacity building and employment. It effectively prevents and strikes out at terrorism and extremism, and at the same time maintains social stability and improves people's lives, with its impoverished population and poverty incidence markedly reduced. From 2013 to the end of 2019, Xinjiang wiped out poverty in 25 poor counties and 3,107 poor villages, and the poverty incidence dropped from 19.4 percent to 1.24 percent. From 2014 to the end of 2019, a total of 2.92 million people from 737,600 households shook off poverty. By the end of 2020, poverty will be completely eliminated in Xinjiang. Xinjiang has worked out a new approach to addressing some of the global challenges: protecting human rights while combating terrorism and extremism, and pursuing sustainable development while eliminating poverty.

Responding to the ILO's Decent Work Agenda. The ILO has launched an agenda to promote decent work for all, aiming to achieve all-round human development. The agenda, which is integral to respecting and protecting human rights, embodies the consensus of the international community. The Chinese government always puts people first and has actively responded to the ILO's agenda by implementing the *Decent Work Country Program for China (2016-2020)* and incorporating the concept of decent work into national policies and development plans. Xinjiang has put into practice relevant policy measures of the national government, focusing in particular on respecting workers' choices, protecting their rights and interests, improving their workplace environment and working conditions, and recognizing their contributions. This ensures that people from all ethnic groups work in a decent environment with freedom, equality, safety, and dignity. Conforming to the *Constitution*, the *Labor Law*, and the *Employment Promotion Law* of the country, and respecting local conditions, Xinjiang has launched a package of effective policy measures to ensure stable employment for all residents. In recent years, Xinjiang's registered urban unemployment rate has remained below 3.5 percent. This enables the local people enjoy the right to work to the greatest extent possible, and has laid a solid foundation for raising the human rights to life and development to a higher level across a broader sphere.

Conclusion

Chinese President Xi Jinping, also general secretary of the CPC Central Committee and chairman of the Central Military Commission, has emphasized that employment is pivotal to people's wellbeing. *The Global Employment Agenda* adopted by the ILO states that employment is central to poverty reduction. Having decent work is of vital importance to one's survival and growth, a harmonious and happy family life, and the long-term stability of society. The proactive polices to ensure employment and job security adopted by the local government of Xinjiang have effectively protected all ethnic groups' basic labor rights, greatly improved their living and working conditions, and fully satisfied their aspirations to create a better life.

For years, certain international forces, guilty of ideological bias and prejudiced against China, have been applying double standards in Xinjiang, criticizing "breaches of human rights" while ignoring the tremendous efforts Xinjiang has made to protect human rights. They have fabricated facts to support their false claims of "forced labor" in Xinjiang, and smeared the local government's work on employment and job security. Their acts amount to a denial of the fact that the local people in Xinjiang enjoy the right to work, aspire to move out of poverty and backwardness and are working towards that goal. Such groundless allegation would be strongly opposed by everyone who values justice and progress.

Respecting and protecting human rights are principles enshrined in the *Constitution* of China. The CPC and the Chinese government have always prioritized the protection of the citizens' rights to work and employment, and have taken a resolute stance against forced labor and eradicated it in any form. Xinjiang's policies and practices concerning employment and job security comply with China's *Constitution* and relevant laws, conform to international labor and human rights standards, and support the will of all ethnic groups to live a better life. They have served to meet the people's needs, improve their wellbeing, and win their support.

Work helps to make a difference and create happiness. Looking forward, Xinjiang will continue its commitment to the people-centered philosophy of development, adhere to the principle that employment is of paramount importance to people's wellbeing, implement the strategy of giving priority to employment, and introduce more proactive policies to boost employment. With tireless efforts it will strive to grow employment in volume and quality, to meet the growing expectation of all ethnic groups for a better life.

China's Armed Forces:
30 Years of UN Peacekeeping Operations

The State Council Information Office of
the People's Republic of China

September 2020

Preface

This year marks the 75th anniversary of victory in the Chinese People's War of Resistance Against Japanese Aggression and the World Anti-Fascist War. It is also the 75th anniversary of the founding of the United Nations (UN) and the 30th year since China's armed forces first participated in UN peacekeeping operations (UNPKOs).

Peace is an ever-lasting aspiration of the Chinese people and the salient feature of China's development. Since its founding, the People's Republic of China (PRC) has been firmly committed to the path of peaceful development; it has made a significant contribution to world peace and development while realizing its own development. China has always resolutely safeguarded the UN-centered international system and the basic norms governing international relations underpinned by the purposes and principles of the UN Charter, and worked with countries around the world to uphold multilateralism, equity and justice.

China takes concrete actions to safeguard world peace and has actively participated in the UNPKOs. China is the second largest contributor to both peacekeeping assessment and UN membership fees, and the largest troop-contributing country (TCC) among the permanent members of the UN Security Council. Over the past 30 years, China's armed forces have resolutely delivered on the purposes and principles of the UN Charter, and sent over 40,000 peacekeepers to 25 UN peacekeeping missions. They have faithfully performed their duties and made a positive contribution to world peace and common development. They have stood fast as a disciplined force for peace and justice.

In the new era, China's armed forces comprehensively implement the pledges announced by President Xi Jinping during the UN Leaders'

Summit on Peacekeeping. To contribute to building a community with a shared future for mankind, China's armed forces have stepped up their support for and participation in the UNPKOs, bringing greater confidence and hope for peace and development to areas beset by conflict. As a critical element and key force in the UNPKOs, China's armed forces in the new era have instilled more positive energy into world peace and development.

The world is undergoing profound changes unseen in a century. Despite mounting risks and challenges, peace and development remain the overriding theme of the times. No matter how the international landscape evolves, China will always strive to maintain world peace, promote global growth, and uphold international order. China's armed forces will always be a force of justice for world peace and development.

The Chinese government is issuing this white paper to review the glorious journey of China's armed forces in the UNPKOs over the past 30 years, to expound their ideas on safeguarding world peace in the new era, and to elaborate on the efforts they make.

I. Embarking on Missions for World Peace

UN Peacekeeping, as an instrument developed for peace, has made a significant contribution to world peace. In 1971, China recovered its legitimate seat in the UN and began to play a more active role in international affairs. After reform and opening up began in 1978, China gradually increased its involvement in UN peacekeeping affairs. In April 1990, China's armed forces dispatched five military observers to the United Nations Truce Supervision Organization (UNTSO) and embarked on a new voyage as a participant in the UNPKOs. In the past three decades, China's armed forces have engaged in the UNPKOs with courage and determination, always aspiring to fulfill their missions of meeting the responsibilities of a major country, safeguarding world peace, and contributing to the building of a community with a shared future for mankind. China's Blue Helmets have become a key force in UN peacekeeping.

China's armed forces participate in the UNPKOs, because the pursuit of peace is in the genes of the Chinese nation. The Chinese nation values peace and harmony. Ideas such as "unity of man and nature" "harmony among all nations" "harmony without uniformity" and "kindness towards fellow human beings," voice the mind of the Chinese people on the universe, international relations, society and ethics. The pursuit of peace, amity and harmony has long been the primary aspiration of our nation. The philosophy of upholding peace, harmony, cooperation and common development has been passed down from generation to generation in China. For millennia, peace has been in the veins and the DNA of the Chinese nation. It is a consistent goal of China's armed forces.

China's armed forces participate in the UNPKOs, because the Chinese people care about the wellbeing of humanity. The Chinese people always dream of living in a harmonious world where everyone belongs to one and the same family. They advocate that "a just cause should be pursued for the common good" and that one should put concern for the wellbeing of other people before personal interests. They hope for a better life not only for themselves, but also for other peoples across the world. Chinese service members join the UN efforts to bring hope and promote peace.

China's armed forces participate in the UNPKOs, because serving the people is the fundamental purpose of the people's armed forces. China's armed forces come from the people, have their roots in the people, developed to serve the people, and fight for the people. They serve the people wholeheartedly at all times and under all circumstances, remain close to the people, and always put the people's interests first. With love and humanity, Chinese peacekeeping troops make efforts to bring peace and happiness to people in mission areas.

China's armed forces participate in the UNPKOs, because China honors its responsibilities as a major country. As a founding member of the UN and a responsible member of the international community, China honors its obligations, firmly supports the UN's authority and stature, and actively participates in the UNPKOs. China is a permanent member of the UN Security Council, and therefore, it is incumbent on China as a major country to play an active part in the UNPKOs. World peace is indivisible and humanity shares a common destiny. To participate in the UNPKOs is integral to China's joint efforts with other countries to build a community with a shared future for mankind.

China's armed forces commit themselves to the following policy stances on UN peacekeeping:

Upholding the purposes and principles of the UN Charter. China always abides by the primary principles of the UN such as sovereign equality of all members and settlement of international disputes by peaceful means. It respects the social systems and development paths independently chosen by other countries, and respects and accommodates the legitimate security concerns of all parties.

Following the basic principles of the UNPKOs. China always adheres to the basic principles of UN peacekeeping, including consent of the host nation, impartiality, and non-use of force except in self-defense and defense of the mandate. It respects the territorial integrity and political independence of sovereign states, always remains impartial, and strictly fulfills the mandate of the Security Council.

Championing the vision of global governance based on extensive consultation, joint contribution and shared benefits. China stays committed to building a world of lasting peace through dialogue and consultation, to combining its efforts with others to bring about a world of common security for all, and to creating a world of common prosperity through win-win cooperation, an open and inclusive world through exchanges and mutual learning, and a clean and beautiful world by pursuing green and low-carbon development.

Pursuing common, comprehensive, cooperative and sustainable security. China always respects and ensures the security of each and every country. It upholds security in both traditional and non-traditional fields, promotes the security of both individual countries and broader regions through dialogue and cooperation, and focuses on development and security so that security would be durable.

Staying committed to peaceful means in settling disputes. China advocates that disputes and differences between countries or within a country should be resolved through peaceful means. Countries should increase mutual trust, settle disputes and promote security through dialogue. Willful threat or use of force should be rejected.

Building stronger peacekeeping partnerships. China strives to bring about greater involvement of host nations, TCCs and fund contributing countries (FCCs) through UN peacekeeping reform. It leverages the role of regional and sub-regional organizations, and promotes closer partnerships in peacekeeping operations.

II. A Key Force in UNPKOs

Over the past 30 years, China's armed forces have contributed a growing number of peacekeepers across an expanding range of deployments. From a few military observers at the outset of its involvement, China's armed forces are now sending both formed units and military professionals. Chinese military peacekeepers serve on the UN missions in engineer, medical, transport, helicopter, force protection and infantry units, and as staff officers, military observers and seconded officers. Chinese military peacekeepers have left their footprints in over 20 countries and regions including Cambodia, the Democratic Republic of the Congo (DRC), Liberia, Sudan, Lebanon, Cyprus, South Sudan, Mali and the Central African Republic. They have made a tremendous contribution to facilitating the peaceful settlement of disputes, safeguarding regional security and stability, and promoting economic and social development in host nations.

1. Ceasefire Supervision

Ceasefires are supervised to ensure that conflicting parties abide by their agreements. It was the earliest function of UN peacekeeping, and the first task undertaken by Chinese military peacekeepers. Since 1990, in addition to military observers, more military professionals have been involved in UN peacekeeping as staff officers and seconded officers. In the past three decades, China's armed forces have sent 2,064 military professionals to 25 missions and UN headquarters (UNHQ). Thirteen of them have been appointed to key positions as force commander, deputy force commander, sector commander, and deputy sector commander. In August 2020, 84 military professionals were working on missions and at UNHQ on patrols, observation, ceasefire supervision, liaison, negotiation, command and control, and operations planning.

Military observers are deployed in conflicts to gather information for decision making. Their lives are often threatened by armed conflicts. On July 25, 2006, during the Israel-Lebanon conflict, Du Zhaoyu, a young Chinese military observer deployed in south Lebanon, bravely remained at his post, fulfilled his duty, and made the ultimate sacrifice for peace. He was posthumously awarded First Class Merit by the Chinese military and the Dag Hammarskjöld Medal by the UN.

2. Stabilizing the Situation

Promptly stabilizing the situation paves the way for the peace process. This is a main task of UN peacekeeping missions, and an important area to which Chinese peacekeeping troops have expanded their functions in recent years. The security situation in some mission areas is challenging, marred by frequent conflicts, terrorist attacks and violent riots. Among all peacekeeping units, it is the infantry battalions that are mainly tasked with armed patrol, separating conflicting parties, riot control, cordoning, and search. They are the backbone for UN peacekeeping and the stabilizers of security.

In January 2015, the Chinese People's Liberation Army (PLA) dispatched an infantry battalion of 700 troops to the United Nations Mission in South Sudan (UNMISS), the first organic unit of its kind to operate overseas in a peacekeeping mission. Over the past five years, six rotations have been committed to UNMISS. The Chinese infantrymen worked day and night amid the rattle of gunfire and the rumble of explosions in the mission area. As of August 2020, these battalions had completed 51 long-range and 93 short-distance patrols, 314 armed escorts, and over 30,000 hours of patrols in weapons-free zones, making a significant contribution to stabilizing the local situation. In August 2018, when a large riot erupted in Juba, capital of South Sudan, the Chinese infantry battalion acted immediately on orders and quelled the violence decisively and promptly.

3. Protecting Civilians

The Protection of Civilians (POC) is an important part of the UNPKOs. It is a duty that Chinese military peacekeepers resolutely undertake. The Chinese people suffered immensely from the scourge of war in modern times, and Chinese service members know only too well the value of peace and life. In war-torn mission areas, Chinese military peacekeepers maintain peace with their sweat, youth and lives.

In July 2016, an armed conflict broke out in Juba between government and opposition forces. Heavy weapons including tanks, large-caliber artillery, and armed helicopters were employed by both sides in fierce exchange of fire, putting a large number of civilians in severe danger. The Chinese infantry battalion, together with peacekeepers from other countries, was responsible for protecting civilians in downtown Juba and over a hundred surrounding villages. Facing a raging storm of gunfire and artillery bombardment, the Chinese infantrymen risked their lives to build a defense for life and prevented the militants from approaching the POC camp, and ensured the safety of over 9,000 civilians. Corporal Li Lei and Sergeant Yang Shupeng sacrificed their lives in the action. They lived up to the solemn pledge and sacred obligation of protecting lives and safeguarding peace with bravery and sacrifice. They were posthumously conferred First Class Merit by the Chinese military and the Dag Hammarskjöld Medal by the UN.

4. Providing Force Protection

Force protection is vital to securing the personnel and assets of UN peacekeeping missions. As an important contributor to the UNPKOs, China's armed forces have been active in sending in troops to the UN missions to provide reliable force protection.

In December 2013, China's armed forces dispatched a force protection unit of 170 troops to the United Nations Multidimensional Integrated Stabilization Mission in Mali (MINUSMA) to conduct guard duties and VIP protection at the Sector East Headquarters. This was the first time that China's armed forces had dispatched troops to carry out force protection duties for the UNPKOs. Mali is among the most dangerous mission areas, afflicted by frequent suicide attacks, roadside bombs and other terrorist assaults. Over the past seven years, China's armed forces have sent 1,440 troops for force protection in eight rotations to MINUSMA. The units have fulfilled their tasks effectively in the hazardous southern edge of the Sahara Desert, including over 3,900 armed patrols and armed escorts. They have earned themselves the reputation of "des troupes d'élite" of Sector East. On May 31, 2016, First Sergeant Shen Liangliang was killed trying to prevent a terrorist vehicle laden with explosives from crashing into the UN camp. He was posthumously conferred First Class Merit by the Chinese military and the Dag Hammarskjöld Medal by the UN. On the occasion of the 70th anniversary of the founding of the PRC, First Sergeant Shen Liangliang was conferred the national honorary title of People's Hero.

On March 12, 2017, an intense conflict broke out in Yei, a border town in South Sudan. Seven UN civilian staff were caught in the crossfire and they were at severe risk of losing their lives. The Chinese infantry battalion immediately sent in 12 officers and soldiers to the rescue. Despite threats and dangers in their way, they outmaneuvered the militants, defeated three interception attempts, and successfully evacuated the trapped personnel. This timely and efficient operation was hailed and publicized as an exemplary model of rescue operations by UNMISS.

5. Deploying Enabling Capabilities

Force enablers such as engineer, transport, medical, and helicopter units play an irreplaceable role in the UNPKOs. Currently, the majority of Chinese peacekeeping troops perform such enabling tasks. On UN peacekeeping missions, Chinese military peacekeepers in the logistic support units have become the embodiment of China's quality, speed and standards through their skills, professionalism and dedication.

In January 2020, some terrorists attacked the Tessalit Camp in the

Sector North of MINUSMA and wounded more than 20 people. The Chinese medical unit in Sector East was rushed in by air and evacuated seven injured Chad peacekeepers to the Chinese medical camp. All the wounded were saved by prompt emergency treatment. In May 2020, despite the ongoing COVID-19 pandemic and a tense security situation, the Chinese engineer unit built a bridge over the Sopo River in South Sudan to the highest quality standards. This bridge created a transport route between Wau and Raga, which was highly commended by the local government and residents.

In the past 30 years, China's armed forces have contributed 111 engineer units totaling 25,768 troops to eight UN peacekeeping missions in Cambodia, the DRC, Liberia, Sudan, Lebanon, Sudan's Darfur, South Sudan, and Mali. These units have built and rehabilitated more than 17,000 kilometers of roads and 300 bridges, disposed of 14,000 landmines and unexploded ordnance, and performed a large number of engineering tasks including leveling ground, renovating airports, assembling prefabricated houses, and building defense works. Twenty-seven transport units totaling 5,164 troops were dispatched to the UN peacekeeping missions in Liberia and Sudan. They transported over 1.2 million tons of materials and equipment over a total distance of more than 13 million kilometers. Eighty-five medical units of 4,259 troops were sent to six UN peacekeeping missions in the DRC, Liberia, Sudan, Lebanon, South Sudan, and Mali. They have provided medical services to over 246,000 sick and wounded people. Three helicopter units totaling 420 troops were sent to Sudan's Darfur. They completed 1,951 flight hours, transported 10,410 passengers and over 480 tons of cargo in 1,602 sorties.

6. Sowing the Seeds of Hope

It is the common aspiration of all peoples throughout the world to live a better life. Far from home, Chinese military peacekeepers have made concrete efforts to bring peace and hope to war-afflicted peoples.

To actively facilitate humanitarian assistance. Over the past 30 years,

China's peacekeeping troops worked extensively and effectively with international humanitarian agencies, and have played an active role in resettling refugees and internally displaced persons (IDPs), distributing food, building refugee and IDP camps, and carrying out disaster relief tasks. In April 2020, Uvira in eastern DRC was struck by a rare flood, which posed a severe threat to the lives and property of the locals. The Chinese engineer unit was assigned to disaster relief work at the most critical moment and rushed to help reinforce levees and restore damaged bridges. They have given the locals access to help and protection, and effectively ensured the safety and security of the affected population.

To participate extensively in post-conflict reconstruction. In a post-war country or region, when a peace agreement is reached, it is essential to restore livelihoods and social order in order to prevent the recurrence of conflict and achieve lasting peace and stability. Chinese peacekeeping troops have played an active role in post-conflict reconstruction of host nations. They built important infrastructure, monitored elections, trained local doctors and nurses, and promoted environmental protection. Their efforts have been acclaimed by the governments and peoples of host nations. Darfur lies on the edge of a desert with complex geology. It is one of the regions afflicted by the world's most severe water shortages. From 2007 to 2013, Chinese military engineers drilled 14 wells in the most difficult circumstances, and effectively alleviated the problem of water scarcity for the locals.

To pass on love and care. Chinese military peacekeepers are not only guardians of peace but also messengers of friendship. The Chinese medical units in the DRC ran a twinning project in SOS Children's Village Bukavu to offer help. Touched by the love and care from the units, children in the village called the female members their Chinese mothers. The consistent efforts of the Chinese units over the past 17 years have won widespread praise from the locals. In UNMISS, Chinese military peacekeepers provided agricultural techniques, farming tools and vegetable seeds to local people. They were invited by local middle schools to teach lessons on

Chinese culture and language, which were very popular with the students.

Over the past 30 years, China's armed forces have contributed more than 40,000 service members to 25 UN peacekeeping missions. Sixteen Chinese military peacekeepers have sacrificed their lives for the noble cause of peace. As of August 2020, 2,521 Chinese military peacekeepers were serving on eight UN peacekeeping missions and at UNHQ. Chinese service women are playing an increasingly important role in peacekeeping. More than 1,000 female peacekeepers have worked in medical support, liaison, coordination, demining, explosive ordnance disposal, patrol, observation, gender equality promotion, protecting women and children, and other fields. They demonstrated the talent and professionalism of Chinese women on their UN missions. Chinese peacekeeping troops have been commended by the UN and the international community for their contribution. They have won honor for their country and military. On October 1st, 2019, Chinese military peacekeepers were reviewed for the first time by the country and the people in the parade celebrating the 70th anniversary of the PRC.

III. Implementation of Pledges Announced at the UN Summit

On September 28, 2015, President Xi Jinping addressed the Leaders' Summit on Peacekeeping at UNHQ and announced six measures that China would take to support UN peacekeeping. The Chinese government and armed forces have faithfully implemented the decisions and directions of President Xi Jinping, and taken concrete steps to honor their promises. Important progress has been made over the past five years. China's armed forces have expanded the composition of their peacekeeping troops from single service to multiple military branches, enabling Chinese peacekeepers to perform diverse tasks in addition to enabling functions. The objectives of China's peacekeeping efforts have extended beyond conflict prevention to building lasting peace. As a result, the peacekeeping capacity of China's armed forces has been further strengthened.

1. A Peacekeeping Standby Force in Position

Rapid deployment of peacekeeping forces means greater opportunities to maintain peace and protect lives. China's armed forces fully support the UN in developing the Peacekeeping Capability Readiness System (PCRS) and reinforcing UN rapid deployment capacity. In September 2017, China completed the registration of a UN peacekeeping standby force of 8,000 troops. This force has 28 units in ten categories – infantry, engineer, transport, medical, force protection, rapid response, helicopter, transport aircraft, UAV, and surface ship units. In October 2018, after a satisfactory Assessment and Advisory Visit (AAV) by a UNHQ team, 13 of these units were elevated to PCRS Level 2. In 2019 and 2020, six units were upgraded to PCRS Level 3 from Level 2. The Chinese standby force has been trained in strict compliance with the UN criteria and maintained the requisite degree of preparedness. It is now a well-trained, well-equipped and disciplined specialized force. China has become the country with the largest number of standby peacekeeping troops of the most diversified profile. In addition, in June 2016, the Chinese Ministry of Public Security set up a permanent peacekeeping police squad, the first of its kind in the world. The squad was pledged to the PCRS Rapid Deployment Level (RDL) in October 2019.

2. More Enabling Capabilities to the UNPKOs

Enabler troops including engineer, transport and medical units provide vital support to peacekeeping missions. They play an important part in promoting the effectiveness of UN missions, facilitating post-conflict reconstruction and improving lives in host nations. China traditionally deploys hard-to-source enabler troops. After the Leaders' Summit on Peacekeeping in 2015, China responded actively to the UN call for more enabler assets including engineering and medical capabilities. Twenty-five rotations of engineer and medical units totaling 7,001 troops have been committed to missions in the DRC, South Sudan, Sudan's Darfur, Mali and Lebanon. As of August 2020, six Chinese engineer units of 1,188 troops and four medical units of 199 troops were serving on UN missions. In the danger, turbulence and harsh conditions of mission areas, Chinese military peacekeepers have successfully performed all tasks entrusted by the UN including building paved roads and bridges, clearing mines and explosives, providing medical services, and supporting reconstruction in host nations. They have contributed to the local peace process and promoted the public image of UN peacekeepers.

3. Training Foreign Peacekeepers

China's armed forces are willing to share their peacekeeping assets in a spirit of win-win. They have actively helped other TCCs improve training, build capability to respond to complex situation, and better perform in the UNPKOs. In the past five years, China has provided 20 training programs to over 1,500 peacekeepers from more than 60 countries, covering civilian protection and courses for senior mission officials, trainers, military professionals, and female officers. The Chinese military provided assistance in demining and trained more than 300 professionals from countries including Cambodia, Laos, Ethiopia, Sudan, Zambia, and Zimbabwe. The Chinese Ministry of Public Security also trained more than 1,000 foreign peacekeeping police officers.

4. Military Aid Gratis to the African Union (AU)

Africa has the greatest need for peacekeeping. In order to help the African countries improve their ability to maintain peace and stability, and provide African solutions to African issues, the PLA has honored China's commitment of gratis military aid to the value of USD100 million to support the African Standby Force and the African Capacity for Immediate Response to Crisis. The first installment of the aid including military equipment and supplies has been delivered to the AU, and Chinese military experts have been sent to complete the hand-over and provide end-user training. The PLA has agreed with the AU on the arrangement of the next aid installments.

5. The First Peacekeeping Helicopter Unit in Operation

The PLA helicopter unit made its first flight on a peacekeeping mission in August 2017. China's armed forces deployed their first peacekeeping helicopter unit of 140 troops to the African Union-United Nations Hybrid Operation in Darfur (UNAMID). The unit was composed of four medium multi-purpose helicopters and tasked with force delivery, operational support, search and rescue, medical evacuation, and logistic supply. The unit adapted itself to the unknown complexities of overseas missions and fulfilled multiple high-risk tasks. It has become an essential airborne arm of UNAMID and a pillar of the UN peacekeeping operations in Darfur.

6. China-UN Peace and Development Fund in Support of the UNPKOs

To support the UN efforts for peace and advance multilateral cooperation, China has established a China-UN Peace and Development Fund. From 2016 to 2019, the fund financed 52 peace and security projects to a total value of USD33.62 million. Twenty-three of these projects were in support of the UNPKOs, which cost USD10.38 million. The goal of these projects is to strengthen coordination and planning of the UNPKOs, increase African peacekeeping capacity, provide protection for peacekeepers, and improve lives in Sudan's Darfur, Mali and other mission areas.

IV. Active Efforts for Greater International Cooperation

World peace is the responsibility of all countries and peacekeeping calls for expanding multilateral cooperation. China's armed forces have cooperated on peacekeeping with over 90 countries and 10 international and regional organizations. They have enhanced mutual understanding, shared experience, extended practical cooperation, strengthened bilateral and multilateral relations, and promoted peacekeeping capability through exchange of visits, expert discussions, joint exercises and training, and personnel training.

1. Strengthening Strategic Communication to Build Consensus on Peacekeeping

Better strategic communication with the UN leadership is an important means to move the UNPKOs forward. Since 2012, President Xi Jinping has had 11 meetings with UN Secretary-Generals, proposed Chinese ideas and Chinese solutions for world peace and development on multiple international occasions, and reiterated China's support for the UNPKOs. In 2015, President Xi Jinping attended the Leaders' Summit on Peace-keeping at UNHQ and presented proposals that the basic principles of peacekeeping should be strictly followed, the peacekeeping system needs to be improved, rapid response needs to be enhanced, and greater support and help should be given to Africa. Accordingly, China's armed forces are resolved to implement the consensus reached by the leaders. They have strengthened communication with relevant UN agencies, attended several sessions of the UN Peacekeeping Defense Ministerial and the UN Chiefs of Defense Conference, and actively promoted peacekeeping cooperation.

China's armed forces are committed to strengthening bilateral and multilateral communication for better understanding and mutual trust. They have carried out active peacekeeping cooperation with the militaries of countries including Russia, Pakistan, Cambodia, Indonesia, Vietnam, France, Germany, the UK, and the US. Through reciprocal visits, China's armed forces and their foreign counterparts have strengthened communication on policies, made cooperation plans, and advanced friendly state-to-state and military-to-military relations. In May 2010, the first China-US consultation on the UNPKOs was held in Beijing. In April 2015, the defense ministers of China and Vietnam signed a memorandum of understanding (MOU) on peacekeeping cooperation between the two ministries in Beijing. That same year, China conducted the first BRICS consultation on the UNPKOs with Brazil, Russia, India and South Africa. In February 2017, the first China-UK dialogue on peacekeeping operations was held in the UK. In April 2018, military advisers of Russia, France, the UK and the US to the UN Military Staff Committee visited China and exchanged extensive views on the UNPKOs with the Chinese side. In May, the defense ministries of China and Pakistan signed a protocol on policy collaboration with regard to the UNPKOs. In October, the German defense minister visited the Training Base of the Peacekeeping Affairs Center of the Chinese Ministry of National Defense (MND), and a peacekeeping delegation from the Chinese MND visited the German Armed Forces United Nations Training Centre.

2. Contributing Chinese Wisdom and Sharing Experience

Sharing experience and learning from each other is an effective approach to improving the UNPKOs. China's armed forces have actively conducted international exchanges on peacekeeping. The PLA sent delegations to visit the peacekeeping training facilities of countries including Argentina, Finland and Germany, and received more than 180 visits from other countries and international organizations including the UN and the AU. China has hosted over ten international events on peacekeeping, including the Sino-UK Seminar on Peacekeeping Operations, the International Seminar on Challenges of Peace Operations – Into the 21st Century, the China-ASEAN Seminar on Peacekeeping Operations, and the 2009 Beijing International Symposium on UN Peacekeeping Operations. Meanwhile, Chinese peacekeeping troops in Mali, Sudan, South Sudan, the DRC, Liberia, and Lebanon have exchanged experience with their counterparts from France, Senegal and Spain.

China's armed forces have participated extensively in UN peacekeeping consultations and policy-making, and provided input on the UNPKOs. They have played a dynamic role in the Special Committee on Peacekeeping Operations of the UN General Assembly and the TCC Contingent-Owned Equipment (COE) Working Group, invited officials from the UN High-level Independent Panel on Peace Operations and the UN Security Council to China, and offered suggestions on reforming UN peacekeeping, raising its effectiveness, and ensuring the safety and security of peacekeepers. Expert meetings have been hosted by China to draft and review documents including the *United Nations Peacekeeping Missions Military Engineer Unit Manual* and the *Military Peacekeeping-Intelligence Handbook,* and Chinese experts have been sent to participate in updating the manuals of UN peacekeeping infantry, force protection, aviation, transport, medical support units and civil-military cooperation.

3. Extending Cooperation on Joint Exercises and Training to Build Capability

Joint exercises and training are important as a means of improving the UN's peacekeeping capability and its talent pool. To learn from each other and improve skills, China's armed forces have conducted various peacekeeping exercises and training with the UN, and with relevant countries and regional organizations. In June and July 2009, China and Mongolia held a joint exercise codenamed Peacekeeping Mission-2009 in Beijing. In addition, China's armed forces have sent military personnel to participate in multilateral engagements including the ADMM-Plus Experts' Working Group Table-Top Exercise on Peacekeeping Operations in the Philippines in February 2014, the Khan Quest multinational peacekeeping exercises in Mongolia from 2015 to 2019, the ADMM-Plus Experts' Working Group on Peacekeeping Operations and Humanitarian Mine Action field training exercises in India in March 2016 and in Indonesia in September 2019, peacekeeping table-top exercises in Thailand in May 2016 and May 2018, and the multinational computer-assisted command-post exercise Viking 18 in Brazil in April 2018.

China's armed forces established a specialized peacekeeping training institution in June 2009. Since then, the PLA has run over 20 international training programs for UN peacekeepers, including the UN Military Observers Course, the UN Staff Officers Course, the UN Peacekeeping Training of Trainers Course for Francophone Countries, and the UN Senior National Planners Course. The PLA has also invited UN experts and senior instructors from other countries for pre-deployment training of Chinese peacekeeping troops and military professionals, and sent instructors to assist peacekeeping training in countries including Australia, Germany, the Netherlands, Switzerland, Thailand, and Vietnam. More than 100 PLA officers have attended courses or observed exercises hosted by the UN or other TCCs.

V. Contributing to Building a Community with a Shared Future for Mankind

The world is going through profound changes unseen in a century, and the COVID-19 pandemic is accelerating such changes. Uncertainties and destabilizing factors in the international security situation are on the rise, and there are diverse threats to world peace. The UNPKOs are faced with multiple challenges, including increasing constraints, heavier tasks, and a more complex security environment. China will continue to play its part as a permanent member of the UN Security Council, firmly support and participate in the UNPKOs, actively respond to the Action for Peace-keeping (A4P) initiative, and support reasonable and necessary reforms in the UNPKOs. China will contribute its fair share to building an open, inclusive, clean, and beautiful world that enjoys lasting peace, universal security and common prosperity.

1. Upholding the Vision of a Community with a Shared Future for Mankind and Working Together to Promote World Peace

In today's world, people in conflict-ridden areas are still suffering. They have a deep yearning for peace, higher hopes of the UN, and greater expectations of peacekeeping operations. Countries should treat each other with respect and equality. Disputes and problems should be settled through dialogue and consultation with the maximum sincerity and patience. No country should willfully resort to threat or use of force, or undermine world peace and the national interests of sovereign states. Instead, countries should commit themselves to raising the awareness that people across the world are members of a community of shared destiny.

They should uphold humanitarianism, and increase support for and participation in the UNPKOs. China will continue to fulfill its responsibilities as a major country, scale up support for and involvement in the UNPKOs, and join forces with other countries to promote a sound and reasonable UN peacekeeping reform. China's armed forces will endeavor to play a stronger role in the UNPKOs, comprehensively improve peacekeeping capability, faithfully fulfill their responsibilities, and contribute more to world peace.

2. Improving the Peacekeeping System and Addressing Both the Symptoms and Root Causes of Conflict

Only by giving equal attention to development and security and by addressing both the symptoms and root causes of conflict can sustainable peace be assured. Peacekeeping operations should be aligned with preventive diplomacy and other peace-related endeavors, and at the same time coordinated with political mediation, rule of law, national reconciliation, and improvement of living standards. China supports the UN in improving the peacekeeping system. With a focus on the primary tasks of the UNPKOs, a bigger share of limited resources should be allocated to development. China advocates that the rights of host-nation governments to independently choose social systems and development paths based on their national conditions, and local people's rights to subsistence and development should be respected. Only then will host nations be able to focus on development and reconstruction so that peacekeeping gains and sustainable peace are secured. In the UNPKOs, China's armed forces will, as always, contribute to a safe and stable environment for countries and regions in conflict. They will actively participate in medical support and health care, humanitarian assistance, environmental protection, improving lives, and social reconstruction, and provide more public services to enable the local people to enjoy the benefits of peaceful development.

3. Pursuing Extensive Consultation, Joint Contribution, and Mutual Complementarity and Building a New Type of Peacekeeping Partnership

Both TCCs and FCCs are important contributors to the UNPKOs. In peacekeeping, all countries should shoulder their respective responsibilities, follow the principles of consultation and collaboration, and leverage each other's strengths for greater synergy. China supports the UN's efforts to improve peacekeeping partnerships by strengthening coordination among the Security Council, the Secretariat, TCCs and host nations, and optimizing the UN's coordination and collaboration with regional and sub-regional organizations. China's armed forces will actively respond to the triangular cooperation initiated by the UN, and provide all possible support to other TCCs and regional and sub-regional organizations in terms of technology, equipment, personnel and funding.

4. Supporting the UN Efforts to Refine Security Council Mandates and Improve Peacekeeping Effectiveness

Security Council mandates are the basis and guidelines for UN peacekeeping missions, and a decisive factor in the legitimacy and effectiveness of the UNPKOs. When developing and renewing peacekeeping mandates, it is necessary to take into account various factors such as national conditions and the actual needs of host nations, and the capability of the TCCs. It is also important to reset the priorities and main lines of action at each phase in accordance with changing needs. China supports the establishment of an accountability mechanism for peacekeeping performance by the UN, the economic use of resources, and the employment of advanced technology with a view to improving the effectiveness of the UNPKOs and fulfilling the role they are expected to play. China is in favor of the UN measures in helping developing countries build peacekeeping and stabilization capability, improving troop and equipment capacities, and enabling peacekeeping forces to perform their duties. China's armed forces will continue to train more excellent professionals for other countries.

5. Giving Full Play to the PCRS and Enhancing Rapid Response

The PCRS is an important guarantee for the UN's rapid response to crises and conflicts. China supports the UN in strengthening the PCRS and will first select and deploy the units of the standby force that meet the UN standards. China's armed forces will follow the PCRS criteria, continue to build the 8,000-troop peacekeeping standby force and maintain a high level of preparedness. Surface ships, rapid response units and other capabilities can be provided to the UNPKOs if needed.

6. Proactively Addressing Risks and Threats and Ensuring the Safety and Security of Peacekeepers

The operational environment of the UN missions is becoming more hostile and complicated. Only by ensuring the personal safety and security of peacekeepers can the mandates of UN Security Council be effectively fulfilled. With a view to fully protecting the safety, security and health of peacekeepers, China advocates a systematic approach to addressing the increasing traditional and non-traditional security threats, and stands for comprehensive UN solutions to strengthen information collection and sharing, reinforce early warning and risk awareness, upgrade security equipment and facilities, improve medical services, and enhance the prevention and control of infectious diseases.

Closing Remarks

Seventy-five years ago, people across the world won an epic victory against fascism, following a heroic struggle and huge sacrifice. A UN-centered international system was then established. Looking back through history, people are more keenly aware that peace has not come easily and to safeguard it requires great effort. At present, humanity is at a cross-roads: Peace or war, cooperation or confrontation, progress or regress – these are significant choices that all countries need to make.

Peace needs to be fought for and safeguarded. China is firmly committed to the path of peaceful development, and hopes that other countries will also pursue peaceful development. Only when all countries do so, can common development, peaceful coexistence, and world peace be secured. As always, China's armed forces will continue to provide unfailing support for the UNPKOs, fulfill their commitments to safeguarding peace, and bring greater confidence and hope to conflict-ridden areas and local people. China is ready to join hands with all peace-loving nations to champion and pursue multilateralism, and uphold the international system centered on the UN and the basic norms of international relations underpinned by the purposes and principles of the UN Charter. China will exert itself in building a community with a shared future for mankind, and in making the world a better place.

Annex I
Timeline of Activities in UNPKOs

In April 1990, China's armed forces dispatched five military observers to UNTSO and embarked on a new voyage as a participant in the UNPKOs.

In April 1992, China's armed forces dispatched an engineer unit of 400 troops to UNTAC. This was the first formed military unit committed by China to the UNPKOs.

In September 2000, Chinese President Jiang Zemin addressed the UN Security Council summit and expanded on China's stance on the functions of the Security Council, the UNPKOs and African issues.

In December 2001, the Peacekeeping Affairs Office of the MND of the PRC was established. The office took on the responsibility for coordinating and managing the peacekeeping affairs of China's armed forces, and conducting international peacekeeping exchanges.

In February 2002, China officially joined the United Nations Standby Arrangement System (UNSAS) level 1 and specified one engineer battalion, one level-2 hospital and two transport companies as UN peacekeeping standby units. These were pledged to deploy to mission areas within 90 days of a request made by the UN.

In April 2003, China's armed forces dispatched an engineer unit of 175 troops and a medical unit of 43 troops to MONUC.

In December 2003, China's armed forces dispatched an engineer unit of 275 troops, a transport unit of 240 troops and a medical unit of 43 troops to UNMIL.

In April 2006, China's armed forces dispatched an engineer unit of 182 troops to UNIFIL.

In May 2006, China's armed forces dispatched an engineer unit of 275 troops, a transport unit of 100 troops and a medical unit of 60 troops to UNMIS.

In January 2007, China's armed forces dispatched an additional medical unit of 60 troops to UNIFIL and expanded the engineer unit to 275 troops.

In February 2007, during his state visit to Liberia, Chinese President Hu Jintao visited China's peacekeeping troops deployed on the UN mission there, and wrote words of encouragement: "Fulfill missions faithfully and safeguard world peace."

In September 2007, Major General Zhao Jingmin was appointed as Force Commander of MINURSO. He was the first Chinese military officer to assume a senior command position in the UN peacekeeping forces.

In November 2007, China's armed forces dispatched a multipurpose engineer unit of 315 troops to UNAMID. The unit was the first UN peacekeeping force to enter the mission area.

In June 2009, the Peacekeeping Center of the MND of the PRC was established, which took over the responsibility for peacekeeping training, research and international cooperation for China's armed forces.

From June to July 2009, China's armed forces held a joint exercise codenamed Peacekeeping Mission-2009 with their Mongolian counterparts. This was China's first joint peacekeeping exercise with a foreign force.

In September 2010, the Peacekeeping Affairs Office of the MND of the PRC and the UN Department of Peacekeeping Operations (UNDPO) co-hosted the UN Senior Mission Leaders' Course in Beijing, China – the first senior-level peacekeeping training program held by China's armed forces.

In March 2011, UN Training of Trainers Course was co-hosted by the Peacekeeping Affairs Office of the MND of the PRC and the UNDPO for the first time.

In July 2011, Chinese engineer and medical units committed to UNMIS were transferred to the newly-established UNMISS. The transport unit completed its tasks and returned home.

In June 2013, UN Secretary-General Ban Ki-moon paid a visit to China, during which he visited the Peacekeeping Center of the MND of the PRC.

In December 2013, China's armed forces dispatched an engineer unit of 155 troops, a force protection unit of 170 troops and a medical unit of 70 troops to MINUSMA.

In October 2014, the Peacekeeping Affairs Office of the MND of the PRC hosted the International Forum for the Challenges of Peace Operations 2014 in collaboration with the China Institute for International Strategic Studies and Folke Bernadotte Academy of Sweden. Eighty-six delegates from the UN and 19 countries participated in the event.

In January 2015, China's armed forces dispatched the first infantry battalion of 700 troops to UNMISS.

In April 2015, the defense ministers of China and Vietnam signed an MOU on peacekeeping cooperation.

In May 2015, China's armed forces dispatched an additional construction engineer unit of 200 troops to UNIFIL.

In June 2015, China's armed forces sent troops to participate for the first time in the Khan Quest multinational peacekeeping exercise in Mongolia.

In June 2015, the UN Peacekeeping Operations Protection of Civilians Course was co-hosted by the Peacekeeping Affairs Office of the MND of the PRC and the United Nations Entity for Gender Equality and the Empowerment of Women (UN Women).

In September 2015, Chinese President Xi Jinping addressed the Leaders' Summit on Peacekeeping at UNHQ and put forth four propositions and six measures that China would take to support and improve the UNPKOs.

In November 2015, China's armed forces held a photo exhibition entitled "In Course of Peace – Celebrating the 25th Anniversary of China's Armed Forces in UN Peacekeeping Operations" at UNHQ.

In July 2016, during his visit to China, UN Secretary-General Ban

Ki-moon visited the first peacekeeping helicopter unit to be dispatched to Sudan's Darfur by China's armed forces.

In January 2017, Chinese President Xi Jinping delivered a keynote speech entitled "Work Together to Build a Community with a Shared Future for Mankind" and provided a profound, comprehensive and systematic analysis of the vision of building a community with a shared future for mankind at the UN Office at Geneva.

In June 2017, China's armed forces dispatched the first helicopter unit of 140 troops to UNAMID.

In September 2017, the 8,000-strong Chinese peacekeeping standby force completed its PCRS registration.

In December 2017, as deputy chair of the expert working group, China hosted the drafting of *UN Military Peacekeeping-Intelligence Handbook*.

In May 2018, China and Pakistan signed a protocol on policy collaboration with regard to the UNPKOs in Islamabad.

In June 2018, the Peacekeeping Affairs Office was restructured into the Peacekeeping Affairs Center of the MND of the PRC, and the Peacekeeping Center into the Training Base of the Peacekeeping Affairs Center of the MND of the PRC.

In September 2018, representatives of China's peacekeeping troops attended the 2018 Beijing Summit of the Forum on China-Africa Cooperation (FOCAC).

In October 2018, 13 units of the Chinese peacekeeping standby force passed the UN assessment and were elevated to PCRS Level 2.

In December 2018, as deputy chair of the expert working group, China hosted the updating of the *United Nations Peacekeeping Missions Military Engineer Unit Manual*.

In 2019 and 2020, six units of the Chinese peacekeeping standby force passed the UN assessment and were elevated from PCRS Level 2 to Level 3.

In October 2019, a grand celebration was held in Beijing to mark the

70th anniversary of the founding of the PRC. The Chinese military peace-keepers were reviewed by the country and the people for the first time in a National Day military parade.

Annex II
Participation in UN Peacekeeping Missions

NO.	UN PEACEKEEPING MISSIONS	PERIOD OF PARTICIPATION
1	United Nations Truce Supervision Organization (UNTSO)	April 1990 – present
2	United Nations Iraq-Kuwait Observation Mission (UNIKOM)	April 1991 – January 2003
3	United Nations Mission for the Referendum in Western Sahara (MINURSO)	September 1991 – present
4	United Nations Advance Mission in Cambodia (UNAMIC)	December 1991 – March 1992
5	United Nations Transitional Authority in Cambodia (UNTAC)	March 1992 – September 1993
6	United Nations Operation in Mozambique (ONUMOZ)	June 1993 – December 1994
7	United Nations Observer Mission in Liberia (UNOMIL)	November 1993 – September 1997
8	United Nations Observer Mission in Sierra Leone (UNOMSIL)	August 1998 – October 1999
9	United Nations Mission in Sierra Leone (UNAMSIL)	October 1999 – December 2005
10	United Nations Mission in Ethiopia and Eritrea (UNMEE)	October 2000 – August 2008
11	United Nations Organization Mission in the Democratic Republic of the Congo (MONUC)	April 2001 – June 2010
12	United Nations Mission in Liberia (UNMIL)	October 2003 – December 2017
13	United Nations Operation in Côte d'Ivoire (UNOCI)	April 2004 – February 2017
14	United Nations Operation in Burundi (ONUB)	June 2004 – September 2006
15	United Nations Mission in Sudan (UNMIS)	April 2005 – July 2011

NO.	UN PEACEKEEPING MISSIONS	PERIOD OF PARTICIPATION
16	United Nations Interim Force in Lebanon (UNIFIL)	March 2006 – present
17	United Nations Integrated Mission in Timor-Leste (UNMIT)	October 2006 – November 2012
18	African Union-United Nations Hybrid Operation in Darfur (UNAMID)	November 2007 – present
19	United Nations Organization Stabilization Mission in the Democratic Republic of the Congo (MONUSCO)	July 2010 – present
20	United Nations Peacekeeping Force in Cyprus (UNFICYP)	February 2011 – August 2014
21	United Nations Mission in South Sudan (UNMISS)	July 2011 – present
22	United Nations Organization Interim Security Force for Abyei (UNISFA)	July 2011 – October 2011
23	United Nations Supervision Mission in Syria (UNSMIS)	April 2012 – August 2012
24	United Nations Multidimensional Integrated Stabilization Mission in Mali (MINUSMA)	October 2013 – present
25	United Nations Multidimensional Integrated Stabilization Mission in the Central African Republic (MINUSCA)	January 2020 – present

Annex III
Service Personnel Fatalities on
UN Peacekeeping Missions

NO.	NAME	UN PEACEKEEPING MISSIONS	DATE OF DEATH
1	Liu Mingfang	UNTAC	January 21, 1993
2	Chen Zhiguo	UNTAC	May 21, 1993
3	Yu Shili	UNTAC	May 21, 1993
4	Lei Runmin	UNIKOM	May 7, 1994
5	Fu Qingli	MONUC	May 3, 2003
6	Li Tao	UNMIL	August 11, 2004
7	Zhang Ming	UNMIL	October 24, 2005
8	Du Zhaoyu	UNTSO	July 25, 2006
9	Xie Baojun	UNMIS	May 28, 2010
10	Zhang Haibo	UNMIL	September 11, 2014
11	Shen Liangliang	MINUSMA	May 31, 2016
12	Li Lei	UNMISS	July 10, 2016
13	Yang Shupeng	UNMISS	July 11, 2016
14	Fu Sen	UNMISS	November 26, 2019
15	Wang Xudong	UNMISS	February 15, 2020
16	Chen Shun	UNAMID	August 6, 2020

Energy in China's New Era

The State Council Information Office of
the People's Republic of China

December 2020

Preamble

Energy is the foundation and driving force for the progress of human civilization. It matters to the economy, to people's lives, to national security, and to the survival and development of humanity. It is of vital importance in advancing social and economic development and public welfare.

Since the founding of the People's Republic of China (PRC) in 1949, under the leadership of the Communist Party of China (CPC), a relatively complete energy industry system has been established. This has largely been achieved through self-reliance and hard work. Since the launch of the reform and opening-up policy in 1978, to adapt to the rapid development of the economy and society, China has promoted the development of energy in a comprehensive, coordinated and sustainable manner. Today, China has become the world's largest energy producer and consumer. Its transition to efficient energy utilization has been the fastest in the world.

Since the 18th CPC National Congress in 2012, China has entered a new era, as has its energy development. In 2014, President Xi Jinping put forward a new energy security strategy featuring Four Reforms and One Cooperation[1], pointing out the direction for the quality growth of the energy industry with Chinese characteristics in the new era. China upholds the

---

[1] The new energy security strategy featuring Four Reforms and One Cooperation was put forward by Xi Jinping at the conference of the Leading Group for Financial and Economic Affairs under the CPC Central Committee held on June 13, 2014. Four Reforms and One Cooperation refer to: one reform to improve the energy consumption structure by containing unnecessary consumption; one reform to build a more diversified energy supply structure; one reform to improve energy technologies to upgrade the industry; one reform to optimize the energy system for faster growth of the energy sector; comprehensive cooperation with other countries to realize energy security in an open environment. – Tr.

vision of innovative, coordinated, green, open and shared development with focus on high quality and restructuring of the supply side. It has been working on all fronts to reform the ways energy is consumed, to build a clean and diversified energy supply system, to implement an innovation-driven energy strategy, to further the reform of the energy system, and to enhance international energy cooperation. China has entered a stage of high-quality energy development.

A thriving civilization calls for a good eco-environment. Facing increasingly severe global problems such as climate change, environmental risks and challenges, and energy and resource constraints, China embraces the vision of a global community of shared future and accelerates its transformation towards green and low-carbon development in economy and society. In addition to promoting clean and low-carbon energy use domestically, China has been an active participant in global energy governance, exploring a path of worldwide sustainable energy alongside other countries. At the general debates of the 75th United Nations General Assembly in September 2020, President Xi pledged that China will scale up its Intended Nationally Determined Contributions by adopting more vigorous policies and measures, striving to have carbon dioxide emissions peak before 2030 and to achieve carbon neutrality before 2060. In the new era, China's energy strategy will provide forceful support for sound and sustained economic and social development, and make a significant contribution to ensuring world energy security, addressing global climate change, and boosting global economic growth.

The Chinese government is publishing this white paper to provide a full picture of China's achievements in its energy development and its major policies and measures for energy reform.

I. Developing High-Quality Energy in the New Era

China's energy strategy in the new era endeavors to adapt to domestic and international changes and meet new requirements. China will continue to develop high-quality energy to better serve economic and social progress, support the Beautiful China and Healthy China initiatives, and build a clean and beautiful world.

1. The New Energy Security Strategy

In its energy plans for the new era, China has adopted a new strategy featuring Four Reforms and One Cooperation.

– **One reform to improve the energy consumption structure by containing unnecessary consumption.** China is determined to carry out the principle of prioritizing energy conservation, and has tightened the control of total energy consumption and energy use intensity, and enforced energy conservation in all areas of social and economic development. It resolves to adjust its industrial structure. It emphasizes energy conservation in the process of urbanization, and works to develop a green and low-carbon transport system. China encourages hard work and thrift and calls people to conserve energy and work and live with green energy, and move faster towards an energy-saving society.

– **One reform to build a more diversified energy supply structure.** In the direction of green development, China has been vigorously promoting the clean and efficient utilization of fossil energy, prioritizing the development of renewable energy, developing nuclear power in a safe and orderly manner, and raising the proportion of non-fossil energy in the energy supply structure. China has intensified efforts for the exploration and exploitation of oil and gas resources, to increase reserve and production volumes. China has been building the production, supply, storage and sales systems for coal, electricity, oil and gas, while improving energy transportation networks, storage facilities, the emergency response system for energy storage, transportation and peak load management, and enhancing its supply capacity for safer and higher-quality energy.

– **One reform to improve energy technologies to upgrade the industry.** China is implementing the innovation-driven development strategy, building a system that nurtures innovation in green energy technologies, and upgrading energy technologies and equipment in an all-round way. China has strengthened basic research on energy, innovation in generic and disruptive technologies, and original and integrated innovation. China has started to integrate digital, big-data and AI technologies with technologies for clean and efficient energy exploration and exploitation, with a focus on smart energy technologies, to turn these technologies and related industries into new growth drivers for industrial upgrading.

– **One reform to optimize the energy system for faster growth of the energy sector.** China is determined to promote energy market reform, to marketize energy commodities and form a unified and open market with orderly competition. China is furthering energy pricing reform, to create a mechanism in which the market determines the price. China has been working to modernize its law-based energy governance system, developing new models of efficient energy management, and pushing forward reforms to streamline government administration, delegate powers, improve regulation, and upgrade service. It has strengthened planning and policy guidance for the energy sector, and improved the regulatory system of the energy industry.

– **Comprehensive cooperation with other countries to realize energy security in an open environment.** Under the principle of equality and mutual benefit, China is opening its door wider to the world. China promotes green and sustainable energy under the Belt and Road Initiative

(BRI), and endeavors to improve energy infrastructure connectivity. China has been an active participant in global energy governance, increasing energy cooperation and exchanges with other countries, and facilitating international trade and investment in the energy sector. China has joined the international community in building a new model of energy cooperation, maintaining energy market stability, and safeguarding common energy security.

2. Guiding Philosophies for Energy Policies in the New Era

– **Putting people first.** China upholds the principle of energy development for the people, by the people and answerable to the people. Its primary goal is to ensure energy supply for people's life and to ensure that the poverty-stricken population have access to electricity. To this end, China has been improving energy infrastructure related to people's life and public services, and has integrated energy development with poverty eradication. China has launched programs on poverty reduction through energy support, which exemplify the fundamental role of energy supply, infrastructure and services in the battle against poverty.

– **Promoting a clean and low-carbon energy.** China embraces the vision of harmonious coexistence between humanity and nature, directing its efforts towards clean and low-carbon energy. China promotes green energy production and consumption, and has improved the relevant structures accordingly. China is increasing the proportion of clean energy and non-fossil energy at the consumption stage, reducing carbon dioxide emissions and pollutant discharge by large margins, and working hard to accelerate its transformation towards green and low-carbon development for the Beautiful China initiative.

– **Ensuring the core status of innovation.** China is focusing on transforming the energy sector through technical advancement. China is actively promoting independent innovation in energy technologies, and increasing sci-tech input in the national energy development. With enterprises playing a key role in innovation, China has been promoting close collaboration along the energy industrial chain between enterprises, universities and research institutes, to reduce technology imports and boost independent innovation so as to develop a new model where innovations of both upper and lower streams well interact and coordinate with each other.

　– **Pursuing development through reform.** China will fully leverage the decisive role of the market in allocating energy resources, and ensure the government better play its part in this regard. It is endeavoring to advance market-oriented reform in the competitive areas of the energy sector, further display the role of the market mechanism, and build a high-quality energy market system. China has highlighted the guiding role of its energy strategy and planning, formed a law-based governance system and a regulatory system in the energy industry, and improved the financial and fiscal systems that support green and low-carbon energy transformation. All these measures aim to unlock potential and provide support for quality growth of the energy sector.

　– **Building a global community of shared future.** Confronted by the severe impact of climate change, China advocates a global community of shared future, greater international cooperation on energy governance, and a new round of energy reform directed towards clean and low-carbon development. China has joined other countries in seeking sustainable energy and building a clean and beautiful world.

II. Historic Achievements in Energy Development

China is committed to driving an energy revolution. As a result, major changes have taken place in the production and use of energy and historic achievements have been realized in energy development. Energy production and consumption are being optimized, energy efficiency has increased significantly, and energy use has become more convenient for both work and life. China's capacity to ensure energy security has been strengthened. All this provides important support to quality economic development, victory in the battle against poverty, and building a moderately prosperous society in all respects.

1. Growing Capacity to Ensure Energy Supply

A diversified energy production infrastructure consisting of coal, oil, natural gas, electricity, nuclear energy, new energy and renewable energy is in place. Preliminary calculations show that China's primary energy production in 2019 reached 3.97 billion tons of standard coal, making it the world's largest energy producer.

Coal remains the basic energy source. Since 2012, the annual production of raw coal has ranged between 3.41 and 3.97 billion tons. Crude oil production remains stable. Since 2012, the annual production of crude oil has ranged between 190 and 210 million tons. The production of natural gas has increased notably, from 110.6 billion cu m in 2012 to 176.2 billion cubic meters in 2019. China's electricity supply capacity has risen to a cumulative installed capacity of 2.01 billion kW in 2019, up 75 percent since 2012, and an electricity output of 7.5 trillion kWh, up 50 percent. Renewable energy resources have expanded rapidly, with cumulative installed capacities of hydropower, wind power, and solar photovoltaic (PV) power each ranking top in the world. As of the end of 2019, the total installed capacity of nuclear power plants under construction and in operation reached 65.93 million kW, the second largest in the world. The installed capacity of nuclear power plants under construction ranked first.

Energy transport capacity has risen remarkably. China has built natural gas trunk lines measuring over 87,000 km, oil trunk lines totaling 55,000 km, and 302,000 km of electricity transmission lines of 330 kv or more.

The energy reserve system has been steadily improved. China has built nine national oil reserve bases; it has achieved preliminary results in building a natural gas production, supply, reserve and sale system; the coordinated guarantee system for coal production and transport is sound; the country has become a global leader in operating a secure and stable power grid; and its capacity in comprehensive energy emergency response has been strengthened significantly.

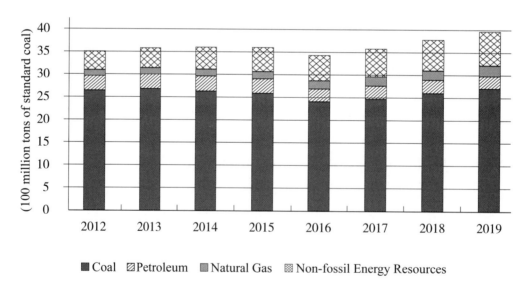

Figure 1   China's Energy Production (2012-2019)

Source: National Bureau of Statistics

Panel 1	**China's Renewable Energy Exploitation Ranks First in the World**

As of the end of 2019, China's total installed capacity of power generation using renewable energy resources reached 790 million kW, accounting for about 30 percent of the global total. The total installed capacity of hydropower reached 356 million kW, wind power 210 million kW, solar PV power 204 million kW, and biomass power 23.69 million kW. All of these ranked first in the world. Since 2010, China has invested a total of about US$818 billion in new energy power generation, accounting for 30 percent of the global total investment over the same period.

Heating-supply using renewable energy has been widely adopted. By the end of 2019 the total surface area of solar panels on solar water heaters had reached 500 million sq m. The total floor area of buildings heated using shallow, medium and deep geothermal energy exceeded 1.1 billion sq m.

A complete industrial chain has been formed in the manufacture of wind power and solar PV power generation equipment, with the scale of output and level of technology leading the world. In 2019, the output of polysilicon accounted for 67 percent of the global total. The figure for solar PV cells was 79 percent, and for solar PV modules 71 percent. Solar PV products were exported to more than 200 countries and regions. The production of complete wind power assemblies accounted for 41 percent of the world total, making China a key player in the global industry chain of wind power equipment manufacture.

2. Remarkable Achievements in Optimizing Energy Conservation and Consumption

Significant improvement has been made in energy efficiency. Since 2012, energy consumption per unit of GDP has been reduced by 24.4 percent, equivalent to 1.27 billion tons of standard coal. From 2012 to 2019, China saw an average annual growth of 7 percent in the economy, while annual energy consumption rose by only 2.8 percent.

The shift towards clean and low-carbon energy consumption is accelerating. Preliminary calculations show that in 2019, coal consumption accounted for 57.7 percent of total energy consumption, a decrease of 10.8 percentage points from 2012; the consumption of clean energy (natural gas, hydropower, nuclear power, wind power) accounted for 23.4 percent of total energy consumption, an increase of 8.9 percentage points over 2012. Non-fossil energy accounted for 15.3 percent of total energy consumption, up 5.6 percentage points against 2012. With this China has reached the target of raising the share of non-fossil energy to 15 percent in total energy consumption by 2020. The number of new energy vehicles is rising rapidly. In 2019 the total number of new energy vehicles reached 3.8 million, with 1.2 million new energy vehicles going on road that year. Both of these figures represent more than half of the global totals. As of the end of 2019, there were 1.2 million electric-vehicle charging stations nationwide, constituting the largest charging network in the world, and effectively improving energy efficiency and optimizing energy consumption in the transport sector.

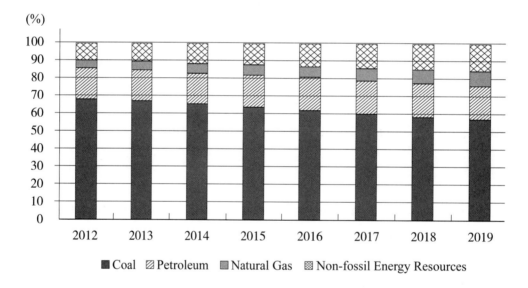

Figure 2   China's Energy Consumption Structure (2012-2019)

Source: National Bureau of Statistics

3. Rapid Improvements in Energy Technology

China continues to pursue technological innovation in the energy sector. Its energy technologies are continuously improving, and technological progress has become a basic driver for the transformation of the energy industry. There are complete industrial chains for the manufacturing of clean energy equipment for hydropower, nuclear power, wind power, and solar power. China has successfully developed and manufactured the world's largest single-unit hydropower generators, with a capacity of 1 million kW; it is able to manufacture a full range of wind turbines with a maximum single-unit capacity of 10 mw; and it continues to establish new world bests in the conversion efficiency of solar PV cells. China has built a number of nuclear power plants using advanced third-generation technologies, and made significant breakthroughs in a number of nuclear energy technologies such as new-generation nuclear power generation and small modular reactors. Its technological capabilities in oil and gas exploration and development keep improving. It leads the world in technologies such as the high-efficiency development of low-permeability crude oil and heavy oil, and a new generation of compound chemical flooding. The technology and equipment for shale oil and gas exploration and development have greatly improved, and successful natural gas hydrate production tests have been completed. China is developing green, efficient and intelligent coal mining technology. It has achieved mechanization in 98 percent of its large coal mines, and mastered the technology for producing oil and gas from coal. It has built a safe, reliable, and world-leading power grid which is the largest across the globe, with reliability of supply at the forefront of the world. A large number of new energy technologies, new businesses, and new models such as "Internet +" smart energy, energy storage, block chain, and integrated energy services are booming.

4. Significant Progress in Eco-Environmental Friendliness of the Energy Sector

China sees green energy as an important measure to enhance eco-environmental progress, and resolutely fights pollution, especially air pollution. Its capabilities in clean coal mining and utilization have greatly improved, and significant results have been achieved in regulating coal mining subsidence areas and building green mines. It has amended the *Law on Air Pollution Prevention and Control* to strengthen the prevention and control of pollution from coal and other energy sources, and ensure that more environmentally friendly energy sources are used to replace coal in equal or reduced amount in newly-built, renovated, or expanded coal-consuming projects in key areas for air pollution control. The green development of the energy sector has significantly improved air quality, and the emissions of sulfur dioxide, nitrogen oxides and soot have dropped notably. Green development of the energy sector has played an important role in reducing carbon emissions. By 2019, carbon emission intensity in China had decreased by 48.1 percent compared with 2005, which exceeded the target of reducing carbon emission intensity by 40 to 45 percent between 2005 and 2020, reversing the trend of rapid carbon dioxide emission growth.

Panel 2　Achievements in Clean Development of Fossil Energy

Clean coal mining capacity has increased significantly. China is actively promoting clean coal mining technologies such as cut-and-fill mining and water-preserved mining, and strengthening the comprehensive utilization of coal mine resources. In 2019, the coal washing rate reached 73.2 percent, the comprehensive utilization rate of mine water reached 75.8 percent, and the land recovery rate for farming reached 52 percent.

China has built the world's largest clean coal power supply system. It has rolled out ultra-low emission transformation of coal-fired power plants. As of the end of 2019, the total capacity of ultra-low-emission coal power generating units reached 890 million kW, accounting for 86 percent of the total installed capacity of all coal power generating units. Coal-fired power generation units with a total capacity of more than 750 million kW have undergone energy-saving transformation. As a result, the coal consumption of coal-fired power generation has been reduced year by year.

Remarkable results have been achieved in the replacement and transformation of coal-fired furnaces and kilns. Over 200,000 small coal-fired boilers

---

have been phased out, and coal-fired boilers below 35 t/h in key pollution control areas have been basically eliminated. Clean fuel substitution is being implemented for industrial kilns that use coal, petroleum coke, and heavy oil as fuel.

The environmental standards of vehicle fuel have been steadily raised. Through a special campaign to upgrade the quality of refined oil products, the standards of gasoline and diesel for vehicles have been upgraded rapidly, from the National III emission standard in 2012 to the National VI emission standard in 2019, significantly reducing vehicle exhaust emissions.

5. Continuous Improvement in the Energy Governance Mechanism

China is making every effort to ensure that the market plays a greater role in the energy sector. Now, in a better business environment and a more viable market, market entities and individuals enjoy more convenient services and find it easier to start businesses. Market access for foreign capital in the energy sector has been extended, private investment is growing, and investment entities have become more diverse. Policies on power generation and consumption plans have been relaxed in an orderly manner, trading institutions can operate independently and in accordance with regulations, and the power market has further developed. China has accelerated reforms such as the deregulation of the oil and gas exploration market and the circulation of mining rights, reform of the pipeline network operation mechanism, and the dynamic management of crude oil imports. It has improved the construction of oil and gas trading centers. China encourages the market to play a decisive role in determining energy prices. It has further relaxed control on the prices in competitive areas, and has preliminarily established a reasonable pricing mechanism for power transmission and distribution and oil and gas pipeline networks. It coordinates energy reform with law-based governance, and the legal framework regarding the energy sector has been improved. An energy governance mechanism covering strategies, plans, policies, standards, supervision, and services is in place.

6. Solid Benefits for People's Lives

Ensuring public wellbeing and improving people's lives is China's fundamental goal in energy development. China is ensuring that urban and rural residents have access to basic energy supply and services, as a fundamental element in building a moderately prosperous society in all respects and supporting rural revitalization. From 2016 to 2019, the total investment in transforming and upgrading rural power grids reached RMB830 billion, and the average power outage time in rural areas was reduced to about 15 hours per year. The quality of power services for rural residents has improved significantly. From 2013 to 2015 China implemented an action plan to ensure access to electricity for every citizen, and completed this historic task by the end of 2015. It has implemented poverty alleviation projects based on solar PV power generation, and other energy-related poverty alleviation projects. China prioritizes poverty-stricken areas in planning energy development projects and has introduced energy projects for the benefit of the rural residents. This has promoted economic development in poverty-stricken areas and raised

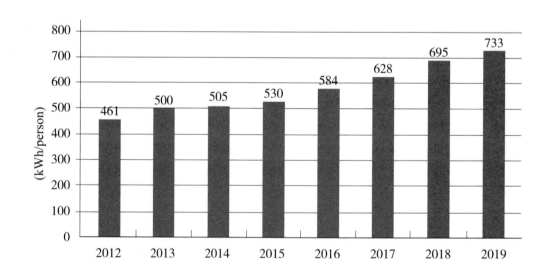

Figure 3   China's Per Capita Household Electricity Consumption (2012-2019)

Source: China Electricity Council

the incomes of the poor. It has improved the infrastructure for natural gas utilization, supplied natural gas to more areas, and improved its ability to ensure gas supply for people's daily life. Significant progress has been made in clean heating in northern China, with improvements in the energy use and living environment of urban and rural residents. As of the end of 2019, clean heating in northern China covered a floor space of 11.6 billion sq m, an increase of 5.1 billion sq m over 2016.

III. An All-Round Effort to Reform Energy Consumption

China perseveres with its fundamental national policy of conserving resources and protecting the environment. Prioritizing energy saving, it understands that energy conservation means increasing resources, reducing pollution, and benefiting humanity, and exercises energy saving throughout the whole process and in all areas of economic and social development.

1. Implementing a Dual Control System of Total Energy Consumption and Energy Intensity

A dual control system of total energy consumption and energy intensity is in place. China sets the targets of total energy consumption and energy intensity for different provinces, autonomous regions and municipalities directly under the central government and applies oversight and checks over the performance of local governments at all levels. It has introduced the energy-saving index into the performance evaluation system of eco-environmental progress and green development, to guide the transformation of the development philosophy. It breaks down the dual control targets of total energy consumption and energy intensity for key energy consumers, and evaluates their performance accordingly to strengthen energy-saving management.

2. Improving Laws, Regulations and Standards for Energy Conservation

China has revised the *Energy Conservation Law.* It has put in place an energy-saving system in key areas including industry, construction and transport as well as in public institutions. It continues to improve the supporting legal institutions for energy conservation supervision, energy-efficiency labeling, energy-saving checks on fixed assets investment projects, and energy conservation management of key energy consumers. It has strengthened standard-setting as a constraining factor and improved energy-saving standards system. It has carried out 100 projects to upgrade energy efficiency standards, enacted more than 340 national energy-saving standards, including almost 200 mandatory standards, covering most high energy-consuming industries and final energy consumption products. China has strengthened oversight over energy-saving law enforcement, reinforced operational and post-operational supervision, and exercised strict accountability for law enforcement to ensure the effective implementation of energy conservation laws, regulations, and mandatory standards.

3. Improving Energy-Saving and Low-Carbon Incentives

Corporate income tax and value-added tax incentives are awarded to energy-saving businesses. China encourages the imports of energy-saving technologies and equipment, and controls the exports of energy-intensive and heavy-polluting products. China is improving the green financial system, and makes use of energy efficiency credits and green bonds to support energy conservation projects. It is exploring new ground in pricing to advance green development. Differential pricing, time-of-use pricing, and tiered pricing for electricity and natural gas have been adopted. China is improving its policies of environment-friendly electricity pricing to arouse the enthusiasm of market entities and the public in energy conservation. It has conducted trials of paid use of and trading in energy-using right in four provinces and cities including Zhejiang, and carbon emissions trading in seven provinces and cities including Beijing. The government is promoting energy performance contracting (EPC) and developing integrated energy services, and encourages innovations in energy-saving technology and business models. It has strengthened the management of demand-side power use and implemented a market response mechanism to guide the economical, orderly and rational utilization of electricity. A "leader board" of best energy-savers has been put in place to increase the efficiency of final energy consumption products, energy-intensive industries, and public institutions.

4. Improving Energy Efficiency in Key Areas

China is doing all it can to optimize the industrial structure, develop advanced manufacturing, high-tech industry and modern services with low energy consumption, and promote the intelligent and clean transformation of traditional industries. China has sped up the transformation to green, recycling and low-carbon industry, and implemented green manufacturing on all fronts; put in place monitoring, law enforcement and diagnostic mechanisms for energy conservation, and carried out energy efficiency benchmarking; raised the energy-saving standards of new buildings, expanded the energy-saving renovation of existing buildings, and improved the structure of energy consumption in construction. It is developing a highly efficient and comprehensive transport system with lower energy consumption, promoting the use of clean energy in transport, and enhancing energy efficiency of vehicles and other means of transport. It is building energy-saving public institutions, to set an example for the rest of society. A market-oriented system of green technology innovation will be put in place to encourage the R&D, transfer and popularization of green technology. China is promoting national key energy-saving and low-carbon technologies, particularly for the transport sector, and energy-saving industrial equipment. The government encourages extensive public involvement in energy conservation, and is raising public awareness of frugality, promoting simple, modest, green and low-carbon lifestyles, and opposing extravagance and excessive consumption.

Panel 3 Growing Momentum for Energy Conservation in Key Areas

Strengthening energy conservation in the industrial sector. China has tightened supervision of energy conservation over major national industrial projects, conducted diagnosis of industrial energy saving, and promoted industrial energy conservation and standardization of green manufacturing and growth. A "leader board" of energy efficiency has been introduced for selecting model enterprises in 12 key industries, including steel and electrolytic aluminum. China has taken action to manage the demand-side industrial power users, issued the "Guidelines for Power Demand-side Management in the Industrial Sector", and selected 153 industrial enterprises and parks as models. It is also cultivating energy service integrators in a bid to integrate modern energy services and industrial manufacturing.

Enhancing energy conservation in the construction sector. Building energy efficiency standards are being rigorously enforced in new construction projects. China has piloted ultra-low and near-zero energy consumption buildings, and undertaken energy-saving renovation of existing residential buildings. It is improving energy efficiency in public buildings, and applying renewable energy in construction. By the end of 2019, 19.8 billion sq m of energy-efficient buildings had been erected, accounting for more than 56 percent of existing buildings in urban areas. In 2019, the floor area of new energy-efficient buildings in urban areas exceeded 2 billion sq m.

Promoting energy conservation in transport. China has improved public transport services and promoted multimodal transport. It has built or renovated more electric railway lines, popularized natural gas vehicles (NGVs), developed energy-saving and new energy vehicles, and improved facilities for battery charge and replacement and hydrogen fuel. Docked ships and civil aircraft are encouraged to use shore power, and CNG (compressed natural gas) filling stations and LNG (liquefied natural gas) fueling stations have been built for NGVs. Obsolete energy-wasting vehicles and ships have been phased out. By the end of 2019, China had built more than 5,400 port facilities for shore power supply and over 280 LNG-powered ships.

Reinforcing energy conservation in public institutions. China has conducted quota management of energy, and published a "leader board" of efficient energy users from public institutions including government bodies, schools and hospitals.

China is promoting green building, green office, green travel, green dining room, green IT, and green culture. It has established more than 3,600 energy-saving demonstration units in public institutions.

5. Promoting Clean Final Energy Consumption

Focusing on the Beijing-Tianjin-Hebei region and its surrounding areas, the Yangtze River Delta, the Pearl River Delta and the Fenwei Plain (the Fenhe Plain, the Weihe Plain and their surroundings in the Yellow River Basin), China is working to reduce and find substitutes for coal consumption, and taking comprehensive measures to control the use of bulk coal. It is promoting clean and efficient coal-fired furnaces, and replacing inefficient and highly-polluting coal with natural gas, electricity and renewable energy. Now, fiscal and price policies are in place to support clean heating in winter in northern China to improve air quality. China is replacing coal and oil with electricity in final energy consumption, and popularizing new energy vehicles, heat pumps, electric furnaces, and other new forms of energy consumption. It has strengthened the development and connectivity of natural gas infrastructure, and made the use of natural gas more efficient in urban areas, as well as in industrial fuel, power generation, and transport. It is promoting natural gas CCHP (combined cooling heating and power), decentralized renewable energy, and multi-energy coordination and energy cascade use in final energy consumption.

Panel 4   Rising Green and Low-Carbon Energy Consumption

Expanding the use of electric power in final energy consumption. The "Guiding Opinions on Advancing the Replacement by Electric Energy" has been issued to replace coal and oil with electricity in residential heating, manufacturing, and transport, and to raise the level of electrification of every part of society. In 2019 China used 206.5 billion kWh of electricity to replace less environmentally friendly forms of energy, an increase of 32.6 percent over the previous year.

Strengthening bulk coal management. China has issued the "Implementation Plan for Upgrading Coal-fired Furnaces for Energy Conservation and Environmental Protection", to improve the efficiency of furnace systems and promote gas-fired furnaces, electric furnaces, and biomass briquette furnaces as per local conditions. China is eliminating small coal-fired boilers in key areas of air pollution control. Restricted zones forbidden to highly polluting fuels have been designated according to air quality control targets.

Advancing clean heating in northern China. China has issued the "Clean Heating Plan for Northern China in Winter (2017-2021)" to integrate public well-being with environmental control, adopt heating methods suited to local conditions, and promote clean heating. By the end of 2019, the clean heating rate in northern China hit 55 percent, an increase of 21 percentage points over 2016.

IV. Building a Clean and Diversified Energy Supply System

Proceeding from its basic national conditions and current stage of development, China gives priority to eco-environmental conservation and pursues green development. It seeks growth while protecting the environment, and believes that a sound eco-environment better facilitates growth. It focuses on supply-side structural reform in the energy sector – giving priority to non-fossil energy, promoting the clean and efficient development and utilization of fossil energy, improving the energy storage, transportation and peak-shaving system, and developing coordinated, complementary, and diverse energy sources in different regions.

1. Prioritizing Non-Fossil Energy

The development and utilization of non-fossil energy is a major element of transitioning to a low-carbon and eco-friendly energy system. China gives priority to non-fossil energy, and strives to substitute low-carbon for high-carbon energy and renewable for fossil energy.

Facilitating the use of solar energy. In line with the principles of driving technological progress, reducing costs, expanding the market and improving the system, China is promoting the use of solar energy in an all-round way. It makes overall planning of geographical layout of solar PV generation bases and market accommodation, with emphasis on both centralized and decentralized power generation. It has implemented a "leader board" incentive to encourage solar PV power generation, and allowed projects to be allocated through market competition, so as to accelerate progress in relevant technologies and reduce costs. As a result,

China's solar PV industry has become internationally competitive. The country is improving grid access and other services for decentralized solar PV power generation, and coordinating the development of solar PV power, agriculture, animal husbandry, and desertification control to form a diversified model of solar PV power generation. China is also industrializing solar thermal power generation through demonstration projects, and providing market support for related industrial chains. It has expanded the market for and utilization of solar thermal energy, and introduced centralized hot water projects in industry, commerce and public services to pilot solar heating.

Developing wind power. On the basis of balancing wind power development with power transmission and accommodation, China is taking steps to exploit wind power and building large-scale wind power bases. Based on the principles of overall planning and coordination, and efficient utilization and development of centralized and decentralized wind power both onshore and offshore, it is taking active measures to develop decentralized wind energy in the middle and eastern parts of the country, and offshore wind farms. It gives priority to wind power projects that deliver electricity at affordable prices, and encourages project allocation through market-oriented competition. China also promotes wind power production through large-scale development and utilization of wind power, which helps to boost industry innovation and international competitiveness, and improve the industrial service system.

Developing green hydropower. China considers eco-environmental conservation to be a priority and pursues green development. While protecting the eco-environment and relocating the residents, China develops hydropower in a rational and orderly way, giving equal importance to development and conservation, and emphasizing on both the construction and consequent management of the facilities. Focusing on major rivers in the southwest, China is building large hydropower bases and controlling the construction of small and medium-sized hydropower stations in the basin areas. China seeks the green development of small hydropower stations, and has increased investment in river ecology restoration. It is also improving policies for relocated residents to share the benefits from hydropower projects, thus giving a boost to local economic and social development and helping the relocated population get out of poverty. As in any resource development program, the goals are always set for a better economy, better environment, and better benefits for the people.

Developing safe and structured nuclear power. Nuclear security is the lifeline in developing nuclear power. China attaches equal importance to safety and the orderly development of nuclear power. It has strengthened whole-life management and supervision of nuclear power planning, site selection, design, construction, operation, and decommissioning, and adopted the most advanced technologies and strictest standards for the nuclear power industry. China is improving the multilevel system of regulations and standards on nuclear energy and safety and strengthening relevant emergency plans, legal system, institutions and mechanisms, in its effort to establish a national emergency system that effectively responds to nuclear accidents. China has strengthened nuclear security and nuclear material control, rigorously fulfilling its international obligations towards nuclear security and non-proliferation, and keeping a good nuclear security record. So far, the nuclear power units in operation are generally safe, and there have been no incidents or accidents of level 2 or above on the International Nuclear and Radiological Event Scale.

Developing biomass, geothermal and ocean energy in accordance with local conditions. China is adopting advanced technologies that meet environmental protection standards to generate power by means of urban solid waste incineration, and upgrading biomass power generation to cogeneration of heat and power. It is growing biogas into an industry and transforming methane use in rural areas. In industrializing liquid biofuel production by means of non-food biomass, it avoids using crops as raw materials and occupying arable land, strictly controls the expansion of fuel ethanol processing capacity, and focuses on improving the quality of biodiesel products. China is engaged in innovative geothermal power generation, providing urban central heating, and building demonstration zones for efficient production and utilization. It is also reinforcing R&D and pilot demonstrations on harnessing ocean power such as tidal and wave energy.

Increasing the overall utilization rate of renewable energy. China guarantees full acquisition of all renewable energy generated. It has implemented a clean energy accommodation action plan and is adopting various measures to promote the use of clean energy. It is improving the overall planning of the power sector, optimizing the power supply structure and layout, and allowing the market to function as a regulator, to form institutional mechanisms conducive to the use of renewable energy and make the power system more flexible and better at coordinating energy use.

China has put in place a mechanism for accommodating power generated from renewable energy, which determines on an annual basis the minimum proportion of renewable energy to be consumed in each province and equivalent administrative unit, and requires suppliers and users to work together to achieve this goal. The country uses the power grid as a platform for optimizing resource allocation. It facilitates optimal interaction and coordination of power source-grid-load-storage, and improves the appraisal and supervision of different sectors in accommodating power generated from renewable energy. Renewable energy use rate has increased significantly: In 2019 the national average consumption rate of wind power was 96 percent, that of solar PV power was 98 percent, and that of water energy in major river basins reached 96 percent.

Panel 5 The Zhangjiakou Renewable Energy Demonstration Zone

In 2015, the state approved the plan for the Zhangjiakou Renewable Energy Demonstration Zone, which proposes "three major innovations", "four major projects" and "five major functional areas". The three major innovations are institu-

---

tional innovation, business model innovation and technological innovation. The four major projects are large-scale renewable energy development, large-capacity energy storage, intelligent power transmission, and diversified application and demonstration. The five major functional areas are a low-carbon Olympic area, a high-tech incubator, a comprehensive business district, a high-end equipment manufacturing area, and an agricultural recycling demonstration area.

By the end of 2019, the total installed capacity of renewable energy power generation in Zhangjiakou City reached 15 million kW, accounting for more than 70 percent of the total installed power generating capacity in the region. With more than 8 million sq m of floor space being heated by wind power, and 285 million kWh of renewable energy being accommodated by the green data center, renewable energy accounted for 27 percent of regional energy consumption. As of 2019 about 3,000 new energy vehicles had been sold, and a number of hydrogen fuel cell buses had been put into operation. The Zhangbei 500-kv flexible DC power grid test and demonstration project and the Zhangbei-Xiongan 1,000-kv ultrahigh voltage AC transmission and transformation project contributed to coordinated development of green energy in the Beijing-Tianjin-Hebei Region.

By 2030, Zhangjiakou's energy supply will be largely based on renewable energy: Eighty percent of its power consumption will be renewable, as will the energy used by all of its public transport, and residential, commercial and public buildings, and its industrial enterprises will all achieve zero carbon emissions.

2. Promoting Clean and Efficient Development and Utilization of Fossil Energy

China coordinates the development and utilization of fossil energy and eco-environmental protection in accordance with its resource endowment and the bearing capacity of natural resources and the environment. It promotes advanced production capacity while phasing out outdated capacity. It also promotes the clean and efficient utilization of coal and the exploration and development of oil and gas, and works to increase reserves and production, so as to be more self-sufficient in oil and gas.

Facilitating the safe, smart and green utilization of coal. China strives to build an intensive, safe, efficient and clean coal industry. It is furthering supply-side structural reform in the industry, improving the coal production capacity replacement policy, speeding up the decommissioning of outdated production facilities, and releasing high-quality capacity in an orderly manner. As a result, the configuration and production capacity of the coal mining sector have seen notable improvement, and large modern coalmines have become the mainstay. From 2016 to 2019, China cut more than 900 million tons of outdated coal production capacity per year on average. It has also increased input in production safety, and improved the mechanism to ensure workplace safety in the long run. Coalmines are becoming highly automated and intelligent by employing more machines and applying information technology, which also make them safer and more efficient. China promotes green mining at large coal bases and facilitates their green transformation by applying coal washing and processing technology, building a circular economy in mining areas and protecting the eco-environment. A number of green mines have been built with improved utilization of various resources in an all-round way. China has taken action to promote the clean and efficient utilization of coal, and increased the quota of coal consumption on power generation. Progress has also been made in coal-to-liquid (CTL) and coal-to-gas (CTG), the precision utilization of low-rank coals, and other industrialized demonstration projects of intensive coal processing.

Promoting the clean and efficient development of thermal power. China has been optimizing coal-fired power and upgrading technology to steadily reduce excess capacity. It has improved the early warning mechanism for risk control in coal-fired power planning and construction, and moved faster to phase out outdated capacity. By the end of 2019, China had phased out more than 100 million kW of outdated coal power capacity, and the ratio of coal-fired power in total power generation had dropped from 65.7 percent in 2012 to 52 percent in 2019. China has taken action to upgrade coal-fired power plants to reduce emissions, and adopted stricter standards for energy efficiency and environmental protection. The efficiency and pollutants control levels of coal-fired power units are on par with world advanced levels. China has also begun to develop natural gas power where appropriate. It encourages adding peak-shaving natural gas power stations to power load centers to improve power security.

Increasing the production of natural gas. In order to increase domestic natural gas supply, China has strengthened basic geological surveying and resource evaluation, and stepped up scientific and technological innovation and industrial support for conventional natural gas production. It is also making breakthroughs in unconventional natural gas exploration and development, such as shale gas and coal-bed gas, and is working on large-scale shale gas exploitation. It is improving relevant policies for the exploitation and utilization of unconventional natural gas. Focusing on the Sichuan, Ordos and Tarim basins, it has built a number of natural gas production bases with an output of more than 10 billion cu m. Since 2017, natural gas output has been increasing by more than 10 billion cu m per year.

Panel 6   Breakthroughs in the Exploration of Unconventional Natural Gas

Shale gas. Major breakthroughs have been made in the exploration and development of marine shale gas. China has built national shale gas pilot zones in Changning-Weiyuan (Sichuan Province), Zhaotong (Yunnan Province) and Fuling (Chongqing City) to promote large-scale development of shale gas. The annual output exceeded 15 billion cu m in 2019.

Coal-bed gas. Two major coal-bed gas industrial bases have been established in Qinshui (Shanxi Province) and eastern Hubei, making an important contribution to the development of green and low-carbon economy in coal-rich areas. In 2019, the extraction volume of coal-bed gas (coal-mine methane) exceeded 18 billion cu m.

Tight gas. Important progress has been made in the exploration and development of tight sandstone gas, which has directly led to the rapid growth of tight gas output in the Ordos Basin and central Sichuan.

Raising the level of oil exploration, development and processing.
China has strengthened domestic oil exploration and development, fur-

thering related institutional reforms and promoting scientific and technological R&D and the application of new technologies. It has intensified the exploration and development of low-grade resources, and increased crude oil reserves and production. It has developed advanced oil recovery technologies, increased the recovery ratio of crude oil, and ensured steady output at old oilfields in the east, including the Songliao and Bohai Bay basins. Focusing on the Xinjiang region and the Ordos Basin, it has increased the reserves and production of new oilfields in the west of the country. It has also strengthened offshore oil and gas exploration and development in the Bohai Sea, the East China Sea and the South China Sea, and are advancing deep-sea cooperation with other countries. The output of offshore oilfields was about 40 million tons in 2019. China is also transforming and upgrading its oil refining industry to produce better refined oil products and improved fuel quality, which will reduce exhaust gas pollution of vehicles.

3. Improving the Energy Storage, Transportation and Peak-Shaving System

China coordinates the transportation of various energy resources such as coal, electricity, oil, and gas. It has built interconnected transmission and distribution networks and established a stable and reliable energy storage, transportation and peak-shaving system, to enhance its emergency response.

Strengthening energy transmission and distribution networks. China has been building cross-provincial and cross-regional key energy transmission channels, to connect major energy producing and consumption regions, and promote the complementary and coordinated development between regions. It has improved the capacity of existing railway lines for transporting coal, and seen that more coal is transported by rail with higher efficiency. It has enhanced the connectivity between main natural gas pipelines and provincial pipelines, liquefied natural gas receiving terminals, and gas storages, and is building a unified national network. A natural gas transportation system that is flexible, safe and reliable has taken shape. China has steadily built trans-provincial and trans-regional power transmission channels, and expanded the scope of clean energy allocation in the northwest, north, northeast and southwest. It has improved the main framework of the regional power grid and strengthened internal grid building at the provincial level. It has also carried out flexible HVDC pilot projects, and is working on the Internet of Energy (IoE) and a multilevel power system that is safe, reliable, and of a reasonable size.

Improving energy reserves for emergency response. China has integrated state, corporate, strategic and commercial reserves to achieve higher reserves for oil, natural gas and coal. It has improved the national oil reserve system and accelerated the construction of oil reserve bases. It has set up a multilevel natural gas storage and peak-shaving system, with local governments, gas suppliers, pipeline transportation enterprises and urban gas services fulfilling their respective responsibilities. It has also put in place a coal reserve system with enterprises playing the main part out of their social responsibility and local governments playing a supporting role. China has improved the national emergency mechanism for large-scale power outages, made power supply more reliable, and enhanced its emergency response. It has established a guarantee system for energy transmission and distribution that matches its energy reserve capacity, a standardized system for oil procurement, storage, replacement and use, and a supervisory mechanism for implementation.

Enhancing the energy peak-shaving system. China attaches equal importance to the supply side and the demand side. It strives to increase the peak-shaving capacity with sound market mechanism and strong technological support, so as to use the energy system in an efficient and all-round way. It has accelerated the construction of pumped-storage power stations, built natural gas peak-shaving power stations as appropriate, and implemented power flexibility transformation projects in existing coal-fired CHP cogeneration units and coal-fired power generating units, so as to improve the peak-shaving performance of the power system, and promote clean energy accommodation. It is optimizing energy storage, power generation from new energy sources and the operation of the power system, and carrying out electrochemical energy storage and other peak-shaving pilot projects. It has promoted the construction of facilities for natural gas storage and peak shaving, improved the market-oriented mechanism of auxiliary services, and enhanced the peak-shaving capacity of natural gas. China has also improved its policies on electricity and gas prices to guide power and natural gas users to participate in peak shaving and peak shifting, so as to enhance the response on the demand side. It has improved the system for interrupting or adjusting electricity and natural gas load to tap the demand-side potential.

4. Supporting Energy Development in Rural and Poor Areas

China has implemented the strategy of rural revitalization to improve energy security in rural areas, so that the residents can have a better sense of gain, happiness and security.

Improving rural energy infrastructure. Making electricity accessible to all is a basic condition for building a moderately prosperous society in all respects. China implemented a three-year action plan to ensure power access for people without electricity, and had achieved this goal by the end of 2015. China attaches great importance to the renovation and upgrading of the rural power grid and makes great efforts to strengthen the weak links in the process. It has carried out targeted programs for renovating and upgrading power grid in small towns and central villages[1], connecting motor-pumped wells in rural plain areas to the grid, and supplying poor villages with electricity for industrial and commercial use. Since 2018, it has been focusing on upgrading the power grid in severely impoverished areas and border villages. China has built natural gas

---

[1] The central village is a rural community composed of a number of administrative villages with a certain population size and relatively complete public facilities. – *Tr.*

branch pipelines and infrastructure to expand the coverage of the pipeline network. To improve energy infrastructure in rural areas, it has built supply outlets for liquefied natural gas, compressed natural gas, and liquefied petroleum gas in areas not covered by natural gas pipelines, and developed renewable energy sources adapted to local conditions.

Carrying out targeted poverty alleviation through energy projects. Energy is a driving force for economic development, and also an important impetus for poverty alleviation. China makes sound plans for the exploitation of energy resources in poor areas, introducing major energy projects in these areas to improve their capability to sustain themselves, thus adding new momentum to the local economy. It has given priority to energy development projects in old revolutionary bases, ethnic minority areas, border areas and poor areas, and built power transmission bases for sending surplus clean electricity to other parts of China, contributing significantly to local economic growth. In developing hydropower, China has followed a sustainable development path by ensuring smooth relocation and resettlement of residents, and by making sure those involved have the means to better themselves, so that the poor share more of the benefits of resource development. China has also increased financial input and policy support for clean energy such as biomass, wind power, solar power, and small hydropower stations in poverty-stricken areas. It has adopted various models integrating solar PV power and agriculture to reduce poverty, and built thousands of "sunshine banks" in poor rural areas.

Using clean energy for heating in rural areas in north China. Winter heating is of great importance in northern China. To ensure that the residents stay warm in winter while reducing air pollution, China has launched clean heating programs in rural areas in accordance with local conditions. In this new scheme enterprises assume the main responsibility and governments provide support to ensure affordable heating for the people. China has been steadily replacing coal with electricity and natural gas for centralized heating, and supported the application of clean biomass fuel, geothermal energy and solar energy in heating, as well as the use of heat pumps. At the end of 2019, the rate of clean-energy heating in the rural areas of north China was about 31 percent, up 21.6 percentage points from 2016. By 2019 about 23 million households in rural areas in northern China had replaced bulk coal with clean energy, including 18 million households in the Beijing-Tianjin-Hebei region, its surrounding areas and the Fenhe-Weihe River Plain.

Panel 7   Achievements in Rural Energy Development and Poverty Alleviation

A new round of upgrading of rural power grids. In 2017, China completed the renovation and upgrading of rural power grids in small towns and central villages, electrified motor-pumped wells, and supplied poor villages with electricity for industrial and commercial use, benefiting 78,000 villages and 160 million rural residents. The country electrified 1.6 million motor-pumped wells, benefiting more than 10,000 townships and 10 million hectares of farmland. It also provided electricity to 33,000 villages. In 2019, China completed a new round of rural grid transformation and upgrading, achieving a supply reliability rate of 99.8 percent and an integrated voltage qualification rate of 97.9 percent. Stable and reliable power supply services have been provided to all rural areas in China.

Universal access to electric power. From 2013 to 2015, the state allocated RMB24.78 billion to extend power grids to areas without electricity, benefiting some 1.55 million people. It carried out an independent solar PV power supply project, providing electricity to 1.19 million people. By the end of 2015, China had achieved full electricity coverage for its entire population.

Poverty alleviation through solar PV power generation. Poverty alleviation through solar PV power generation is one of the top 10 targeted poverty alleviation projects in China. Since 2014, the state has formulated relevant plans, introduced fiscal, financial and pricing policies, strengthened power grid building and operation services, and promoted various solar PV poverty alleviation projects funded by the government and implemented by enterprises. China has built a total of 26.36 million kW of solar PV power stations for this purpose, benefiting nearly 60,000 poor villages and 4.15 million poor households. The facilities now earn about RMB18 billion from power generation and provide 1.25 million public welfare jobs every year.

V. Leveraging the Role of Innovation as the Primary Driver of Development

China has seized the opportunities presented by the new round of scientific and technological revolution and industrial transformation. In the energy sector, it has implemented a strategy of innovation-driven development to increase its capacity for scientific and technological innovation and address major issues and challenges, such as energy resource constraints, environmental protection, and climate change, through advances in technology.

1. Improving Top Level Design for Energy Policies Relating to Scientific and Technological Innovation

China has made energy a vital part of its innovation-driven development strategy, and given more prominence to innovation in energy science and technology. Modern energy technology that is safe, clean and of high efficiency is a key strategic sector and a national priority in the country's "Outline of Innovation-driven Development Strategy". Accordingly China has drawn blueprints for sci-tech innovation in energy and resources, made strategic plans for scientific and technological development of the resources and energy industry till 2035, and proposed major measures and tasks for innovation in energy science and technology. These are all aimed to enhance the role of scientific and technological innovation in driving and underpinning the energy sector.

By making plans for technological innovation in energy and creating the "Innovation Action Plan of Energy Technological Revolution (2016-2030)", China has charted the roadmap and identified its priorities. Through deeper reform, China is establishing an energy science and technology system in which technological innovation is directed by the government and led by the market, and engages the whole of society, with enterprises playing a major role and all stakeholders coordinating with each other. At the same time China has increased investment in scientific and technological innovation in key energy fields and emerging energy industries, stepped up efforts to cultivate professionals in these areas, and endeavored to help all entities involved to improve their capacity for innovation.

2. Creating Diversified Platforms for Technological Innovation in Energy at Various Levels

On the strength of leading enterprises, research institutions and universities, China has created a number of high-standard platforms for technological innovation, and inspired enthusiasm for innovation among all parties involved. Amid efforts to promote scientific and technological advances in energy, China has established more than 40 key national laboratories and a group of national engineering research centers that focus on research into technologies for safe, green and intelligent coal mining, highly efficient use of renewable energy, energy storage, and decentralized energy systems. It has also built more than 80 national energy R&D centers and key national energy laboratories for research in the key areas of coal, oil, natural gas, coal-fired power, nuclear power, renewable energy and energy equipment, all of which cover the vital and frontier areas of energy innovation. Adapting to their own needs and the needs of the industry, large energy enterprises have made continuous efforts to build up their scientific and technological capacity, and have established some influential research institutions in their respective fields. In keeping with the industrial strengths of their regions, local governments have adopted various measures to expand their scientific and technological capacity. Encouraged by the policy of "public entrepreneurship and public innovation", all entities in Chinese society are actively engaged in scientific and technological innovation, and a large number of new energy technology businesses have been established.

3. Promoting Coordinated Scientific and Technological Innovation in Key Realms of the Energy Sector

China has implemented major scientific and technological initiatives and projects to achieve leapfrog development in key energy technologies. Focusing on its strategic industrial goals, China has rolled out a project on oil and gas technology whose emphasis is making breakthroughs in petroleum geology theory and key technologies for high-efficiency exploration and exploitation, as well as finding technology solutions to low-cost, high-efficiency exploitation of unconventional sources of energy, including shale oil, shale gas and gas hydrates. China has launched a project in nuclear power technology to advance research on core technologies of a third-generation pressurized water reactor and a fourth-generation high-temperature gas cooled reactor. The goal is to boost the country's independent innovation in nuclear power technology. In the field of key generic technologies, China has planned for and carried out research into new energy vehicles, smart grid, smart coal mining, clean and efficient use of coal and new energy-saving technology, renewable energy and hydrogen energy, among others. To achieve its major strategic goals, China has given priority to research in basic physics and chemistry concerning clean and efficient use and conversion of energy, in the hope that advances in basic research will lead to breakthroughs in applied technologies.

Panel 8	Breakthroughs in Key Energy Technology and Equipment

Renewable energy technology and equipment. China has mastered key technologies in hydropower, wind and solar energy, and leads the world in the design and manufacturing of complete sets of hydropower generators. New technologies are replacing existing ones at a rapid pace in the whole industrial chain of wind and solar PV electricity, the cost has been falling sharply, and a cohort of internationally competitive companies have emerged. China has also made remarkable progress in biomass energy, geothermal energy and ocean energy technologies.

Power grid technology and equipment. China has fully mastered technologies for ultra-high voltage power transmission and distribution, and conducted demo applications of advanced power grid technologies such as VSC-HVDC and multi-terminal DC transmission. It is making strong headway in the fields of smart grid and large-scale power system control, and leads the world in power transmission and distribution technology and equipment.

Nuclear power technology and equipment. China has mastered the technology to design and build GW-class nuclear power plants with pressurized water reactors. The equipment and the third-generation nuclear power technology developed independently by China are globally advanced. Major progress has been made on the No. 5 unit of Fuqing Nuclear Power Plant, the world's first pilot project using the Hualong-1 design with China's own intellectual property rights. Pilot projects for the pressurized water reactor CAP1400 and high-temperature gas cooled reactor are proceeding smoothly, and breakthroughs have been made in multiple frontier technologies including those associated with fast reactors and advanced small modular reactors.

Technology and equipment for oil and gas exploration and exploitation. China has developed advanced technologies to explore low-permeability oil fields and heavy oil reservoirs, put into industrial application the technology to safely and efficiently explore mega-sized, ultra-deep gas fields with high sulfur content, and developed a fracturing technology for the formation with ultra-high pressure. It has made important progress in key technologies and equipment for deep sea exploration and exploitation. China has independently developed 3,000-m deep-water semi-submersible drilling platforms, exemplified by HYSY 981, as well as the drilling rigs Bluewhale I and Bluewhale II. All of this marks technological breakthroughs in offshore extraction of natural gas hydrates.

Technology and equipment for clean and efficient coal-fired power genera-tion. China has the capacity to independently develop and build ultra-supercritical coal-fired power generator sets, and brought down coal consumption in power generation to 256 grams of standard coal per kWh. It leads the world in coal-fired power generation in the technologies of air cooling, double reheating, circulating fluidized beds, and ultra-low emissions. China has also built a 100,000-ton-class demo unit for carbon capture, utilization and storage.

Technology and equipment for safe, green and intelligent exploration and use of coal. With its technologies for safe and green extraction of coal among the best in the world, China is transforming coal production to automated, mechanized and intelligent operations. It has developed complete sets of procedures and tech-nologies for deep processing of coal with its own intellectual property rights, such as those for coal gasification and CTL production.

4. Launching Major Energy Projects to Upgrade Energy Tech-nologies and Equipment

In a global trend of transition to green and low-carbon development in the energy sector, China has accelerated the upgrading of conventional energy technologies and equipment, and is replacing them with new ones at a faster pace. It has redoubled efforts to make independent innovations in emerging energy technologies, and achieved a marked improvement in clean, low-carbon energy technologies. By launching major equip-ment manufacturing projects and major demonstration projects, China has made breakthroughs in the trials, demonstration, application and popu-larization of key energy technologies. It has improved the measurement, standard setting, testing, and certification systems of energy equipment, and built up its capacity to research, develop, design and manufacture complete sets of important energy equipment.

To achieve secure energy supply, develop clean energy, and encour-age the clean, efficient use of fossil fuels, China concentrates on making breakthroughs in key technologies in energy equipment manufacturing, solving bottleneck issues involving materials and accessories, and promoting technological innovation along the whole industrial chain. China has launched major demonstration projects for advanced energy technologies and equipment in such fields as clean and intelligent coal mining, washing and selection, the exploration and exploitation of deep-water and unconventional oil and gas resources, oil and gas storage and transport, clean and efficient coal-fired power generation, advanced nuclear power technologies, power generation from renewable sources, gas turbine, energy storage, advanced power grid, and deep processing of coal.

5. Supporting the Development of New Technologies and New Business Forms and Models

The world now stands at the confluence of a new round of technological revolution and an industrial revolution. New technological breakthroughs have accelerated industrial transformation, giving rise to waves of new business forms and models in the energy sector. China has made strenuous efforts to integrate energy technologies with modern and advanced information, material and manufacturing technologies, and has rolled out the "Internet +" intelligent energy program to explore new models of energy production and consumption. It has stepped up efforts to innovate and upgrade intelligent solar PV power generation, integrate the development of solar PV power generation with agriculture, fishery, animal husbandry and construction, and open new space for the complimentary application of solar PV power generation, creating new models in the utilization of new energy.

China has picked up its pace in developing industrial chains in the production, storage, transport and application of green hydrogen, hydrogen-fuel cells, and hydrogen-powered vehicles. It supports the application of energy storage technologies at multiple points in energy production and utilization, and the complementary development of energy storage and renewable energy. By supporting the construction of micro-grids for new energy, China has established regional systems of clean energy supply that integrate power generation, storage and utilization. It promotes new comprehensive energy services and strives for complementary, coordinated and efficient end use of various forms of energy. With pilot and demonstration projects leading the way, a series of new energy technologies and new business forms and models have emerged, triggering a fusion of innovative development in China's energy sector.

VI. Deeper Reform of the Energy System in All Areas

China will fully leverage the decisive role of the market in allocating energy resources, and ensure the government better play its part in this regard. It will extend market-oriented reform in key areas and on vital issues to remove institutional barriers, solve the problem of an incomplete market system, provide strong institutional guarantees for China's energy security and boost the high-quality development of the energy sector.

1. Creating an Energy Market with Effective Competition

China is working hard to cultivate a variety of market entities, break up monopolies, ease market access, and encourage competition. It is building an energy market system that is unified, open, competitive and yet orderly, removing market barriers, and making the allocation of energy resources more efficient and fairer.

Diversifying market entities. China supports a variety of market entities to operate in segments of the energy sector that are not on the entry negative list, in accordance with the law and on equal footing. China has extended systemic reform of oil and gas exploration and exploitation and opened up the market in this regard. It has implemented competitive trading of oil and gas exploration blocks, and adopted a more rigorous exit mechanism for oil- and gas-bearing zones. China encourages qualified enterprises to import crude oil. It has reformed the oil and gas pipeline operation system to separate transport from sales. In an effort to reform electricity distribution, China is opening up electricity distribution and sales to non-government investment in an orderly manner, and is separating power grid enterprises' secondary business from their core business. New market entities are being cultivated in the fields of electricity distribution and sales, energy storage, and comprehensive energy services. Meanwhile China is extending reform of energy SOEs, supporting development of the non-public sector, and conducting active yet prudent mixed-ownership reform in the energy industry to boost the vitality and motivation of energy enterprises.

Building an energy market system that is unified, open, and competitive yet orderly. China has established trading platforms for coal, electricity, petroleum and natural gas to facilitate interaction between demand and supply. A modern coal market system is under construction. Futures trading of thermal coal, coking coal and crude oil and spot trading of natural gas are under way. Restrictions have been lifted on the generation and consumption of electricity by commercial consumers. An electricity market is under way to incorporate medium- and long-term trading, spot trading and other forms of trading of electricity. China is also working to build a unified electricity market across the country and a national carbon emissions trading market.

Panel 9   Breakthroughs in Market-Oriented Reform of the Electricity Sector

Improving the price regulation system for electricity transmission and distribution. China has established a preliminary regulatory framework based on allowing recovery of costs plus reasonable profits, and changed the profit model of power grid enterprises. This lays the foundations for further market-oriented reform of the electricity sector.

Supporting independent and procedure-based operation of electricity trading agencies. China has established two regional trading agencies, in Beijing and Guangzhou, and 33 agencies at the provincial level. It is also working to improve the management of trading agencies by transforming them into joint stock companies.

> **Opening up electricity distribution and sales business.** China encourages the participation of non-government investment in electricity distribution, and encourages qualified enterprises to engage in electricity sales. This will give consumers more choice. By the end of 2019 the country had launched 380 pilot reform projects to expand the business of electricity distribution, and the number of companies selling power that were registered with electricity trading agencies had risen to proximately 4,500.
>
> **Developing the electricity market.** China has lifted restrictions on electricity generation and consumption in an orderly manner, promoted mid- and long-term trading of electricity, and rolled out a pilot program for spot trading in eight regions. It is developing the market for supporting services among five trans-regional and 27 provincial power grids. In 2019 market-based transactions in electricity totaled 2.71 trillion kWh, accounting for 37.5 percent of China's power consumption for that year.

2. Improving the Market-Based Mechanism for Deciding Energy Prices

Following the principle of "allowing for more competition in electricity generation, sales and consumption while tightening government regulation of power grid, transmission and distribution", China has lifted price control over competitive areas and links. The goal is to allow prices to reflect market demand, and thereby guide the allocation of resources. It has also conducted strict government oversight of the determination of pricing to cover reasonable costs.

Lifting price control over competitive links in an orderly manner. China is steadily fostering a market-based pricing mechanism of commercial electricity generation and distribution, and allowing prices to be decided by electricity users, sellers and producers through market-based modalities. China has extended reform of the price-setting mechanism for on-grid electricity from coal-fired power plants, and introduced a market-based pricing mechanism in which electricity prices may fluctuate above or below the benchmark. Steady progress has been made in determining the price of on-grid electricity from new wind and solar PV power plants through competitive bidding. Relevant parties are encouraged to negotiate on the basis of sharing risks and benefits, and set through market-based modalities the price for trans-provincial or trans-regional transmission of electricity. The pricing mechanism for oil products is being improved. Reform is ongoing in having the market determine gas prices. China has enforced progressive pricing for household consumption of electricity and gas across the nation, ensuring basic living needs are met while encouraging conservation.

Appropriately deciding prices for natural monopoly operations. Allowing recovery of costs plus reasonable profits, China has set appropriate transmission and distribution prices for power grids and gas pipelines. It has analyzed costs and verified prices for electricity transmission and distribution over two regulatory periods. China has also stepped up the price regulation of gas transmission and distribution and analyzed gas costs in order to establish a price regulation system that covers the whole process of gas transmission and distribution.

**Panel 10   Progress Made in the Marketed-Oriented
Reform of Oil-Gas Sectors**

Reforming the oil-gas exploration and exploitation system. As the reform of mineral resource management proceeds, China has put in place a system in which owners of prospecting rights can extract the oil or gas reserves they have discovered after reporting to relevant authorities, and qualified market entities are allowed to prospect and extract conventional oil and gas. China has completed several rounds of competitive trading of prospecting rights for oil and gas, and pressed ahead with competitive trading of oil and gas exploration blocks to open the sector to other market entities in addition to state-owned oil enterprises. China has also adopted a more rigorous block exit mechanism to enforce more exits.

Reforming the system for operating oil and gas pipelines. In 2019 China founded PipeChina, which is controlled by state capital and funded by diverse investors – a move to promote fair competition in the upper- and lower-reaches markets. China is opening up oil and gas pipeline facilities to all eligible users, and supports connectivity between and equal access to such facilities.

Reforming the pricing mechanism for oil and gas products. China has shortened the adjustment period for refined oil products, and gradually lifted price control over unconventional gas. The retail gas price has been overhauled to better reflect changes in the cost, demand and supply. Price supervision and regulation have been heightened for gas transmission and distribution, and intermediate links on the gas supply chain have been cut back. In 2017 China reviewed and determined transmission prices for long-distance pipelines.

Improving the management system for import and export of oil and gas products. China has refined its import and export policies for oil products. By encouraging qualified non-state enterprises to import crude oil, China has made the sector more diverse, orderly and dynamic.

3. Innovative Management of the Energy Sector and Improved Government Services

Working to become a service-oriented government, the Chinese government has further transformed its functions, streamlined administration, delegated powers, improved regulation and upgraded services. It employs strategic plans and macro-policies on energy, and mobilizes resources for major undertakings. Better oversight and regulation of the energy market will deliver better results and promote fair competition among all market entities. Putting people and lives above everything else, China has remained firm in its commitment to safe production in the energy industry.

Igniting the vitality of market entities. China has extended reform in the energy sector to delegate powers, improve regulation, and upgrade services. This includes reducing approval by the central government for energy projects and delegating the approval power to local authorities for some projects. The requirement for government review and approval has been rescinded for energy projects about which market entities can decide at their own discretion. The number of items of preliminary review has been slashed and the threshold for market access has been lowered, while supervision during and after production has been enhanced and standardized. "Access to electricity" services have been improved. As a result the time, procedures and cost needed for businesses to connect to the power grid have all been cut down. In addition, China has promoted the "internet plus government services" model, and expanded the practice of providing all energy-related government services at one simple window in localities where all relevant authorities have outlets, thereby improving one-stop services.

Panel 11   Better Electricity Access for Businesses

Increasing electricity access to improve the business environment is key to giving market entities and the general public a stronger sense of fulfillment and greater satisfaction. China has promoted a service to connect small and micro businesses applying for low capacity to the power grid without visits to government offices, government approval or investment by the applicants. At the end of 2019 this service had been made available in all municipalities directly under the central government, provincial capitals, and capitals of autonomous regions, and the procedure could be completed within 30 working days. World Bank reports show that from 2017 to 2019, the average number of steps required for a business to connect to the grid in China was cut from 5.5 to 2, resulting in marked reduction in the amount of time and money they spent in the process, and China's ranking on the Getting Electricity Indicator rose all the way from No. 98 to No.12.

Guiding the allocation of resources. In addition to other plans, including special plans and action plans, China has drawn up and implemented the "Strategy for Energy Production and Consumption Revolution (2016-2030)" for developing the energy sector. These define the overall goals and key tasks, and guide investment in the sector. In order to encourage market entities to appropriately explore and utilize energy resources, China has refined its fiscal, taxation, industrial, financing, and investment policies, implemented a nationwide *ad valorem* tax on crude oil, natural gas and coal, and raised excise tax on oil products. It is building a green finance incentive system to promote new energy vehicles and develop clean energy. China also encourages Renminbi settlement for trading in bulk energy commodities.

Promoting fair competition. China has overhauled the government's regulatory power and responsibilities, and gradually transformed regulation of the electricity sector to comprehensive regulation of the entire energy sector. It has tightened regulation of electricity transaction, distribution and supply, the market order, equitable connection to the power grid, and grid investment, cost and efficiency. China has also reinforced oversight of the opening of oil and gas pipeline facilities to all eligible users, increased information transparency of pipeline operators, and increased the utilization rate of these facilities. Random inspection by randomly selected staff and prompt release of inspection results have been expanded to the whole energy sector. Efforts have been intensified to establish a credit system in the energy industry, created in accordance with law lists of entities that have committed serious acts of bad faith, and to take joint punitive action against such acts, hence increasing the effectiveness of credit regulation. China exercises prudential regulation of new business forms to develop new drivers of growth. It also keeps energy hotlines open to ensure oversight by the public.

Ensuring production safety. China has improved the accountability system for coal mine safety, raised the efficiency of coal mine supervision, regulation and law enforcement, created a standardized management system for coal mine safety, and built up its capacity for disaster prevention and control. As a result coal mine safety has much improved. Enterprises share the main responsibility for power safety, industry regulators share the regulatory responsibility, and local authorities have the overall responsibility for safety in their respective jurisdictions. Oversight and management have been improved to ensure cybersecurity of the electricity system, as well as the safety and quality of electricity construction projects. Safety risks in the supply of electricity are manageable in general, and there has been no instance of extensive blackout. Meanwhile, through stronger safety regulation of the entire oil and gas industrial chain, China has maintained safety in oil and gas production. Thanks to sustained efforts to improve its system and capacity for nuclear safety regulation, China's nuclear power plants and research reactors are generally safe and secure, and the quality of nuclear projects under construction is well controlled as a whole.

4. Improving the Rule of Law in the Energy Sector

Implementation of the rule of law is essential in the energy sector. It stabilizes expectations and creates long-term benefits. China aligns law making with reform and development in the energy industry, and has amended or abolished laws and regulations incompatible with the needs of reform and development in the sector. China adheres to the principle that administrative bodies must fulfill their statutory obligations and must not take any action that is not mandated by law, and sees that the government fully performs its functions in accordance with the law.

Improving the system of energy laws. More laws and administrative regulations concerning the energy sector have been formulated or amended. Supervision and inspection of the enforcement of energy laws and regulations has been intensified. The work to enact, amend or repeal regulations and normative documents in the fields of electricity, coal, oil, natural gas, nuclear power and new energy has been accelerated, in order to incorporate reform results into China's laws, regulations and major policies.

Improving law-based governance of the energy sector. China is working to ensure law-based governance and see that the rule of law materializes in the entire process of making, enforcing, overseeing and managing energy strategies, plans, policies and standards. To raise awareness of the law, it is developing a new paradigm that features interaction and mutual support between the government and enterprises, which will help create an enabling environment across the nation for respecting, studying and observing the law. China has adopted new practices in administrative law enforcement by introducing a nationwide system for disclosing information on administrative law enforcement, a system for recording the entire enforcement process, a system for reviewing the legality of major enforcement decisions, and an accountability system. China will ensure that the channels for applying administrative reconsideration and filing administrative lawsuits remain open, that cases are handled in accordance with laws and regulations, that the legitimate rights and interests of administrative counterparts are protected in accordance with the law, and that people can see in every case that justice has been served.

VII. Strengthening International Energy Cooperation Across the Board

China bases international cooperation on the principle of mutual benefit and win-win results while embracing the concept of green development. It is endeavoring to ensure energy security in an open environment, open its energy sector wider to the world, promote high-quality Belt and Road cooperation, actively engage in global energy governance, guide global cooperation in climate change, and build a global community of shared future.

1. Opening the Energy Sector Further to the World

China is committed to a stable global energy market and is opening its energy sector wider to the world. It has greatly eased market access for foreign investment, and has built a market-based international business environment that respects the rule of law to facilitate free trade and investment. It has adopted pre-establishment national treatment plus a negative list, reducing restrictions on access to the energy sector for foreign investment. It has lifted the restrictions for foreign investment to enter the sectors of coal, oil, gas, electric power (excluding nuclear power), and new energy. It is promoting the energy industry in pilot free trade zones such as Guangdong, Hubei, Chongqing and Hainan, and supports further opening up of the entire oil and gas industry in the China (Zhejiang) Pilot Free Trade Zone. International energy companies such as ExxonMobil, GE, BP, EDF and SIEMENS are steadily expanding investment in China. Major foreign investment projects such as Tesla's Shanghai plant are well under way. Foreign-funded gas stations are spreading.

In 2017, the "Catalogue for the Guidance of Industries for Foreign Investment" was revised. For the first time this gave a negative list for foreign investment access to be adopted across the whole country. The Special Administrative Measures (Negative List) for Foreign Investment Access under the Catalogue were separately released in 2018. Equal treatment has since been given to domestic and foreign investment in all sectors outside the negative list.

The Negative List for foreign investment issued in 2018 removed the following access restrictions:

• Construction and operation of power grids (with Chinese party as the controlling shareholder)

• Exploration and exploitation of special and rare kinds of coal (with Chinese party as the controlling shareholder)

• Manufacturing of complete vehicles using new energy (the proportion of Chinese shares shall not be less than 50%)

• Construction and operation of gas stations (in the case of the same foreign investors selling product oil of different varieties and brands from multiple suppliers through more than 30 chain gas stations, the Chinese parties shall be the controlling shareholders)

The Negative List issued in 2019 removed the following access restrictions:

• Exploration and exploitation of oil and natural gas (including coal-bed gas and excluding oil shale, oil sand, shale gas and so on) (limited to Sino-foreign equity or contractual joint ventures)

• Construction and operation of pipeline networks for gas and heat supply in cities with a population of more than 500,000 (with Chinese party as the controlling shareholder)

2. Promoting Energy Cooperation Among BRI Countries

China follows the principles of extensive consultation, joint contribution and shared benefits, and pursues open, green and clean governance in its energy cooperation with BRI countries towards high-standard, people-centered and sustainable goals. It attempts to bring benefits to more countries and their people while maintaining its own development trajectory, and to create conditions favorable to further common development.

Pragmatic and mutually beneficial energy cooperation. China engages in extensive cooperation with over 100 countries and regions around the world in terms of energy trade, investment, industrial capacity, equipment, technology, and standard setting. The high standards of Chinese enterprises are much sought after by partner countries for their energy projects, which help to turn local resource advantages into development strengths. They will also drive technical progress in these countries, create more jobs, stimulate the economy, and improve people's lives. In this way China and its BRI partners will grow together by leveraging and incorporating their respective strengths. China builds cooperation with countries and large transnational corporations in the field of clean energy through third-party markets, to create an energy cooperation framework which is open, transparent, inclusive, and mutually beneficial. In 2019, China established Belt and Road energy partnerships with 30 countries.

A silk road with green energy. China is the largest renewable energy market and the largest clean energy equipment manufacturer in the world. It is actively working towards green and low-carbon global energy transition by engaging in extensive cooperation in renewable energy. Its efforts can be seen in cooperation projects such as the Kaleta hydropower project in Guinea, the Kaposvar PV power station project in Hungary, the Mozura wind park project in Montenegro, Noor Energy 1 – the CSP+PV solar power project in Dubai of the UAE, the Karot hydropower project and the first phase of the solar PV power project in the Quaid-e-Azam Solar Park in Pakistan. The wide application of renewable energy technologies in the Chinese market is helping to reduce the cost of renewable energy across the globe and accelerate the green transition process.

Greater energy infrastructure connectivity. China is promoting transnational and cross-regional energy infrastructure connectivity, creating conditions for complementary cooperation and reciprocal trade in energy resources. A batch of landmark energy projects such as the China-

Russia, China-Central Asia and China-Myanmar oil and gas pipelines have been completed and brought into operation. China has now connected its grid with the power grids of seven neighboring countries, giving a strong boost to energy infrastructure connectivity and realizing optimal allocation of energy resources on a larger scale, which facilitates economic cooperation within the region.

Wider global energy access. China actively implements the UN sustainable development goal of ensuring "access to affordable, reliable, sustainable and modern energy for all". It also takes an active part in global cooperation on expanding energy access. To improve energy access in partner countries and benefit ordinary people, China has employed multiple financing methods to develop electric power projects using grid-connected, microgrid, or off-grid solar systems according to local conditions, and donated clean cooking stoves to regions still using traditional cooking fuels.

3. Actively Participating in Global Energy Governance

As a staunch supporter of multilateralism, China builds bilateral and multilateral energy cooperation based on mutual benefit and win-win results. It supports the role of the International Energy Agency (IEA) and relevant cooperation mechanisms in global energy governance, promotes global energy market stability and supply security, and the green energy transition within the framework of international multilateral cooperation, and contributes ideas and solutions to the sustainable development of global energy.

Engagement in multilateral energy governance. China is an active participant in international energy cooperation under multilateral mechanisms such as the UN, G20, APEC and BRICS. It is making positive progress in joint research, releasing reports and founding agencies. China has set up intergovernmental energy cooperation mechanisms with over 90 countries and regions, and established ties with over 30 international organizations and multilateral mechanisms in the energy sector. Since 2012,

China has become a member state of the International Renewable Energy Agency (IRENA), an observer country to the Energy Charter Treaty, and an affiliate of the IEA.

A facilitator in regional energy cooperation. China has built regional energy cooperation platforms with ASEAN, the League of Arab States, African Union, and Central and Eastern Europe, and organized forums on clean energy at the East Asia Summit. It has also facilitated capacity building and cooperation on technological innovation and provided training for 18 countries in clean energy use and energy efficiency.

Panel 13   China's Efforts to Improve the Global Energy Governance System

Within the framework of international multilateral cooperation, China actively promotes the formulation and implementation of initiatives on global energy market stability and supply security, the transition to green and low-carbon energy, greater access to energy, and higher energy efficiency.

• Advocate of a global energy network to meet global power demand with clean and green alternatives

• Facilitator of the G20 Energy Efficiency Leading Programme, the Enhancing Energy Access in Asia and the Pacific: Key Challenges and G20 Voluntary Collaboration Action Plan, and the G20 Voluntary Action Plan on Renewable Energy

• Co-host of the International Forum on Energy Transitions in cooperation with the IRENA and other international organizations

• Proponent of the Shanghai Cooperation Organization Energy Club

• Host of the APEC Sustainable Energy Center in China

• Proponent of the BRICS Energy Research Cooperation Platform

• Founding member of the IEA's new Energy Efficiency Hub

---

4. Joining Forces to Tackle Global Climate Change

Embracing the vision of a global community of shared future, China works together with other countries to address global climate change and promote the transition to green and low-carbon energy.

Strengthening international cooperation on climate change. With support from the UN, World Bank, Global Environment Facility, Asian Development Bank, and countries such as Germany, China is focusing on green and low-carbon energy transition and developing extensive and sustainable bilateral and multilateral cooperation with other countries in exploiting renewable energy and showcasing pilot low-carbon cities through experience sharing, technical exchanges, and project dovetailing.

Supporting capacity building in developing countries to address climate change. China is committed to deeper South-South climate cooperation. It provides support to the least developed countries, small island countries, African countries and other developing countries in their response to climate change. Since 2016, China has set up 10 pilot low-carbon industrial parks, launched 100 mitigation and adaptation programs, and provided 1,000 training opportunities on climate change cooperation in developing countries to help them develop clean and low-carbon energy and jointly address global climate change.

5. China's Proposals for Developing Synergy on Sustainable Global Energy Development

Humanity has entered an era of connectivity when maintaining energy security and addressing global climate change have become major challenges confronting the whole world. The ongoing Covid-19 pandemic highlights all the more the interdependent interests of all countries and the interconnection of all peoples. China proposes that the international community should work together on the sustainable development of global energy, address the challenges of climate change, and build a cleaner and more beautiful world.

Jointly promoting the transition to green and low-carbon energy to build a cleaner and more beautiful world. It requires the joint effort of all countries to address the challenge of climate change and improve the global eco-environment. All countries should choose the green development path, adopt green, low-carbon and sustainable working practices and lifestyles, promote energy transition, and address problems relating to energy. We should join forces to tackle global climate change and make our contribution to building a cleaner and more beautiful world.

Jointly consolidating multilateral energy cooperation to accelerate the green economic recovery and growth. We should improve international governance and maintain an open, inclusive, balanced and reciprocal multilateral framework for international energy cooperation. We should expand communication and pragmatic cooperation in the energy sector to promote economic recovery and integrated development. We should strengthen transnational and cross-regional innovation on clean-energy and low-carbon technologies, and cooperation on technology standards, to promote energy technology transfer and rollout and improve international IPR protection.

Jointly facilitating international investment in energy trading to protect global market stability. We should eliminate energy trade and investment barriers, facilitate trade and investment, cooperate on energy resources and industrial capacity as well as infrastructure, improve connectivity, and promote efficient resource allocation and greater market integration. We should embrace the principles of extensive consultation, joint contribution and shared benefits, seek the greatest common ground to promote the sustainable development of global energy, and jointly maintain global energy security.

Jointly improving energy access in underdeveloped areas to address energy poverty. We should join forces to realize the sustainable goal in the energy sector, and ensure access to basic energy services such as electricity for people in need in underdeveloped countries and regions. We should help underdeveloped countries and regions to popularize advanced green energy technologies, train energy professionals and improve energy services to integrate the efforts on green energy development and the elimination of energy poverty.

Conclusion

China is embarking on a new journey towards a modern socialist country in all respects. In this new development stage, it will remain committed to an energy revolution, and move faster to build a clean, low-carbon, safe and efficient energy system, to lay a solid foundation for basically achieving socialist modernization in 2035 and becoming a great modern socialist country by the middle of the 21st century.

The world today is experiencing a scale of change unseen in a century. The eco-environment has a direct bearing on human existence and its sustained development. Countries of the world need to work in solidarity to cope with the challenge. China will embrace the vision of a global community of shared future, work together with all countries to expand cooperation on global energy governance, promote the sustainable development of global energy, and protect global energy security. This is part of our commitment to realizing more inclusive, balanced and equal development for all, and to building a clean, beautiful, prosperous and habitable world.

Sustainable Development of Transport in China

The State Council Information Office of
the People's Republic of China

December 2020

Preface

Transport is an important service industry – a basic, leading and strategic sector of the economy underpinning sustainable development.

Since the founding of the People's Republic of China in 1949, and particularly since the beginning of reform and opening up in 1978, under the leadership of the Communist Party of China (CPC), China has followed a strategy of coordinating the development of its transport industry with its economy and society, and ensuring harmony between the transport system and the natural environment. Based on a self-reliant approach, China has made a great effort to create a transport industry that fully responds to public needs. Remarkable results have been achieved, and a once-backward transport industry with a weak base has been hugely improved, providing strong support for economic and social development and creating an outstanding transport system with Chinese characteristics.

Since the 18th CPC National Congress held in November 2012, under the guidance of Xi Jinping Thought on Socialism with Chinese Characteristics for a New Era, China has made historic progress in its transport system. The industry has entered a golden period characterized by infrastructure improvements, better services, and high-quality transformation and development. China leads the world in terms of the scale of its transport infrastructure. Its transport service and support capacity has steadily improved, its capacity for technological innovation has markedly strengthened, and the modernization of management has made huge steps forward in this sector. As a result, the public now enjoys higher-quality travel experiences, and China is on the way to becoming a world leader in transport.

The world today is undergoing levels of change unseen in a century, and the future of all countries is linked in ways that are unprecedented. In this context, the role of transport in enhancing connectivity and people-to-people bonds is growing in importance. As a major country that shoulders its responsibilities, China is committed to implementing the United Nations 2030 Agenda for Sustainable Development. It takes an active part in global transport governance, and looks to strengthen international exchanges and cooperation, so as to contribute Chinese wisdom and strength to sustainable development throughout the world and help to build a global community of shared future.

The Chinese government is publishing this white paper to provide a full picture of China's achievements in the field of transport, and to share with the international community China's strategy and activities in building a sustainable transport system.

I. A New Path for Transport in the New Era

China's transport industry has followed a new path to keep up with the new development dynamic, serving high-quality domestic development and high-standard opening up. China is taking advantage of a period of golden opportunities to improve infrastructure, upgrade services and make transformation in order to build a comprehensive transport system that is intelligent, safe, and green.

1. Building the Transport System That the People Need

China is committed to satisfying public needs and serving public interest in developing its transport industry. In the new era, China adheres to a people-centered approach to governing and developing the sector based on public collaboration and participation for the benefit of all. It is dedicated to building the transport system that the people need.

– Public participation. China must concentrate its efforts on solving the most pressing, immediate transport issues that concern the people the most, encourage them to become involved in the governance of transport, and boost their initiative and creativity.

– Benefit for all. China should guarantee equitable and efficient access to basic public services in urban and rural areas, and ensure that transport development is sustainable and beneficial to all.

– People-centered development. Public satisfaction is the ultimate criterion for evaluating government work. In the light of public expectations in the new era, China focuses on building a high-quality transport industry through supply-side structural reform, meeting the transport needs of diverse groups, and bringing the people a stronger sense of gain, happiness and security.

2. Leading Economic Development

A nation and its economy can only be strong when its transport system is well-developed. Transport plays a leading role in economic and social development. China ensures that it can play this role to the full by always planning for the future and maintaining an appropriate pace of growth.

– Priority in planning. Priority has been given to transport when implementing strategies for coordinated regional development, including the Beijing-Tianjin-Hebei Region, the Yangtze River Economic Belt, the Yangtze River Delta, and the Guangdong-Hong Kong-Macao Greater Bay Area, and when facilitating major programs such as poverty eradication, rural revitalization, and new urbanization.

– Future-oriented planning. In formulating comprehensive transport plans, and in building a comprehensive and multidimensional transport network, China has adopted future-oriented plans for infrastructure construction to accommodate new industrialization, information technology, urbanization, and agricultural modernization. The goal is to bolster economic and social development now and in the future.

– The leading role of transport. Transport should play a key role in making the best use of land, facilitating cross-region industrial transfer, improving the spatial layout of urban areas, and promoting economic exchanges and trade. China gives full play to the leading role of new internet-based transport business forms in fostering driving forces for economic development and accelerating the rise of new forms of economic activity.

3. New Development Philosophy as Guide

Implementing the vision of innovative, coordinated, green, open, and shared development is the key to developing China's transport industry in the new era. China works to steer the future of transport with the new development philosophy, updating concepts, adopting new approaches, resolving difficulties and boosting strengths.

– Building a modern comprehensive transport system that is safe, convenient, efficient, green and economical. China aims to build a high-quality rapid transit network, an efficient regular artery network, and an extensive basic service network. China is moving faster in building a comprehensive and multidimensional and interconnected transport network that traverses the whole country and connects it to the world.

– Advancing supply-side structural reform in transport. China reduces the structural, institutional, technical, administrative, and service costs of transport, helps logistics industry to reduce costs and increase efficiency, so that transport can play the principal role in boosting the development of the logistics industry.

– Improving the business environment. In promoting law-based governance of the country, China properly defines the fiscal powers of the central and local governments in the field of transport and their responsibilities for expenditure, further streamlines administration and delegates powers, strengthens regulation, and provides better services to the transport industry. Efforts have been made to build a new supervision mechanism based on credit, and provide a business environment that is based on market principles, governed by the rule of law, and aligned with international standards.

– Strengthening drivers of development. China encourages and regulates new forms of business in the transport industry, accelerates the transformation of growth drivers, and strives to establish a multilevel transport service system offering high quality and diverse options.

4. Reform and Opening Up as a Driving Force

Further reform and opening up provides a powerful driving force for steady progress in the transport industry. China perseveres with its reform to build the socialist market economy, and creates stronger synergy between a well-functioning market and an enabling government, so as to unleash the productivity of the transport industry.

– Making the transport industry more market-oriented. China ensures that the market plays the decisive role in resource allocation, and that the government plays its role better. The state has lifted restrictions on access to the transport market and is promoting changes for higher quality, efficiency and impetus. It is crucial to rely on the market to tackle insufficient development while better playing the role of the government in addressing unbalanced development, so as to improve the transport market and increase the vitality of the transport industry.

– Pursuing high-standard opening up. China pursues development with its doors open wide and encourages "bringing in" and "going global" in transport development. Focusing on facilitating cooperation under the Belt and Road Initiative, China makes great efforts to promote land, sea, air and cyber connectivity, and coordination of policies, rules and standards, so as to ensure higher-level connectivity with other countries and facilitate international transport.

5. Innovation as Support

Innovation is a prime mover in transport development. With technological innovation as a locomotive, China promotes innovation in management, institutions and culture, improves its innovation system and environment, and optimizes its human resources in support of the transport industry.

– Increasing the durability of the transport system through upgrading infrastructure construction and maintenance technologies. China strengthens the disaster-resistance, early warning and monitoring capacity of its transport infrastructure, and improves its engineering technologies for high-speed rail, expressways, mega bridges and tunnels, deep-water ports, large airports and other projects.

– Advancing the digital economy and the sharing economy through developing intelligent transport. China fosters a new transport system by promoting coordinated innovation in business models and forms, products, and services, and improving the efficiency of comprehensive transport networks.

– Raising the quality of the transport industry through digital, internet-based, intelligent and green technologies. China endeavors to seize the historic opportunities provided by a new round of global technological revolution and industrial transformation, and use new technologies and new business models and forms to promote sustainable development of its transport industry.

II. China's Growing Strength in Transport

In the new era, China is accelerating the high-quality development of its transport industry – it is seeing consistent progress in infrastructure construction, marked improvements in transport capacity, quality and efficiency, stronger technological support, greater accessibility and convenience, and more efficient freight transport. China is building up its strengthen in transport.

1. Creating a Comprehensive Infrastructure Network

China has taken advantage of a key window of opportunity to optimize the configuration of transport infrastructure and build it into a comprehensive network. The country has advanced supply-side structural reform in transport by brining into service a group of passenger and freight hubs. The scale, quality and coverage of the comprehensive transport network have been significantly increased.

Forming a basic network for comprehensive transport infrastructure. By the end of 2019, China had a total of 139,000 km of rail track, of which high-speed lines represented 35,000 km, and a total of more than 5 million km of highways, of which expressways represented 150,000 km. The country had 23,000 operative berths, including 2,520 berths of 10,000-tonne-class or above, and 127,000 km of navigable inland waterways. There were 238 certified civil airports throughout the country. The long-distance oil and gas pipelines totaled 156,000 km with better connections achieved. The total network length of postal and express delivery services approximated 41 million km; every township had a post office and every village was provided with postal services. A comprehensive and multidimensional transport network has been put in place to give strong support to the sustained, rapid and healthy development of society and the economy.

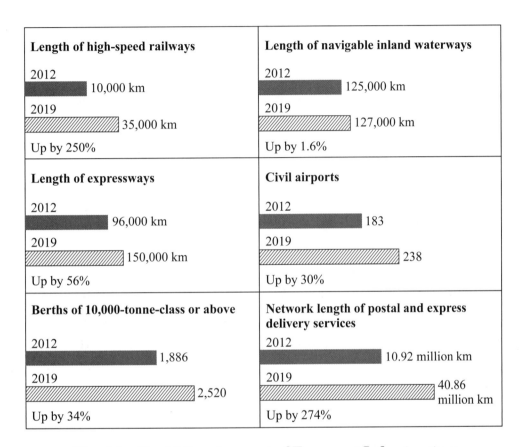

Chart 1   Rapid Development of Transport Infrastructure

Connecting the main transport corridors. The main transport corridors will be further expanded and connected to ensure China's territorial and energy security, and strengthen economic and political connections between regions. The state has devised ten vertical and ten horizontal transport corridors. Economic belts and city clusters are thriving along the transport corridors between Beijing and Shanghai, between Beijing and Guangzhou, along the Yangtze River and the coastlines, and near the ports in the Yangtze River Delta and Pearl River Delta and along the Bohai Sea Rim. They are becoming the most economically dynamic and populous areas in the country. Two thirds of the cities and 80 percent of the GDP of the Yangtze River Delta are concentrated along the high-speed transport corridors between Shanghai and Nanjing, and between Shanghai and Hangzhou. A rapid intercity transport network featuring high-speed railways, intercity railways and high-grade highways has been put in place in the Guangdong-Hong Kong-Macao Greater Bay Area.

A trunk network of gas pipelines is improving with the capacity to transmit gas from west to east China, from Sichuan to east China and from Shaanxi to Beijing, and to bring gas from offshore. Coal logistics corridors are better configured, and a railway corridor for energy transport running across the country has taken shape. The main logistics corridors for grain have been connected, and the container volumes of unprocessed grain, bulk grain and refined grain have increased significantly, along with improved efficiency in grain logistics. Flow of people and goods is more convenient between regions. An open and comprehensive transport network that crosses the whole country and connects with the world has taken shape.

Building integrated transport hubs. By giving full play to the hub economy and actively fostering new drivers of growth, China has promoted the integration of transport, logistics, and information with society and the economy. Considering the national urban configuration, the country has built international transport hubs in Beijing, Shanghai and Guangzhou, and created more transport hubs at national and regional levels. Highlighting the need for integrated transport terminals, a group of such projects have been completed, such as the Beijing Daxing and Shanghai Hongqiao hubs, integrating airport transport seamlessly with high-speed and standard rail, and urban passenger transport.

The configuration of freight terminals and logistics parks has been optimized for multimodal and multilevel transport. A number of modern logistics hubs, such as Yangshan Port in Shanghai and the railway inland port in Zhengzhou, have helped to improve the transshipment capacity, enhance multimodal transport, and create a comprehensive transport system. The integration of various transport methods at these hubs provides strong support for optimizing the economic structure and modernizing the economic system.

Panel 1   Beijing Daxing International Airport

On September 25, 2019, Beijing Daxing International Airport opened for business. After full completion, the airport is expected to cover 45 square kilometers and have six runways to handle over 100 million passengers per year.

Renewable energy accounts for 16 percent of the airport's energy use, and over 60 percent of operational vehicles in the airport control area are powered by new energy. All facilities are environment-friendly, 70 percent of which meet the highest green building standards in China. The airport has the world's largest terminal, which is both functional and aesthetic.

The construction took less than five years and the airport entered service smoothly, fully demonstrating China's strengths in engineering and infrastructure, and the Chinese spirit. The airport is China's new gateway to the world and new source of national development.

Strengthening systematic planning for urban transport infrastructure. By the end of 2019, the total length of urban roads across the country was 459,000 km, the road area per capita 17.36 sq m, the road network density in the urban built-up areas was 6.65 km/sq km and the road area ratio 13.19 percent. The government has strengthened planning for a comprehensive urban transport network and improved effective transport connections between cities and neighboring areas.

With a concept of "narrower roads and a denser network", China has built an urban road network featuring a reasonable composition of expressways, arterial roads, sub-arterial roads and branch roads friendly to green travel. The transport authorities have improved road space allocation to fully ensure the needs of green travel and regulated the provision of traffic safety and management facilities. The country has carried out campaigns to clear up sidewalks and build bike paths to improve the environment for green travel.

2. Optimizing Transport Capacity and Quality

China has made all-round improvements to the quality of transport. The rapid growth of Internet Plus Transport and other new business models has offered more equitable access to more diversified services of higher quality, facilitating the movement of people and goods, and strengthening the accessibility and support functions of transport. Transport is playing a stronger role in supporting the nation's economic and social development, and in promoting investment, stimulating consumption, and sustaining growth.

Enhancing freight transport capacity. China is one of the busiest freight hubs in the world. The increasing demand for freight capacity requires China to accelerate multimodal transport, create efficient and innovative transport links such as rail-highway, air-rail, rail-waterway and river-sea transport, ship-to-ship transfer, and roll-on/roll-off shipping.

China has also implemented programs to raise railway transport capacity, upgrade waterway transport, and regulate highway freight transport. The freight transport structure has been optimized, overall transport efficiency has improved, and logistics costs have been lowered. A marked decrease has been seen in transport pollution. The construction of pipelines for crude oil, refined oil and natural gas is accelerating. The proportion of rail transport in total freight transport is increasing. Visible results have been achieved in shifting more freight transport from road to railway. The cargo throughput and container throughput in China's ports both rank first in the world. Express delivery continues to flourish, and has led the world for the past six years. Substantial growth in transport service capacity has accelerated progress in reducing costs, increasing efficiency, and upgrading the logistics industry.

Meeting the public's expectation for quality travel. Passenger transport is becoming more professional and personal, meeting the public's expectation for a better, faster, more convenient, more comfortable, and satisfying travel experience. With road transport as the base and high-speed rail and civil aviation as the direction of future development, the

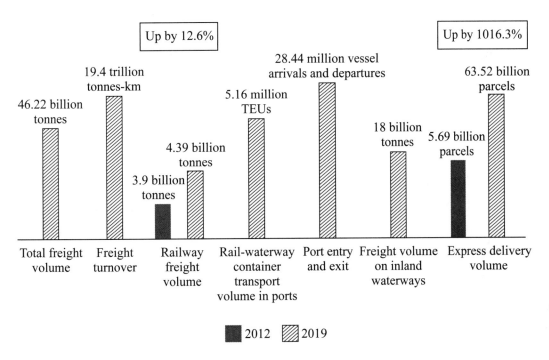

Up by 12.6%

Up by 1016.3%

28.44 million vessel
arrivals and departures

19.4 trillion
tonnes-km

63.52 billion
parcels

46.22 billion
tonnes

5.16 million
TEUs

4.39 billion
tonnes

18 billion
tonnes

5.69 billion
parcels

3.9 billion
tonnes

Total freight volume | Freight turnover | Railway freight volume | Rail-waterway container transport volume in ports | Port entry and exit | Freight volume on inland waterways | Express delivery volume

■ 2012 ▨ 2019

Chart 2　Freight Transport in 2012 and 2019

Panel 2　China's Postal Services

China has the world's largest postal system servicing its 1.4 billion people. An express delivery network connecting urban and rural areas, covering all corners of the country and reaching the world is in place. Remarkable progress has been made in express delivery in three respects: improving the service network in west China, promoting the sales of industrial products in rural areas and agricultural products in urban areas, and encouraging express delivery enterprises to expand their cross-border business. There are 54,000 postal outlets across the country, the coverage of express delivery in township outlets is 96.6 percent, and all administrative villages have direct access to postal services.

A host of competitive and robust market entities have emerged in the delivery industry, resulting in one enterprise with annual revenues exceeding RMB100 billion and five others exceeding RMB50 billion. China has become the fastest growing and most dynamic delivery market, with its package volume overtaking the combined figure in the US, Japan and Europe and ranking first in the world for the past six years.

transport service structure is improving. The trend is for passengers on middle- and long-distance journeys to shift from highway travel to high-speed rail and planes. By the end of 2019, 12 billion trips had been made on high-speed rail, and its share of total rail passenger transport had risen from 4.5 percent in 2007 to 65.4 percent.

The transport capacity and service during the Chinese New Year holiday, National Day holiday, and other travel peaks have significantly increased. People can now take a trip whenever they want, and enjoy quality and professional service that makes travel a comfortable and satisfying experience.

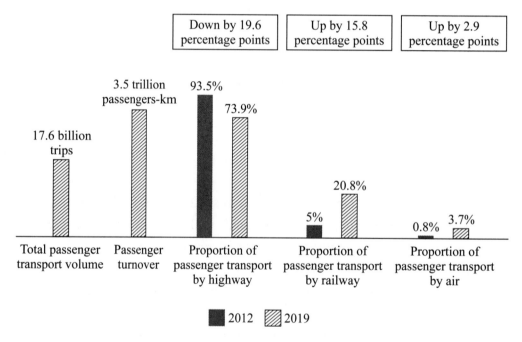

Chart 3 Passenger Transport in 2012 and 2019

Prioritizing the sustainable development of urban public transport. Modern cities aspire to provide high-quality public transport, and take effective measures to strengthen urban traffic management and enhance the life quality of urban citizens. Great efforts have been made to improve urban rail services. By the end of 2019, a total of 40 cities had opened urban rail transit lines, with 6,172.2 km of track. While the role of rail transit is increasingly visible, the number of people using public transport for travel is also growing, and the level of comfort is improving.

Rapid development has also been seen in non-motorized transport. More than 70 cities have released administrative measures to regulate bike-sharing, and over 360 cities provide bike-sharing services. Public transport offers convenient travel by meeting the public's diverse travel needs.

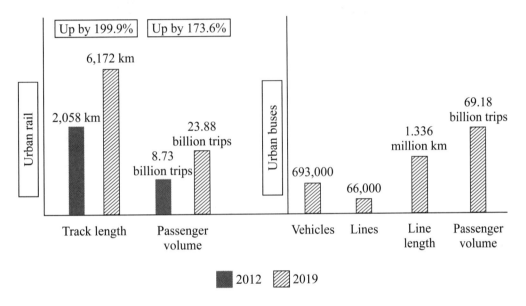

Chart 4   Urban Public Transport in 2012 and 2019

Panel 3   The Transit Metropolis Project

Public transit is the top priority of urban transport development. In 2012, China initiated a transit metropolis demonstration project, ratifying 87 cities in three batches to launch the project. By the end of 2019, 14 cities were classified as national transit metropolis models. The public transport service system with transit metropolises as the benchmark has promoted the healthy and sustainable development of urban transport and created a significant impact on the urban economy.

Ensuring equal access to basic public services. To promote social harmony, the Chinese government is committed to ensuring equal access to public transport services. Low-fare low-speed trains in remote areas which stop at every small station and have a similar function to buses, serve as a bridge between mountainous villages and cities. These trains provide a convenient public welfare service to people along the line and facilitate their efforts towards a better life.

The nationwide expansion of highway passenger transport and rural logistics has helped to integrate rural and urban areas. By the end of 2019, integration of rural and urban transport had been piloted in 52 counties; 95 percent of urban districts and counties nationwide had achieved AAA ratings in urban-rural transport integration, and 79 percent had achieved AAAA ratings.

Accessible transport provides convenience for people with disabilities, and barrier-free access has been implemented at public transport hubs including train stations, highway service areas, passenger ship terminals, airports, and postal outlets. Further measures are being implemented to provide universal services and help people share in the fruits of transport development.

Panel 4   Accessible Transport

An accessible environment is a prerequisite for people with disabilities to engage in social life on an equal basis, and an important indicator of social progress. China is developing and improving its transport infrastructure to create an accessible travel environment offering full coverage, seamless connection, and safe and comfortable facilities.

Full provision of accessible facilities has been achieved in the passenger transport sector in many provinces. Accessible passenger vehicles have been introduced across the country. More than 3,400 EMU (electric multiple unit) trains provide priority seating for people with disabilities. Courtesy seating is reserved on public transport. Low-floor buses and barrier-free taxis are in use. LCD displays and

---

audible stop announcement systems are provided on city buses. Postal offices provide door-to-door delivery services to people with severe disabilities, text messaging services to people with hearing impairments, and deliver publications in Braille for free.

An accessible environment in the transport sector enables people with disabilities to get out of their home and fully engage in social life.

Encouraging new models and forms of business in transport. Internet Plus models in transport are having a profound impact on the way people travel. By the end of 2019, more than 400 cities across the country had online car-hailing services, with daily usage averaging 20 million trips. Bike-sharing has effectively bridged the last kilometer in urban travel, with daily usage averaging more than 45.7 million trips.

The penetration of Internet Plus into freight logistics is accelerating, and inspiring organizational innovations. The 95306 online platform for railway freight services was put in place. In 2019, the online rail freight service handling rate rose to 85 percent. 229 non-truck operating common carriers integrated 2.11 million freight vehicles, improving the utilization rate by 50 percent, lowering the freight transaction cost by six to eight percentage points compared with traditional ways. The integration of the internet and high-speed railway network has seen remarkable results. In 2019, a total of 3.57 billion tickets were sold on 12306.cn, China's official website for booking train tickets. Electronic tickets can be bought at almost all railway stations. China is on the way to achieving full WIFI coverage in high-speed trains and stations. It has also made innovations to roll out services such as online meal booking, wireless charging and intelligent interaction.

By the end of 2019, over 98 percent of the bus terminals at the county level and above offer province-side online ticket booking services. The new online and offline forms of passenger transport such as car-hailing, bike-sharing, and car-sharing services, and new forms of business such as facial recognition check-in at railway stations, paperless boarding at airports, drone delivery, contactless delivery, intelligent parking, and customized passenger transport services have brought convenience to people and injected fresh momentum to economic growth.

Supporting major strategies for regional development. China has strengthened the transport configuration to support and serve the strategy to coordinate the development of the Beijing-Tianjin-Hebei Region, the Yangtze River Economic Belt, the Guangdong-Hong Kong-Macao Greater Bay Area and other regions. The country has accelerated to build multi-junction transport matrices for world-class city clusters, and a first-class comprehensive transport system in the Xiong'an New Area. Efficient connections between trunk, intercity, suburban and urban rail have been achieved, with a focus on facilitating Beijing-Tianjin-Hebei integration.

In its efforts to systematically manage major waterways, China has mitigated the traffic bottleneck along the Three Gorges Dam, improved the function of the Yangtze River as the golden waterway, and endeavored to build a transport corridor along the Yangtze River Economic Belt. To create a modern and comprehensive transport network in the Guangdong-Hong Kong-Macao Greater Bay Area, the country has opened up transport corridors in the east, west and north of Guangdong connecting the Greater Bay Area with surrounding provinces and regions, and aimed to build an international overland transport corridor linking the pan-Pearl River Delta with the Association of Southeast Asian Nations (ASEAN).

To support the Hainan Free Trade Port, China has built a multi-junction, province-wide transport matrix of railways, intercity rail, and main highways in Hainan, focusing on the Haikou-Chengmai-Wenchang Economic Integration Circle and the Greater Sanya Tourism Economic Circle. To promote better and integrated transport in the Yangtze River Delta, the country has built a multilevel, well-connected transport network with Shanghai, Nanjing, Hangzhou, Hefei, Suzhou, Wuxi, Changzhou and Ningbo as the junctions.

In line with the need for eco-environmental conservation and territorial space development in the Yellow River Basin, China has coordinated the development of the transport corridors, hubs and network in the river basin. Targeted transport measures in various regions have been designed to support their respective strategies.

3. Moving from Follower to Leader in Transport Technology

China's capacity for innovation in transport has strengthened – it possesses self-developed core technologies, and has made major breakthroughs in transport infrastructure and equipment. Capacity for sustainable development is growing. China is making steady progress from a follower to a leader in transport technology.

World-leading mega-projects. China leads the world in technology for railways at high altitudes and in extremely low temperatures, and for high-speed and heavy-haul railways. It has solved the most challenging technical problems confronting highway construction in difficult geological conditions such as plateau permafrost, expansive soil, and desert. It also leads in core technologies for building deep-water offshore ports, improving massive estuary and long waterways, and building large airports.

The Beijing-Guangzhou High-speed Railway, the longest high-speed rail line in the world, has been completed. The Lanzhou-Urumqi High-speed Railway has the world's longest line that has been built at one go. The Harbin-Dalian High-speed Railway, the world's first high-speed rail line operating at low temperatures in winter is open to traffic. The Datong-Qinhuangdao Heavy-haul Railway ranks top in the world in terms of annual transport volume. The Xueshan No. 1 Tunnel, the world's highest of its kind, built in Golog Tibetan Autonomous Prefecture, Qinghai Province, has been opened to traffic. The section of the Sichuan-Tibet Railway between Ya'an and Nyingchi is under construction.

Other notable mega-projects include the Hong Kong-Zhuhai-Macao Bridge, the Xi'an-Chengdu High-speed Rail cutting through the Qinling Mountains, the container terminal at Yangshan Port, the automated container terminal at Qingdao Port, and the deep-water channel improvement project in the Yangtze River Estuary.

China leads the world in the total length and number of highway bridges and tunnels in service and under construction. It has seven of the ten longest cable-stayed bridges, six of the ten longest suspension bridges, six of the ten longest cross-sea bridges, and eight of the ten highest bridges in the world.

Panel 5   Hong Kong-Zhuhai-Macao Bridge

The 55-km-long Hong Kong-Zhuhai-Macao Bridge entered service on October 23, 2018. This sea-crossing mega-project is a joint project between Hong Kong SAR in the east and Zhuhai and Macao SAR in the west, and links all three. The bridge is making a significant contribution to the development of the Guangdong-Hong Kong-Macao Greater Bay Area.

In the course of construction, the most challenging technical obstacles were overcome, such as the rapid creation of artificial islands, the design of an undersea tube tunnel, and the composite coating of the tunnel. The bridge is the largest and most technologically complex transport project in China, and it has set many world records. It embodies China's national strength, capacity for independent innovation, and national aspiration to strive for world-class standards. It represents the Chinese people's dreams, solidarity, confidence, and path to rejuvenation.

Major breakthroughs in transport equipment technology. Aiming to develop cutting-edge core technologies, China has substantially improved the level of its independent research in key transport equipment technology. China has set a world record by successfully testing its self-developed Fuxing EMU trains running at 420 km/h in intersection and coupled operations. The Fuxing EMUs have been running at 350 km/h – the highest operating speed in the world – on the Beijing-Shanghai High-speed Rail, the Beijing-Tianjin Intercity Rail and the Beijing-Zhangjiakou High-speed Rail. China became the first in the world to realize autopilot on trains running at a speed of 350 km/h. 600 km/h prototype maglev trains and high-speed free gauge trains running at a speed of 400 km/h that can change tracks and are capable of making international trips have rolled off the production line.

Major breakthroughs have been achieved in tunneling technology – earth pressure balance, hard rock, and slurry shield machines with the world's largest operating diameters have been developed. The fuel-efficient and new energy vehicle industry is prospering, keeping abreast of the latest international advances. The manufacturing technologies for special marine engineering machinery vessels and complete sets of large automated and specialized container handling equipment rank top in the world. China has also made innovative breakthroughs in 300-meter saturation diving. The C919 large passenger aircraft has made its maiden flight. The ARJ21 regional jet is now in commercial service.

The sorting technology in express delivery is developing rapidly. China leads the world in building ocean-going vessels, high-speed EMU trains, high-power locomotives, and marine engineering machinery. Its burgeoning equipment technology in large aircraft and new-generation intelligent connected vehicles is on the way to becoming a major international calling card for China's manufacturing.

Panel 6   China's High-Speed Rail

China has built a complete technological system for high-speed rail – its overall engineering level is in the vanguard of international standards and in some sectors its technological strength even leads the world. By the end of 2019, the total length of high-speed railway lines across the country exceeded 35,000 km, making up more than two thirds of the world's total. It has created basic "travel circles" that take one to four hours to commute between large/medium-sized cities and adjacent ones, and 30 minutes to two hours to commute within city clusters.

With the eight vertical and eight horizontal trunk railway lines as the main corridors, China has built world-class high-speed trains running at 350 km/h on the Beijing-Tianjin, Shanghai-Nanjing, Beijing-Shanghai, Beijing-Guangzhou, and Harbin-Dalian lines. The high-speed trains have operated accident-free for 7.5 billion km. They handled 2.36 billion passengers in 2019.

China's high-speed rail shows how quickly the country is capable of implementing major projects. The high-speed rail is opening new fields for quality economic growth, injecting new vitality into economic and social development, and paving the way to a better life for the Chinese people.

Expedited development of intelligent transport. China is developing transport featuring Internet Plus to fully integrate modern information technology with transport management and services. The country has applied emerging technologies such as 5G, big data, and artificial intelligence to transport infrastructure and equipment, and has made breakthroughs in research and development of intelligent transport. Electronic ticketing and online booking have become increasingly popular in railway, highway, waterway and civil aviation passenger services, the application of IT in transport management has significantly increased. By the end of 2019, 229 airports and major airlines have realized paperless travel.

China has removed all expressway toll booths at provincial borders across the country. Positive results have been achieved in the application of new technologies such as Electronic Toll Collection (ETC) on expressways. By the end of 2019, there were more than 200 million ETC users across the country. Round-the-clock, all-weather and full-coverage monitoring of the road network and information distribution are strengthening.

The BeiDou Navigation Satellite System (BDS) has been applied to 7.6 million vehicles on the road, 33,300 postal and express delivery trucks, 1,369 public service vessels, 10,863 maritime navigation facilities, 109 coastal ground-based augmentation stations, 352 general-purpose aircraft, and three transport aircraft. The Beijing-Zhangjiakou High-speed Rail featuring autopilot is the first in the world to use the BDS. Intelligent highway technologies are further promoted, and intelligent port and shipping technologies are widely used. Intelligent delivery outlets are found everywhere in all major cities, and automated sorting has been adopted by all major distribution centers of express delivery enterprises.

China has released administrative rules on road testing of self-driving vehicles, technical guidelines on the construction of enclosed testing fields for autopilot, and rules on intelligent ships. It has built a test area for unmanned cargo ships and piloted the use of drones in delivery services.

Panel 7   Yangshan Port in Shanghai

Phase IV of Yangshan Port in Shanghai is the world's largest fully automated container terminal. It is a key symbol of China's integration into the global economy. Phase IV of the Yangshan Port covers 2.23 million square meters and has a 2,350-meter wharf for seven container ship berths.

An automated operating system developed in China is being used at the port. It is connected to the data information platforms of Shanghai Port to realize automated traffic scheduling. The port embodies the landmark upgrading of China's port industry in terms of operating models, technology application, and equipment manufacturing.

III. A Key to Poverty Alleviation and Moderate Prosperity

Achieving moderate prosperity in China's rural areas – the key for completion of this overall national task – hinges largely on the improvement of the transport network there. China is very conscious of the role of transport in poverty alleviation, and sees it as an important support to all-round moderate prosperity across the country, the modernization of agriculture and rural areas, and shared benefits from reform and development. Therefore, it makes every effort to remove the transport bottlenecks that hinder the development of rural areas, providing a solid foundation for rural people to escape from poverty and move to moderate prosperity.

1. Winning the Battle Against Poverty Through Transport

Poverty alleviation has been raised to the top of the agenda for transport in the new era. The transport authorities have improved the planning and policy system for poverty alleviation, created new work models, and prioritized the planning, funding, coordination and implementation of poverty alleviation-oriented transport projects and measures. Through these extraordinary steps and efforts, China is counting on transport to facilitate its campaign against poverty.

Better planning for transport projects to alleviate poverty. China has improved the top-level design and policy framework of poverty alleviation-oriented transport projects. It has devised strategies, implementation programs, and action plans in this regard, including the *Outline of Poverty Alleviation-Oriented Transport Projects in Contiguous Poverty-Stricken Areas (2011-2020),* the *Plan for Transport-Driven Poverty Alle-*

viation During the 13th Five-Year Plan Period (2016-2020), the *Opinions on the Implementation of the Plan to Further Leverage Transport to Support Poverty Alleviation*, involving 1,177 counties, cities and districts in old revolutionary base areas, areas with large ethnic minority populations, border areas, and poor areas.

Taking severely impoverished areas as the priority, China has moved faster to upgrade national expressways and national and provincial highways, and prioritized transport projects that provide villages and households with better access to roads. It has worked to renovate and expand trunk and rural roads, improve the quality, safety and environment of transport infrastructure, and leverage local resources through transport.

Breaking new ground in targeted transport-driven poverty elimination. China has intensified coordinated planning in this field by formulating and improving a system in which a five-year plan, a three-year action plan and annual plans operate as a unit. Detailed annual programs are made at the provincial level to ensure the plans are carried out in alignment.

China has increased its effort to help impoverished people access education and build aspirations. In addition to providing them with useful information, knowledge, skills training and technologies, it has also encouraged them to find work on rural road construction projects, and employed workers from poverty-stricken households to carry out road maintenance.

Increasing investment in poverty alleviation-oriented transport projects. The state has steadily increased the central government subsidy as a proportion of transport project investment for impoverished areas. From 2012 to 2020, over RMB1.46 trillion, or 61.3 percent of total road construction funds from vehicle purchase tax, was directed to poor areas, which mobilized another RMB5.13 trillion of social investment. The average contribution from vehicle purchase tax to national expressway projects rose from 15 percent during the 12th Five-year Plan period (2011-2015) to 30 percent during the 13th Five-year Plan period (2016-2020), and the increase in national highways was from 30 percent to 50 percent. Government subsidies from vehicle purchase tax to asphalt and concrete road projects for towns, townships and administrative villages rose to an average of 70 percent or more of project costs.

By optimizing the disposition of central budget investment, vehicle purchase tax, and other funds, China has lent more financial support to ensure the implementation of these policies and projects.

Focusing on severely impoverished areas. The most arduous tasks in achieving moderate prosperity throughout the country are in the rural areas, especially in severely impoverished areas. Therefore, China has underlined the primary role of transport in poverty elimination, and increased support to these locations, giving preference to the "three areas and three prefectures"[1] when allocating new funds, planning new projects and formulating new measures. From 2016 to 2020, China spent RMB274.6 billion from vehicle purchase tax on transport projects in the "three areas and three prefectures", including RMB78.1 billion on rural road projects.

2. Promoting High-Quality Transport in Poor Areas

Good roads are key to prosperity in all sectors. Aiming to build high-quality rural roads that are properly built, operated, managed, and maintained, China has created a safe and easily accessible transport network that links villages, towns and townships in impoverished areas and connects them with other parts of the country. It has improved passenger and

---

[1] The "three areas and three prefectures" are national-level severely impoverished areas, with harsh natural and economic conditions. The "three areas" refer to the Tibet Autonomous Region, prefectures and counties with large Tibetan populations in Qinghai, Sichuan, Gansu and Yunnan provinces, and the Hotan, Aksu, Kashgar prefectures and the Kizilsu Kirgiz Autonomous Prefecture in southern Xinjiang. The "three prefectures" refer to the Liangshan Yi Autonomous Prefecture in Sichuan Province, the Nujiang Lisu Autonomous Prefecture in Yunnan Province, and the Linxia Hui Autonomous Prefecture in Gansu Province.

freight transport services in urban and rural areas, and expanded bus services to more villages. The backward nature of transport in poor areas has gone through a complete transformation.

Establishing a comprehensive transport network in poor areas. Inadequate transport infrastructure is one of the most formidable challenges confronting poverty-stricken areas. To resolve this challenge, the state subsidized the upgrading of 17,000 km of national expressways and 53,000 km of national highways, and the building of 2,365 km of inland waterways from 2016 to 2019. By now, almost all county seats in poor areas have access to highways of Grade II or above, with many of the counties having expressways, and some having railways or even airports. A high-grade inland waterway network linking trunk rivers and tributaries continues to improve. Through such efforts, a comprehensive transport network is taking shape in poor areas rapidly, and the gap between in and outside of these areas is shrinking.

Achieving notable results in building high-quality rural roads. Two hundred pilot counties have led the development of high-quality rural roads that are properly built, operated, managed, and maintained. China has strengthened regulation and exercised strict quality control of rural road projects, making seven key pieces of information available to the public: construction plans, subsidy policies, tendering, construction management, quality supervision, fund management, and project delivery and review. The country has improved the configuration of the rural road network, promoted the road chief system nationwide, and enhanced the long-term mechanism for building high-quality rural roads. A five-tiered accountability system has been implemented, clearly defining responsibilities for road management at provincial, city, county, township, and village levels. In the process of reforming public institutions and township government institutions, the rural road management system in counties and towns has also been improved.

The transport departments have strived to increase public satisfaction with rural roads, and promoted the practice of packaging road maintenance contracts with construction projects. The beautiful countryside program has served to improve the environment along rural roads.

Passenger transport resources in urban and rural areas are being co-ordinated, and new modes of passenger transport are being explored in rural areas. The resources of transport departments, postal agencies, supply and marketing cooperatives, and e-commerce companies have been integrated to improve logistics in poor rural areas.

These measures have achieved solid results, bringing business and funds to rural areas, especially those suffering from poverty.

Panel 8   High-Quality Rural Roads

The program to build high-quality rural roads that are properly built, operated, managed, and maintained is an important symbol of social transformation in China's rural areas in the new era. By the end of 2019, rural roads accounted for 83.8 percent of the total length of roads in China, and classified highways made up 93.2 percent of rural roads. In 2019, 98.8 percent of rural roads were subject to government maintenance plans, and 83 percent were ranked as in medium, good or excellent condition. Bus services were accessible to 99.8 percent of administrative villages. The government has subsidized the upgrading of 59,000 km of roads to serve resource transport, tourism and business development in poor areas, resolving long-standing travel obstacles there.

The interconnected network of high-quality rural roads has shortened the time for traveling between urban and rural areas, greatly improved working and living conditions in rural areas, transformed rural society and provided remote villages with access to modernity. The movement of people and goods has brought knowledge, information and funds into poor areas, helping people there open their minds, abandon outdated social mores, and promote healthy practices through cultural exchanges. Thus, poor people can have access to a better education and become more confident in their ability to lift themselves out of poverty. This has laid a solid foundation for farmers to achieve prosperity through education.

Making travel easier and more convenient. Due to the significant improvement in rural roads, the days in which travelers had to trudge through dust and mud on dirt roads are gone. All towns, townships and administrative villages with feasible conditions had been connected to asphalt and concrete roads by the end of 2019, and to bus services by September 2020.

Integrated road passenger transport in urban and rural areas has made progress. A passenger transport network with county seats as centers, towns and townships as junctions, and administrative villages as points has taken shape. China's 600 million rural people now enjoy easy and convenient access to better roads and bus services between villages and between urban and rural areas.

3. Helping Farmers Improve Their Lives Through Transport

Better transport has cleared the bottlenecks that delayed economic and social development in poor areas, supporting farmers' efforts to rise out of poverty and achieve moderate prosperity, reinforcing China's endeavors to modernize agriculture and rural areas, and laying a solid foundation for rural revitalization in the new era.

Smoothing farmers' path to moderate prosperity through rural roads. To achieve the goal of greater connectivity, from 2012 to 2019 China built or upgraded 2.09 million km of rural roads, including about 1.1 million km in poor areas, bringing the total length of rural roads to 4.2 million km, and connecting another 51,000 administrative villages in poor areas with asphalt and concrete roads. From 2016 to 2019, China built 96,000 km of asphalt and concrete roads in poor areas to reach natural villages with relatively large populations, and implemented a safety program on 458,000 km of rural roads, effectively preventing and reducing accidents.

The transport authorities have issued *Administrative Measures for Rural Road Construction*, *Administrative Measures for Rural Road Quality*, and *Administrative Measures for Rural Road Maintenance*, and formulated or modified relevant technical standards and specifications. The government issued the *Opinions on Furthering Institutional Reform of Rural Road Management and Maintenance* and put in place other auxiliary mechanisms to ensure long-term results in this field. From 2012 to 2019, the number of administrative villages with access to bus services increased by 54,000.

To develop logistics in rural areas, China has stepped up the construction of a three-tiered rural logistics network at county, township and village levels, which collected and delivered more than 15 billion parcels in 2019. Logistics companies are now able to offer better delivery services between urban and rural areas by transporting industrial products to the countryside and agricultural products to cities, and providing delivery services to the door.

Facilitating poverty alleviation through railways. China has accelerated the implementation of railway construction plans, and increased railway coverage to give poor areas better access to the rail network. By the end of 2019, RMB3.3 trillion, or 78 percent of total investment in railway infrastructure, has gone into railway projects in the 14 contiguous poverty-stricken areas, old revolutionary base areas, areas with large ethnic minority populations, and border areas. The new railways connect 274 national poor counties, integrating them into a larger "high-speed rail economic circle".

Big data analysis is employed to optimize passenger train schedules for poor areas. In 2019, an average of 2,328 passenger trains ran every day with stops in poor areas, and 594 special tourist trains were arranged to poor areas, which promoted tourism, retail and catering businesses and helped stimulate consumption in areas along the lines. To transport agricultural products from poor areas, railway transport services effectively scheduled freight trains such as point-to-point trains, express container trains and high-speed express trains, which have transported 1.71 billion tonnes of freight since 2018.

Delivering tangible benefits by advancing Transport Plus ini-

tiatives. China encourages new business models such as Transport Plus Tourism, Transport Plus Business, and Transport Plus Poverty Alleviation, and promotes the extensive integration of transport and business in poverty-stricken areas. From 2012 to 2019, China built or upgraded 59,000 km of roads serving resource transport, tourism and business development in poor areas.

The Transport Plus Express Delivery poverty alleviation projects integrate resources from different sectors, including transport, supply and marketing cooperatives, retail and e-commerce, and postal services. Drones have been tested to deliver parcels in rural areas. In 2018, China's postal service companies completed a total of rural e-commerce transactions worth RMB1.4 trillion.

Other new models, such as Transport Plus Agriculture Plus E-commerce, Transport Plus Culture Plus Tourism, Transport Plus Employment Plus Public Welfare, have also played their part in poverty alleviation. Distinctive local businesses have emerged and flourished along with the newly built roads, creating a path to wealth for rural people.

Reinforcing China's efforts to build a beautiful countryside through rural transport. Transport departments have actively participated in the socialist new countryside program, and used rural road construction to expand the effort to maintain a clean environment and foster social etiquette and civility in the countryside. Trees have been planted and village profiles enhanced along the roads, turning rural roads into an attractive element of local scenery.

Interconnected roads help improve people's lives and environment in rural areas, enhance public services such as education, health care, and culture, and promote integrated urban-rural development. Following the rapid expansion of rural roads, the vast countryside is finding greater prosperity and becoming more attractive.

IV. Modernization of Transport Governance

China is the largest developing country in the world. The complexity and rapid development of its sizable transport sector have created difficulties in managing the industry. Based on national conditions and drawing on international experience, China has devoted serious effort to modernizing its transport governance. Through reform and innovation, the country has unleashed the vitality of technology and market, increased efficiency and facilitated the high-quality development of the industry.

1. Reforming the Transport Governance System

Basing itself on the present while focusing on long-term development, China has reformed its comprehensive transport management and improved related laws and regulations. At present, a unified, open, competitive and orderly transport market is in place, and a transport governance system that meets the needs of the country's development in the new era has been steadily improved.

Upgrading comprehensive management. With the focus on advancing supply-side structural reform and improving transport governance, China has furthered reform of the management institutions and mechanisms. As part of the "large government departments" reform in 2013 to optimize administrative functions, a basic institutional framework was formed under the Ministry of Transport, which brought the National Railway Administration, Civil Aviation Administration of China and State Post Bureau under its management. The country has advanced corporate reform of the China Railway Corporation and the China Post Group Corporation. The two companies, restructured into China State Railway Group Co., Ltd and China Post Group Co., Ltd, have established a modern corporate governance structure and a modern state-owned enterprise system with Chinese characteristics. Reform has been accelerated at the provincial level, and most provinces have begun to put in place comprehensive transport management institutions or operational coordination mechanisms.

As National Railway Administration and China State Railway Group Co., Ltd were set up, separation of government administration from the management of enterprises was achieved in the railway sector. Reform of the civil aviation institutions and mechanisms for airport public security, pricing, investment access, and air traffic control is proceeding in a well-planned manner. Reform of the postal service has been proceeding steadily, with improved supporting measures for postal reform.

China has steadily promoted reform of administrative law enforcement by reorganizing and streamlining law enforcement teams and their functions. A comprehensive administrative law enforcement system that is authoritative and efficient, balances powers with responsibilities, and features effective regulation and high-quality service is now in place. The country has established a basic mechanism for comprehensive transport planning and coordination, which helps the connection and balanced development of railways, highways, waterways, civil aviation and postal services.

Thanks to these reforms, China has further modernized its capacity for transport governance by optimizing the institutions and mechanisms for comprehensive development, integrating different modes of transport, and boosting driving forces from within the industry.

Developing law-based government departments for transport. Implementing the Xi Jinping Thought on the Rule of Law in developing law-based government departments, China has exercised the rule of law in all aspects of transport, including planning, construction, operation, management and workplace safety, providing a solid guarantee for building China's strength in transport. A system for law-based government administration has taken shape, and the working mechanisms for legislation, supervision over law enforcement, administrative review and response to lawsuits, and public education on the law and the rule of law have gradually improved. The government has stepped up the pace to introduce legislation on railways, highways, waterways, civil aviation and postal services, and as a result a broad framework of laws and regulations is now in place.

Focusing on major national strategies and areas relevant to the industry, China has formulated and revised key laws and regulations on railways, highways, maritime traffic safety, ports, waterways, civil aviation, and postal services. China has also promulgated and revised urgently needed provisions and measures for ensuring safe navigation when overwater and underwater activities take place, and for standardization in the transport industry, and has progressively overhauled normative documents.

Advancing reforms to improve the business environment. China has remained problem-oriented, accelerated the transformation of government functions, furthered reforms to streamline administration, delegate power, improve regulation and upgrade services, and continued to improve the business environment. It has gradually relaxed restrictions on market access in the transport sector, removed unreasonable and unnecessary fines and inspections, and established catalogues of fees charged to enterprises. Tax and fee reduction policies have been implemented to lower logistics costs. The government has strengthened in-process and follow-up oversight, cleared intermediary services from the list of items of administrative examination and approval, and furthered reform in the business sector.

Oversight conducted through the random selection of both inspectors and inspection targets and the prompt release of results has been implemented. China has made use of information technologies such as big data, cloud computing and internet of things to promote the nationwide parallel licensing system for inter-provincial heavy cargo. It has also accelerated the establishment of a new market supervision mechanism based on credit, coordinated the regulation of new business forms, and created innovative and integrated online and offline regulation models to make the market environment fairer and more orderly.

China has improved administrative approval services regarding transport, and enabled access to government services via a single website to make it easier for people to get their problems solved by one single department and with one-stop service, thus significantly improving the efficiency of public services.

Reforms designed to streamline administration, delegate power, improve regulation, and upgrade services have optimized the business environment, stimulated the vitality of the transport sector, raised the efficiency of government services, and promoted the healthy development of the industry.

2. Pursuing Green Development

Acting on the understanding that lucid waters and lush mountains are invaluable assets, China has improved the system for promoting eco-civilization in the transport sector, achieved real results in energy conservation and carbon reduction, and increased environmental friendliness.

Comprehensive energy conservation, emissions reduction and low-carbon development. China has worked hard to conserve energy, reduce emissions, and develop low-carbon transport to boost economic development. It has strictly implemented a system that controls both the total amount and intensity of energy consumption to improve the overall efficiency of transport. The national railway electrification rate has reached 71.9 percent. There are now more than 400,000 buses and 430,000 trucks using new energy, 180,000 natural gas vehicles, and 290 liquefied natural gas (LNG) ships. About 14 percent of airport vehicles and facilities are run on new energy sources, substitute facilities for aircraft auxiliary power units (APUs) are in full use, and the numbers of postal vehicles run on new and clean energy and those that are in service in key regions are steadily increasing. More than 7,400 charging piles have been built and operated in 942 expressway service areas across the country, more than 5,800 sets of shore power facilities have been built at ports, covering over 7,200 berths, and container terminals at major ports along the Yangtze and coastlines have switched from oil to electricity for power. The annual energy saved by green transport provinces and cities, green highways, green ports and other demonstration projects has exceeded 630,000 tonnes of coal equivalent. The central government has used vehicle purchase tax funds to support the construction of comprehensive passenger terminals, freight hubs, and port railways, and coordinated the development of road-rail, sea-rail and other multimodal forms to restructure the transport network.

Strengthening the intensive and economical use of resources. In taking responsibility for the country's long-term development and for future generations, the Chinese government is endeavoring to transform the extensive use of transport resources to an approach that is intensive and economical. By implementing national planning for land use, drawing red lines to protect ecosystems and permanent basic cropland, and to restrict unlimited urban development, China has promoted the integrated intensive and efficient use of railways, highways, waterways, civil aviation, postal services and associated resources along these passages of transport.

China has strengthened the protection and comprehensive utilization of land resources along highways and railways and reduced the impact on the surrounding environment by building low embankments or building bridges and tunnels instead of roads. It has reinforced eco-environmental protection and green development and maintenance of waterways, promoted the beneficial use of dredged sediments from waterways, strengthened the administration, supervision and efficient use of port shorelines, and explored systems for paid use of shoreline resources.

China has promoted the recycling of waste pavement, asphalt, used tires, construction scrap and other materials. It has also attached great importance to the green treatment, reduction and recycling of delivery packaging, and promoted the replacement of disposable plastic woven bags with recyclable transit packaging, with the utilization rate of electronic waybills reaching 98 percent.

Strengthening the prevention and control of atmospheric and water pollution. China uses the strictest systems and laws to control environmental pollution from transport. It has set up the Domestic Emission Control Areas (DECAs) for Atmospheric Pollution from Vessels along coastlines and the main streams of the Yangtze and other major rivers, and implemented measures to limit the sulfur content of fuel oil used by international vessels entering Chinese waters in accordance with international conventions. It has promoted the use of clean energy and installation of exhaust gas cleaning equipment on vessels, and established a mechanism for ensuring the supply and joint supervision of low-sulfur fuel oil.

The country has implemented the national mandatory standards for water pollutant discharge from vessels, built receiving and treatment facilities for oily wastewater, chemical tank-cleaning wastewater, sanitary sewage and garbage from vessels in ports, and carried out dust pollution control at ports. It has implemented the Blue Sea Action[1] plan along the coast to salvage sunken ships and objects that are at risk of polluting the oceans and affecting the safety of maritime transport.

China has also accelerated the management, phase-out and renewal of old and high-energy consuming, high-emission vehicles and construction machinery, and introduced an emission inspection and mandatory maintenance program for motor vehicles. By replacing subsidies with incentives, the central government has helped the Beijing-Tianjin-Hebei Region and its surrounding areas, and the Fenhe-Weihe River Plain, to phase out commercial diesel trucks at or below China III emission standards. A three-year action plan to readjust the transport structure has been

---

[1] The Blue Sea Action is a public welfare program approved by the State Council as a major measure to promote eco-civilization and related national strategies, and to build green and safe transport. Since 2014, the transport rescue and salvage departments have carried out the action plan for six consecutive years, salvaging a total of 79 sunken ships.

carried out across the country. From 2012 to 2019, motor vehicle pollutant emissions decreased by 65.2 percent nationwide.

Panel 9   DECAs

China attaches great importance to the prevention and control of transport pollution, and has issued a series of policy documents, including the *Implementation Plan on Domestic Emission Control Areas in Waters of the Pearl River Delta, the Yangtze River Delta and Bohai Sea Rim (Beijing, Tianjin, Hebei)*, the *Implementation Scheme of the Domestic Emission Control Areas for Atmospheric Pollution from Vessels*, and the *Implementation Scheme of the Global Marine Fuel Oil Sulfur Limit by 2020*. With its initial focus on the Pearl River Delta, the Yangtze River Delta, and the Bohai Sea Rim (Beijing, Tianjin and Hebei), China has set the goal of controlling and reducing emissions of atmospheric pollutants including sulfur oxides (SOx), nitrogen oxides (NOx), particulate matters (PMs) and volatile organic compounds (VOCs) from vessels and improving the air quality of coastal areas and inland river port cities.

Since the launch of the scheme, pollutant emissions have been remarkably reduced. At present, the DECAs have further expanded to coastal areas and the main streams of the Yangtze and Xijiang rivers, and stricter control standards have been proposed for the waters in Hainan. The implementation of DECAs is an important step in achieving continuous improvement of air quality, meeting people's expectation for a better life, and advancing our campaign to prevent and control air pollution and to keep our skies blue. It is also a key element of China's participation in global environmental governance.

Intensifying eco-environmental protection and restoration. China has strictly enforced the red lines for protecting the ecosystems and has put in place a system for protecting and restoring ecosystems. In building transport infrastructure, it has adopted a model of "avoidance, protection and restoration", and promoted eco-friendly route planning and site selection and design. Particular efforts have been made to avoid farmland, forestland, wetland and other types of territorial space with key eco-environmental functions.

China has carried out afforestation programs along railways, highways and waterways to improve eco-environmental functions and landscape quality. In railway and highway construction projects it makes provision for wildlife corridors. The wildlife corridors built on the Qinghai-Tibet Railway have guaranteed the safe migration of Tibetan antelopes and the movement of other plateau animals. In the construction of ports and the renovation of waterways, China has focused on reducing impacts on aquatic ecology and life, building fishways and facilitating fish migration. It has implemented more than 50 million square meters of eco-environmental restoration along highways and ports.

The country has also addressed the problems of illegal docks and sand mining along the Yangtze River. By the end of 2019, it had closed or rectified 1,361 illegal docks, improving the eco-environment and ensuring flood control, water supply and navigational safety along the river.

3. Strengthening Safety Management and Emergency Response

Upholding the sanctity of human life, China has improved the capacity of the transport industry to deal with public emergencies and in particular major public health emergencies, strengthened safety management and emergency response, and coordinated development and safety, so as to provide safe transport to the public and support economic and social development.

Traffic safety management has significantly improved. Putting prevention first and adopting a comprehensive approach, China has further enhanced the system for ensuring safe transport, and improved the mechanism for controlling workplace risks and removing hidden dangers, with the goal of preventing serious and major traffic accidents and ensuring workplace safety.

No major railway accidents have occurred since 2012. In 2019, railway accident fatalities had dropped by 46.1 percent compared with 2012, the death rate per billion tonne-km by 53.8 percent; the number of serious and major traffic accidents on ordinary roads had lowered by 55.9

percent, and the number of fatalities by 60 percent. In water traffic, there were no serious accidents in 2019, and the number of serious accidents and deaths both decreased by 68.5 percent and 69.4 percent respectively compared with 2012. Civil aviation has achieved a new safety record of almost 81 million hours of continuous safe flight in 112 months.

Emergency response has markedly improved. China has strengthened emergency response capacity, prevented and defused major safety risks in a timely manner, and effectively responded to disasters and accidents of all kinds. It has carried out projects to secure safety of high-speed railways, built a security system combining manpower, equipment and technology, and improved the security conditions along high-speed railway lines, removing 64,000 potential risks from the routes. Efforts have also been made to improve the safety of standard rail lines. The country has carried out safety and security projects covering 889,000 km of roads at or above the township level, renovated 47,000 unsafe bridges, and effectively disciplined the operation of transport vehicles.

China has strengthened maritime rescue and reinforced emergency response to major offshore oil spills. It has established a fast and efficient approach to maritime search and rescue that follows unified government leadership with the main responsibility on local authorities, and enlists help from both professional forces and the public in line with the principle of proximity and convenience. China is now equipped with more than 70 professional rescue vessels, more than 120 salvage vessels, more than 20 specialized rescue aircraft, and more than 20 emergency rescue teams. It has built a maritime search and rescue capability composed of professional rescue and salvage forces, the armed forces, government forces and social forces. From 2012 to 2019, the government organized 16,000 maritime search and rescue operations, dispatching 72,000 vessels and 2,780 aircraft, and rescued 11,000 vessels and 122,000 people in distress, with a success rate of 96.2 percent.

The capacity to deal with public emergencies has distinctly improved. China has enhanced its emergency response systems and capabilities, and has responded rationally and efficiently to various public emergencies. After Covid-19 struck, the Chinese government made resolute decisions to block the transmission of the virus and ensure the continuity of the transport network, the channels for emergency transport, and the transport of goods and materials essential for work and daily life. It introduced a series of timely policies and measures:

• ensuring the rapid handling and delivery of emergency supplies by rail;

• prioritizing and expediting free road access for emergency transport vehicles;

• giving priority to emergency transport waterway vessels in passing through locks, being piloted, anchoring and docking;

• allowing each Chinese airline to operate only one route per country with no more than one flight per week;

• matching supply and demand between air transport enterprises and international trade and foreign-funded enterprises; and

• opening fast postal channels.

These measures stopped any spread of the virus by means of transport and ensured the availability of emergency supplies and daily necessities, providing strong support for the all-out war against the epidemic.

Panel 10   Transport Plays an Important Role in Covid-19 Response

During the fight against the epidemic, the transport sector has played an important role in curbing the spread of the virus, providing timely medical supplies and maintaining people's daily life. A total of 1.59 million tonnes of medical supplies and daily necessities and 5.8 million tonnes of thermal coal and fuel oil arrived in Hubei Province by railway, highway, waterway, civil aviation and postal express delivery. More than 40 million workers in the sector worked day and night in the front line, and millions of couriers pressed ahead with their work in the face of snow, wind and danger.

Transport services resumed through a region-specific and multilevel approach. Expressway tolls were waived nationwide. With Covid-19 prevention and control measures in place, railways, highways, waterways, urban buses, subways and taxis continued their services, effectively guaranteeing the transport of supplies for work and daily life.

V. Building a Global Community of Transport for All

Pursuing a mutually beneficial strategy of opening up, China expands cooperation with other countries in the field of transport, actively promotes global connectivity and engages in global transport governance. It earnestly fulfills its international responsibilities and obligations and pursues win-win results and common development through cooperation in wider fields and at higher levels, contributing to building a global community of transport for all, and promoting a global community of shared future.

1. Contributing to Belt and Road Cooperation

The Belt and Road Initiative embodies great dreams. Following the principles of extensive consultation, joint contribution and shared benefits, China joins hands with other countries to accelerate cooperation in infrastructure connectivity and build a high-quality development path that is inclusive and beneficial to all – a road of peace, cooperation and prosperity.

Promoting connectivity of transport infrastructure. China recognizes the importance of transport in promoting global connectivity and shared prosperity, and thus strengthens win-win cooperation with other countries in transport connectivity. Steady progress has been achieved in cooperation on the Pakistan Main Line 1 (ML-1) upgrading project, the China-Nepal Cross-border Railway, the China-Laos Railway, the China-Thailand Railway, and the Jakarta-Bandung High-speed Rail. With the joint efforts of Chinese enterprises and their international partners, the

Mombasa-Nairobi Railway, the Addis Ababa-Djibouti Railway, and the Orange Line metro train project in Lahore, Pakistan have been completed. More than 31,000 China Railway Express Trains have made transcontinental voyages to Europe, reaching 92 cities in 21 European countries.

Cooperation between China and relevant countries has brought a number of road and bridge projects to completion, including the Havelian-Thakot section of the Karakoram Highway and the Sukkur-Multan section of the Peshawar-Karachi Motorway, the Kunming-Bangkok Expressway, the Heihe-Blagoveshchensk Highway Bridge, the Tongjiang-Nizhneleninskoye Railway Bridge and other road and bridge projects.

China has participated in the construction and operation of the Port of Piraeus in Greece, the Port of Colombo in Sri Lanka, the Gwadar Port in Pakistan and other overseas ports. With the active participation and joint efforts of the countries concerned, a connectivity framework consisting of six corridors, six routes and multiple countries and ports has taken shape.

A comprehensive, multilevel infrastructure network with railways, highways, shipping and aviation at its core is forming rapidly. As a result, the costs of cross-regional trade and goods movement have been gradually reduced, facilitating the orderly flow and optimal allocation of resources and other production factors across regions.

Facilitating international transport. China actively promotes the coordination of policies, rules and standards among countries so as to provide institutional support for connectivity. Under the framework of Belt and Road cooperation, it has signed 22 agreements on international road transport with 19 countries, reached bilateral agreements with Belgium, the UAE, and France on mutual recognition and exchange of motor vehicle driving licenses, and concluded 70 bilateral or regional shipping agreements with 66 countries and regions, with its shipping services covering all costal countries along the Belt and Road.

China has also signed agreements with 26 countries and regions on unilateral or mutual recognition of seafarer's certificate of competency, and signed a memorandum of understanding on electronic certificates with Singapore to facilitate customs clearance of ships and the application of electronic certificates in the global shipping industry. An international railway cooperation mechanism has been established for China Railway Express to Europe, and China has signed postal cooperation agreements with 22 countries, realizing regular outbound mail traffic of China Railway Express.

China has signed bilateral intergovernmental agreements on air transport with 100 countries. By the end of 2019, Chinese and foreign airlines were operating air routes in China reaching 54 countries, with 6,846 round-trip flights every week. China has signed regional air transport agreements with ASEAN and the European Union.

China has established a cooperation mechanism for maritime search and rescue with Japan, the Republic of Korea, and Russia, and signed a departmental memorandum of understanding on maritime search and rescue with the National Search and Rescue Agency of Indonesia.

Thanks to these measures, China can enjoy closer cooperation, more convenient exchanges, and more shared interests with other countries along the Belt and Road.

2. Promoting Reform of Global Transport Governance

Currently, global transport governance faces a series of new challenges. To better facilitate and support global development, it urgently needs reform and innovation. China firmly supports multilateralism, actively promotes the evolution of the global transport governance system, and contributes China's vision and approach to global transport governance.

Participating in global transport governance. As a major country that shoulders its international responsibilities and obligations, China has become a party to nearly 120 multilateral agreements on transport; it has taken an active part in the UN Economic and Social Commission for Asia and the Pacific (ESCAP), the Organisation for Cooperation between

Railways (OSJD), the International Union of Railways (UIC), the World Road Association (PIARC), the International Transport Forum (ITF), the International Maritime Organization (IMO), the International Civil Aviation Organization (ICAO), the Universal Postal Union (UPU) and other international organizations. China has been reelected as a Category (a) Council member of the IMO and member of the councils of the UPU. It has hosted the World Transport Convention and other international conferences.

China is committed to undertaking all transport-related actions under the framework of the UN 2030 Agenda for Sustainable Development. It works with other developing countries to promote reform of global governance for sustainable transport, with the goal of creating a favorable international environment for developing countries.

Contributing to global climate governance. China attaches great importance to tackling climate change, actively undertakes international responsibilities and obligations that are commensurate with its stage of development and national conditions, and enforces a national strategy to proactively respond to climate change. It has played a leading role in formulating and implementing IMO's initial strategy on the reduction of greenhouse gas (GHG) emissions from ships, and worked hard to safeguard the interests of developing countries during the formulation and implementation of the market-based measure – Carbon Offsetting and Reduction Scheme for International Aviation. China strives for the establishment of a fair and rational global climate governance system directed towards cooperation and win-win results, with the goal of contributing to global eco-environmental progress and sustainable development.

3. Strengthening International Exchanges and Cooperation

In the spirit of equality and mutually beneficial cooperation, China seeks closer and broader cooperation with other countries on transport, to facilitate an open world economy.

Broadening the global network of partnerships. Through mechanisms such as the Transport Cooperation Sub-Committee of the Committee for Regular Meetings between Chinese and Russian Heads of Government, the China-US Transportation Forum, and the China-CEEC Transport Ministers' Meeting, China furthers cooperation in sustainable development of transport and plays a constructive role in building a new model of international relations.

Adhering to the principles of amity, sincerity, mutual benefit, and inclusiveness in its relations with its neighbors, China strengthens its cooperation with neighboring countries in transport. The following mechanisms have been established: the China-Japan-Korea Ministerial Conference on Transport and Logistics, the Meeting of SCO Ministers of Transport, the ASEAN and China Transport Ministers Meeting, the Joint Committee on Coordination of Commercial Navigation on Lancang-Mekong River among China, Laos, Myanmar and Thailand, mechanisms for the use and management of China-Russia and China-DPRK transboundary waterways, the Asia-Pacific Heads of Maritime Safety Agencies (APHoMSA) forum, and the China-ASEAN Maritime Consultation Mechanism. China has participated in transport cooperation under the Greater Mekong Subregion (GMS), the Central Asia Regional Economic Cooperation (CAREC) and other frameworks, contributing substantially to regional economic development.

Guided by the principle of pursuing the greater good and shared interests, China actively engages in international programs on enhancing maritime capability and technological cooperation, and provides support and aid for other developing countries in infrastructure construction, planning and capacity building. Through broad and in-depth exchanges and cooperation, China has broken new ground in opening up featuring mutually beneficial market-based cooperation, experience-sharing and mutual learning.

Engaging in international cooperation in fighting Covid-19. The coronavirus is a common foe of all of humanity. China strengthens transport cooperation in Covid-19 prevention and control with other countries and promotes a global community of health for all. At China's initiative, the IMO recommended and forwarded a number of protocols from China to its 174 member states and relevant international organizations, including *Guidelines for Covid-19 Prevention and Control for Seafarers on Board Vessels* and *Guidelines for Covid-19 Prevention and Control for Ports and Their Frontline Staff*. The Civil Aviation Administration of China shared with its counterparts in more than 40 countries *Preventing Spread of Coronavirus Disease 2019 (COVID-19) Guideline for Airlines* and *Preventing Spread of Coronavirus Disease 2019 (COVID-19) Guideline for Airports*. Via the UPU, China Post shared the *Handbook for New Coronavirus Prevention and Control* with 192 member states of the union.

China attended the Special Session of the Eighth China-Japan-Korea Ministerial Conference on Transport and Logistics, the China-ASEAN Transport Ministers' Special Meeting on Covid-19, and the 19th China-ASEAN Transport Ministers' Meeting via video links, and joint statements were issued after the events.

China has established domestic fast channels for the transport of materials to assist in the battle against Covid-19, and set up special task forces for international logistics. Through multimodal methods such as multi-stop chartered flights, commercial flights, sea-land multimodal freight and China Railway Express to Europe, it provides full support for transporting aid materials. So far, 294 batches of supplies have been provided to 150 countries and 7 international organizations, and 35 teams totaling 262 medical experts have been dispatched to aid 33 countries.

VI. Future Prospects for China's Transport

The 19th CPC National Congress laid out the goals for realizing basic socialist modernization by 2035 and developing China into a great modern socialist country by the middle of the century. The Fifth Plenary Session of the 19th CPC Central Committee proposed that we should accelerate the effort to build China into a country with a strong transport industry, which would bring in a period of good opportunities for the sector's development.

A high-quality transport industry is a matter of urgency. Decisive progress has been made in China's endeavors to secure a decisive victory in building a moderately prosperous society in all respects. The country has entered a new stage of development and worked to put into practice the new development philosophy, with a higher requirement and providing more room for transport to contribute to the new development dynamic. The Chinese people's expectations of a better life have been growing in a multi-tiered and multi-faceted way, producing stronger and more diverse demands for transport services.

A new round of technological revolution and industrial transformation is gaining momentum and bringing tremendous changes to transport. Meanwhile, China is faced with a more complex international environment and increasing instability and uncertainty. The worldwide spread of Covid-19 has led to a level of profound worldwide change unseen in a century. Unilateralism, protectionism and hegemonism have seriously impeded international industry and supply chains. Climate change has posed real and potential threats to eco-environmental security and economic and social development.

Facing these changes in the international and domestic situation,

China is moving faster in developing a national comprehensive and multidimensional traffic network, and reinforcing its strength in transport to satisfy the needs of its people, ensure adequate support for transport, and become a world leader in this field. They involve both opportunities and challenges.

China will adapt to changes in work and daily life, develop transport services that fully respond to public needs, and improve the efficiency and service quality of a comprehensive transport network. To serve the exploitation and protection of its land resources, and to ensure coordinated development between rural and urban areas and between regions, China will improve its all-round transport support capabilities, maintain a future-oriented approach to the development of its transport infrastructure, and optimize the leading role of transport in bolstering economic and social development. To serve high-quality economic development, China will transform the growth model of its transport industry, pursue safe, intelligent and green transport, improve its capacity in safety management and emergency response and rescue, and modernize its transport governance. To support opening up on all fronts, China will strengthen the connectivity of transport infrastructure and improve the globally-oriented network of transport services.

China moves faster to become a world leader in transport. In its endeavors to build a high-quality transport system fit for a new stage of development, China is committed to people-centered development, and pursues supply-side structural reform as its main task. Giving priority to transport in future plans, China will shift its focus from speed and scale to quality and efficiency, from independent initiatives to integrated multi-modal development, and from traditional drivers to innovative forces. Our country will build a modern comprehensive transport system that is safe, convenient, efficient, green and economical, equipped with world-class facilities, technology, management and services.

By 2035, China will have built up significant strength in transport. A modern comprehensive transport system will be in place to substantially improve public satisfaction levels and better support national modernization. Equipped with an advanced express network, sound trunk network, and extensive basic network, the system will raise the coordinated transport development in urban and rural areas to new heights.

The National 1-2-3 Travel Circle (one hour to commute in cities, two hours to travel within city clusters, and three hours to travel between major domestic cities) and the Global 1-2-3 Logistics Circle (one day to deliver within China, two days to deliver to neighboring countries, and three days to deliver to major global cities) will take initial shape, providing convenient combined transport of passengers, and economical and efficient multimodal transport of goods. China will make marked progress in developing intelligent, safe, green and shared transport, easing urban traffic congestion, and creating a barrier-free travel system.

The country will establish a sci-tech innovation system for transport, develop advanced and safe key equipment, train high-caliber professionals, and create a sound market environment. China will achieve the basic modernization of its transport governance. Its international competitiveness and influence in transport will be improved markedly. China will make all-round progress in transport to meet the people's growing expectation for a better life and provide powerful support for achieving basic socialist modernization.

Conclusion

China is engaged in an all-out effort to build a great modern socialist country. Transport will play a stronger part in leading economic and social development. China will implement the new development strategy and develop safe, convenient, efficient, green and economical transport to lay a solid foundation for achieving basic socialist modernization by 2035 and becoming a great modern socialist country in all respects by the middle of the century.

At present, the world is facing challenges from the Covid-19 pandemic and economic recession. Transport can play an important role in binding countries together and promoting economic growth during this difficult time. Upholding the vision of a global community of shared future, China will continue to implement the UN 2030 Agenda for Sustainable Development and strengthen international exchanges and cooperation on transport. China will work with all other countries to promote global connectivity and stronger people-to-people ties, and make a greater contribution to building a better world.

责任编辑：刘敬文

图书在版编目（CIP）数据

中国政府白皮书汇编.2020/中华人民共和国国务院新闻办公室 著. —北京：人民出版社，
　外文出版社,2021.3
ISBN 978－7－01－023264－5

Ⅰ.①中…　Ⅱ.①中…　Ⅲ.①国家行政机关-白皮书-汇编-中国-2020　Ⅳ.①D62

中国版本图书馆 CIP 数据核字(2021)第 048046 号

中国政府白皮书汇编（2020 年）
ZHONGGUO ZHENGFU BAIPISHU HUIBIAN（2020NIAN）

中华人民共和国国务院新闻办公室

人民出版社
外文出版社 出版发行
（100706　北京市东城区隆福寺街 99 号）

中煤（北京）印务有限公司印刷　新华书店经销

2021 年 3 月第 1 版　2021 年 3 月北京第 1 次印刷
开本：889 毫米×1194 毫米 1/16　印张：32
字数：326 千字

ISBN 978－7－01－023264－5　定价：150.00 元

邮购地址 100706　北京市东城区隆福寺街 99 号
人民东方图书销售中心　电话 （010）65250042　65289539